Secure Blockchain and Quantum Technologies for 6G-Enabled Internet of Things

Scrivener Publishing
100 Cummings Center, Suite 541J
Beverly, MA 01915-6106

Publishers at Scrivener
Martin Scrivener (martin@scrivenerpublishing.com)
Phillip Carmical (pcarmical@scrivenerpublishing.com)

Preface

Networks of the 21st century are achieving revolutionary progress through the convergence of next-generation technologies including 6G networks and related digital platforms. *Secure Blockchain and Quantum Technologies for 6G-Enabled Internet of Things* helps us explore how emerging wireless systems will improve secure blockchain and quantum technology management in an IoT setting. With 6G emerging technology that takes enormous leaps beyond its precedents to provide ultrahigh speed transmission combined with nearly instant response over AI-based networks and it easily connects to quantum technology platforms. This book explains the basic features of 6G technology including its advanced spectrum usage methods and AI control systems alongside its ability to make next-generation IoT solutions function as expected.

The book focuses on security issues caused by rising global interconnectedness. The rise of 6G network elements creates a new security vulnerability because existing security systems cannot protect all the connected devices. DLTs act as essential systems by distributing validated records and letting users create self-executing contracts. The book shows how new consensus methods help 6G grow while using less power and explains how to make SDN and network slicing work together. The book explains quantum-resistant cryptography before blockchain to explain how future quantum computers could break regular encryption systems. The research discusses how QKD security measures combined with post-quantum algorithms and quantum AI protect IoT environments against advanced cyberthreats in 6G networks.

This book stands out because it merges academic research with practical benefits through its multiple subject connections. The content moves beyond predictions to explore actual network applications through smart grids that use blockchain to secure energy deals and other examples. The text examines both policy and ethical standards along with data security controls and public impact of widespread connectivity. Research from business experts and practical experiments support this book equally for scientists, engineers and executives who create 6G telecommunications systems.

This book *Secure Blockchain and Quantum Technologies for 6G-Enabled Internet of Things* offers a guide to future technology development instead of just technical information. This book shows future directions for 6G and blockchain technology evolution with quantum technologies while addressing key challenges of IMT-2030 standards. Through its complete presentation the book shows readers both important information and promising research paths for the future of secure quantum network development.

Acknowledgements

We express our sincere gratitude to all the contributors—researchers, practitioners, and visionaries—who have shaped the chapters of this book. Your insights and expertise are the cornerstone of this volume. We also acknowledge the support of institutions, peer reviewers, and technical editors who helped bring this effort to fruition.

Above all, this book is a tribute to the enduring spirit of innovation and collaboration that defines our journey toward a smarter, more secure, and more connected world.

1

Harnessing 6G for Diverse IoT Applications

A. Saran Kumar[1]*, K. Dhana Shree[2], M. Nivaashini[3], V. Praveen[4], S. Priyanka[5] and Muhammad Nawaz Khan[6]

[1]Department of Artificial Intelligence and Data Science, Coimbatore Institute of Technology, Coimbatore, India
[2]Department of Computer Science and Engineering, Sri Ramakrishna Engineering College, Coimbatore, India
[3]Department of Artificial Intelligence and Data Science, Sri Eshwar College of Engineering, Coimbatore, India
[4]Department of Computer Science and Engineering, Bannari Amman Institute of Technology, Erode, India
[5]Department of Artificial Intelligence, Kongu Engineering College, Erode, India
[6]Department of Higher Education Archives and Libraries, Khyber Pukhunkhwa, Pakistan

Abstract
The sixth generation is called 6G in the network field. The main objective of moving to 6G is to support high-speed connectivity with reduced latency and high flexibility in wireless services. Due to its lower latency property, it can support high levels of business applications and digital platform experiences such as video conferencing, remote monitoring, digital games, and automated self-driving cars. The internet of things (IoT) is a grooming area, defined as a collection of different components such as sensors, software and other hardware components over the internet. In this chapter, the role of 6G network in IoT is discussed with its major role in different industries. Recently, many industries require a high-level data transferring mechanism with standard security concerns. IoT is collecting many data through its components and transfers it to different places. To connect these two major concepts, 6G with IoT is considered by all grooming industries. Also, this chapter discusses the working principle, security measures, and IoT roles in industries.

**Corresponding author*: saran.cit92@gmail.com

T. Perarasi, M. Karthiga, S. Sountharrajan, E. Suganya and Balamurugan Balusamy (eds.) Secure Blockchain and Quantum Technologies for 6G-Enabled Internet of Things, (1–16) © 2026 Scrivener Publishing LLC

Keywords: 6G network, IoT, industry applications, role of 6G, fastest network

1.1 Introduction

Telecom industry entered into a new transformation of mobile technology with improved features. The existing 2G, 3G and 5G network based services supported the development in field of high speed data connectivity and reliable communication [1]. The 6G technology bit that's different from the existing communication technologies defined as follows:

- ***Very High Speed Broadband communications***
  - In case of moving for broadband communications, there is a need to consider many factors such as rural or urban area, cost, availability and how it's incorporated with other services.
- ***Ultra High reliability and Low latency***
  - Low latency is defined as the processing of large volume of data with minimum amount of delay. Reliability aspect is defined as uninterrupted connection for entire duration.
- ***Larger volume of machine type communications***
  - The capacity to connect a large number of devices at once should greatly improve with 6G networks. Supporting the vast array of sensors, actuators, and other devices present in contemporary industrial settings requires this functionality.

1.1.1 6G Systems – Transforming the Technologies

A computerized change is occurring in pretty much every industry, upsetting and making us reevaluate our methods of performing. Through an extraordinary capacity to share data, individuals and ventures are working together more, making arrangements that consolidate various subject matters and upsetting customer action plans [2]. This inter-industry transformation has made a need to advance remote availability for the fifth era of portable innovation as shown in Figure 1.1.

The advanced change, enabled by broadband, cloud, and versatility, is happening in almost every industry, upsetting us and forcing us to reevaluate our working practices [3]. As the 6G era begins, new applications for innovation are emerging as users and businesses begin to identify cycles and channels that will improve their quality of life and their businesses. The core of this technological revolution is wireless connectivity.

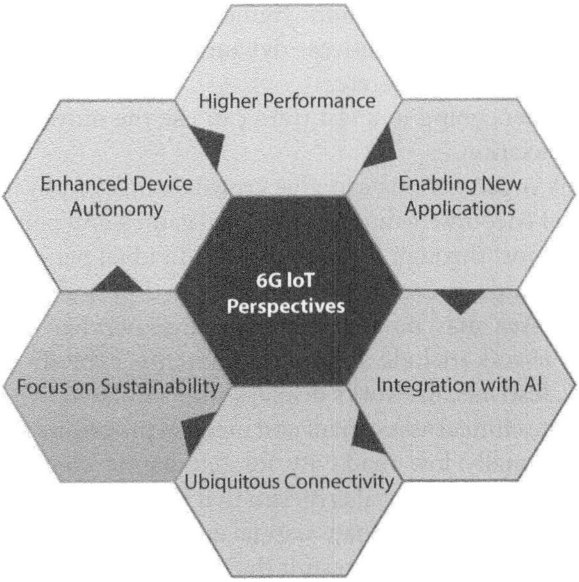

Figure 1.1 Perspectives of 6G network-based IoT.

Newer business opportunities are emerging for individuals from various companies as well as for those who have historically shown interest in the value chain, such as telecom administrators. Indeed, even the value chains are going through a change, with substance and start-to-finish administrations getting always significant. New plans of action are being made with an emphasis on conveyed cloud. An extraordinary capacity and capability to share data is prompting a more noteworthy level of coordinated effort among individuals and a wide range of various enterprises [4].

1.1.2 6G Network for Communication

A few industry bodies have set the necessities as far as what 6G really is [5]. Here, we investigate various promising use cases that speak to different key areas: specifically, the car business, development, energy, wellbeing, producing, media, retail, and transport.

- Expanding autonomous driving is made possible by autonomous vehicle control, which also helps people and brings about a number of benefits. Some of these benefits include increased profitability, enhanced personal satisfaction, and reduced rush-hour traffic.

- Intelligent transportation frameworks (ITSs) encourage effective traffic executives, dynamic traffic rerouting, and traffic signal control, etc.
- Passengers going in a fast train can use the movement time for relaxation.
- Arena organizations can give crowds a mix of physical and virtual encounters during shows and games, and permit public support through the sharing of individual perspectives.
- Large outdoor events held for a limited period in a designated area may be attended by a large number of people. Such events include sports tournaments, exhibitions, concerts, festivals, fireworks displays, and similar activities.
- Remote clinical assessment and medical procedure empower exceptionally low inactivity for tele-haptic control so the specialist gets material criticism that is intended to be undefined from or better than manual employable strategies.
- Shopping centers can permit the conveyance of customized shopping encounters.
- Smart city networks incorporate distant monitoring of the city framework, ongoing traffic data, and public safety alerts for improved crisis reaction times.
- Teleportation in a brilliant matrix network is the capacity to respond to quick changes in the stock or use of assets to evade dominant framework disappointments which harm gear clients the burden of intensity blackouts.

1.2 The Evolution of 6G Network System

The 6G framework would suggest significant changes in the execution and sending of systems administration foundation, in light of software-defined networking (SDN) and network functions virtualization (NFV). Organization activities and administrations are turning out to be cloud-empowered in almost every industry; and the broadcast communications industry is no exception – however, it is unmistakable from different enterprises attributable to the dispersed idea of organization tasks [6]. This presents a significant opportunity to create value from distributed storage and cloud computing for specific customers and services as well. The principal areas of the 6G framework are remote access, transport, cloud, applications, and the executives including organization as shown in Figure 1.2.

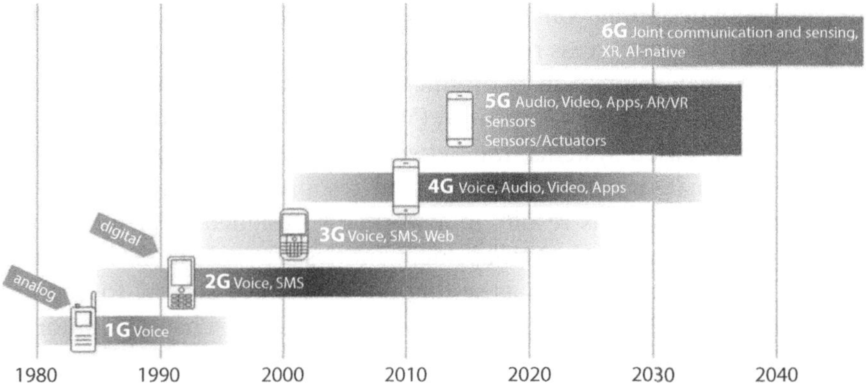

Figure 1.2 Evolution of 6G networks.

1.2.1 Wireless Access

A single key segment of 6G radio access is a creative air interface called New Radio (NR), which is planned basically for new range groups. In industry and the scholarly world, it is observed that the achievement of 6G will rely upon a variety of range resources with a length of low, medium and high range groups. During conversations in WRC-15, accentuation has commonly been set on high range groups, for example, millimeter wave groups, although numerous organizations additionally understand that low groups under 6GHz will be critical to giving the vital inclusion and data transfer capacity [7].

1.2.2 Network Applications

Organization applications, for example, Evolved Packet Core (EPC), voice over LTE (VoLTE), and future 6G center organization capacities will be cloud-empowered: that is, they will be able to execute in the SDN/NFV cloud climate. For instance, the core network organization can send in a nearby worker in a manufacturing plant to help with particularly short reaction times. At the same time, it should be possible to support the factory with communication services from a centrally located VoLTE installation, for example [8].

1.2.3 Management

The organization of executive elements in 6G frameworks will enable the automation and orchestration of lifecycle management processes, and will be capable of designing complex, dynamic systems involving applications, cloud, and transport access resources.

Network management in 6G frameworks requires additional effort to integrate Virtual Network Functions (VNFs) deployed in cloud data centers. In cloud-based systems, the network is expected to coordinate and manage automated tasks and distributed resources through centralized administration [9]. This results in a workflow designed to achieve optimal network performance. Management entities are evolving from issuing explicit configurations (such as setting up a switch or server) to distributing policies, KPIs, and target objectives, which each subsystem autonomously and locally optimizes [10].

Investigation and protection are basic capacities that would be viewed as a component of 6G organization [11]. An investigation is a vital tool for expanding the computerization of tasks by giving expectation knowledge that can be applied consequently.

1.3 The 6G System

The 6G framework is built on "adaptable" radio access hubs; it's circulated and incorporated in server farms taking into account adaptable assignment of outstanding burdens. These hubs and server farms are associated with programmable vehicle organizations [12]. The vehicle networks are interconnected through backbone hubs, which transfer data from the access hubs to the data centers where most of the information is stored and the network is managed. Furthermore, the management of applications, cloud, transport, and access resources is primarily centralized in the data center, but these resources can also be flexibly allocated as needed.

1.3.1 Network Division

The strategy of network cutting takes into consideration the meaning of various sensible networks (or cuts) on top of a similar actual foundation. Assets can be devoted only to a solitary cut or divided among various cuts. There are various kinds of assets; for example, computing, storage, transport, VNFs, and so on [13].

A network cut is worked to address an ideal conduct from the organization. Such conduct can be related to security, information stream seclusion, nature of administration, dependability, autonomous charging, etc. A network cut may uphold one or numerous administrations, and can be utilized to make a virtual administrator organization. Network cutting can be utilized for a few uses: a total private organization, a duplicate of a public organization to analyze assistance, or a devoted organization for a particular help.

1.3.2 Industry Automation

The industry automation uses case needs cMTC services. The most critical prerequisites are minimal idleness and high reliability; for example, phone automation in a factory. In useful terms, perhaps the main difficulties would be able to help cMTC business administrations where high-grade network cut needs to give the necessary degrees of accessibility, vigor and versatility to assaults [14].

The proposed article focuses on the impact of 6G Networks on various IoT-based platforms. It also examines the unique features of 6G and the advantages in adopting the 6G networks over the IoT based applications. The study also analyzes the limitations in existing 3G and 5G networks to extend the reliable and fast network communication to IoT networks [15].

The GSMA intelligence finds the total number of IoT inter-connections will increase to 25.2 billion by 2025. The wide area of cellular technologies utilizes licensed spectrum, such as GSM, LTE and 6G network communications to join more range of devices and geographical regions.

The existing 5G Networks will keep on supporting 6G networks to give adequate network inclusion and ability to expand the network inclusion worldwide. The 6G networks together with the gigantic number of static and versatile IoT gadgets improves the wide scope of correspondence as far as speed, data transmission and quality of services (QoS).

The Mobile IoT devices are mainly divided into following types:

- Enhanced mobile broadband (eMBB)
- Massive IoT and critical communication (mMTC)
- LTE for machines (LTE-M) and Narrowband-IoT (NB-IoT) technologies

1.3.3 6G Networks in Industrial IoT (IIoT)

The Industrial IoT design supports enhanced data generation which is completely automatic, like data transfer, data processing and actuation between canny machines. A high level of security and reliability are the main requirements which are preferred by industrial IoT applications.

The 6G networks are used to control and monitor the Industrial IoT machine activity from remote locations. For the purpose of sense degradation, connected machine tools in the IoT applications are using the 6G network. Also, it uses the same for wear and tear in real time and makes use of it for taking corrective action. In the current scenario, many IoT-based industries are using a huge number of sensors, and all the sensors are distributed in well-structured manner for performing the monitoring in many aspects such as structural and environmental. In addition to that, sensors are used to track the asset, monitoring all the processes and optimization purposes [16].

1.3.4 Automotive and Mobility Models

Seamless service, high quality of services, navigation service, and other additional services are depending on the high bandwidth connectivity. The reduced latency also plays a vital role in automotive and mobility models. From the experimental experiences, it's proved that the high bandwidth connectivity and minimal latency can help improve the fuel efficiency and driver's requirement in the plantation process based on the automatic process.

In the forthcoming days, service or costs will be optimized in providing automatic or remote driving and remote support such as transportation management, through high bandwidth and low latency network connections. In the current network architectures, many divisions are made to support greater flexibility. This also helps in managing same network architecture in efficient ways. The main objective of introducing many divisions are to allocate every division to some predefined tasks or functions to manage troubleshooting in an easy way [17].

Car manufacturers are mainly sharing their data with different stakeholders to support all facilities to their customers in their supply chain. In this scenario, the data-based business models are helping them to share the traffic information and patterns related to driving with their other stakeholders such as fleet managers and insurance companies. This will help them get information soon after verified by all the stakeholders.

1.3.5 Automated Connected Vehicles

Many researchers are focusing on autonomous vehicle to support driverless vehicle on public roadways. This field is attracting many researchers due to its automatic driving mechanism and effective methodology. Apart from the driverless facility in the autonomous vehicles, many other new facilities are also adopted. Some of those facilities are automatic music streaming, weather prediction and reporting, communication establishment between other vehicles on the same road, with road infrastructure and also vehicles in pedestrians. To enable all autonomous vehicles to extend this facility, they should adopt specific characteristics and leverage IoT concepts to optimize processes in a simplified manner [18]. The driverless vehicle system eliminates many of the barriers present in traditional vehicles operated by human drivers. But it's not completed due to some of the disadvantages which arise while using autonomous vehicle in roadways.

1.3.6 Augmented and Virtual Reality

The augmented reality and virtual reality incorporate the 6G network communications in the operation to enhance the process in real time scenario. The model requires enormous amount of network bandwidth which automatically launch the application on the virtual platform. The advancements in 6G technology significantly improve real-time data capture and communication activities. The virtual view of the various construction design environment and industrial machine communication and monitoring activities are established in an effective manner.

1.3.7 Media and Content

Media is very huge industry which transfers huge amount of data to different places within a fraction of seconds. Their main requirement is to contact different people in different locations within no time, to distribute data among them. If the communication is fast, then their role will reach the people in quick manner than the competitors in the market. 6G facility can support transferring high volume of data, superior quality video content in real-time applications using its high data transmission and low inactivity property. Also, this property can enable the people to use the mobile phone to see the media contents and live streaming. IoT can provide weather prediction through sensors, along with other sensors that deliver related content to the media. Live telecasting using small sensor based cameras also can be supported by IoT. All these facilities can make the media industry stronger than the traditional networking methods [19].

Another key division of media industry is advertising. Advertising relies on data about people's requirements and regional industry needs. Using this data, companies can effectively promote their products in each region. In this process, 6G and IoT play a major role. Individual industry can have its own private network to share all these, but it makes industry to invest a lot during its initial phase. Many resources are needed to manage and run all these in perfect manner. 6G can support private as well as public network facility to the industry.

The above mentioned scenario motivating media and substance players to utilize 6G use cases for all their experiments. Every media operation is not performed individually by their own industry. For all their data transferring and related operations, they are depending on mobile operators because they are working within a smaller ecosystem. Some business models are established between them like revenue shares business model with involvement of different stakeholders. Cloud based facilities are also adopted by many industries for sharing all type of media content in secured and reliable manner between different set of people and to handle large amount of data.

1.3.8 Gaming Industry

The gaming industry generates huge volume of revenue in the digital market. The technological advancements support the gaming industry to introduce the number of new gaming applications. The existing model supports wide range of gaming application with limited speed and bandwith capacity. The reduced latency and improvised network connection through 6G networks may increase the revenue of the gaming industry through advanced feature enhancements. In game industry due, to 6G involvement, it can support the following things for improvements:

- Mobile cloud based advance gaming techniques
- High level efficient streaming technique and facility
- Multiplayer gaming platforms in a single game
- Advertisement using dynamic methods
- Mobile battery support for long duration
- Better mobile game development as required by players

1.3.9 Smart City

The major objective of any smart city infrastructure is to enhance the development of smart ecosystem in all sectors. The sectors include connected vehicles, linked to traffic lights and utilization of some mass digitization in all the public sectors. In case of crime scenes, police officers are in the situation of transmitting high quality voice data and video footages over the smart phones. Smart city includes many other facilities such as air quality monitors in entire city to educate people on potential hazards [20]. Hospitals, fire service, police department and other multiple departments should be connected in network to share their data within a second for providing better service in the city. To support this 6G network, IoT can be used which will support efficient data management through its network slicing methodology.

1.3.10 Health Care Management

Healthcare management or healthcare administration becomes a booming technology which cares about many subfields such as patient information exchange, hospital administration, public health systems and its network and other medical infrastructures. Nowadays, many hospitals adopt the AR/VR concept for remote based surgery training for the junior doctors. To make all the above mentioned successful, the wired high latency and low bandwidth network infrastructures are useless. To overcome this, 6G based network infrastructure came with adequate low latency and high level bandwidth capacity.

Pharmaceutical data also managed through this network to deal efficient diagnostics and make surgery in accurate manner. Another important field is data analytics based medical administration.

Preparing junior physicians for medical procedures can be enhanced using AR/VR supported by low-latency, high-bandwidth 6G networks. Wired connections in operating rooms could be replaced with secure, low-latency wireless links enabled by 6G. Remote real-time diagnostics can be improved by delivering high-quality video streams over 6G. Robots could be employed for drug administration, assisting with diagnostics, and even performing surgeries, with 6G providing the necessary low latency and high-speed connectivity. Data analysis across medical records, such as CT scans, can further support patient prioritization.

6G needs to give similar latency as wired organizations without any interference, as patient's well-being is of vital significance. Low cost for cell availability for analytic gadgets is offering a high performance to fiber network.

Remotely connecting a countless number of gadgets in a safe and cost-proficient manner is most preferable as wired associations are costly and unbendable. Empowering virtual control of machines with low inertness in 6G network is a significant advantage. This prompts cost improvement as less CPUs are required on one side. A collection of distributed computing, eMBB and mMTC can be utilized to send the data progressively in high goal. iNetwork cuts can be held for explicit capacities.

1.3.11 Construction Industry

The construction industry is increasingly adopting remote construction operations, which require massive amounts of data [21]. By leveraging 6G technology, with its high efficiency and low latency, these industries can enable real-time autonomous construction through remote methods. The construction industry can adopt Building Information Modeling (BIM) tools through virtualization methods or by leveraging 6G technology, which offers ultra-low latency. When combined with IoT, 6G contributes to several areas in construction, such as drone operation and data management, support for mine workers, and the handling of construction machinery. By improving efficiency, it helps save time and space while also enhancing worker safety.

1.3.12 Pharmaceutical Industry

The pharmaceutical industry heavily relies on supply chain data to improve the efficiency of medicine production and to ensure that medicines reach all levels of people within the distribution chain. This industry handles and transfers massive volumes of data across multiple locations. In such a scenario, a robust network infrastructure is essential, as it must support the connection of a large number of sensors and the processing of sensor-generated data. So 6G network and IoT based strong connectivity is required by the pharmaceutical industry. In pharmaceutical industry, drug discovery process is a complicated process which requires data from multiple sources. To manage this situation 6G supports and it will provide efficient platform for drug discovery process [22].

In India, pharmaceutical industries are contributing major role all over the world. If 6G based IoT is incorporated with such industries, then it will be a more beneficial to rule over the world in drug discovery and delivery process. Security for the data which we are transferring should be highly confidential and the data which we are collecting from the sensors should be transferred in a secured manner. To achieve this objective, the 6G platform is providing high level security mechanism in low cost. This is the main reason for integrating 6G based technologies for the pharmaceutical industries.

1.3.13 A Significant Quantity of Widely Distributed Devices

An example of a traditional use case—the vast array of topographically dispersed devices—is managed by MMTC. It might have to do with devices connected to traffic stop meters in urban areas, or resource tracking in contemporary sites; for example, most of these devices have long battery lives (over 10 years), little effort/unpredictability (half duplex, low power, single antenna), and overall better inclusion (a 15-20dB preferred connection edge over LTE). They mostly generate traffic on the uplink and are typically static. NB-IoT was recently finalized by the 3GPP in 2016, and it addresses most of these needs [23].

1.3.14 Transport

The vehicle area conveys a network between distant locales and gear/gadgets. Backhaul serves the two sides of the transmission – for instance, to associate a base station (BS) to an access network or a middle office – while front take is a term used when the BS antennas are associated with a distant incorporated radio recurrence (RF) unit, or to a halfway found baseband (BB) unit [24]. In addition to providing administrators with broad access to the network's versatile front-haul and back-haul, the transport domain can also offer various customer-facing network services, such as Layer 2 or Layer 3 VPNs.

1.3.15 Cloud and Fog Networks

The cloud and fog computing technologies offer a wide range of IT infrastructure as services to the end users. The model allows the user to provide the computing resource from the remote data center. The data center can be viewed as an enormous amount of computing resources pooled under the data center infrastructure. The advancement in the field of 6G network communication directly supports the cloud and fog based service model with enhanced network communication. The low latency on the network communication is directly mapped into the functionalities of the fog network and its operations. The cloud-based infrastructure also requires a very high-performance computing network to provide cloud-based services to its end customers. The 6G networks can be used in various levels of cloud, grid and fog-based service layers to improve the Quality of services (QoS) in various inherent technologies [25].

Because the cloud enables the foundation to grow and shrink naturally, when an application requires more resources, it finds a new instance of that application and removes it when its load decreases. It is challenging to achieve such flexible scaling when the application is run on specialized hardware. In a virtualized cloud environment, information security will ensure that only authorized access is allowed to the framework application's data store. Similarly, the framework application may be sent in a distributed virtual farm (DC) that spans multiple physical server farms [26].

1.4 Conclusion

The research article examines the advantages of utilizing 6G networks across various IoT-based platforms. It highlights how the 6G framework, with its upgraded capabilities, can drive transformative changes across industries. Beyond enhancing communication, 6G plays a crucial role in advancing businesses and society as a whole. Moreover, 6G networks expand public connectivity, making new applications more feasible. As a result, both the Internet of Things and the broader Networked Society will be significantly strengthened by the adoption of 6G.

As a hallmark of contemporary network architecture, access, transit, and cloud are divided into building blocks (counting SDN and NFV), network applications, and the executives (counting coordination and computerization), 6G frameworks will give a more elevated level of reflection that will rearrange the administration. The 6G design won't just be cost-effective to work; it will have light-footed and adaptable systems set up for the quick presentation of administrations. The 6G networks become the key element to transform the IoT platform into next level.

AI disclosure statement: The author confirms that no artificial intelligence (AI)-generated content or AI-assisted writing tools were used in the preparation of this chapter (including summaries and the abstract). All text, analysis, and conclusions are the result of the author's original work.

References

1. Agyapong, P.K., Iwamura, M., Staehle, D., Kiess, W., Benjebbour, A., Design considerations for a 5G network architecture. *IEEE Commun. Mag.*, 52, 11, 65–75, 2014.
2. Bhuiyan, M.Z.A., Wang, G., Tian, W., Rahman, M.A., Wu, J., Content-centric event-insensitive big data reduction in internet of things, in: *GLOBECOM 2017-2017 IEEE Global Communications Conference*, IEEE, pp. 1–6, 2017, December.
3. Borgia, E., Gomes, D.G., Lagesse, B., Lea, R., Puccinelli, D., Special issue on "Internet of Things: Research challenges and Solutions". *Comput. Commun.*, 89, 1–4, 2016.
4. Castillejo, P., Martínez, J.F., López, L., Rubio, G., An internet of things approach for managing smart services provided by wearable devices. *Int. J. Distrib. Sens. Netw.*, 9, 2, 190813, 2013.

5. Mohsan, S.A.H., Mazinani, A., Malik, W., Younas, I., Othman, N.Q.H., Amjad, H., Mahmood, A., 6G: Envisioning the key technologies, applications and challenges. *Int. J. Adv. Comput. Sci. Appl.*, 11, 9, 2020.
6. Gupta, A. and Fernando, X., Exploring secure visible light communication in next-generation (6G) internet-of-things, in: *2021 International wireless communications and mobile computing (IWCMC)*, IEEE, pp. 2090–2097, 2021, June.
7. Abbas, M.T., Grinnemo, K.J., Ferré, G., Laurent, P., Alfredsson, S., Rajiullah, M., Eklund, J., Towards zero-energy: Navigating the future with 6G in Cellular Internet of Things. *J. Network Comput. Appl.*, 103945, 2024.
8. Serôdio, C., Cunha, J., Candela, G., Rodriguez, S., Sousa, X.R., Branco, F., The 6G ecosystem as support for IoE and private networks: Vision, requirements, and challenges. *Future Internet*, 15, 11, 348, 2023.
9. Miraz, M.H., Ali, M., Excell, P.S., Picking, R., A review on Internet of Things (IoT), Internet of everything (IoE) and Internet of nano things (IoNT). *2015 Internet Technologies and Applications (ITA)*, pp. 219–224, 2015.
10. Mohjazi, L., Selim, B., Tatipamula, M., Imran, M.A., The journey toward 6G: A digital and societal revolution in the making. *IEEE Internet Things Mag.*, 7, 2, 119–128, 2024.
11. Chataut, R., Nankya, M., Akl, R., 6G networks and the AI revolution—Exploring technologies, applications, and emerging challenges. *Sensors*, 24, 6, 1888, 2024.
12. Rahman, M.A., Ali, J., Kabir, M.N., Azad, S., A performance investigation on IoT enabled intra-vehicular wireless sensor networks. *Int. J. Automot. Mech. Eng.*, 14, 1, 3970–3984, 2017.
13. Priyanka, S., Praveen, V., Sivapriya, G., Meenakshi Dhanalakshmi, M., Hindrance detection and avoidance in driverless cars through deep learning techniques, in: *Advances in Deep Learning Applications for Smart Cities*, pp. 69–100, IGI Global Scientific Publishing, 2022.
14. Saran Kumar, A., Priyanka, S., Praveen, V., Sivapriya, G., AI-Enabled Threat Detection and Security Analysis. *Wireless Commun. Cybersecur.*, 175–197, 2023.
15. Jain, P., Gupta, A., Kumar, N., A vision towards integrated 6G communication networks: Promising technologies, architecture, and use-cases. *Phys. Commun.*, 55, 101917, 2022.
16. Polese, M., Giordani, M., Mezzavilla, M., Rangan, S., Zorzi, M., 6G enabling technologies, in: *6G mobile wireless networks*, pp. 25–41, Springer International Publishing, Cham, 2021.
17. Javeed, D., Saeed, M.S., Ahmad, I., Adil, M., Kumar, P., Islam, A.N., Quantum-empowered federated learning and 6G wireless networks for IoT security: Concept, challenges and future directions. *Future Gener. Comput. Syst.*, 2024.
18. Hakeem, S.A.A., Hussein, H.H., Kim, H., Vision and research directions of 6G technologies and applications. *J. King Saud Univ. Comput. Inf. Sci.*, 34, 6, 2419–2442, 2022.

19. Padhi, P.K. and Charrua-Santos, F., 6G enabled tactile internet and cognitive internet of healthcare everything: Towards a theoretical framework. *Appl. Syst. Innovation*, 4, 3, 66, 2021.
20. Alsamhi, S.H., Hawbani, A., Sahal, R., Srivastava, S., Kumar, S., Zhao, L., Curry, E., Towards sustainable industry 4.0: A survey on greening IoE in 6G networks. *Ad Hoc Networks*, 103610, 2024.
21. Wang, M., Zhu, T., Zhang, T., Zhang, J., Yu, S., Zhou, W., Security and privacy in 6G networks: New areas and new challenges. *Digital Commun. Networks*, 6, 3, 281–291, 2020.
22. Bakar, K.B.A., Zuhra, F.T., Isyaku, B., Sulaiman, S.B., A review on the immediate advancement of the Internet of Things in wireless telecommunications. *IEEE Access*, 11, 21020–21048, 2023.
23. Jiang, W., Han, B., Habibi, M.A., Schotten, H.D., The road towards 6G: A comprehensive survey. *IEEE Open J. Commun. Soc.*, 2, 334–366, 2021.
24. Tataria, H., Shafi, M., Molisch, A.F., Dohler, M., Sjöland, H., Tufvesson, F., 6G wireless systems: Vision, requirements, challenges, insights, and opportunities. *Proc. IEEE*, 109, 7, 1166–1199, 2021.
25. Raikwar, T., Suman, P.N., Chandan, R.K., Mishra, G.K., Rusia, R.K., The Road Ahead of 6G: Exploring the Future of Wireless Connectivity. *Microwave Rev.*, 29, 2, 2023.
26. De Alwis, C., Kalla, A., Pham, Q.V., Kumar, P., Dev, K., Hwang, W.J., Liyanage, M., Survey on 6G frontiers: Trends, applications, requirements, technologies and future research. *IEEE Open J. Commun. Soc.*, 2, 836–886, 2021.

2

Demystifying 6G: Unlocking the Potential of the Next Generation Wireless Networks

G. Amuthavalli[1]*, U. Palani[2] and M. Bavethra[2]

[1]Department of Electronics and Communication Engineering, Sri Venkateshwaraa College of Engineering & Technology, Puducherry, India
[2]Department of Electronics and Communication Engineering, IFET College of Engineering, Villupuram, India

Abstract

The vision of 6G is to provide sustainable solutions in all aspects and to be a trendsetter in improving the quality of human life by connecting the needs of the human world with the physical and digital worlds. Amongst the different stages of the framework of International Mobile Telecommunications (IMT) defined by the International Telecommunication Union (ITU), IMT-2030, aka 6G, is the forthcoming generation to achieve the following goals: Inclusivity, Ubiquitous Connectivity, Sustainability, Innovation, Enhanced Security and Resilience, Standardization and Interoperability, and Interworking. In this chapter, unlocking the potential of the next generation of wireless networks is being done by traversing through the usage scenarios of extended 5G for 6G, which are immersive communication, massive communication and hyper reliable and low latency communication, and also exploring the three newer usage scenarios of 6G: ubiquitous connectivity, AI and communication, and integrated sensing and communication. The demystification of 6G is being done by unveiling the enhanced capabilities of 6G such as security and resilience, reliability, latency, mobility, connection density, area traffic capacity, spectrum efficiency, user experienced data rate and peak data rate and significantly, the pivotal role of its newer capabilities: coverage, sensing-related, applicable AI-related, sustainability, interoperability and positioning. The 6G is envisioned to utilize a wide range of frequency bands ranging from Sub-1 GHz up to frequency bands above 100 GHz with technology trends and enablers for the use cases. The anticipated perspective of the timeline for 6G is the possible

**Corresponding author*: amuthavalli.phd1@gmail.com

T. Perarasi, M. Karthiga, S. Sountharrajan, E. Suganya and Balamurugan Balusamy (eds.) Secure Blockchain and Quantum Technologies for 6G-Enabled Internet of Things, (17–36) © 2026 Scrivener Publishing LLC

deployment around the year 2030 with potential introduction, adding the capabilities and supporting the continuous evolution of its features. This chapter reveals the potential characteristics of 6G in expanding the next generation wireless networks to achieve an outstanding Intelligent Human Machine Interface communication in the realm of all the possible applications.

***Keywords*:** IMT-2030, 6G, demystifying, wireless networks, AI sensing, intelligent communication, sustainability, ITU-R

2.1 Introduction to the Evolution of Wireless Networks

Wireless Networks have evolved rapidly over the last four decades, with a new generation in every ten years, bringing its unique capabilities. The zeroth generation provided simple radio communication functionality before the period of 1980s. The first generation of wireless networks introduced voice communication using analog technology with a data rate of 2.4 Kbps in the 1980s. The second generation transitioned analog networks to digital networks, which supported the basic data services such as short messaging services along with voice communication with a data rate of 64 Kbps. The third generation improvised with multimedia message services and video calls at 2 Mbps data rate by introducing an internet broadband service. In the fourth generation, improved broadband services with applications, such as communication with Internet Protocol (IP) and online gaming, with the data rates from 100 to 1000 Mbps. The fifth-generation of wireless networks focused on improving the standards and quality of services with a high maximum data rate, reliable low latency communication, massive communication, network softwarization by connecting the devices/things/entities through internet of things with 1 – 20 Gbps of data rate. The wireless communication networks with services have evolved with their key features as depicted in the Figure 2.1.

The key challenges, such as data rate of very high value, less latency, faster than 5G, more efficiency, more bandwidth efficiency, demand for devices to be connected, etc., are key driving components for the revolution of 6G [2]. The white paper of Ericsson's view [3], as in the Figure 2.2 emphasized the timeline, which provided the information on the completion of 5G advanced with MIMO, XR, mobility, energy efficiency, and AI/ML features released in 2024 and followed by the studies and specification of 6G in 2028.

The organization of this Chapter is as follows: Section 2.2 discusses the need for technological evolution with 6G and the motivation behind it;

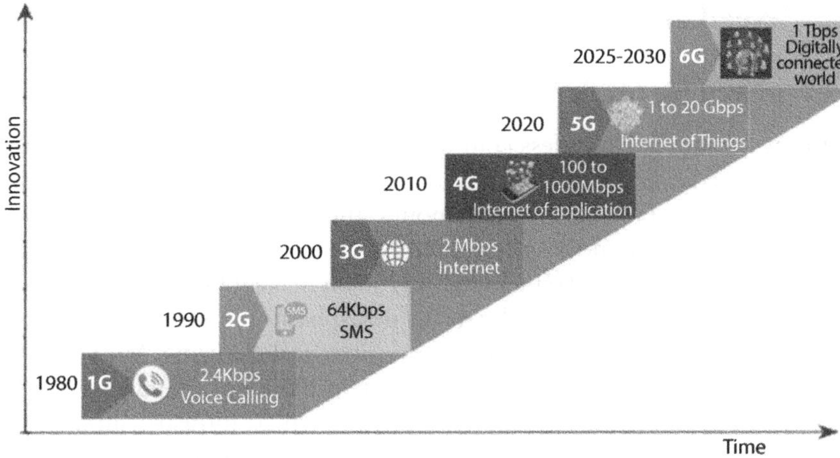

Figure 2.1 Features of wireless communication networks – evolution perspective.

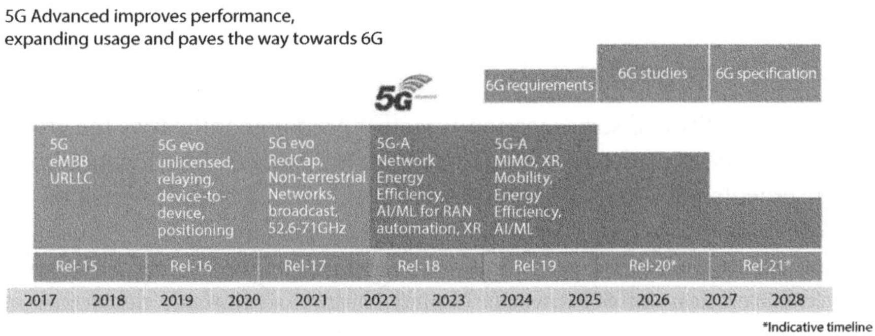

Figure 2.2 Ericsson's view on 5G advanced and 6G timeline. (Source: White Paper, Ericsson BNEW-22:024836).

Section 2.3 elaborates on the capabilities of 6G under two sub-sections: 2.3.1, which highlights the enhanced capabilities of 6G over 5G, and 2.3.2, which presents the new capabilities of 6G. Section 2.4 emphasizes the usage scenarios, classified into enhanced and new usage scenarios for 6G. Section 2.5 focuses on candidate technologies, detailing the technology trends and enablers that are critical for implementing any emerging network generation. Section 2.6 discusses the spectrum of 6G; and the last Section 2.7 concludes with the research scope of 6G for its successful implementation in the near-future 2030.

2.2 Need and Motivation

2.2.1 Need for 6G

With the evolution of wireless communication, the generational change has been witnessed every 10 years. The convergence of many technologies is taking place and need for 6G is of paramount importance. The substantial correlation between 6G and Edge Computing, Internet of Things (IoT), High Performance Computing (HPC) [16], and so on makes 6G an inevitable one. The prime focus of 6G is to accelerate the next-phase of Industrial Revolution by interconnecting human, machine and biological elements. Most significantly, 6G aims to expand the frontiers of applications, unlocking new realms of possibilities across the domains such as super-smart infrastructure, transportation networks, cyber-physical continuum, smart and intelligent healthcare with extended reality (XR) and robotic surgery, autonomous system, industrial automation and manufacturing, brain-computer interface (BCI), haptic communication, internet of everything (IoE) [7], and so on.

2.2.2 Motivation Towards 6G

The sustainability and socio-economic factors predominantly drive the growing development of the 6G technology, despite its need. The technological advancements pave the way to think about the underserved population by democratizing the efforts of providing access to connectivity and ensuring it irrespective of their socio-economic status and geographical origin. The societal considerations of 6G towards United Nations sustainable development goals (SDG) are expectedly enabled to achieve the following goals [5, 6]:

Inclusivity and Ubiquitous Connectivity: The 6G contributes towards hyperconnectivity by meaningfully connecting the unconnected devices and bridging them to attain maximum feasibility with affordable access to everyone. The underserved regions are covered by addressing all the challenging scenarios and promoting the digital inclusion for an affordable broadband connectivity [4].

Sustainability: The advent of technological generations ensures the responsibility of not affecting the range of environmental options. The 6G envisaged to support the efficient deployment with a plan of maintenance and services, thereby reducing the environmental impact with the consideration of climate change in achieving the environmental sustainability goals (ESG) and SDGs. The implementation of 6G requires efficient resource utilization by minimizing power consumption through energy-efficient solutions and reducing greenhouse gas emissions [4–6]. The diverse needs of real end-users and leveraging the circular economy must be prioritized with a promotional perspective of environmental and socio-economic sustainability.

Innovation: The development of 6G fosters innovation by introducing novel solutions to address emerging challenges, thereby driving positive transformations in both economies and human lives. It enhances user experiences by unlocking new capabilities and facilitating connectivity, improved productivity and efficient resource management [4–6].

Enhanced Security and Resilience: The advent of 6G focuses on assessing the expected future risks and provides potential security solutions with the efforts of mitigating the assessed risks. By integrating resilient strategies within the infrastructure, malicious elements that disrupts operational processes will be addressed and thus broader societal and economic goals are achieved by a self-protective network structure [4–6].

Standardization and Interoperability: The standardization and interoperability of 6G ensure its implementation through technical and quality standards, enabling seamless connectivity across communication services and among different services or network operators, regardless of the telecommunication infrastructure or manufacturer [4–6]. 6G is expected to establish an ecosystem with standardized and interoperable interfaces, thereby promoting seamless communication through its functional compatibility and interoperability.

Interworking: 6G provides user flexibility through interworking and supports continuity in communication services. Regardless of the network generation, users are expected to migrate smoothly from existing networks to 6G, thereby achieving the objectives of required inclusivity, equity, and ubiquitous connectivity [4–6].

2.3 Unlocking the 6G Capabilities

The motivation of societal considerations aligned with the Sustainable Development Goals (SDGs) can be realized by unveiling the capabilities of 6G and applying them across diverse usage scenarios. The recommendations of ITU-R M.160-0 [5], as illustrated in Figure 2.3 and ITU-R

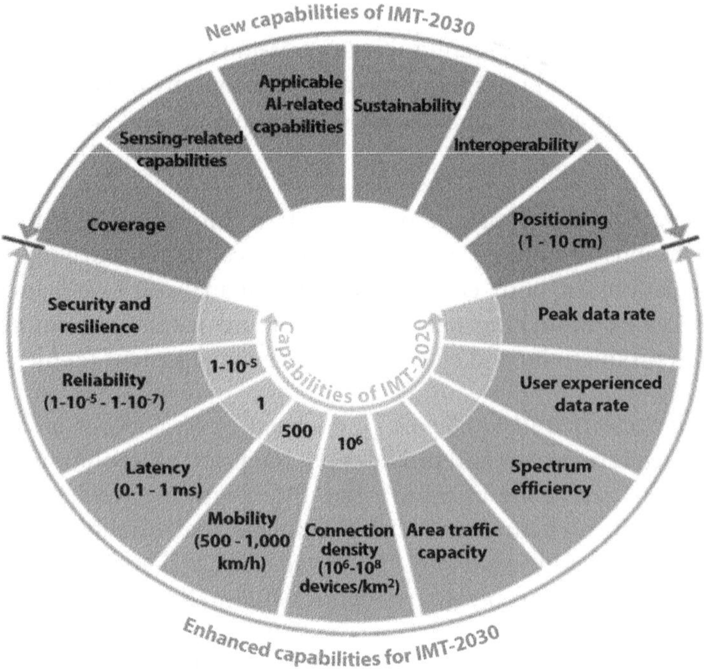

Figure 2.3 Palette diagram of capabilities of IMT-2030 aka 6G (Source: Recommendation ITU-R M.2160-0(11/2023)).

M.2083 [6], describe the new capabilities of IMT-2030(6G) along with the enhanced capabilities of IMT-2020.

According to the ITU-R recommendations/reports [5], and [6], the capabilities are defined with range of values and the targets are estimated and developed by equally prioritizing research and investigation for each of its usage scenario.

The existing nine capabilities of 5G such as the "peak data rate, spectrum efficiency, the user achievable data rate, the traffic capacity, the connection density, mobility, latency, reliability, security and resilience [5]," are improvised and included as enhanced capabilities in 6G technology. In addition, six new capabilities such as "coverage, sensing-related functions, sustainability, interoperability, and positioning [6]," are introduced. Together, these enhanced and new capabilities enable 6G to deliver a more immersive and real-time user experience.

2.3.1 Enhanced Capabilities of 6G

Maximum data rate: The maximum data rate or peak data rate gives the speed at which the data are transmitted in a period of time over the network. The ITU-R M.2083 recommended data rate of 20 Gbit/s considered ideal conditions of the communication device and any values such as 50 to 200 Gbit/s are considered for specific scenarios.

User achievable data rate: A user can experience the data rate based on the coverage area of their device; and the target user area with a value of 10 Mbit/s is recommended in ITU-R M.2083 [5]. In 6G, the enhanced capability envisions greater values, with research target set at such as 300 and 500 Mbit/s depending on the usage scenario.

Bandwidth efficiency: Bandwidth efficiency is the average data rate and can be transmitted over a unit of spectrum or bandwidth in a coverage area. Compared to the research target values of existing 5G capabilities, the bandwidth or spectrum efficiency can be enhanced nearly three times greater than that of it, and also even greater values can be considered for other usage scenarios.

Traffic Capacity of an Area: The traffic capacity of the area is referred to the total throughput of the traffic served for a geographical area. According to the ITU-R M.2083 recommendation, 10 Mbit/s/m^2 is the area traffic capacity of IMT-2020. The greater values such as 30 and 50 Mbit/s/m^2 are considered for building up the 6G system with enhanced capability.

Connection Density: Connection density refers to the number of devices of a network per unit area are connected and/or accessible totally. Nearly 10^6 – 10^8 devices/km^2 are recommended as research target values in the ITU-R M.2160-0 [6].

Mobility: Mobility refers to ability of a network to maintain seamless data transfer and quality of service at higher user speeds, supported by radio nodes and multi-layer radio access technologies. According to ITU-R M.2160, the research target for 6G mobility is in the range of 500 – 1000km/h.

Latency or Network Delay: It is the delay time taken in between by the network to send a packet of certain size from the source and to receive the same at the destination and the recommended research target according to ITU-R M. 2160 is 0.1 - 1ms.

Communication Reliability: When a pre-defined volume of data is transmitted successfully within a pre-determined time duration [5, 6], for a given probability and the research target is recommended [4], $1\text{-}10^{-5}$ to $1\text{-}10^{-7}$ range of values for the communication reliability.

Security, Privacy and Resilience: The digitalization pace is prone to vulnerabilities such as cyber security threats and the communication systems with 6G technology are made by focusing more on the disturbed privacy and security and building up a system by integrating resilience strategies like disruption mitigation and recovery during natural disasters and any man-made cyber-attacks.

2.3.2 New Capabilities of 6G

Coverage: Coverage in general can be defined as the network's ability to provide undisrupted communication by avoiding pathloss services in the desired area, whereas link budget analysis provides better performance enhancement by considering distance between the edges in a single cell [6], in such a way the coverage capability of the network is focused in 6G.

Sensing Related Capabilities: The accuracy, detection rate, resolution, and false alarm are the metrics used for measuring the sensing related capabilities of IMT-2030. The capabilities [6], refer to the ability of the radio interface system to support functionalities such as object detection, angle estimation, range, localization, velocity, imaging, and mapping [5].

Applicable AI-related Capabilities: The artificial intelligence (AI) - enabled application has more functionalities like distributed data processing and learning, AI-based model inference, mode execution, and intelligent computing [18]. A key capability of IMT-2030 is to provide all those functionalities across the entire system, thereby enabling seamless operation of AI-driven applications.

Sustainability: The quantifiable measure of sustainability is energy efficiency, which represents the voluminous of information bits that are being transmitted or received for a unit of energy consumption in bit/joule [5]. To minimize the overall power consumption, energy efficiency can be improved appropriately by optimizing the resource equipment longevity, repair, reuse and recycling [4]. More specifically, sustainability can be referred to as the ability to minimize the carbon footprint of the environment.

Interoperability: The functionalities between different entities of the system are enabled based on the inclusivity of the member and transparency to provide effective communication through radio interface thereby supporting the diversified services in the IMT-2030 ecosystem [6].

Positioning: Positioning refers to the approximate position of connected devices in the ecosystem. The calculation of finding the difference between actual horizontal and vertical position of the connected devices and the recommendation according to ITU-R for its research target is 1-10 cm.

2.4 Usage Scenarios of 6G

The capabilities of 6G provide prospects towards sustainability in the digital transformation and thereby expanding the way the users are benefited out of the technology in their applications. To improvise the overall performance of the 6G systems, common design principles are built up which could be applicable to all the usage scenarios. The three usage scenarios of 5G are enhanced from "eMBB-enhanced Mobile Broad Band" to

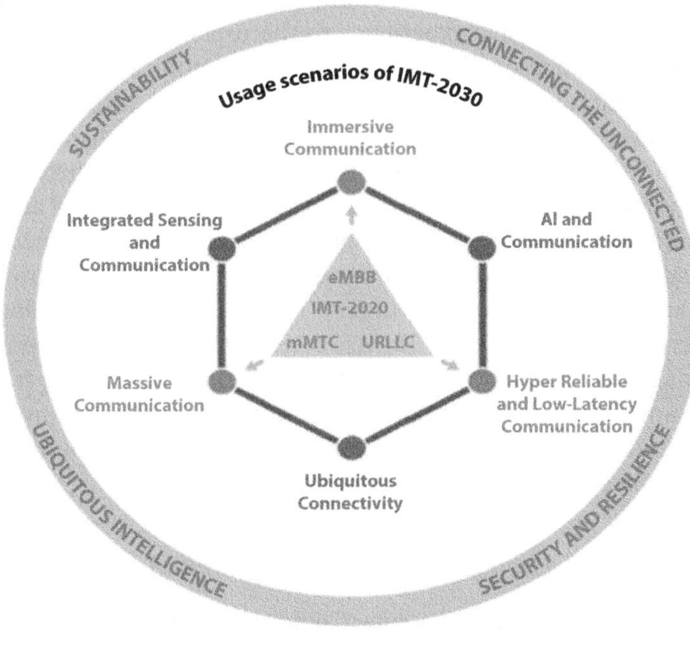

Figure 2.4 IMT-2030 aspects (Source: Recommendation ITU-R M.2160-0(11/2023)).

"Immersive Communication", "URLLC- Ultra Reliable and Low Latency communication" to "Hyper Reliable and Low Latency Communication (HRLLC)", "nMTC-massive Machine Type Communication" to "Massive Communication" as depicted in Figure 2.4 [4].

The following usage scenarios which were not actually designed for the previous generations of IMT systems [6], are introduced in 6G as:

- "Integrated Sensing and Communication" - To support and integrate the sensing ability of all the networks or systems and integrate them with communication
- "AI and Communication" – To support the network through Artificial Intelligence and Communication
- "Ubiquitous Connectivity" – To provide the inclusivity and connectivity by connecting the unconnected

2.4.1 Usage Scenarios of 6G-Extension of 5G

2.4.1.1 Immersive Communication

The usage scenario enhanced mobile broad band (eMBB) is extended to immersive communication by shifting the paradigm of communication to the level of rich and interactive communication between the machines, which gives an immersive experience to the users. It is expected to have a profound influence on the landscape of communication [15, 17] and enrich the communication of experience of the users with the following aspects: delivering 3D images with parallax information, haptic information, extended reality, 3D telepresence, interactive sports through ultra-realistic online support, interactive rich experience in learning and so on. From gaming to industrial control applications relevant to commercial and enterprise scenarios, in which the representative use cases are immersive gaming and entertainment, telesurgery, immersive learning, holographic teleconference, and metaverse. The use cases are with many challenges like communication reliability, multi-modal communication, delay, transmission rate and so on. The realization of immersive communication happens when advancement in each layer, i.e., from physical layer to the application layer solutions, with user behavior prediction.

2.4.1.2 Hyper Reliable and Low Latency Communication

The Hyper Reliable and Low Latency Communication (HRLLC) is derived [8], from the extension of URLLC as recommended by ITU-R M.2083.

It is required to support the time-critical applications, where time-synchronized operations are significant for data delivery within specific latency bounds; otherwise, severe consequences will end up in failure of application. The key performance indicator such as data rate, connection density, precise positioning, energy efficiency, communication reliability gives the best communication, which is hyped by including round-time latency [15]. The applications which are critically dependent on time are industrial automation, drone control, cloud gaming, tele-operated driving, autonomous interaction and control of machines or vehicles, emergency services, monitoring of electrical transmission and distribution, and virtual/augmented reality and telesurgery [26].

2.4.1.3 Massive Communication

The massive Machine Type Communication (mMTC) of 5G is extended as Massive Communication for 6G networks. The 6G connectivity are envisaged to connect massive number of devices/machines/entities/users with the goal of providing inclusivity and ubiquitous connectivity. The multiple input multiple output (MIMO), millimeter and Terabit communication are the new paradigms of 6G wireless communication, which are to be explored to expand the use cases to home automation, smart cities, smart transportation, logistics and supply chain management, health agriculture [4], for which massive number of machine type devices with battery or long-life batteries are connected. Based on the use cases, various data rates, less power consumption, high connection density support, use cases dependency, mobility, more coverage, high security and communication reliability [5, 6] are required by the usage scenarios.

2.4.2 New Usage Scenarios

2.4.2.1 Integrated Sensing and Communication

The new usage scenario, called as Integrated Sensing and Communication combines the communication and sensing capabilities. These capabilities enable sensing-assisted communication, in which communication efficiency is improved by sensing; also, enable communication-assisted collaborative sensing [19], in which more accurate information is obtained by joint-sensing communication. The use cases of 6G, which require spatial data of connected and unconnected devices, can be broadly categorized for outdoor and indoor applications. The wider outdoor use cases rely on the complete network to receive the spatial coordinates for the real-time tracking, without any collision with other devices in the traffic management and routing of autonomous unmanned assisted vehicles (UAVs). In the case of indoor or restricted-area applications, tracking, monitoring and managing people or animals or any other devices are to be done for the detection of fall, recognizing gesture or posture, assisting navigation with spatial accuracy to avoid risks in industries. The sensing and communication capabilities can be enhanced with the support of artificial intelligence, extended reality and digital twin concepts and significantly, high-precision positioning and localization, imaging and mapping capabilities, estimation of range, velocity and angle, and detection of objects [20].

2.4.2.2 Artificial Intelligence and Communication

The usage scenario artificial intelligence (AI) and communication integrating the AI-driven network to make intelligent communication system [16, 18]. The AI applications such as big data analytics, data caching, mobility management, intelligent resource management, massive MIMO and beam forming, channel coding, and network management strengthen the next generation wireless networks. The AI-enabled wireless communication faced the following challenges: massive data handling, AI algorithm complexity, interference management, energy efficiency, privacy and security and regulatory and ethical issues. Also, AI driven beam forming and antenna arrays, autonomous networks, quantum-assisted AI, AI enabled satellite networks, AI for sustainability, AI-enabled network slicing and distributed machine learning for communication [13].

2.4.2.3 Ubiquitous Connectivity

Focusing on bridging the digital divide, the usage scenario enhances the connectivity between the uncovered areas with population from rural and remote areas through interworking with IMT and non-IMT systems [4], with the inclusive of typical use cases, but not limited to IoT and broad band communication of mobile networks [5, 6].

2.5 Technology Trends and Enablers of 6G

The capabilities and usage scenarios of 6G or IMT-2030 would provide application scenarios with the features of immersive, intelligent and ubiquitous [22], for each of these technology trends are envisaged for the

Figure 2.5 Candidate technologies of 6G.

development of 6G [25]. The key enabling technologies such as "Terahertz communication, integrated sensing and communication, integrated intelligent and communication, ultra-massive MIMO, reconfigurable intelligent surface, co-frequency co-time full-duplex communication, holographic radio and ultra-low power IoT communication [22]" are used based on the requirements of application scenarios. This is not limited and the other technologies of Non-Terrestrial Networks [29], such as Satellite Fidelity (SaFi) [30], visible light communication, distributed intelligent computing network, UAVs also included in the Figure 2.5 for better understanding of the candidate technologies of 6G.

The key enabling technologies of 6G are discussed below:

2.5.1 Tera Hertz Communication

Higher frequency bands are required to provide more spectrum resources in the applications of big data analytics and immersive experience in the intelligent systems. The Terahertz (THz) waves [7], are in the frequency range of 100GHz to 10THz, which can support "ultra-high transmission rate, ultra-large bandwidths and ability to penetrate non-metallic or non-polarized materials, in holographic communication, short- and medium-range wireless access, data backhaul/fronthaul, micro size communication, high accuracy positioning and high-resolution sensing and imaging [14, 22]". To obtain the THz communication benefits for 6G, the following technical breakthroughs are to be achieved: ultra-large scale array antenna, ultra-high speed baseband signal processing, channel measurement and modeling. The vector network analyzer and external TX front ends are required to support sub-THz frequency bands [11].

2.5.2 Joined Sensing and Communication

In the case of high-frequency and large bandwidth application scenarios, integration of communication system for different types of sensing services and enhancement of communication management with improved QoS and efficiency by using the sensing results are to be done. The application scenarios are further improved with the research of enhanced positioning, high-resolution imaging, simultaneous localization and mapping and gesture and activity recognition [20, 22]. A general test set up like vector signal generator, signal and spectrum analyzer, and radar echo generator are required to measure the receiver performance in terms of BLER and data throughput, and at the same time, object emulation is needed to measure the sensing performance [23].

2.5.3 Integrated Intelligence and Communication

The integration of artificial intelligence (AI) and communication is expected to promote the evolution of communication paradigms [1] and changes in the network architecture using unknown environment modeling, channel prediction, intelligent signal generation and processing, network status trading and intelligent scheduling, and network optimization and deployment [22, 25]. In the 6G research scenario, machine learning [12] is applied to signal processing by replacing the individual or multiple blocks in the chain with trained models to perform channel estimation [28], and equalization. The test and measuring equipment like vector signal generator, oscilloscope, and vector signal explorer software can be used to generate datasets to train machine learning models for the tasks of channel estimation and equalization [24].

2.5.4 Ultra-Massive MIMO

Higher operating frequency bands provide convenient conditions to deploy ultra-large MIMO systems, enabling higher bandwidth efficiency, wider and more flexible network coverage, improved positioning accuracy, and enhanced efficiency [22]. These advancements can be achieved by deploying ultra-large-scale antenna arrays and applying new materials and tools [21]. The research scenarios of ultra-large MIMO are "ultra-massive MIMO baseband processing algorithm, channel state information feedback, intelligent design for ultra-massive MIMO, channel measurement and modeling, distributed ultra-massive MIMO [22, 27]". In the case of ultra-massive MIMO testing, an antenna test system with vector signal generator and a signal and spectrum analyzer is employed. This setup enables the evaluation of the peak-beam performance of the antenna array structure, including measurements such as error vector magnitude (EVM) measurement [23].

2.5.5 Reconfigurable Intelligence Surface

The reconfigurable intelligent surface (RIS) technology is a way to control electromagnetic waves through the radio propagation channel using meta materials with properties, which are unavailable in nature. By enabling the control of its sub wavelength unit cells, a meta material can be programmable and thus reconfigurable [16]. In the myriads of sensing, imaging or communication applications, programmable meta materials combine with software directives becoming capable of adapting to the environment and communicating with other meta materials. For RIS testing, the test environment enables the illumination of RIS modules from different incident angles, while measuring the reflected signals simultaneously at multiple observation angles [23].

2.5.6 Co-Frequency and Co-Time Full Duplex Communication

The traditional duplex communication modes such as Frequency Division Duplex and Time Division Duplex theoretically double the spectral efficiency. To improve the spectral efficiency practically, advancements in the wireless communication theories like "self-interference cancellation, enable simultaneous transmission and reception in the same frequency band [22]". The co-frequency co-time full-duplex technique achieves much higher spectral efficiency and its commercialization can be obtained by addressing the following technical challenges: "suppression of high-power dynamic self-interference signal, novel interference elimination mechanism and novel networking designs [10, 22]".

2.5.7 Holographic Radio Technology

The holographic radio technology dynamically reconstructs the electromagnetic space with precision control in real-time, thereby quasi-continuous and infinite multiplexing space are provided. In smart factories, wireless industrial buses operating in ultra-high traffic density are enabled by holographic radio access with ultra-high capacity/traffic density and ultra-low latency. Before commercializing the technology for 6G, the following research challenges are to be addressed: "fundamental theories and modeling, hardware and physical layer design issues, antenna arrays and high-performance optical computing [22]".

2.5.8 Ultra-Low Power IoT Communication

To address the challenge of working the devices for a very long periods, power-constrained devices are used. The Backscatter communication [9], uses a Back Com device which conveys the data by reflection and modulation of RF signal. In the passive RIS-based communication, research challenges [4] such as low-complexity signal processing and air interface design are unaddressable by the traditional algorithms. To resolve the challenges, cognitive radio can be leveraged through symbiotic radio by enabling backscatter communication within the same spectrum [22].

2.6 Spectrum of 6G

The Ericsson's white paper [11], discusses how the 6G spectrum will be allocated for various use cases. The wide area spectrum of about 3GHz is required for the need for the outdoor and indoor mobility by the use cases like massive digital twins, holographic communication, mobile broad

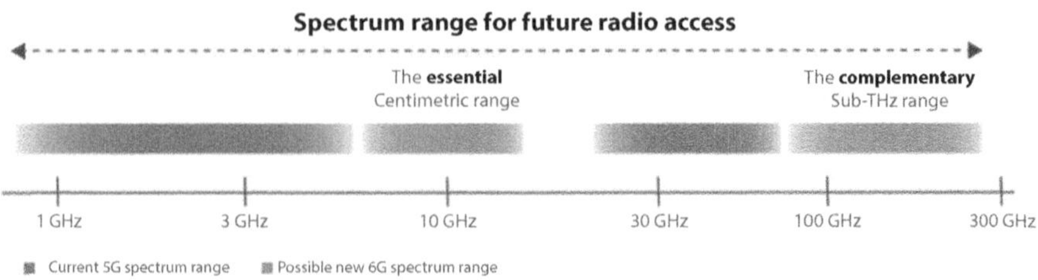

Figure 2.6 Possible new 6G spectrum ranges (Source: White paper, (2024)23:000243 Ericsson).

band communication and Internet of Senses. Since, insufficiency of 3GHz in meeting the demands is visible, an additional spectrum of 1.5 to 2.2 GHz is considered, despite the closeness to the mid-band in its characteristics and re-use of existing bands. For niche scenarios such as remote surgery and high resolution holographic communication, extreme data rates are demanding the spectral resources beyond 10GHz. For this reason, the sub-THz frequency range is identified as a most suitable option as illustrated in Figure 2.6 [11].

2.7 Conclusion and Scope of Research

The 6G or IMT-2030 systems are expected to come up with full of its potential capabilities to unveil the usage scenarios with different use cases in many applications which connects the physical, human and digital world. The recommendations and reports of ITU [5, 6] were reviewed and demystified *via* the 6G by unlocking its potential with its capabilities, usage scenarios and technology trends and enablers for the next generation wireless networks. The use cases of all the anticipated applications of both terrestrial and non-terrestrial IMT systems, and non-IMT systems would be facing the research challenges and issues of their own, for which further investigations have to be done elaboratively on each capability of 6G in each usage scenario and its application for the further development, deployment and successful implementation of 6G.

AI disclosure statement: The author confirms that no artificial intelligence (AI)-generated content or AI-assisted writing tools were used in the preparation of this chapter (including summaries and the abstract). All text, analysis, and conclusions are the result of the author's original work.

References

1. Chataut, R., M., Akl, 6G networks and the AI revolution-Exploring technologies, applications, and emerging challenges. *Sensors*, 24, 6, 1888, 2024.
2. Shafi, M., Jha, R.K., Jain, S., 6G: technology Evolution in Future Wireless Networks. *IEEE Access*, 2024.
3. Paper, W., 5G Advanced: Evolution towards 6G *BNEW-22:024836. Ericsson.*, 2023.
4. Nagaraj, P., Demystifying IMT-2030 or 6G- Capabilities, Usage Scenarios, and Candidate Technologies.

5. *Recommendation ITU-R M.2160-0(11/2023).* M. Series: Mobile and radio determination, amateur and related satellite services. Framework and overall objectives of the future development of 6G and beyond.
6. The ITU-R Framework for IMT-2030 *Recommendation ITU-R-M.2160-0.* Updated in February 2024.
7. Howard, Barsbai, Jalil, Paving the way to Terabit (Tbit) Wireless telecommunications. *Microwave J.*, 67, 2024.
8. Tao, W., Li, W., *et al.*, 6G hyper Reliable and low latency communication-Requirement analysis and POC. *2023 IEEE 98th Vehicular Technology Conference*, pp. 1–5, 2023, October.
9. Guidotti, Vanelli, Jafaari, *et al.*, Role and evolution of Non- Terrestrial Networks towards 6G. *IEEE Access*, 2024.
10. Chowdhury, Shahjalal, Ahmed, *et al.*, 6G wireless communication systems: Applications requirements, technologies, challenges and future research directions. *IEEE Open J. Commun. Soc.*, 1, 957–975, 2020.
11. White paper, 6G spectrum -enabling future mobile life beyond 2030 gftl-23:000243 Ericsson, 2024.
12. Ahammed, Patgiri, Nayak, A vision on the artificial intelligence for the 6G communication. *ICT Express*, 9, 2, 197–210, 2023.
13. Alhammadi, Shayea, Saleh, *et al.*, Artificial Intelligence in 6G Wireless networks: Oppurtunities, Applications & Challenges. *Int. J. Intell. Syst.*, 2024, 1, 8845070, 2024.
14. White Paper, Conceptualizing security in a 6G world. *ABI research*, 2024.
15. Shamsabadi, Yadav, Gadallah, *et al.*, Exploring the 6G potentials: immersive, Hyper-Reliable and low Latency Communication, 2024.
16. White Paper, ICT Orchestration; A Critical Prority for 6G. *ABI research*, 2024.
17. Shen, Gao, Li, *et al.*, Toward immersive communications in 6G. *Front. Comput. Sci.*, 4, 1068478, 2023.
18. E book, Innovating on 6G with Artificial Intelligence. *Microwave J.*, 2024.
19. Bayesteh, Chen, Zhu, *et al.*, Integrated Sensing and communication – From Concept to Practice. *Commun. Huwaei Res.*, 4–25, 2022.
20. Wild, Grudnitsky, Mandelli, *et al.*, 6G integrated sensing and communication: From vision to realization. *2023 20th European Radar Conference*, IEEE, pp. 355–358, 2023, September.
21. Gunduz, Chiariotti, *et al.*, Timely and massive communication in 6G: Pragmatics, learning and inference, in: *IEEE BITS Information Theory Magazine*, 2023.
22. Wang, Du, Wei, *et al.*, Vision, application scenarios, and key technology trends for 6G mobile communications. *Sci. China Inf. Sci.*, 65, 5, 151301, 2022.
23. White paper, Ten key enablers for 6G Wireless communication. *Rohde & Schwartz*, 2024.
24. Perarasi, Gnanaprakash, *et al.*, Channel estimation using Approximate Message Passing based Hybrid-Field for Massive MIMO systems. *2023*

International Conference on intelligent Technologies for Sustainable electric and communication systems, IEEE, pp. 485–489, 2023, December.
25. De Alwis, Kumar, *et al.*, Towards 6G: key technological directions. *ICT Express*, 9, 4, 525–533, 2023.
26. Masaracchia, L., *et al.*, UAV-enabled ultra-reliable low-latency communications for 6G: A comprehensive survey. *IEEE Access*, 9, 137338–137352, 2021.
27. Poongodi, Deepa, Perarasi, *et al.*, Channel Estimation of XL-MIMO in 6G communication system-near field analysis. *2023 Third International Conference on Smart Technologies, Communication and Robotics*, IEEE, pp. 1–4, 2023, December.
28. Poongodi, Deepa, Perarasi, *et al.*, Millimeter wave channel in Urban Micro/Urban macro environments: Pathh Loss Model and its effect on channel capacity. *2022 Smart Technologies, Communication and Robotics*, IEEE, pp. 1–4, 2022, December.
29. Nguyen, S., *et al.*, Emerging Technologies for 6G non-terrestrial-networks: From Academia to Industrial Applications, 2024.
30. Deng, and Yu, Resource Mapping Allocation scheme in 6G Satellite Twin Network. *Sensors*, 22, 15, 5816, 2022.

3

Dynamic Client Selection in Energy-Aware Federated Learning for IoT-Enabled Edge Networks

Gummarekula Sattibabu* **and G. Nagarajan**

Department of Electronics and Communication Engineering, Puducherry Technological University, Pondicherry, India

Abstract

This chapter introduces a novel energy-aware Federated Learning (FL) framework designed for Internet of Things (IoT)-enabled edge networks IoT-enabled edge networks in the context of 6G. The framework enables decentralized model training across IoT devices, preserving data privacy while improving model accuracy. It is particularly suited for resource-constrained IoT devices operating in dynamic environments, leveraging edge computing to minimize latency and energy consumption. The proposed dynamic client selection algorithm evaluates clients based on dataset size, bandwidth, and computational capacity, optimizing the balance between accuracy and energy efficiency. Simulations show significant performance improvements: an increase of 85.57% of the objective function against FedCS, 68.52% against FedAvg, and 57.87% against Fed Energy-based client selection. Such results, therefore, indicate the outstanding capability of the proposed framework for the best possible improvement of energy efficiency and model performance, thus pointing to a scalable method for energy-efficient federated learning across IoT networks.

Keywords: Client selection, data privacy, energy efficiency, edge networks, federated learning, Internet of Things, model accuracy, 6G networks

**Corresponding author*: sattibabu@ ptuniv.edu.in

T. Perarasi, M. Karthiga, S. Sountharrajan, E. Suganya and Balamurugan Balusamy (eds.) Secure Blockchain and Quantum Technologies for 6G-Enabled Internet of Things, (37–68) © 2026 Scrivener Publishing LLC

3.1 Introduction

The energy efficiency demand is critical for the expanding federated learning (FL), particularly for edge IoT networks. Since many devices are battery-powered and resource-constrained, observing the following energy sources is essential. Energy can be rapidly consumed by continuous data sharing and local model training in federated learning, which affects device performance and reduces the lifetime and working efficiency of IoT systems. These problems are addressed in this chapter through the implementation of an energy-efficient dynamic client selection algorithm, which aims to reduce energy expenditure while maintaining effective model performance. This scheme contributes to existing gaps in the literature by promoting a secure balance between energy use and learning efficacy, thus providing a viable solution for energy-efficient FL in IoT environments.

3.1.1 IoT and Edge Computing

The adoption of the internet of things (IoT) and the concept of edge computing [1, 2] has changed how data is created, processed and consumed. The emergence of connected IoT devices is on an exponential growth curve, as illustrated in Figure 3.1 [3].

IoT has already started embedding intelligence in most objects and their surroundings, making it necessary today. IoT-enabled edge networks have

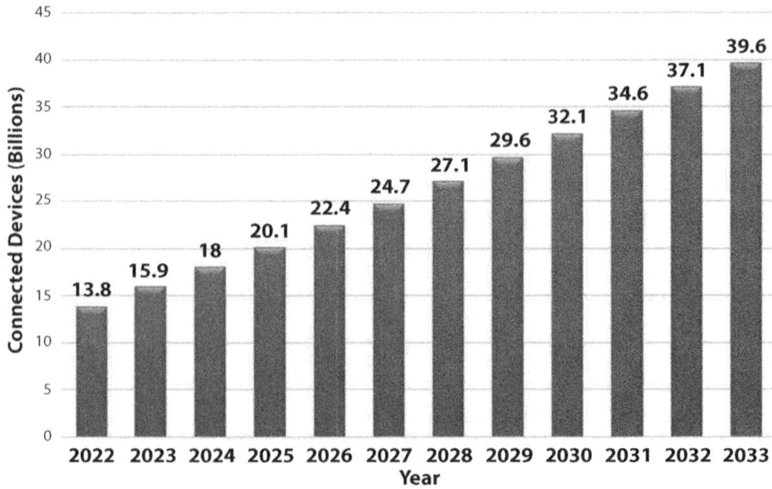

Figure 3.1 The exponential growth in the number of connected devices over time.

become increasingly prevalent, ranging from smart homes to wearable health monitors and from autonomous cars to industrial sensors [4]. These networks perform the analysis and decision-making near where the data is generated, at the network's edge rather than sending data to a central cloud. Moreover, sectors such as agriculture have experienced an enhancement where smart sensors automate irrigation and crop health; retail experiences where continuous data assists in stock availability and increasing the customer experience; and environmental mapping sensors that are not concentrated offer data on airborne and aquatic pollution [5]. As IoT and edge computing are evolving, the need for strong, effective and scalable solutions is quite essential [6]. This methodology is also interconnected to advanced technologies and policies for a broad structural approach to solving the challenges of endlessly complex and diverse data streams for IoT devices with too much data to analyze.

3.1.2 Federated Learning

Federated learning has found its rightful application in the evolution of machine learning by allowing machine learning models to be trained on multiple devices without requiring data to be gathered in one place. This was first put forth by some Google researchers in the year 2016. FL integrates distributed edge devices to perform efficiently without exposing data [7, 8]. This decentralized method effectively plugs into the vast data generated by edge devices, such as smartphones, IoT sensors and edge servers; while using their processing capabilities, they train accurate and efficient models collaboratively. Federated Learning operates on the idea of keeping data decentralized, ensuring it stays on the devices where it is generated. This scheme significantly reduces privacy and security risks typically associated with shifting large volumes of raw data to central servers. Rather than shifting data to the cloud, every device trains its model locally using its stored data. The devices then transmit only the model updates to a central server without sharing the actual data. The server consolidates these updates to refine a global model, which is sent back to the devices. This cycle repeats over several repetitions until the model accomplishes the required accuracy [9].

3.1.3 Challenges

Federated learning states not only privacy concerns but also refers to the latency and bandwidths associated with centralized training. Decentralizing the training process enables edge devices to collaborate in the learning process without compromising their users' data. One of the main issues is the heterogeneity of the devices involved [10]. Another significant challenge is the energy consumption related to federated learning [11]. IoT devices are often battery-powered and have restricted energy resources. The energy consumption in wireless sensor networks happens mainly during data transmission, reception, forwarding and processing [12]. The continuous training and communication required in federated learning can drain these resources quickly; this impact lies on the device's primary functions thereby reducing lifespan. Energy efficiency thus becomes a severe concern in deploying federated learning in IoT-enabled edge networks.

3.1.4 Advancements in Energy-Efficient FL

Researchers have developed various approaches to address these challenges as the federated learning field progresses. Techniques such as dynamic client selection, which logically picks a subgroup of devices to take part in each training round based on their energy levels and computational abilities, are being developed to improve the efficiency and effectiveness of federated learning in IoT-enabled edge networks [13].

3.1.5 Energy Consumption in IoT Devices

A wireless sensor network contains sensor nodes that gather data from the environment [14], and IoT devices, like sensors and smart gadgets, often resource-limited batteries, so energy efficiency is essential. As these devices continuously gather and process data, they require efficient energy usage to sustain their functionality over extended periods. The energy consumption in federated learning rises from two primary activities: local training and communicating model updates [15]. Local training involves rigorous computation, which can quickly deplete the battery of resource-constrained devices. On the other hand, communication involves transmitting model updates to the central server and receiving the updated global model, which also consumes substantial energy, especially in networks with limited bandwidth [16].

3.1.6 Energy-Aware Dynamic Client Selection Architecture

The dynamic selection of participating clients is essential for optimizing energy efficiency federated learning. Dynamic client selection comprises choosing a subgroup of devices to participate in each training round based on their current energy levels, computational abilities and other relevant issues [17]. Dynamic client selection is intended to balance the energy consumption across all devices in the network. The system follows decisions about which devices should participate in the next training round by periodically assessing each device's energy levels and computational load. Higher energy devices are reserved with lower current workloads; they are given priority to ensure no single device is overburdened. Figure 3.2 shows a fundamental federated learning system with an FL server managing a global model and multiple IoT clients handling local models.

IoT clients, such as routers, laptops and phones, indicate an IoT-enabled network, with the base station denoting the edge network infrastructure. The diagram indicates energy awareness through the potential for dynamic client selection based on energy levels, optimizing energy consumption across the network.

Also, dynamic client selection has the flexibility to adjust to changing conditions in real time. For instance, during rush hour, some sensors in a smart city architecture may have high data rates [18]. Algorithms for dynamic selection can detect these conditions and change the participation

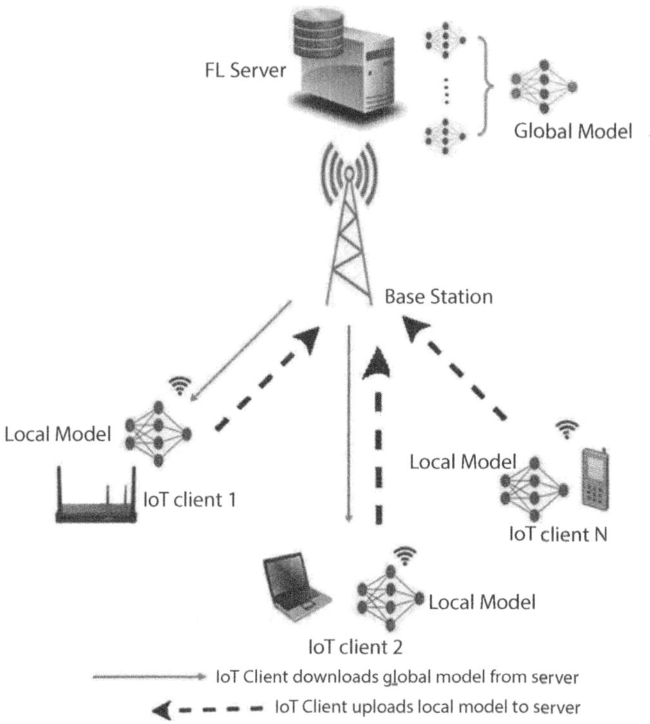

Figure 3.2 Federated learning enabled IoT network.

of those sensors as necessary, thereby avoiding unnecessary energy usage while maintaining constant data collection and processing.

3.1.7 Benefits of Energy-Aware Algorithms

Energy-aware algorithms improve the efficiency of federated learning [19]. These algorithms can seamlessly integrate models for energy consumption, which predict how much energy an array of devices will use based on their assigned tasks and working conditions. The forecasts can be used in selecting clients, providing a good balance between efficiency in training and saving energy by sustaining an acceptable level of learning accuracy and preserving the lifetime of devices [20]. Generally, the dynamic selection of contributing clients in federated learning denotes a considerable energy efficiency and sustainability advancement for IoT-enabled edge networks [21].

3.1.8 Chapter Objectives and Structure

The main objective of this chapter is to address the gap by proposing a fundamental energy-aware dynamic client selection algorithm. This methodology is focused on distributing energy consumption to balance among the devices for improving the sustainability and efficiency issues of federated learning within edge networks. The essential contributions of this work include the development of a novel algorithm for dynamic client selection, comprehensive evaluations of its performance and look into its effect on energy consumption and learning accuracy.

This chapter is organized as follows: Section 3.2 explains motivation and related works about federated learning. Section 3.3 presents the system model of the client selection approach. Section 3.4 presents the proposed work for the dynamic client selection and its workflow design for implementation. Simulation results and analysis are presented in Section 3.5. Finally, Section 3.6 concludes the chapter with a conclusion and discussion of future research directions and possible applications of IoT related to 6G networks.

3.2 Motivation and Related Works

This research is motivated to increase the efficiency and sustainability of federated learning in IoT-enabled edge networks. Considering the challenges in client selection, mainly in terms of device capability, data quality, communication efficiency, and energy constraints, this chapter shall develop a more robust and dynamic approach to client selection in FL.

3.2.1 Client Selection in FL for IoT

This section will discuss why client selection becomes important in IoT environments, how it poses challenges and what must be considered to achieve an efficient, energy-aware, and dynamic client selection strategy.

3.2.1.1 Client Selection in Federated Learning (FL)

Selection of the client in federated learning (FL) forms the function to choose a subset of clients participating in model training at each step. FL allows for cooperatively training models in various devices without the central data storage. Next, the client downloads the global model from the selected list, performs local training using its private data, and uploads the updated model parameters. The server aggregates all these updates to improve the overall global model [22].

3.2.1.2 Importance in IoT-Enabled Networks

Client selection is critical in IoT-enabled networks because of the constraints on IoT devices, including limited battery life, computational powers, and memory [23]. Choosing the right clients results in high-quality data, thus improving the model's accuracy and performance. An effective client selection minimizes latency, communication overhead, and network congestion, which play a considerable role in bandwidth-limited IoT environments. Furthermore, the energy-efficient clients' selection elongates the operational life of battery-operated IoT while ensuring sustainable functionality that allows for energy-conscious federated learning [24].

3.2.1.3 Factors and Key Considerations of Client Selection in IoT-FL

The challenges and critical factors in IoT-FL client selection are mainly based on the heterogeneity of device capabilities; for instance, some devices have limited CPU power, memory, and energy levels [11, 13]. Effective selection must avoid overburdening weaker devices to maintain reliable communication while addressing dynamic network conditions, including bandwidth fluctuations and periods of temporarily interrupted connectivity. Heterogeneity requires selecting clients with high-quality data to enhance the performance of the model [25]. Furthermore, energy efficiency is critical for battery-powered devices for long-term involvement without resource depletion. These factors are considered for energy-aware selection methods to improve performance and sustainability in large-scale IoT networks.

3.2.2 Criteria for Client Selection

The major criteria for client selection depend on the device's capability, quality and quantity of data, and communication efficiency [26]. All criteria are critical as they guide the optimization of the FL process, balancing performance and resource utilization. In selecting the best clients for federated learning (FL) in IoT-enabled networks, the criteria must confirm efficiency and effectiveness in the training processes [27].

3.2.2.1 Device Capability

In Federated Learning, the IoT devices must be examined based on their computational power, their memory capacity, and their battery life to confirm efficient training and client selection, with the computational power to be measured through a series of benchmarking tests, past performance data, and conditions on the devices, which allow for selecting the appropriate devices that can quickly handle complicated computations and much larger data sets. Memory capacity is required to prevent interruption, which can be assessed by sketching available memory and matching it to the FL model's needs. The battery's life is essential in holding up the training cycle in battery-powered devices [28]. It entails monitoring the battery level constantly, and an estimate of energy usage during rounds should be computed to identify devices with better battery levels that should not shut down in mid-training. By concentrating on all these aspects, client selection is adequate and energy-aware.

3.2.2.2 Data Quality and Quantity

In federated learning (FL), the model's performance is greatly influenced by the quality and quantity of data available to each client. High-quality data is to be obtained through proper labeling, cleaning and significance to the task, leading to more accurate and generalizable models [29]. The quantity of data, evaluated by measuring data volume and ensuring the data allocation line up with the model's requirements, provides strong training signals but demands high computational resources. Client selection is based on the criteria of weighted selection, and clients are assigned weights defined by the quality and quantity of their data or threshold, which sets the minimum standard that clients must be selected [30]. Ensuring high-quality and sufficient data on selected clients is essential for achieving the desired model performance and energy efficiency.

3.2.2.3 Communication Efficiency

In IoT-related federated learning networks, communication efficiency with limited bandwidth is critical. Techniques like data compression, sparse updates and local aggregation are used to minimize communication overhead [31]. Reducing latency comprises selecting clients close to the server, continuously checking network conditions to choose clients with better connectivity and permitting multiple clients to update simultaneously. Optimization policies also include client scheduling that is network situation-aware and adjusts the frequency and size of updates based on the prevailing network conditions [32]. These methods help to reduce the energy consumed in communication processes, in line with targets in energy-aware federated learning.

3.2.3 Related Works for Client Selection in Federated Learning

Many factors influence client selection in federated learning (FL) for IoT applications. First, the heterogeneity of systems and statistical features among clients play an essential role [33, 34]. This includes variations in CPU frequency, dataset sizes, data delivery patterns, and training efficiency. Multi-modal data also challenges client selection since traditional methods may exhibit modality-level bias, resulting in slow, effective data exploitation [35]. Second, factors like hardware specifications, computational resources, and data delivery imbalance among the clients' client selection policies must be optimized to improve FL convergence and reduce its training latency [34, 36]. FL can enhance model performance and training efficiency in IoT environments by addressing these issues through adaptive and fair client selection mechanisms.

The other factors include optimizing for latency, accuracy and energy consumption over multiple rounds [37], considering bandwidth and energy constraints on IoT devices and edge servers [38], addressing potential misbehavior of participating worker nodes and the cost of hiring clients [39], grouping user devices with similar preferences for personalized models and managing communication resources efficiently [40], and dealing with the volatility of the learning environment, client population, data, training status and transmitting status to enhance client selection in volatile federated learning [41]. Considering these factors, federated learning systems' total performance must be improved, ensuring energy efficiency and model accuracy.

Based on Table 3.1, several limitations relevant to the concept of federated learning for IoT-enabled edge networks with a client selection approach are discussed below:

Table 3.1 Some of the federated learning methods in IoT-enabled edge networks.

Author(s), year, ref no.	Method used	Contribution	Challenge(s)	Key difference with proposed work
Zhang *et al.* (2024) [33]	IGPE algorithm for client selection.	Addresses heterogeneity.	Systems (CPU, dataset, transmission) and statistical (non-IID data) heterogeneity.	IGPE handles static heterogeneity, while the proposed method adapts to dynamic energy conditions.
Chen *et al.* (2023) [34]	FedGRA: Adaptive client selection with low overhead.	Analyzed client selection impact; proposed lightweight method.	Device and data heterogeneity, inefficiency of random selection.	FedGRA focuses on communication efficiency; the proposed method on energy efficiency.
Fan *et al.* (2024) [35]	CMSFed for multi-modal data balance.	Introduced a new training loss for modality balance.	Modality-level data imbalance.	CMSFed balances data types, while the proposed work optimizes energy for IoT constraints.
Zhu *et al.* (2023) [36]	Multi-armed bandit for adaptive client selection.	Proposed an asynchronous FL framework with sub-linear regret performance.	Training latency, fairness, unknown channel conditions.	Multi-armed bandit focuses on latency; the proposed method targets energy-aware client selection.

(*Continued*)

Table 3.1 Some of the federated learning methods in IoT-enabled edge networks. (*Continued*)

Author(s), year, ref no.	Method used	Contribution	Challenge(s)	Key difference with proposed work
Ji *et al.* (2023) [37]	ITMCS for client selection and bandwidth allocation.	Optimized latency, accuracy and energy consumption in wireless FL.	Mixed-integer problem formulation over rounds.	ITMCS focuses on complex, round-based optimization; proposed method prioritizes scalable, real-time energy management.
Li *et al.* (2023) [38]	Energy-aware D2D-assisted FL.	Formulated energy-aware D2D assisted FL; energy-efficient DNN model training.	Bandwidth and energy constraints on IoT devices.	Energy-aware D2D-assisted FL focuses on efficient DNN training, while the proposed approach emphasizes adaptability and dynamic client selection.
Tan *et al.* (2024) [39]	Reputation-based Stochastic Integer Programming (SCS).	Optimizes client selection based on reputation.	Misbehavior and hiring costs of clients.	SCS optimizes based on client reputation to mitigate risks; the proposed method emphasizes energy efficiency in resource allocation.

(*Continued*)

Table 3.1 Some of the federated learning methods in IoT-enabled edge networks. (*Continued*)

Author(s), year, ref no.	Method used	Contribution	Challenge(s)	Key difference with proposed work
Li *et al.* (2022) [40]	Clustered FL with DRL for edge association.	Investigated accuracy and communi-cation cost in clustered FL.	User data distribution disparities.	Clustered FL with DRL targets communication efficiency and accuracy, while the proposed method prioritizes energy efficiency through dynamic selection.
Shi *et al.* (2023) [41]	CU-CS: Combinatorial Multi-Arm Bandit (C2 MAB) for client selection.	Convergence analysis for non-convex and strongly convex cases.	Limited bandwidth, changing client population.	CU-CS addresses client selection under bandwidth constraints, while the proposed method highlights adaptability to IoT resource limitations.

3.2.3.1 *Heterogeneity in Systems and Data*

Zhang *et al.* [33], developed the IGPE algorithm to address client heterogeneity (CPU, dataset, transmission) and statistical heterogeneity (non-IID data) in federated learning. However, its real-world application can be complex and may impact overall system performance, highlighting the need for more practical solutions. Chen *et al.* [34], introduced a method to handle both device and data heterogeneity in federated learning. Their method addresses the differences in device abilities and data distributions among clients. However, they come across challenges with the inefficiency of random selection schemes. Competently managing this heterogeneity without compromising performance remains an ongoing challenge.

3.2.3.2 *Communication Overhead and Latency*

Chen *et al.* [34], developed the method FedGRA uses to address the communication overhead reduction. Their method is designed to improve communication efficiency; however, sustaining low communication overhead and effective client selection in a dynamic IoT environment remains challenging. Zhu *et al.* [36], proposed a method to reduce the training latency in federated learning in an online multi-armed bandit approach. Although their procedure is designed to accept the training time, unpredictable channel state information situations and equity problems among clients remain challenging. In real-world applications, these problems can be manifested by increased latency and communication difficulty. Ji *et al.* [37], focused on optimizing wireless federated learning with latency and energy minimization. Their method solves the mixed-integer problem for many rounds and formulates it in a significantly modified way as a multi-round. It shows that addressing each factor efficiently is tricky to balance.

3.2.3.3 *Energy Constraints*

The approach presented by Li *et al.* [38], focuses on energy D2D-assisted federated learning by considering IoT devices' energy limitations. Even though their technique aims to optimize energy consumption while maintaining model performance and reliable communication, striking a balance between these aspects remains a hurdle in energy-restricted settings. In another study, Tan *et al.* [39], introduced a reputation-conscious stochastic integer programming method to address issues related to client misconduct and compensation expenses in federated learning protocols. Dealing with these problems in their own way is one thing; handling them efficiently without using energy presents a real challenge.

3.2.3.4 *Volatile Client Population*

Shi *et al.* [41], introduced the CU-CS technique to address the difficulties of changing client numbers and limited bandwidth in learning systems. Despite their efforts to tackle these issues successfully, ensuring consistent and dependable client engagement is an obstacle in the dynamic landscape of IoT-enabled edge networks.

3.2.3.5 Accuracy and Performance Trade-Offs

Li *et al.* [40], investigated clustered federated learning and deep reinforcement learning to improve accuracy and lower communication costs in their study. Although their approaches appear promising, they face obstacles such as differing user data distributions and suboptimal clustering that may hinder their efficacy and impact performance. Fan *et al.* [35], CMSFed method was introduced to address modality level bias, in modal federated learning. Even though their method deals, with bias enough to some extent, it faces challenges with gathering data accurately, which might affect how well the model works in situations where different data types are involved.

The new method effectively overcomes the shortcomings of the mentioned strategies, which are elaborated in the "Proposed Work" section of this chapter.

3.3 System Model

This section presents the system model for the proposed energy-aware federated learning technique, which highlights how the dynamic client selection improves energy efficiency and learning accuracy in IoT-enabled edge networks.

3.3.1 Clients Data

The adaptive client selection strategy mainly depends on the client's data, which essentially consists of client dataset information for modeling the client data accurately, bandwidth information and transmission power for the proposed system model. This section specifies the parameters used in the simulation for evaluation of the system.

3.3.1.1 Client Dataset Information

The dataset sizes are consistently distributed between 2 and 10 MB to simulate faithful scenarios. The dataset size is denoted by a matrix with dimensions of $T_{round} \times$ Number of Clients during each training round. Each entry in this matrix specifies the data size (in bytes) available for a specific client at a training round. This distribution represents a range of client capabilities and the availability of data.

3.3.1.2 *Client Bandwidth Information*

The bandwidth values were distributed uniformly throughout 50 KHz to 100 KHz for the case of practical flexibility. The interval describes the fluctuations in network conditions and client capabilities. The bandwidth allocated to a client at each iteration in the round is determined from a T_{round} x Number of Clients dimensional matrix. Each matrix entry represents bandwidth (in KHz) assigned to a specific client in a given round.

3.3.1.3 *Client Transmission Power Information*

The transmission's power level is regularly varied between 4 and 10 dBm so that the variation of different power levels can be represented accurately. These variations arise from the difference in client transmission capability and the given network environment. Each matrix entry corresponds to the power level (in dBm) assigned to a specific client for a particular round.

3.3.2 System Model Components

The system model presents three key components: energy consumption, training time, and accuracy related to FL. All these factors play an essential role in understanding the overall performance and efficiency of the system. The following sections contain detailed system models and equations for each element, showing how a method is proposed to calculate energy consumption and estimate training time and FL accuracy.

3.3.2.1 *Energy Consumption Model*

In federated learning, the total energy consumption E_{total} will be the summation of the energy used for facilitating computations, E_{cmp} and the energy consumption for communication E_{up} [42].

Computation energy formula:

$$E_{cmp} = I_{local} \cdot \xi \cdot unit_{cost} \cdot D \cdot f^2 \tag{3.1}$$

Communication energy formula:

$$E_{up} = \frac{S \cdot P}{b \cdot log_2\left(1 + \dfrac{P \cdot G}{N_0 \cdot b}\right)} \tag{3.2}$$

Total Energy Consumption formula:

$$E_{total} = I_{global} \cdot (E_{cmp} + E_{up}) \tag{3.3}$$

3.3.2.2 *Training Time of FL*

The total training time T_{total} in federated learning is computed with both computation time T_{cmp} and communication time T_{up} [43].

Computation time formula:

$$T_{cmp} = I_{local} \cdot \frac{unit_{cost} \cdot D}{f} \tag{3.4}$$

Communication time formula:

$$T_{up} = \frac{S}{b \cdot log_2\left(1 + \frac{P \cdot G}{N_0 \cdot b}\right)} \tag{3.5}$$

Total Training Time formula:

$$T_{total} = I_{global} \cdot (T_{cmp} + T_{up}) \tag{3.6}$$

3.3.2.3 *FL Accuracy*

The federated learning model accuracy ϵ is a function of the data size and system parameters [44].

Formula for Individual Client Accuracy:

$$\varepsilon_{individual} = loglog\ (1 + \mu \cdot D) \tag{3.7}$$

Global Model Accuracy:

$$\varepsilon_{global} = log\ \left(1 + \mu \cdot \sum_i D_i \cdot \beta_i\right) \tag{3.8}$$

3.4 Proposed Work

The proposed work optimizes client selection in energy-aware federated learning for IoT-enabled edge networks. This section presents the methodology for optimizing the selection of clients based on their energy consumption and the accuracy they contribute to the global model. Initial screening of clients based on bandwidth and time constraints is crucial to determine an effective client selection strategy.

Bandwidth Constraint: Each client i must have an individual bandwidth b_i that does not exceed the total system bandwidth B.

$$b_i \leq B \tag{3.9}$$

Time Constraint: The total delay T_i for each client i must be less than or equal to the maximum allowable time T_{max}

$$T_i \leq T_{max} \tag{3.10}$$

Accuracy Constraint: Ensure that the combined accuracy of the selected clients meets or exceeds the target accuracy ε_0

The aggregated model accuracy can be formulated based on the individual accuracies of the selected clients. However, in many practical scenarios, this is approximated or derived from the contributions of the selected clients to the global model.

$$\varepsilon_{model} \geq \varepsilon_0 \tag{3.11}$$

The other foundational constraints related to this approach are detailed in the "System Model" section. Specifically, the computation energy calculation is presented in Equation (3.1), the upload energy calculation in Equation (3.2) and the total energy calculation in Equation (3.3). Time delay calculations are elaborated in Equations (3.4), (3.5) and (3.6). Additionally, accuracy calculation formulas are discussed in Equations (3.7) and (3.8).

By considering the above constraints, the objective function calculation can be calculated.

3.4.1 Objective Function Calculation

The objective function for optimizing client selection is defined as:

$$f_{obj} = \frac{\Sigma(r_i, E_i)}{log\left[1 + \mu \Sigma(r_i \cdot D_i)\right]} \tag{3.12}$$

The Equation 3.12 represents an objective function calculation, that is likely used to evaluate the overall system performance by balancing two critical aspects: energy consumption and data relevance in federated learning.

Table 3.2 explains the critical variables used throughout the Federated Learning (FL) framework for IoT-enabled edge networks. The equations from 3.1 to 3.12 have used the variables, they are essential for understanding the notations and meanings related to energy consumption and communication processes. For a clear understanding of each variable stated in these equations, please see Table 3.2.

3.4.2 Workflow for the Proposed System

The workflow of the proposed system involves a comprehensive scheme to optimize client selection in energy-aware federated learning for IoT-enabled edge networks, as shown in Figure 3.3.

The work begins by loading the necessary client data files, including information about the dataset size, bandwidth and transmission power for each client across different training rounds. System parameters like total system bandwidth (B), channel noise power spectral density (N_0), maximum allowable time for each communication round (T_{max}), data size for upload (S), computation cost per data unit, (ξ) and operating frequency of each client (f) are initialized. The accuracy for every client is calculated based on the dataset, followed by computing the computational and upload energy consumption. Thus, the total time consumption for each client is determined.

Preliminary screening tests are conducted to check whether each client's bandwidth and time constraints are met. Parameters for client selection are initialized to the clients that pass this screening and an inner loop is entered to check accuracy and update the objective function. After the objective function is updated, the loop breaks, if accuracy and constraints are met. Otherwise, the index is incremented, and combinations of the choices made by the clients are examined. If there are valid choices,

Table 3.2 Key variables defined in the system model.

Variable	Definition	Variable	Definition
T	Total number of rounds	ϵ_0	Minimum accuracy requirement
N	Number of clients	ϵ_i	Accuracy for client i
D_t	Dataset size for each client at round t	I_{local}	Number of local iterations in each global iteration
$b_{t:}$	Bandwidth of each client at round t	I_{global}	Number of global iterations
$P_{t:}$	Transmission power for every client at round t	D	Size of the local dataset
G_t	Channel gain for every client at round t	S	Size of the transmitted data.
f_t	Frequency for every client at round t	β_i	Client selection indicator (1 if selected, 0 if not)
μ	System parameter for accuracy calculation	r_i	Binary variable indicating if client iii is selected (1 if selected, 0 otherwise)
L	Number of local iterations in each global iteration	E_i	Total energy consumption for client i.
ξ	Effective switched capacitance	D_i	Dataset size for client i.
N_0	Noise power spectral density	f_{obj}	Objective function value.

the objective function is updated. If there are no valid choices, the initial choice made by the client is used. At each step of this algorithm, results are accrued. When the loop is executed at the end, all results are saved in a file, which marks the algorithms termination. This confirms that the best choices for clients are achieved while considering the stipulated constraints and improving energy efficiency and accuracy.

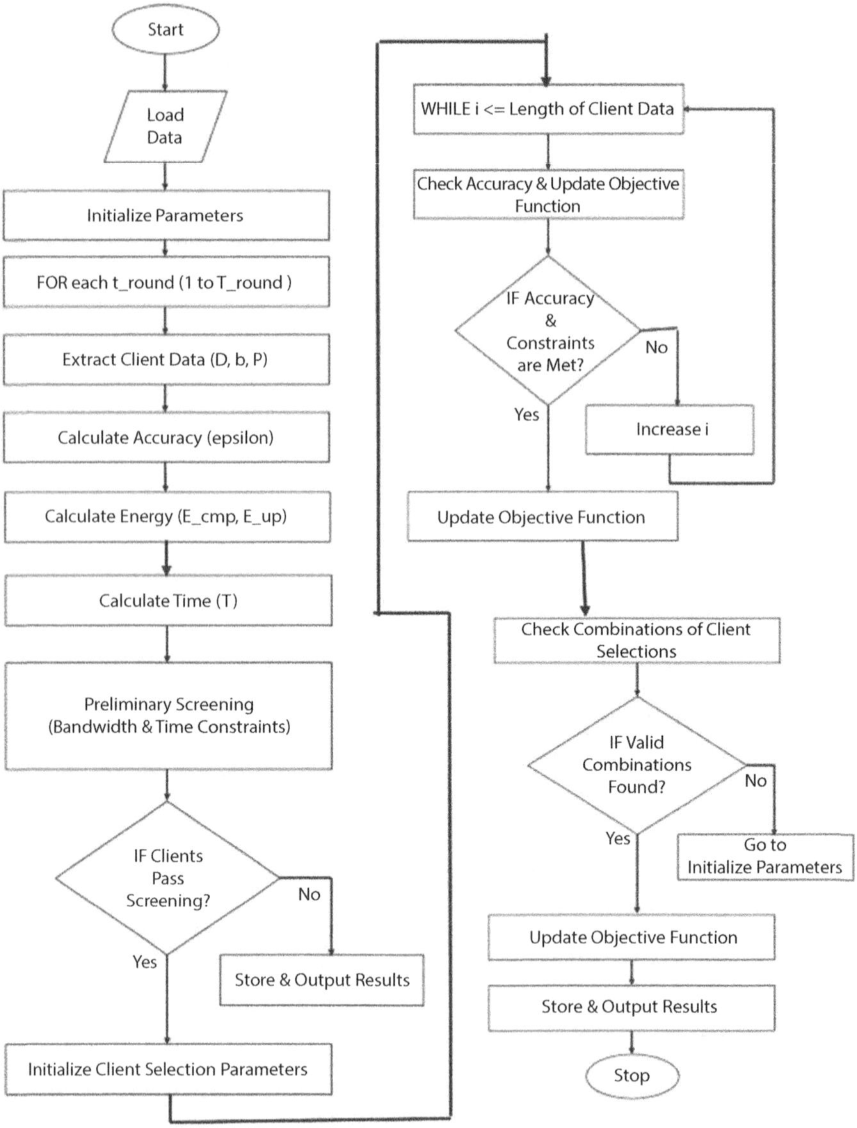

Figure 3.3 Flow chart for the proposed system.

3.4.3 Simulation Tool and Configuration

MATLAB is used as a simulation tool. It is ideal for simulating and suitable for modeling complex systems and algorithms because of its powerful computational and visualization capabilities. The parameters needed for the simulation configuration and their values are shown in Table 3.3. Visualization of data from each client is shown using pre-loaded datasets of different sizes, thus illustrating some common scenarios encountered in federated learning. The proposed Energy-Aware Client Selection scheme

Table 3.3 The parameters required for the simulation.

Parameter	Definition	Value
I	Number of iterations	1000
K	Number of clients	{20, 40, 60, 80, 100}
μ	System parameter	set to 1.7×10^{-8}
B	Total system bandwidth	{1, 3, 5, 7, 9} MHz
$D_{i,k}$	Dataset size for client i, uniformly distributed	[2, 10] MB
$b_{k:}$	Individual client bandwidth, uniformly distributed	[50, 150] KHz
N_0	Channel noise power spectral density	set to 1×10^{-8} W/Hz
T_max	Maximum allowable time for each communication round	set to 5 seconds
S	Data size to be uploaded by each client	10,000 bits (10 kbits)
ξ	Computation cost per data unit	set to 1×10^{-28} cycles/bit
unit_cost	Computational cost per bit, uniformly distributed	[10, 30] cycles/bit
G	Channel gain array for each client	Calculated using $G_i = 40\left[\frac{0.5}{\mu(0.6,1)}\right]^4$ where $\mu(0.6, 1)$ follows a uniform distribution
f	Operating frequency array for each client	Uniformly distributed between 1 GHz and 2 GHz

has been implemented using MATLAB R2021a on a 3.0 GHz Intel Core processor with 12 GB of RAM, thus providing sufficient computational capacities for the analysis and performance evaluation process.

3.4.4 Addressing the Limitations of Existing Works

The following research addresses the shortcomings identified in prior studies related to problems in client selection optimization. With such challenges, the energy-aware federated learning approach addresses many of the elements mentioned, including energy consumption, bandwidth, and precision. Below, the methodology is demonstrated in addressing several of the limitations mentioned above:

Managing Heterogeneity:
The proposed method effectively addresses variations in systems and data by adaptively selecting clients according to dataset size, bandwidth, and transmission energy. This strategy guarantees the optimal selection of clients for every training iteration, thereby mitigating issues arising from multiple clients possessing significantly different capabilities and data attributes.

Reducing Communication Overhead and Latency:
The proposed scheme minimizes communication overhead and latency in training by selecting clients systematically to satisfy specific bandwidth and time constraints. This optimization, therefore, increases efficiency and performance in training models.

Handling Energy Constraints:
To reduce the overall energy consumption and the model's integrity in terms of accuracy, each client is evaluated first before its selection in the given technique. This, in turn, will also eradicate energy constraints and increase an operation's efficiency.

Dealing with Volatile Client Populations:
Implementing this initial screening procedure ensures the retention of clients selected on predetermined criteria such as creditworthiness to confirm dependable clients. This reduces variations among clients since it will constantly point out dependable people.

Improving Accuracy and Performance:
Our proposed approach contains a mechanism to guarantee that the selected clients satisfy the required accuracy conditions. It achieves this

by balancing accuracy and performance effectively, ensuring high-quality results while operating as efficiently as possible.

3.4.5 Comparison with Client Selection Schemes

In connection with the proposed set of federated learning (FL), three different client selection schemes have been tested for effectiveness, and they are:

FedAvg: This scheme follows the principle of randomly choosing clients for the FL training process if the available bandwidth limit is satisfied. However, this approach might be effective in the short run but can have drawbacks in optimally merging the model accuracy and the overall operational efficiency of the process.

FedCS: In this scheme, the FL server selects the clients based on their ability to meet bandwidth constraints. This approach is more efficient than the previous one in the sense that a participating client has the required bandwidth that would enable it to deal with the necessary data transfer making it more efficient than the FedAvg scheme.

Energy-based Client Selection: In this scheme, clients' energy consumption level is established, and those with the best levels are prioritized. From this, the FL server can pick a subsection of clients while adhering to the constraints posed by the bandwidth level of the clients. This scheme aims to reduce energy usage throughout training, which can be beneficial in resource-constrained settings.

Proposed Technique: The proposed scheme presents a novel strategy considering dataset size, bandwidth, transmission power and energy to select the clients. The technique aims at improving the model accuracy while at the same time minimizing energy efficiency and is targeted for energy-resource constrained dynamic IoT environments.

The comparison illustrates how the proposed technique addresses the shortcomings of the other schemes to offer better federated learning in a dynamic environment with varying resource constraints.

3.5 Simulation Results

The simulation evaluates four client selection strategies, and they are Fed-CS (Client Selection), Fed-Avg (Federated Average), Fed-ENE (Energy-based Client Selection), and the proposed dynamic client selection approach (Fed-Proposed) in a federated learning system with a varying client number 20, 40, 60, 80, and 100. The objective value (Obj-Val), the measure of energy consumption and model accuracy, is calculated as the average with a standard deviation over 1000 rounds to ensure the results are dependable. This technique provides an in-depth evaluation of each method's performance and robustness under different client size measures.

Figure 3.4 demonstrates the results of the comparison in a plot for the Ojb-Val metric for various client selection strategies.

From the results, Fed-CS demonstrates poor performance as mentioned earlier, tractable to the confirmed increase of Obj-Val with the leading client numbers, indicating high energy costs and inefficiencies. Fed-Avg performs moderately improved, slowly increasing Obj-Val as the number of clients grows. However, Fed-ENE maintains a stable Obj-Val, representing efficiency in energy-based selection. Notably, the proposed Fed-Proposed approach achieves the lowest Obj-Val across all client numbers, showing a slight downward trend as the number of clients increases, underscoring its effectiveness in reducing energy consumption and enhancing scalability.

The percentage improvement over each traditional method is calculated to quantify the performance improvements achieved by the proposed dynamic client selection approach. The improvement is calculated as:

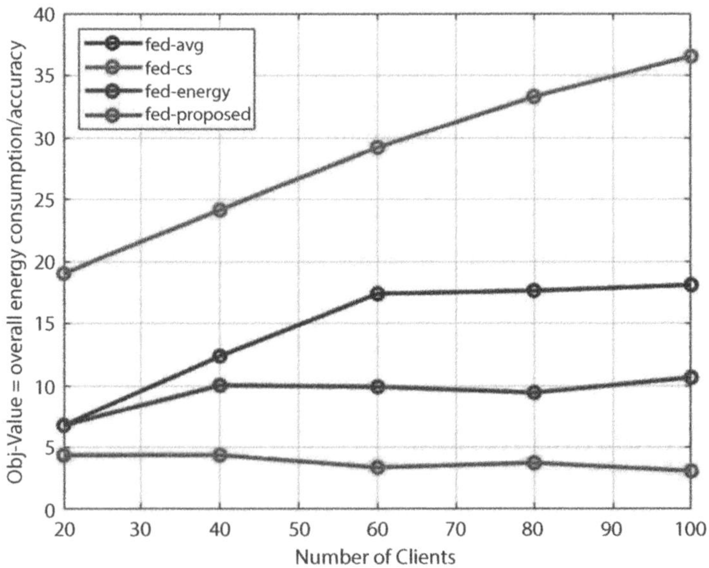

Figure 3.4 Number of clients versus objective value.

$$Improvement\ (\%) = \left(\frac{Value\ of\ baseline\ Method - Value\ of\ Proposed\ Method}{Value\ of\ baseline\ Method} \right) X100$$

The proposed approach shows an average improvement of 85.57% over Fed-CS, 68.52% over Fed-Avg, and 57.87% over Fed-ENE, highlighting its superior efficiency in energy usage and model accuracy across varying client scenarios.

3.5.1 Effect of T_{max} on Qualified Client Numbers and Selection Dynamics

The effect of T_{max} on the number of qualified clients is shown in Table 3.4 and Figure 3.5.

When T_{max} is set to 1 second, very few clients qualify across scenarios due to the strict timing constraint. As T_{max} increases, more clients qualify, with nearly all clients in scenarios of 20 and 40 participants qualifying by T_{max} = 7 seconds. This demonstrates the adaptability of the proposed approach in accommodating diverse client capabilities.

For instance, with T_{max} = 2 seconds, only 7 clients qualify in a 20-client scenario. When T_{max} increases to 6 seconds, almost all clients (19 out of 20) qualify, showcasing the approach's scalability. This flexibility allows

Table 3.4 Qualified clients data.

	No. of clients = 20	No. of clients = 40	No. of clients = 60	No. of clients = 80
T max (sec)	Qualified clients	Qualified clients	Qualified clients	Qualified clients
1	2	3	5	2
2	7	10	14	22
3	10	21	34	43
4	12	28	45	53
5	16	32	50	65
6	19	36	55	71
7	20	38	58	75

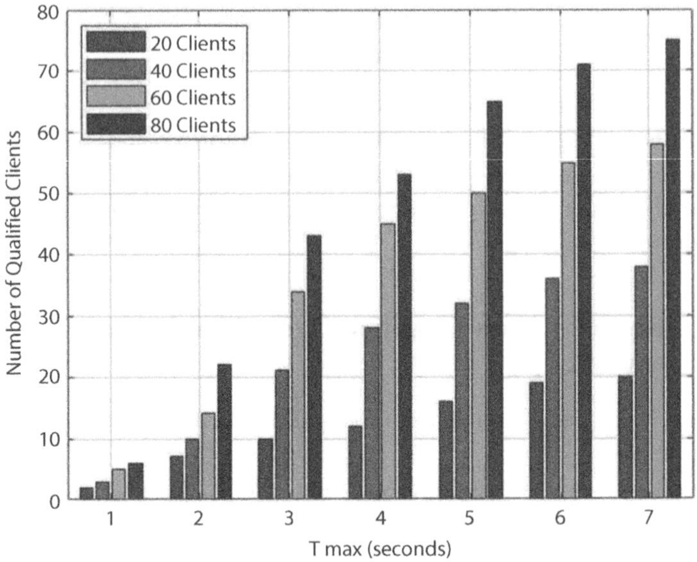

Figure 3.5 Number of qualified clients versus Tmax.

the dynamic selection approach to adjust to network conditions, ensuring optimal resource use and learning performance.

3.5.2 Impact of Tmax and Accuracy Threshold (ε) on Optimization Performance

Increasing T_{max} allows for longer client computations and communications, generally reducing the objective value (f_obj) as more efficient client combinations are selected. For an accuracy threshold of ε = 0.1, f_obj consistently decreases with higher Tmax. However, a lower ε (stricter accuracy requirement, such as ε = 0.08) complicates optimization, limiting viable client combinations. Consequently, at ε = 0.08, f_obj values do not decrease as consistently with higher T_{max}.

Figure 3.6 shows the relationship of f_obj against Tmax for different ε values.

For Tmax = 2 seconds, our f_obj value is 8.4557407 for ε = 0.1 and ε = 0.08, which implies similar client selection under tight time constraints. It is observed from the f_obj, given additional time to the algorithm, decreases more significantly at Tmax = 3 seconds when ε = 0.08 decreases than at ε = 0.1. As computation time increases, the Tmax values are 4 and 5 seconds,

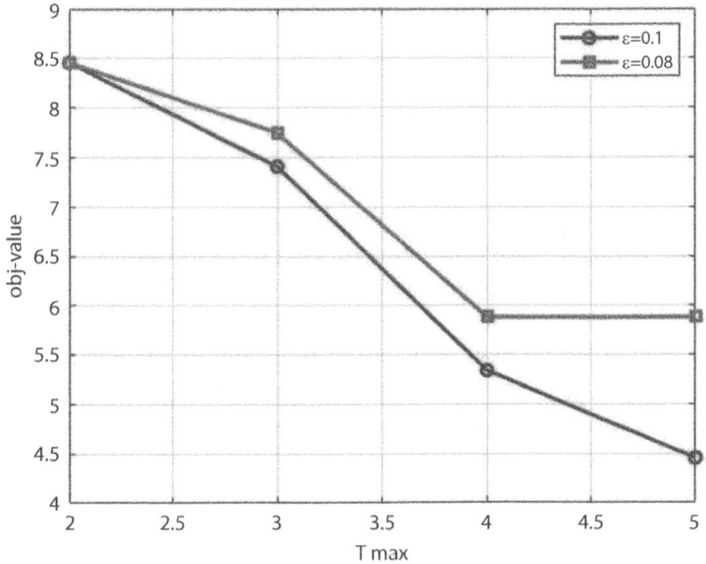

Figure 3.6 Objective function value versus Tmax.

and f_obj values for ε = 0.08 exceed those for ε = 0.1, which indicates that optimization is still impossible. The results in these scenarios show that there are trade-offs between Tmax and ε, and that for maximizing federated learning performance, there is a need to find the balance between time constraints and accuracy necessity.

3.6 Conclusion and Future Work

We proposed a new global Federated Learning (FL) architecture to improve performance and reduce energy consumption in the Internet of Things (IoT)-enabled edge networks as part of next-generation 6G networks. Our approach of dynamically selecting clients outperforms traditional methods by optimizing the overall energy consumed and maintaining model accuracy. Results of extensive simulations validate that this scheme can be flexible to adapt to diverse network conditions and perform adaptability ensuring robustness and scalability. This adaptive approach efficiently addresses the computing and communication overheads, providing a timely solution towards real-world federated learning implementations in resource-limited IoT environments.

The proposed dynamic client selection methodology can yield considerable performance increases. In general, there is an improvement of 85.57%

in the objective function value compared to the FedCS approach, a 68.52% rise relative to the FedAvg technique, and a 57.87% increase against the Fed-Energy strategy. Average statistics indicate that the proposed method is more efficient in enhancing energy efficiency and model accuracy across different client scenarios.

Future work will focus on improving the adaptability of the client selection algorithm. It will be concentrated on optimizing performance with respect to changing bandwidth and varying device conditions for 6G networks. This energy-aware federated learning framework is also applicable to other fields, such as smart cities, health care, and autonomous vehicles, and it is evidenced by high application potential in various IoT contexts. Considering the importance of data privacy, subsequent research endeavors can incorporate advanced methodologies in protecting privacy, namely differential or homomorphic encryption, while keeping the computational complexity and data interchange from inducing excessive overheads.

Future work will precisely remove some barriers that prevent the client selection algorithm from being even adaptive when considering bandwidth volatility and device capabilities expected to be found in the 6G network environment. The FL framework above can be generalized to other fields, such as a smart city, innovative healthcare, or self-driving vehicles, to represent its flexibility and universality to various IoT applications.

Since data privacy is an important issue concerning the federated learning framework, further research may include important privacy-preserving mechanisms such as differential privacy and homomorphic encryption to protect sensitive data with federated learning. The proposed approach can help develop current federated learning architectures by presenting better and safer approaches to solving issues within federated learning, thus allowing safe and efficient implementation in any IoT environment.

AI disclosure statement: The author acknowledges the use of AI-based tools for minor language editing or grammatical correction. However, all intellectual contributions, analyses, and conclusions presented in this chapter are entirely the author's own.

References

1. Saha, R., Misra, S., Chakraborty, A., Chatterjee, C., Deb, P.K., Data-Centric client selection for federated learning over distributed edge networks. *IEEE Trans. Parallel Distrib. Syst.*, 34, 2, 675–686, Feb. 2023, doi: 10.1109/tpds.2022.3217271.

2. Albaseer, A.M., Abdallah, M., Al-Fuqaha, A., Seid, A.M., Erbad, A., Dobre, O.A., Fair selection of edge nodes to participate in clustered federated multitask learning. *IEEE Trans. Network Serv. Management/IEEE eTransactions Network Serv. Manage.*, 20, 2, 1502–1516, Jun. 2023, doi: 10.1109/tnsm.2023.3270168.
3. Statista, Number of IoT connections worldwide 2022-2033, with forecasts to 2030, https://www.statista.com/statistics/1183457/iot-connected-devices-worldwide/, 2024, June 12.
4. Sattibabu, G., Ganesan, N., Prakash, V.C., An exploration of state of art approaches on machine learning based Energy-Efficient routing approaches for wireless sensor networks. *In Adv. Eng. Research/Advances Eng. Res.*, 416–429, 2023, https://doi.org/10.2991/978-94-6463-252-1_45.
5. Jararweh, Y., Fatima, S., Jarrah, M., AlZu'bi, S., Smart and sustainable agriculture: Fundamentals, enabling technologies and future directions. *Comput. Electr. Eng.*, 110, 108799, 2023, https://doi.org/10.1016/j.compeleceng.2023.108799.
6. Hazra, A., Kalita, A., Gurusamy, M., Meeting the requirements of internet of Things: the promise of edge computing. *IEEE Internet Things J.*, 11, 5, 7474–7498, 2024, https://doi.org/10.1109/jiot.2023.3339492.
7. Konečný, J., McMahan, H.B., Ramage, D., Federated Optimization:Distributed optimization beyond the datacenter. arXiv (Cornell University), https://doi.org/10.48550/arxiv.1511.03575, 2015.
8. Konečný, J., McMahan, H.B., Ramage, D., Richtarik, P., Federated Optimization: Distributed machine learning for On-Device intelligence. arXiv (Cornell University), https://doi.org/10.48550/arxiv.1610.02527, 2016.
9. Wahab, O.A., Mourad, A., Otrok, H., Taleb, T., Federated Machine Learning: Survey, Multi-Level Classification, desirable Criteria and future directions in communication and networking systems. *IEEE Commun. Surv. Tutorials/IEEE Commun. Surv. Tutorials*, 23, 2, 1342–1397, Jan. 2021, doi: 10.1109/comst.2021.3058573.
10. Xia, Q., Ye, W., Tao, Z., Wu, J., Li, Q., A survey of federated learning for edge computing: Research problems and solutions. *High-Confid. Comput.*, 1, 1, 100008, 2021, https://doi.org/10.1016/j.hcc.2021.100008.
11. Wen, J., Zhang, Z., Lan, Y., Cui, Z., Cai, J., Zhang, W., A survey on federated learning: challenges and applications. *Int. J. Mach. Learn. Cybern.*, 14, 2, 513–535, 2022, https://doi.org/10.1007/s13042-022-01647-y.
12. Rajendran, S.K. and Nagarajan, G., Network lifetime enhancement of wireless sensor networks using EFRP Protocol. *Wireless Pers. Commun.*, 123, 2, 1769–1787, 2022, https://doi.org/10.1007/s11277-021-09212-6.
13. Khajehali, N., Yan, J., Chow, Y., Fahmideh, M., A comprehensive overview of IoT-Based Federated Learning: focusing on client selection methods. *Sensors*, 23, 16, 7235, 2023, https://doi.org/10.3390/s23167235.
14. Kumaran, R.S. and Nagarajan, G., Mobile sink and fuzzy based relay node routing protocol for network lifetime enhancement in wireless sensor

networks. *Wireless Netw.*, 28, 5, 1963–1975, 2022, https://doi.org/10.1007/s11276-022-02960-8.

15. Imteaj, A., Thakker, U., Wang, S., Li, J., Amini, M.H., A survey on federated Learning for Resource-Constrained IoT Devices. *IEEE Internet Things J.*, 9, 1, 1–24, 2022, https://doi.org/10.1109/jiot.2021.3095077.
16. Sun, Y., Shi, W., Huang, X., Zhou, S., Niu, Z., Edge Learning with Timeliness Constraints: Challenges and Solutions. *IEEE Commun. Mag.*, 58, 12, 27–33, 2020, https://doi.org/10.1109/mcom.001.2000382.
17. Xu, J. and Wang, H., Client Selection and bandwidth allocation in Wireless Federated Learning Networks: A Long-Term Perspective. *IEEE Trans. Wireless Commun.*, 20, 2, 1188–1200, 2021, https://doi.org/10.1109/twc.2020.3031503.
18. Gharaibeh, A., Salahuddin, M.A., Hussini, S.J., Khreishah, A., Khalil, I., Guizani, M., Al-Fuqaha, A., Smart Cities: A survey on data management, security and enabling technologies. *IEEE Commun. Surveys Tutorials/IEEE Commun. Surv. Tutorials*, 19, 4, 2456–2501, 2017, https://doi.org/10.1109/comst.2017.2736886.
19. Li, Y., Liang, W., Li, J., Cheng, X., Yu, D., Zomaya, A.Y., Guo, S., Energy-aware, Device-to-Device assisted federated learning in edge computing. *IEEE Trans. Parallel Distrib. Syst.*, 34, 7, 2138–2154, 2023, https://doi.org/10.1109/tpds.2023.3277423.
20. Shi, D., Li, L., Chen, R., Prakash, P., Pan, M., Fang, Y., Toward Energy-Efficient federated learning over 5G+ mobile devices. *IEEE Wireless Commun.*, 29, 5, 44–51, 2022, https://doi.org/10.1109/mwc.003.2100028.
21. Kaleem, S., Sohail, A., Babar, M., Ahmad, A., Tariq, M.U., A hybrid model for energy-efficient Green Internet of Things enabled intelligent transportation systems using federated learning. *Internet Things*, 25, 101038, 2024, https://doi.org/10.1016/j.iot.2023.101038.
22. Shanmugarasa, Y., Paik, H., Kanhere, S.S., Zhu, L., A systematic review of federated learning from clients' perspective: challenges and solutions. *Artif. Intell. Rev.*, 56, S2, 1773–1827, 2023, https://doi.org/10.1007/s10462-023-10563-8.
23. Aboubakar, M., Kellil, M., Roux, P., A review of IoT network management: Current status and perspectives. *J. King Saud Univ. Comput. Inf. Sci.*, 34, 7, 4163–4176, 2022, https://doi.org/10.1016/j.jksuci.2021.03.006.
24. Wu, J., Drew, S., Zhou, J., FedLE: Federated Learning Client Selection with Lifespan Extension for Edge IoT Networks. arXiv (Cornell University), https://doi.org/10.48550/arxiv.2302.07305, 2023.
25. Srinidhi, N., Kumar, S.D., Venugopal, K., Network optimizations in the Internet of Things: A review. *Eng. Sci. Technol. Int. J.*, 22, 1, 1–21, 2019, https://doi.org/10.1016/j.jestch.2018.09.003.
26. Abdulrahman, S., Tout, H., Mourad, A., Talhi, C., FEDMCCS: Multicriteria Client Selection Model for optimal IoT Federated Learning. *IEEE Internet Things J.*, 8, 6, 4723–4735, 2021, doi: 10.1109/jiot.2020.3028742.

27. Rjoub, G., Wahab, O.A., Bentahar, J., Cohen, R., Bataineh, A.S., Trust-Augmented Deep Reinforcement Learning for federated Learning client selection. *Inf. Syst. Front.*, 2022, https://doi.org/10.1007/s10796-022-10307-z.
28. Nguyen, D.C., Ding, M., Pathirana, P.N., Seneviratne, A., Li, J., Poor, H.V., Federated Learning for Internet of Things: A Comprehensive survey. *IEEE Commun. Surv. Tutorials*, 23, 3, 1622–1658, 2021, https://doi.org/10.1109/comst.2021.3075439.
29. Deng, Y., Lyu, F., Ren, J., Wu, H., Zhou, Y., Zhang, Y., Shen, X., AUCTION: Automated and Quality-Aware client selection framework for efficient federated learning. *IEEE Trans. Parallel Distrib. Syst.*, 33, 8, 1996–2009, 2022, https://doi.org/10.1109/tpds.2021.3134647.
30. Zhu, H., Xu, J., Liu, S., Jin, Y., Federated learning on non-IID data: A survey. *Neurocomputing*, 465, 371–390, 2021, https://doi.org/10.1016/j.neucom.2021.07.098.
31. Lu, S., Li, R., Liu, W., Guan, C., Yang, X., Top-k sparsification with secure aggregation for privacy-preserving federated learning. *Comput. Secur.*, 124, 102993, 2023, https://doi.org/10.1016/j.cose.2022.102993.
32. Alferaidi, A., Yadav, K., Alharbi, Y., Viriyasitavat, W., Kautish, S., Dhiman, G., Federated learning algorithms to optimize the client and cost selections. *Math. Probl. Eng.*, 2022, 1–9, 2022, https://doi.org/10.1155/2022/8514562.
33. Zhang, J., Wang, J., Li, Y., Xin, F., Dong, F., Luo, J., Wu, Z., Addressing Heterogeneity in Federated Learning with Client Selection *via* Submodular Optimization. *ACM Trans. Sens. Netw.*, 20, 2, 1–32, 2024, https://doi.org/10.1145/3638052.
34. Chen, S., Tavallaie, O., Hambali, M.H., Zandavi, S.M., Haddadi, H., Guo, S., Zomaya, A.Y., Boosting Client Selection of Federated Learning under Device and Data Heterogeneity. arXiv (Cornell University), https://doi.org/10.48550/arxiv.2310.08147, 2023.
35. Fan, Y., Xu, W., Wang, H., Ruan, P., Guo, S., Client-wise modality selection for balanced multi-modal federated learning. arXiv (Cornell University), https://doi.org/10.48550/arxiv.2401.00403, 2024.
36. Zhu, H., Zhou, Y., Qian, H., Shi, Y., Chen, X., Yang, Y., Online client selection for asynchronous federated learning with fairness consideration. *IEEE Trans. Wireless Commun.*, 22, 4, 2493–2506, 2023, https://doi.org/10.1109/twc.2022.3211998.
37. Ji, Y., Zhong, X., Kou, Z., Zhang, S., Li, H., Yang, Y., Efficiency-Boosting Federated Learning in Wireless Networks: A Long-Term Perspective. *IEEE Trans. Veh. Technol.*, 72, 7, 9434–9447, 2023, https://doi.org/10.1109/tvt.2023.3250273.
38. Tong, Z., Cai, J., Mei, J., Li, K., Li, K., Dynamic energy-saving offloading strategy guided by lyapunov optimization for IoT devices. *IEEE Internet Things J.*, 9, 19903–19915, 2022. https://doi.org/10.1109/JIOT.2022.3168968.
39. Tan, X., Ng, W.C., Lim, W.Y.B., Xiong, Z., Niyato, D., Yu, H., Reputation-Aware Federated Learning Client Selection based on Stochastic Integer

Programming. *IEEE Trans. Big Data*, 1–12, 2024, https://doi.org/10.1109/tbdata.2022.3191332.
40. Li, Y., Qin, X., Chen, H., Han, K., Zhang, P., Energy-Aware EdGe Association for Cluster-Based Personalized Federated Learning. *IEEE Trans. Veh. Technol.*, 71, 6, 6756–6761, 2022, https://doi.org/10.1109/tvt.2022.3161503.
41. Shi, F., Lin, W., Fan, L., Lai, X., Wang, X., Efficient client selection based on contextual combinatorial Multi-Arm bandits. *IEEE Trans. Wireless Commun.*, 22, 8, 5265–5277, 2023, https://doi.org/10.1109/twc.2022.3232891.
42. Xue, X., Mao, H., Li, Q., Huang, F., El-Latif, A.A., An energy efficient specializing DAG federated learning based on Event-Triggered communication. *Mathematics*, 10, 22, 4388, 2022, https://doi.org/10.3390/math10224388.
43. Li, K., Wang, H., Zhang, Q., FedTCR: communication-efficient federated learning *via* taming computing resources. *Complex Intell. Syst.*, 9, 5, 5199–5219, 2023, https://doi.org/10.1007/s40747-023-01006-6.
44. Khan, L.U., Pandey, S.R., Tran, N.H., Saad, W., Han, Z., Nguyen, M.N.H., Hong, C.S., Federated Learning for edge Networks: Resource Optimization and Incentive Mechanism. *IEEE Commun. Mag.*, 58, 10, 88–93, 2020, https://doi.org/10.1109/mcom.001.1900649.

4

The Connected World: Exploring the Expanding IoT Ecosystem

A. Revathi[1*], R. Kaladevi[2], M. Vimaladevi[1], V. Umarani[3] and S. Mohanaselvi[4]

[1]Department of Computational Intelligence, SRM Institute of Science and Technology, Chennai, India
[2]Department of Artificial Intelligence and Datascience, Saveetha Engineering College, Chennai, India
[3]Department of Computer Science and Engineering, Saveetha Engineering College, Chennai, India
[4]Department of Mathematics, SRM Institute of Science and Technology, Chennai, India

Abstract
The sensors and their enabling technologies have managed communication much easier and cheaper. Internet of Things shortly called IoT consists of sensors that collect data which is then processed using computing resources available in cloud platform. The sensor network consists of controlling software, some hardware components like digital and mechanical gear to govern the network. With robotics, IoT curtails the need for human intervention in the majority of tasks, including mining, disaster relief, and delicate surgery. Things are now communicative and controllable *via* remote systems in a variety of fields, including home automation, industry automation, healthcare monitoring, drones, and sensors in agriculture and defense. This chapter summarizes the importance of IoT in a number of domains, such as weather forecasting, disaster relief, healthcare, agriculture, and home and office automation. The significance of weather forecasting to stakeholders is examined in Section 4.2, along with the numerous sensors and technologies used in the process. Section 4.3 discusses the use of IoT in disaster management using a tsunami early warning system as a case study. The Internet of Medical Things is the subject of Section 4.4. Section 4.5 discusses the IoT's core technologies for industrial automation and optimization. Section 4.6 discusses the different

**Corresponding author*: revathia1@srmist.edu.in

T. Perarasi, M. Karthiga, S. Sountharrajan, E. Suganya and Balamurugan Balusamy (eds.) Secure Blockchain and Quantum Technologies for 6G-Enabled Internet of Things, (69–94) © 2026 Scrivener Publishing LLC

kinds of agricultural sensors and their uses. Section 4.7 provides a summary of the research trends and difficulties in each topic.

***Keywords*:** Internet of things, sensors, agriculture, disaster management, industrial IoT, internet of medical things

4.1 Introduction

Globalization and information and communication technologies provided many technologies and opportunities. The advent of internet made the world communicate in fast pace and information transfer is huge. Through internet telephony and emails, this was achieved. The improvements in mobile technologies provided still more facilities like instant chat, fast transfer of video, audio and image files, mobile banking, instant money transfer *via* Unified Payment Interface. The wireless network standards such as 5G, 6G are designed to connect everything, including gadgets, equipment, and objects. Industry 4.0 refers to "smart manufacturing," in which producers incorporate new technology into every aspect of their business operations, along with AI and machine learning, internet of things (IoT) and cloud services to enhance their operations. This facilitates increased supply, resilience and real-time decision making. The term IoT means network of things or objects in physical which are integrated with sensors, actuators, controling software's and associated to the network to share data with the other end for appropriate action. Object to object communication is possible with the advent of internet of things (IoT) [1].

The field of internet of things is expanding rapidly and attracts widespread uses in various sectors. Connected universe is possible with the advent of portable, wearable and implantable sensors. The physical objects are transformed into ecosystem of information which revolutionize our daily lives. Connected appliances, virtual assistants, security and monitoring system made Smart homes. Smart cities assure smart infrastructure, traffic management, public transport, environment monitoring and waste management. Industrial automation is a major revolution which helps in Predictive maintenance, inventory management, industrial robots, and supply chain management [2]. The role of IoT is vital in healthcare sector to monitor the patients from remote locations, connected medical equipment's, robotic surgery and so on. The more secured Block chain transaction processing technique utilizes IoT. Agriculture is a main area where IoT supports in precision agriculture, livestock monitoring and automated irrigation systems. Apart from the mentioned areas IoT is also useful in disaster management, supply chain, and wildlife monitoring [2].

The internet and mobile technologies, futuristic network technologies, IoT with machine learning and deep learning algorithms are helpful from data collection to data analytics without manual intervention which made the universe more connected. According to experts' prediction, the number of IoT devices are 22 billion by the year 2025. Massive promise for a more automated and connected future exists with the internet of things, (IoT) but it also comes with limitations that need to be addressed—malfunctioning of sensors, energy consumption, interoperability, security and privacy concerns and so on.

IoT is a suitable option for many applications due to its adaptability. Figure 4.1 highlights a few key industries where IoT is marking its significance.

The primary objective of this chapter is to give an overview of how IoT connects physical objects to the digital world. Each section of this chapter summarizes the role of IoT in various sectors including weather management, disaster management, healthcare, industry, and agriculture. For each sector, the important sensors, communication technology are discussed, and emphasized how IoT helps to improve the efficiency and auto mation.

This chapter's road map is as follows. Section 4.2 focuses on Weather forecasting, Section 4.3 covers Disaster management, Section 4.4 address the use of IoT in Medical field (IoMT), Section 4.5 is deals with Industrial automation, Section 4.6 is about smart agriculture. Section 4.7 discusses the existing research and future research needs. Conclusion is given in Section 4.8.

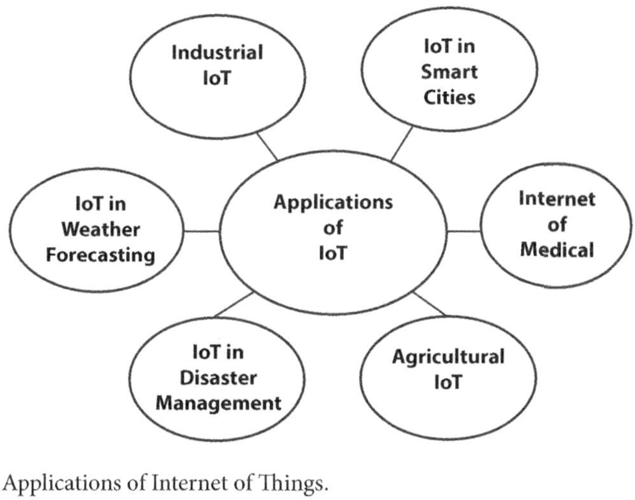

Figure 4.1 Applications of Internet of Things.

4.2 IoT in Weather Forecasting

Weather forecasting is the estimation of climatic condition with the application of principles of physics and various statistical and empirical techniques. It helps us to offer smooth functioning of many important activities. The drastic variations in climate sometimes results in flash-floods that cause significant damage to property and fatalities. The expansion of the internet of things has made it possible to predict real time or almost real time weather condition [3].

The localized sensors facilitate short-term forecasts for small regions by making use of machine learning techniques. Weather monitoring system constantly monitors environmental elements such as humidity, temperature, intensity levels, air quality, and rainfall [4]. In addition, it also monitors the concentration of gases namely carbon dioxide, carbon monoxide, ammonia, hydrogen, and methane to predict the weather condition more accurately [5]. The sensor is handled in the designated servers and it is made available to the public through user friendly interface. These weather data is more useful to farmers to take optimal decision in plant growth.

The system involves various IoT sensors to collect environmental parameters and uses NODEMCU and Arduino UNO. The popular cloud server ThingSpeak enables data transfer and data retrieval becomes the official cloud server, ready to enable data transfer and retrieval irrespective of physical boundaries. The data that resides in cloud server can be accessed anywhere and anytime [6]. The proposed IoT-based weather monitoring arrangement provides information of climate-changing conditions, and the author described the use of IoT in weather prediction. The authors applied swarm intelligence along with simple hardware and software components to accurately predict the output. The authors used thingspeak webserver to store the sensor data collected by them. Thingpad supports the programmer to upload whole sensor data related to weather conditions into the android mobile using API interface key.

Some of the important domains for which weather forecasting is essential is listed below:

Military – Based on the expected weather condition they could plan their battles so that they can maximize the chance of winning the war.
General Public – They're able to take measures against natural calamities such as floods and cyclones to safeguard themselves and their belongings.
Agriculture – Farmers can take intelligent decision based on the likely climate state to maximize the yield.

Transportation – The weather has a major impact on both air and water transportation. Weather has a big impact on an aircraft's takeoff and landing and for water transportation, the two strong influencing factors are storms and strong winds.

The weather forecasting model collects atmospheric conditions such as relative humidity, temperature, precipitation, light intensity and CO_2 level using various sensors that are connected with microcontrollers. The data collected by the sensor are sent to cloud computing platform for processing. The India Meteorological Department (IMD) collects data from several satellites that are in geosynchronous orbit. The Real-Time Analysis of Products and Information Dissemination (RAPID) application process these bits of information and provide interactive visualization. The existing statistical forecasting system is replaced with Multi-Model Ensemble (MME) in IMD to provide more accurate prediction [7].

Weather observation data is used to create weather maps, which are useful for tracking the weather. The locations of areas with high and low pressure can be determined based on the surface air pressure. Cold or warm fronts can be found based on temperature and cloud cover. To evaluate the local weather changes brought about by weather systems, one can follow the path and pace of movement of weather systems, such as cold fronts, warm fronts, and high-pressure zones, on successive weather maps. For example, a cold front brings a sharp drop in temperature, and when an area of low-pressure approaches rain or even thunderstorms often follow.

4.2.1 Challenges in Weather Forecasting

1. Ocean currents largely impacts global weather systems. Since the changes are unpredictable the weather forecasts go sometimes wrong [8].
2. Bay of Bengal influences the weather across the Indian country.
3. It is impossible to account for every aspect of nature in weather forecasting models since they are predicated on specific assumptions.
4. Due to this, weather forecast sometimes goes wrong.
5. It is not always possible to give more accurate input to the model. This is also the reason for forecast model to go wrong.

Both short- and long-term forecast accuracy is increased by IoT-enabled weather monitoring systems. The interconnected sensors help in continuous and precise data collection which pave path for accurate real time analysis. This provides actional insights to communities, industries, and governments to mitigate weather related risks.

4.3 IoT in Disaster Management

Each year, thousands of people are affected by both man-made and natural disasters. Disasters in large-scale results in devastating death toll and extensive physical damage. Natural disasters that cause thousands of life losses and abolished billions of dollars' worth property and habitat every year include floods, earthquakes, volcanic eruptions, hurricanes, landslides, tornadoes, blizzards, tsunamis, cyclones, wildfires, and pandemics [9].

In Semantic Sensor Web (SSW), semantic metadata is added to sensor data to promote interoperability and offer contextual information for situational understanding. The geographical, temporal, and thematic information needed to find and analyze sensor data would be present in a semantic sensor data. Using sophisticated queries, the SSW framework is evaluated over meteorological data [10].

A standard for creating sensor webs called Sensor Web Enablement (SWE) was created by the Open Geospatial Consortium. The SWE is the main element of the model. SWE is an Internet and Web protocol-based interoperability framework for using and accessing sensors and sensor systems [11]. Four web service interfaces and three languages are supported by the suite. These include Web Notification Service (WNS), Sensor Observation and Alert Service (SOS & SAS), Sensor Observation Language (SensorML) [12]. This chapter examines the "tsunami" natural disaster, its detrimental impacts, and the Internet of Things' role in the early indication of tsunami. This system is managed by the Indian National Center for Ocean Information (INCOIS) with the help of various sensors and communication facilities available.

India has a long sealine, spaning over 7500km and around 25% of the population lives in coastal regions. Major population of Indian country is directly or indirectly dependent on the surrounding ocean for various uses and resources, including traditional fishing, high-tech offshore businesses, ports and harbors, shipping, and tourism. Accurate data and forecasts of the state of the ocean at various spatial and temporal scales are necessary for offshore commercial operations, maritime security and safety at sea, and shipping. They also need to monitor oil spills and pollutants for the preservation of the marine ecosystem. Seafaring safety, dangerous chemical trips, fisheries, the oil and gas sector, and national security all depend on accurate ocean current forecasting.

Ocean current provides valuable information for search and rescue, oil spill tracking, safe navigation, distribution, port and coastal infrastructure design, and safe entertaining activities [13].

Global ocean forecasting systems have been validated using ocean currents found by satellite-tracked drifting buoys, which can travel thousands of kilometers and provide worldwide geographic coverage [14].

Aijaz, S. *et al.* [13], found that smaller errors and strong correlation with observations, zonal currents have a greater signal than meridional currents. To predict the coastal populations of India and the allied RIMES countries, INCOIS created an operational ocean forecasting system. Users ranging from fisherman to the Indian Navy and Coast Guard are provided with the forecasts. Daily seven-day advance projections are developed and operationally sent to customers each day. Generally, forecasting systems consist of three separate parts: observations, the data assimilation (DA) technique, and the numerical ocean circulation model.

4.3.1 Role of IoT in Tsunami Warning System

The Tsunami warning system issues warning to the people surrounded by seashore to avoid life loss and goods. It consists of sensors grid and communication infrastructure to detect Tsunami. The presence of seismic observation station at sea floor detects the presence of earthquake. It determines the correct location and depth of earthquake, the cause of tsunami.

The Bottom Pressure Recorders (BPR) could identify and quantify changes in water level of 1 centimeter at ocean depths of up to 6 kilometers. The Indian National Institute of Ocean Technology (NIOT) erected 12 BPRs) to transmit real-time data *via* satellite communication to both the INCOIS in Hyderabad and the NIOT in Chennai at the same time for processing and interpretation. Each BPR is positioned to provide enough warning time and redundancy at the 30- and 60-minute tsunami wave arrival times. They are also sufficiently enough from the seismic zone to allow a clean separation of the tsunami wave signal from the seismic Rayleigh wave.

NIOT has four BPRs stationed in the Bay of Bengal and 2 in Arabian Sea. The timely reception of sensor data is very critical to give timely Tsunami alerts. The end-to-end communication plan using INSAT by Indian Space Research Organization (ISRO) helps to receive timely data. High level of redundancy is maintained to avoid single point failures. Figure 4.2 shows the steps involved in Tsunami early warning station to give alert notice to the government to help evacuate people in surrounding region [15].

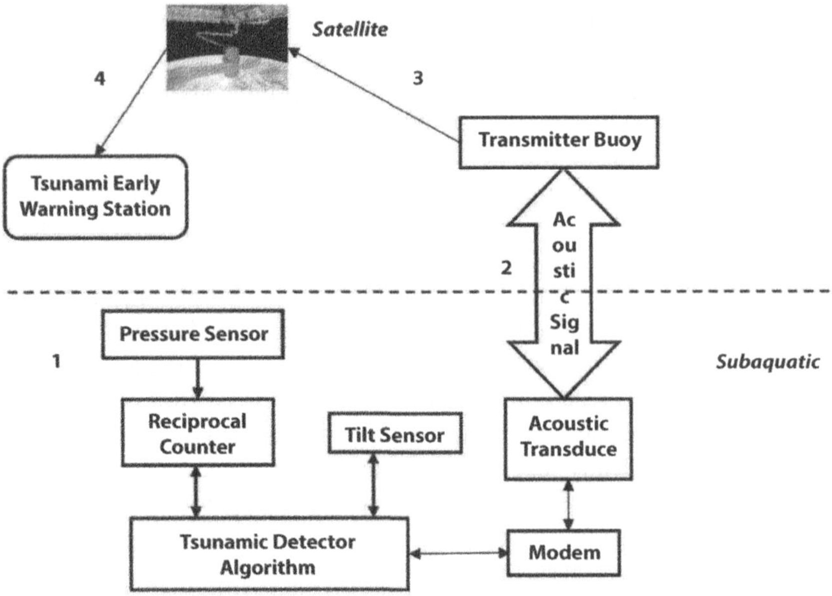

1. The pressure and Tilt sensor to measure water pressure
2. The measurements are sent as Acoustic signal to the Buoy on the surface
3. The Buoy sends signal to the satellite
4. Satellite sends signal to the Early warning station on land

Figure 4.2 Tsunami early warning system.

The National Early Warning Center issues alert to the Ministry of Home Affairs and to the State Emergency Operations Centers using satellite-based virtual private network.

The integration of IoT in disaster management enables preparedness and response through the connected network which can detect and analyze different disasters. The real time monitoring aids to give early warning which minimizes the damages and streamlines recovery efforts in advance.

4.4 IoMT-Internet of Medical Things

The healthcare devices and the API connected to the Internet are coined as IoMT in the healthcare industry. Vantage Market Research states that , the universal IoT market for the healthcare industry is likely to reach USD 190 billion in the year 2028, rising at a composite yearly growth rate of 24.91%. The medical wearables is expected to grow from 20.1 billion USD in 2021 to 83.9 billion USD in 2026 in the global market, predicts Statista.

It consists of remote patient monitoring system, linked inhalers, smart thermometers, and infusion pumps, pulse oximetry, insulin pumps, glucose monitors and heart rate sensors, ingestible sensors and cameras, and magnetic resonance imaging (MRI) machines. The wearable such as the Fitbit or Apple watch collects essential data about persons routine activities, such as the number of steps the person takes or calories burnt. This data is eventually shared for data analysis and history keeping with the watch or another device.

The rise of internet connected sensors in medical equipment reduces needless waste and saves human lives. This makes it possible for medical professionals to collect data automatically and apply decision support criteria, enabling early therapeutic intervention. To support the contemporary idea of IoT, the sensor embedded gadgets communicate with smartphones, social networks, cloud computing and GPS devices. Security threats have to be addressed by the smart device manufacturers since the user's accounts are connected through online. The FDA was forced to provide formal strategies to direct manufacturers of medical devices on how to respond to reports about cyber outbreaks due to the growing number of medical devices that can be hacked [16].

To make individualized and well-informed decisions, the healthcare professionals need to collect required amount of data and analyze and understand it. It all requires more time and work. IoT-based new technologies have the potential to expedite and streamline this process. With the widespread adoption of electronic health registration, there is an increasing amount of digital medical data available. Additionally, medical personnel

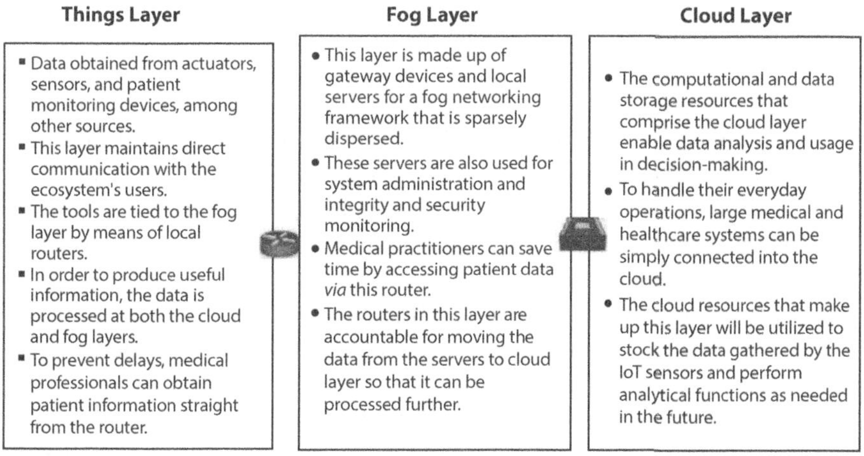

Figure 4.3 Different layers of IMOT.

must be trained in the use of AI-based technologies that are related to IoT [17]. For doctors, the internet of things (IoT) provides a real-time link to care takers, patients and also to the laboratory. Notification of an arrhythmia harming a patient can be sent to a cardiologist, and information regarding hypoglycemia endangering a patient can be sent to a diabetologist. Patients can receive prompt advice and assistance from the experts [18].

Wearable technology and smartphone apps offer symptom monitoring, health education, fitness, collaborative disease management, and cogent care.

The applications which handle real time data mainly relies on sensors for timely prediction of the disease. Authors have shown the flow of sensors data from human body to end users through various tiered technologies [19]. Figure 4.3 presents different layers of IMoT.

4.4.1 Challenges

The fact is that everyday life is still not impacted by IoT and in majority of nations, fifth-generation (5G) wireless technology and Internet of Things services are still not available. According to this, 5G adoption in healthcare represents the first technological obstacle that IoT adoption will encounter [20].

The amalgamation of data is the key challenge to be addressed in the adoption of IMoT. Multiple devices imply multiple data sources. For technical and budgetary reasons, the multitude of wearable sensors and tolls used to collect data devices in the healthcare industry cannot be readily standardized into a single pattern of data collection. Manufacturers are still unable to come to an agreement on standards and communication protocols [21]. For example, diabetic patients may use diverse glucose and signs observing systems also may use various closed-loop insulin pump.

It has been established that practical asset supervision, inventory control, stern quality assurance, product wrapping optimization, and management of supply chain are necessary for IoT financial success in the healthcare industry. Nevertheless, these ideas now seem more industry-focused than health care-focused. It will take close cooperation and in-depth knowledge between economics, healthcare management, and physicians to adapt them to clinical practice [22].

Studies show that the lack of funding for the development of an IoT healthcare network is due to insufficient data and expert knowledge from other healthcare professionals [23].

The main grounds of dispute regarding the handling of sensitive health data include privacy, sharing, autonomy, ownership, consent, and issues with unfamiliar value. The dehumanization and isolation of doctor-patient interactions, the deconstruction of health and comfort, and the dangers of receiving care from non-professionals are alarming ethical developments in the care paradigm [24]. Universal and regional standards, like the EU's General Data Protection Regulation (GDPR) and the UN Declaration of Human Rights, should be fundamental to any relevant law. Services provided by the cloud are required for data processing and storage. Hacking is still a serious risk. The internet of medical things revolutionized the medical field by providing better patient care and personalized care by linking medical devices and sensors. IoT technology enables remote monitoring and promotes preventive care which reshares healthcare industry. IoT is expected to grow exponentially in enhancing the accessibility and quality of healthcare globally.

4.5 IoT in Industrial Automation

IIoT stands for Industrial Internet of Things. In 2011, Chen used the term "IIoT" for the first time. The quantity of articles containing the IIoT keyword has considerably expanded in the last ten years [25]. It's essentially the application of general Internet of Things (IoT) technologies within industrial environments to enhance automation, data collection, and operational efficiencies. It connects industrial machines, sensors, and instruments to a network, enabling them to collect and share data [26]. The industrial IoT can lead to enhanced networking and communication between operators and machines, as well as increased efficiency in production processes. It would be crucial to research, design, and integrate a range of useful sensors in industry to establish complete and effective management systems [27]. To facilitate better industrial trials, such as intelligent IoT-based computer-integrated manufacturing, development is crucial in

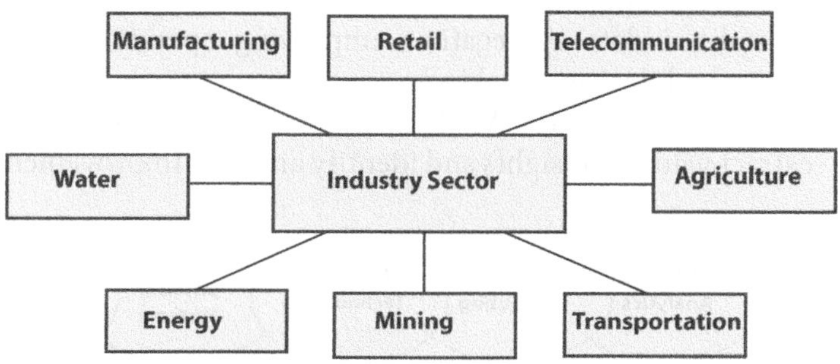

Figure 4.4 Categories of industry sector.

terms of joining many industrial sensors and using and analyzing the data obtained from them [28]. The various businesses that IoT can benefit from are depicted in Figure 4.4.

IIoT uses the data to improve various aspects of industrial operations, including:

- **Predictive maintenance:** Sensors allow for preventive maintenance and save costly downtime by tracking the state of the machinery and forecasting any issues.
- **Process optimization:** Real-time data analysis helps optimize production processes, improve resource utilization, and reduce waste.
- **Remote Observation and Management:** Industrial processes can be monitored and managed remotely, improving efficiency and safety.
- **Enhanced decision-making:** Data-driven insights can help managers make informed decisions about production, resource sharing, and overall business strategy.

4.5.1 Key Technologies

IIoT comprises of various technologies to achieve the proper functioning. Those technologies are depicted in Figure 4.5.

- **Sensors:** Gather data from physical equipment, such as temperature, vibration, pressure, and flow rates.
- **Industrial networks:** Specialized networks connect devices and machines within a factory or industrial setting.
- **Cloud Computing:** Cloud offers scalable storage and computing power, enabling extensive data analysis and remote device management. It supports real-time processing and centralized data aggregation, improving operational efficiency and decision-making.
- **Data analytics, ML, AI:** It analyzes the collected data to extract valuable insights and identify areas for improvement.

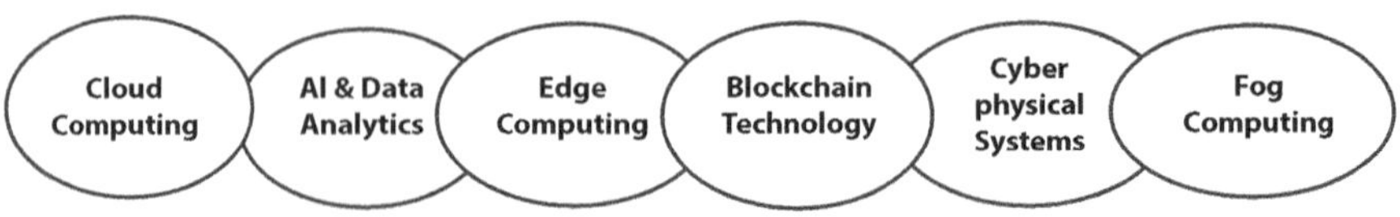

Figure 4.5 Technologies involved in IioT.

It can be used to automate tasks, predict future events, and optimize processes. The ML models are used to analyze data in a rapid speed.

- **Edge Computing:** It processes data directly on devices or local nodes close to the source of data, optimizing latency and real-time processing. It increases efficiency by minimizing the requirement for continuous data transfer to centralized cloud servers. Based on local sensor data (such as temperature and speed), edge computing in smart manufacturing allows for real-time modifications to equipment and procedures.
- **Fog Computing:** It extends the cloud closer to the edge by incorporating additional layers of processing and storage between edge devices and the central cloud, providing a broader network distribution and more robust data handling capabilities. Fog computing analyzes data from multiple manufacturing lines to facilitate supply chain management, quality assurance, and efficiency. Fog computing, however, is linked to long-term environmental data trends that help regulatory compliance and enhance sustainable practices.
- **Blockchain:** It ensures secure and transparent data exchange by providing a decentralized, transaction ledger that cannot be tampered with among devices. It facilitates efficient and trustworthy automation through smart contracts.
- **Cyber Physical systems (CPS):** CPS in IIoT joins physical processes with computational and networking capabilities, facilitating control and monitoring in real time. This enhances system efficiency, reliability, and responsiveness by allowing smooth communication between digital and physical world.

In the context of environmental monitoring, local sensors offer real-time information on the state of the environment, facilitating prompt resolution of problems. The effect of edge computing is this. Fog computing, however, is linked to long-term environmental data trends that help regulatory compliance and enhance sustainable practices.

The term "Industrial Internet of Things" refers to this fourth industrial revolution (IIoT), which focuses on profitability while improving productivity, reliability, and competitive performance. IIoT-enabled technologies have been examined and used in a number of studies, but further investigation is required to fully understand the potential and difficulties they raise. This study investigates IIoT-enabled infrastructure and technologies, their applications, difficulties, and future directions, as well as their role in the expansion of global industry. IIoT applications leverage the intelligence of things to address a variety of industrial matters which includes inadequate cloud strategy, misused supply chains, data privacy concerns, and cost minimization [28].

IIoT is a captivating idea that links the internet to a variety of sensors found around us, creating amazing opportunities for appreciating a magnificent way of life [29]. Due to its ability to integrate the operational technology (OT) and information technology (IT) domains, lower functioning costs, and increased importance in machine-to-machine communication, IIoT is increasingly acknowledged as the most suitable strategy to accomplish production performance.

4.5.2 Benefits of IIoT

- **Increased productivity and efficiency:** By optimizing processes and reducing downtime, IIoT can significantly improve productivity and output.
- **Reduced costs:** Predictive maintenance, improved resource allocation, and lower energy consumption can lead to substantial cost savings.
- **Improved safety:** Potential safety dangers can be recognized and addressed in real time with the use of real time monitoring.
- **Enhanced decision-making:** Data-driven insights can help businesses make better decisions about operations, investments, and overall strategy.

IIoT is a technological advancement that builds on IoT by giving businesses a range of instruments to foster a competitive milieu. Since it caters to the industry, it must adhere to far firmer regulations than those that apply to the consumer sphere. IIoT allows machines to modify their own course of action or to signal other devices to do the same without requiring human intervention. This is accomplished *via* means of actuators and sensors inside an organization and through data gathering, analysis, and exchange. Furthermore, it can facilitate human decision-making by providing real-time data gathering support. Additionally, the data can be stored for later use in maintenance prediction and/or periodic assessment.

4.5.3 Challenges

IIoT services may become unreliable due to certain challenges triggered by heterogeneity, dynamicity, and data volume, all of which are essential for industrial applications. Since the IIoT involves a large number of interconnected devices, a large amount of data must be sent and evaluated quickly. The real-time performance of industrial operations can be impacted by a number of factors, including inadequate device management, a lack of secure services or data confidentiality, individual access and control regulations, ineffective machine error handling, and human error.

Another major challenge is combining various IIoT technology with legacy infrastructure. This adoption and initial invest cost are high. IIoT uses connected sensors and smart gadgets to revolutionize industry operations. It continues to change as technology advances every day and opens up new avenues for growth in the industrial sector.

4.6 IoT in Agriculture

Smart agriculture, often associated with IoT solutions in agriculture, involves the use of IoT sensors to gather environmental and equipment data, allowing farmers to make informed decisions. This technology enhances various aspects of farming, including livestock and crop management. For instance, by using smart sensors to monitor crop conditions, farmers can accurately determine the required amounts of pesticides and fertilizers to achieve optimal efficiency [30].

Additionally, these sensors help farmers better understand their crops, boost productivity, conserve resources, and protect crops from environmental threats or disasters. In livestock management, smart sensors assist with animal identification, monitoring heat cycles, tracking health, and isolating sick animals, as well as tracking herd movements.

The COVID-19 pandemic has positively influenced the adoption of IoT in agriculture, contributing to a compound annual growth rate (CAGR) of 9.9%. Reports indicate that the smart farming market is expected to reach a value of $28.56 billion by 2030.

These agricultural sensors are often integrated into weather stations, drones, and robots. They can be controlled *via* specialized mobile apps, which use wireless connectivity, including Wi-Fi or cellular networks, to operate remotely.

4.6.1 Types of Agriculture Sensors

Sensors and actuators are fundamental components that underpin the Internet of Things (IoT) in agriculture, driving the digital transformation of farming practices. Sensors, such as those measuring soil moisture,

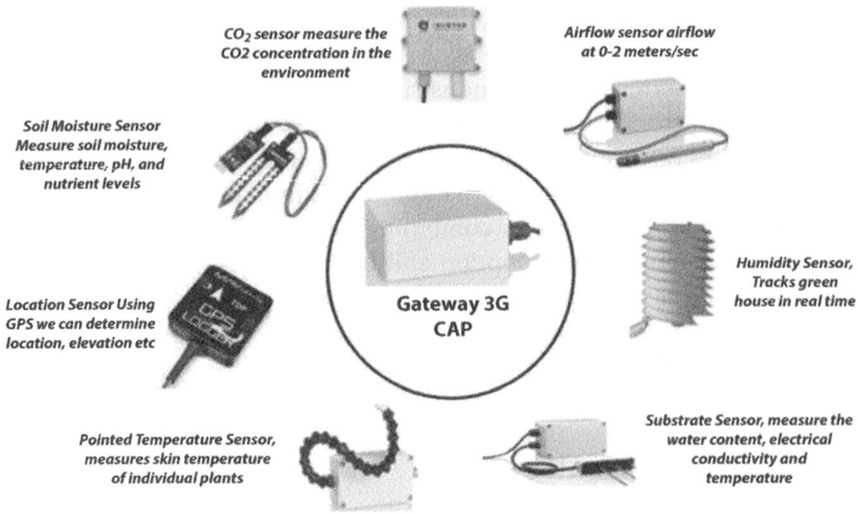

Figure 4.6 Agricultural sensor and its applications.

temperature, humidity, and nutrient levels, collect real-time data from the agricultural environment [31]. This data provides farmers with critical insights into the conditions affecting crop growth and health. Actuators, on the other hand, are devices that execute actions based on sensor data, such as adjusting irrigation systems, activating fertilization mechanisms, or controlling climate conditions within greenhouses. IoT systems enable precise, automated control of various agricultural processes, leading to improved efficiency, resource optimization, and enhanced productivity. Some of them are shown in Figure 4.6.

4.6.2 How IoT Connects World of Agriculture?

IoT devices play a crucial role in connecting people and agricultural information by enabling real-time data collection, analysis, and communication. These devices, equipped with sensors and wireless connectivity, monitor various environmental parameters such as soil moisture, temperature, humidity, and crop health [32]. The data collected is transmitted to cloud platforms, where it can be processed and analyzed using advanced algorithms. Farmers and agricultural managers can access this information through smartphones or computers, allowing them to make informed decisions on irrigation, fertilization, and pest control. The seamless integration of IoT technology enhances efficiency, reduces resource waste, and enables precision agriculture, thereby improving crop yield and sustainability [33].

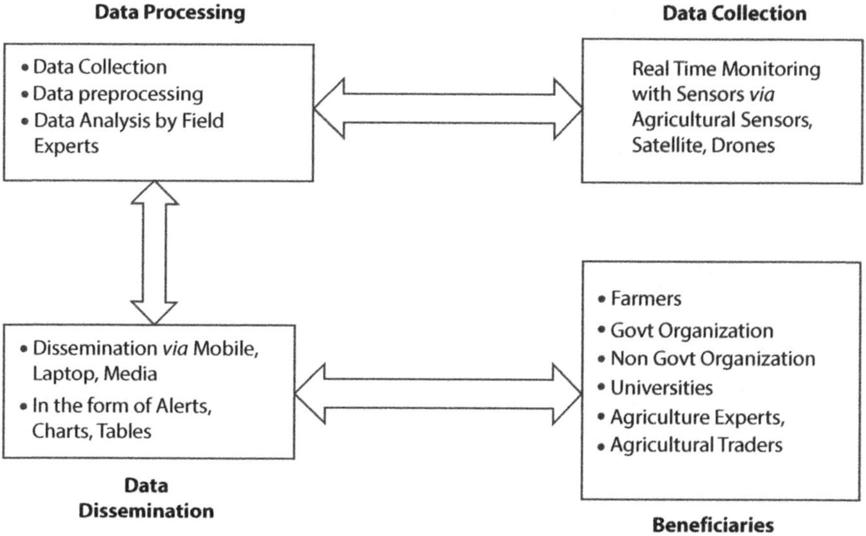

Figure 4.7 Working of IoT in agriculture.

The working of IoT devices from data collection to dissemination is shown in Figure 4.7.

4.6.3 IoT Applications in Agriculture

- Precision Farming: Utilizes data and technology to optimize field-level management of crops, enhancing yield and efficiency.
- Livestock Monitoring: Uses sensors and tracking devices to monitor animal health, behavior, and location, improving livestock management and productivity.
- Smart Greenhouse: Employs sensors and automation to control climate conditions, ensuring optimal growth environments for plants.
- Agriculture Drones: Used for aerial surveys, crop monitoring, spraying, and seeding, providing efficient and precise farm management.
- Monitoring of Climatic Conditions: Involves using sensors and weather stations to track environmental factors, aiding in planning and decision-making.
- Irrigation Monitoring: Uses moisture sensors and automated systems to optimize water usage, conserving resources and improving crop yield.

- Robotics for Weeding, Harvesting, Material Handling: Deploys automated machines to perform labor-intensive tasks, increasing efficiency and reducing labor costs.
- Remote Sensing: Involves using satellite or aerial imagery to assess crop health, soil conditions, and field variability for better resource management.

4.6.4 Challenges of IoT in Agriculture

Connectivity and Infrastructure: Many rural areas lack reliable internet access and infrastructure, which can hinder the implementation of IoT systems. Developing robust and affordable connectivity solutions is crucial to ensure widespread adoption [20].

Data Security and Privacy: The large volumes of data collected by IoT devices raise concerns about data security and privacy. Ensuring secure data transmission, storage, and access is essential to protect sensitive agricultural information from cyber threats [34].

High Costs of Implementation: The initial costs of deploying IoT devices and systems can be high, particularly for small-scale farmers. Addressing the cost barriers through subsidies, scalable solutions, and technological innovations is necessary to make IoT more accessible.

Integration with Existing Systems: Many farms use legacy systems and practices that may not easily integrate with new IoT technologies. Seamless integration and interoperability with existing infrastructure are needed to ensure smooth transitions and efficient use of new technologies [35].

Data Management and Analysis: Handling and analyzing the vast amounts of data generated by IoT devices can be complex. Developing effective data management strategies and tools for real-time analysis and decision-making is crucial for maximizing the benefits of IoT in agriculture.

Technical Expertise and Training: Farmers may lack the technical expertise required to effectively use and maintain IoT systems. Providing adequate training and support is essential for successful adoption and utilization of these technologies.

Strong connectivity options like satellite-based internet and low-power wide-area networks (LPWAN) like LoRaWAN should be deployed in rural regions to guarantee reliable data transfer to mitigate the challenges. Blockchain technology for safe data management, secure access protocols, and end-to-end encryption can all improve data security and privacy. Scalable and modular IoT solutions can be created to overcome high implementation costs, enabling farmers to begin small and grow with the help of government grants and subsidies. Encouraging open standards and APIs will make it easier to integrate current legacy systems and guarantee seamless transitions.

4.7 Recent Research Trends in IoT

The Internet of Things (IoT) is gaining its popularity and shaping our daily life. The two distinct technologies Artificial Intelligence (AI) and IoT can jointly provide innovative viable solutions. It is possible to create intelligent machines by integrating AI with IoT to automate repetitive tasks and to make independent decisions. It offers numerous benefits like minimize downtime, automate various processes, reduce operating costs, enhance productivity, and enable predictive maintenance. From startup to multinational company, every organization needs IoT to compete with its competitors. It is predicted that there will be 25 billion IoT devices in use during the next seven years. The exponential growth rate of the Internet of Things from 2015 to 2025 is depicted in Figure 4.8.

The IoT ecosystem includes sensors, devices, software, hardware and people; all communicate through secured or unsecured private and public networks. The users' smart devices collect their personal data and it

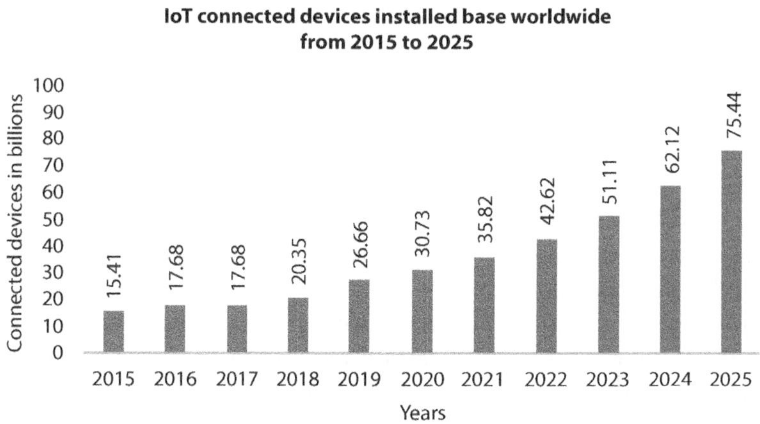

Figure 4.8 Growth of IoT from 2015 to 2025.

is being shared to the network administrators without users' knowledge. Cloud service providers can access users' data which open door for vulnerable security breaches. Intelligent security solution is essential to adopt the IoT techniques in various domains. The intelligent virtual assistants such as Alexa, Google Assistant, and Siri knows more detail about its users. These devices know user preferences, shopping habits, health conditions, travel plans as we have paired these devices with our smart phones. Although these devices deliver to customers a tailored experience, if they end up in the wrong hands, there might be dangerous implications. Many IoT devices come equipped with cameras, microphones, and speakers. Devices used for monitoring babies or the elderly can be hacked from anywhere in the world, potentially putting lives at risk. A survey on IoT says that security is a major barrier to its adoption. As the number of IoT devices rapidly increases, finding effective security solutions becomes increasingly challenging.

Increased use of blockchain technology can improve security. The decentralized block chain technology works well with IoT applications. The government has taken initiative on smart cities to ensure citizen safety, sustainable development, energy efficiency, traffic management and more.

In 2024 5G is one of the emerging technologies for internet of things (IoT). The strong connectivity of 5G technology pave path for more reliable and efficient IoT devices. The major benefits of 5G includes lower latency, network slicing, real-time data processing, and extensive coverage. Statista projects that in 2026 approximately there will be five billion 5G subscriptions worldwide. 5G acts as a base to unlock the full potential of IoT technology.

The other important challenge in using IoT is the scalability [36]. The billions or even trillions of IoT connected devices need to be managed. The addressing mechanisms, power solutions, network protocols of theses IoT devices need to be addressed. The current research applies discrete event simulation to determine scalability issues [37].

In this method, a hypothetical system will be examined under different circumstances and the average of results from multiple replications of the same situation will be obtained. Simulation based solution offers improved results to address scalability.

Blockchain technology has been applied in agriculture to improve traceability and transparency. To promote food safety, Alberta, Canada, for example, started a cattle chain monitoring program that enables customers to track their meat back to certain ranches. A blockchain application follows rice production in Gansu, China, allowing customers to verify the product's quality. Blockchain is being used by Maharashtra, India, to keep an eye on cotton supply lines and guarantee farmers receive fair prices.

The Department of Agriculture in Georgia, USA, implemented IBM Food Trust to improve recall response times and provide quick peach traceability. In a similar vein, the province of Hubei has created a tea traceability system that uses QR codes to connect to blockchain data, guaranteeing consumers authenticity and quality.

Compared to investing in the goods and services of a single company, investing in the Internet of Things (IoT) will be far more complicated. It will even be more complex than investing in e-commerce today. The development of new business models will be necessary in order to see IoT as a "business ecosystem." The acceptance, transmission, and responsible usage of IoT infrastructure, as well as the education of developers, enterprises, and consumers, represent a significant "soft" research problem. The successful integration and deployment of IoT technologies necessitates that standards development organizations (SDOs) tackle this difficulty.

The purpose of the General Data Protection Regulation (GDPR) is to safeguard the privacy and personal information of people living in the European Union (EU) and the European Economic Area (EEA). It imposes strict rules for gathering, storing, processing, and exchanging data. The Cybersecurity Framework from the National Institute of Standards and Technology (NIST) offers a framework of computer security guidelines that private sector firms can use to evaluate and enhance their capacity to stop, identify, and react to cyberattacks.

The Food Safety Modernization Act (FSMA) is a U.S. law that requires manufacturers to use traceability and preventative controls to guarantee the safety of the food supply. The Health Insurance Portability and Accountability Act (HIPAA) sets rules for data security and privacy in the healthcare industry and prevents the disclosure of private patient health information without authorization.

4.8 Conclusion

The internet of things (IoT) has significantly changed our daily lives, making them easier and more comfortable. Applications for IoT can be found in every field, including healthcare, business, agriculture, smart cities, transportation, education, mining, and weather forecasting. In addition to its advantages, the main conclusions of our survey highlight significant issues that must be resolved while utilizing IoT. The main obstacle to the widespread use of IoT technologies is security. Numerous research papers address security challenges when combined with block chain technology. The other major issue is scalability, which can be solved using a mathematical strategy like discrete event simulation. Computationally intensive methods can also be used to handle another issue, which is energy management. Huge volume of sensor devices results in network congestion and this opens avenue for more research on optimized protocols to manage network traffic. Emerging 5G technology addresses network issues and provides reliable communication. This paper addresses the role of IoT in connecting the users and service providers in various application domain, an evidence that IoT will become part of our everyday life.

AI disclosure statement: The author acknowledges the use of AI-based tools for minor language editing or grammatical correction. However, all intellectual contributions, analyses, and conclusions presented in this chapter are entirely the author's own.

References

1. Pereira, A.C. and Romero, F., A review of the meanings and the implications of the Industry 4.0 concept. *Procedia Manuf.*, 13, 1206–1214, 2017, https://doi.org/10.1016/j.promfg.2017.09.032.
2. Kim, M.-Y. and Hwan Lee, K., Electrochemical Sensors for Sustainable Precision Agriculture—A Review. *Front. Chem.*, 09 May 2022.
3. Li, S. J. T. Y. J. P. W., Liu, S.P., Yang, Y.Z., Big Data and IoT in Smart Agriculture: Current Applications, Challenges, and Future Perspectives. *Comput. Electron. Agric.*, 174, 105469, Jan. 2020. doi: 10.1016/j.compag.2020.105469.
4. Muslim, M.A., Setyawan, R.A., Basuki, A., Razak, A.A., Hario, F.P., Fernando, E., IoT based climate monitoring system. *IOP Conference Series: Earth and Environmental Science*, 2021.
5. De Oliveira Filho, J., II, Trichili, A., Ooi, B.S., Alouini, M.-S., Salama, K.N., Self-powered weather station for remote areas and difficult-access locations. *Opt. Express*, 30, 2, 2668–2679, 2022.
6. Ladi, K., V S N Manoj, A., Deepak, G.V.N., IoT Based Weather Reporting System to Find Dynamic Climatic Parameters. *International Conference on Energy, Communication, Data Analytics and Soft Computing (ICECDS-2017).*
7. India Meteorological Department, Ministry of Earth sciences 2021, Government of India accessed 28.7.2024, *https://mausam.imd.gov.in/imd_latest/contents/pdf/forecasting_sop. pdf.*
8. Ocean currents, 2022, accessed 29.7.2024, *https://www.drishtiias.com/to-the-points/paper1/ocean-currents-1.*
9. Khan, S.M., Shafi, I., Butt, W.H., Diez, I.D.L.T., Flores, M.A.L., Galán, J.C., Ashraf, I., A systematic review of disaster management systems: approaches, challenges, and future directions. *Land, 12*, 8, 1514, 2023.

10. Ramar, K. and Mirnalinee, T.T., An ontological representation for tsunami early warning system, in: *IEEE- International Conference on Advances in Engineering, Science and Management 2012(IEEE-ICAESM -2012)*, EVS Pillay Engineering College, Mar 30th&31st, 2012.
11. Damaševičius, R., Bacanin, N., Misra, S., From sensors to safety: Internet of Emergency Services (IoES) for emergency response and disaster management. *J. Sens. Actuator Netw.*, *12*, 3, 41, 2023.
12. Kaladevi, R. and Mirnalinee, T.T., Heterogeneous data management on environmental sensors using ontology mapping. *Lect. Notes Inf. Theory*, 1, 4, 154–158, 2013.
13. Aijaz, S., Brassington, G., Divakaran, P., Régnier, C., Drévillon, M., Maksymczuk, J., Peterson, K.A., Verification and Intercomparison of Global Ocean Eulerian Currents, in: *EGU General Assembly Conference Abstracts*, pp. EGU–2350, 2023, May.
14. Hyder, P., Storkey, D., Blockley, E., Guiavarc'h, C., Siddorn, J., Martin, M., Lea, D., Assessing equatorial surface currents in the FOAM Global and Indian Ocean models against observations from the global tropical moored buoy array. *J. Oper. Oceanogr.*, *5*, 2, 25–39, 2012, https://doi.org/10.1080/1755876X.2012.11020136.
15. Indian Tsunami Early Warning System, 2024, Ministry of Earth Sciences, Government of India, accessed 29.7.2024, https://tsunami.incois.gov.in/TEWS/searlywarnings.jsp.
16. Chacko, A. and Hayajneh, T., Security and Privacy Issues with IoT in Healthcare. *EAI Endorsed Trans. Pervasive Health Technol.*, 4, 14, 2018.
17. Paranjape, K., Schinkel, M., Nanayakkara, P., Short keynote paper:mainstreaming personalized healthcare-transforming healthcare through new era of artificial intelligence. *IEEE J. Biomed. Health Inform.*, 1, 2020, https://doi.org/10.1109/JBHI.2020.2970807.
18. Rayan, R.A., Tsagkaris, C., Romash, I., The Internet of Things for Healthcare: Applications, Selected Cases and Challenges.
19. Al-Kahtani, M.S., Khan, F., Taekeun, W., Application of Internet of Things and Sensors in Healthcare. *Sens. (Basel)*, 22, 15, 5738, 2022 Jul 31. doi: 10.3390/s22155738. PMID: 35957294; PMCID: PMC9371210.
20. Silva, D.G.S.L.N.J.A., Lopes, M.M.T.L.X.J.P., Carvalho, J.R.J.F., IoT in Agriculture: A Survey of the Latest Advances and Challenges. *J. Agric. Food. Chem.*, 68, 2, 552–568, Jan. 2020, doi: 10.1021/acs.jafc.9b06056.
21. Panwar, N., Sharma, S., Singh, A.K., A survey on 5G: the next generation of mobile communication. arXiv:151101643 Cs Math (2015).
22. Psiha, M.M. and Vlamos, P., IoT applications with 5G connectivity in medical tourism sector management: third-party service scenarios. *Adv. Exp. Med. Biol.*, 989, 141–154, 2017, https:// doi.org/10.1007/978-3-319-57348-9_12.
23. Backman, W., Bendel, D., Rakhit, R., The telecardiology revolution: improving the management of cardiac disease in primary care. *J. R. Soc. Med.*, 103, 442–446, 2010, https://doi.org/10.1258/jrsm.2010.100301.

24. Bowes, A., Dawson, A., Bell, D., Ethical implications of lifestyle monitoring data in ageing research. *Inf. Commun. Soc.*, 15, 5–22, 2012, https://doi.org/10.1080/1369118X.2010.530673.
25. Chen, Y., Guo, G., Hu, Y., Ning, B., Wang, W., Spindle and workpiece information collecting for industrial internet of things. *ICIC Express Lett.*, 5, 455–459, 2011.
26. Alabadi, M., Habbal, A., Wei, X., Industrial Internet of Things: Requirements, Architecture, Challenges, and Future Research Directions. in: *IEEE Access*, 10, 66374–66400, 2022, doi: 10.1109/ACCESS.2022.3185049.
27. Li, Y., Gao, M., Yang, L., Zhang, C., Zhang, B., Zhao, X., Design of and research on industrial measuring devices based on Internet of Things technology. *Ad Hoc Netw.*, 102, Article number 102072, 2020.
28. Chen, Y.-Q., Zhou, B., Zhang, M., Chen, C.-M., Using IoT technology for computer-integrated manufacturing systems in the semiconductor industry. *Appl. Soft Comput. J.*, 89, Article number 106065, 2020.
29. Forruque Ahmed, S., Sakib Bin Alam, M., Hoque, M., Lameesa, A., Afrin, S., Farah, T., Kabir, M., Shafiullah, G.M., Muyeen, S.M., Industrial Internet of Things enabled technologies, challenges, and future directions. *Comput. Electr. Eng.*, 110, 108847, 2023. ISSN 0045-7906, https:// doi.org/10.1016/j.compeleceng.2023.108847.
30. Malik, P.K., Sharma, R., Singh, R., Gehlot, A., Satapathy, S.C., Alnumay, W.S., *et al.*, Industrial Internet of Things and its Applications in Industry 4.0: State of The Art. *Comput. Commun.*, 166, 125–39, 2021, https://doi.org/10.1016/J.COMCOM.2020.11.016.
31. Lee, K.R., Taylor, J.M., Huang, R.J., Smart IoT-Based Systems for Precision Agriculture: Advances, Challenges, and Future Trends. *IEEE Access*, 12, 20132–20145, Apr. 2024, doi: 10.1109/ACCESS.2024.3328475.
32. Haque, M.A.A., Khandaker, K.M.M.R., Rahman, M.M., Islam, M.M., A Review of IoT-Based Smart Agriculture: Applications, Challenges, and Future Directions. *IEEE Access*, 9, 21321–21340, 2021, doi: 10.1109/ACCESS.2021.3055405.
33. Kim, W.S., Lee, W.S., Kim, Y.J., A Review of the Applications of the Internet of Things (IoT) for Agricultural Automation. *J. Biosyst. Eng.*, 45, 385–400, 2020, https://doi.org/10.1007/s42853-020-00078-3.
34. Al-Sharekh, S., II and Al-Shqeerat, K.H.A., Security Challenges and Limitations in IoT Environments. *IJCSNS Int. J. Comput. Sci. Network Secur.*, 19, 2, February 2019.
35. Doshi, J., Patel, T., kumar Bharti, S., Smart Farming using IoT, a solution for optimally monitoring farming conditions. *Procedia Comput. Sci.*, 160, 746–751, 2019. ISSN 1877-0509, https://doi.org/10.1016/j.procs.2019.11.016.
36. Stankovic, J.A., Research directions for the internet of things. *IEEE Internet Things J.*, 1, 3–9, 2014.

37. Dyk, M., Najgebauer, A., Pierzchala, D., SenseSim: An agent-based and discrete event simulator for Wireless Sensor Networks and the Internet of Things, in: *Proceedings of the 2015 IEEE 2nd World Forum on Internet of Things (WF-IoT)*, pp. 345–350, Milan, Italy, 14–16 December 2015.

5

Secure Protocols and Blockchain-Based Iot for Smart Home Applications

Senthil Kumaran R.[1*], Prabakaran D.[2], Shyamala R.[3] and S. Hannah Pauline[1]

[1]Department of Electronics and Communication Engineering, SRM Institute of Science and Technology, Kattankulathur, Chennai, Tamilnadu, India
[2]Department of Electronics and Communication Engineering, IFET College of Engineering, Villupuram, Tamilnadu, India
[3]Department of Information Technology, University College of Engineering Tindivanam, Tamilnadu, India

Abstract

Internet of Things is an innovative and magical technology connecting multiple devices, providing access to the device from anywhere in the world. The internet of things (IoT) is capable of connecting multiple devices like computing device, digital device, mechanical and electrical machines, etc. The IoT works on the internet backbone and is capable of transferring data anywhere to the world without the intervention of human to human efforts. The major challenge associated with the IoT environment and its applications like smart home experiences security concern. The attackers tend to observe the traffic pattern, to break the key and to succeed either as active or passive hacker. Hackers exploit the network using Man-in-The-Middle (MiTM) attack, spoofing attack, Insider attack etc. by observing the traffic pattern of the network. To overcome this security concern, this book chapter introduces a security solution for IoT using blockchain technology. This book chapter also describes the numerous platforms for the execution of internet of things and its reference models. The proposed framework is composed of blockchain technology with ethereum platform for connecting and securing the devices connected to the smart home network. A detailed analysis is performed in this chapter and security analysis has been exhibited to prove the supremacy of the framework in terms of security.

**Corresponding author*: sen19841@gmail.com

T. Perarasi, M. Karthiga, S. Sountharrajan, E. Suganya and Balamurugan Balusamy (eds.) Secure Blockchain and Quantum Technologies for 6G-Enabled Internet of Things, (95–116) © 2026 Scrivener Publishing LLC

***Keywords*:** Internet of things, security framework, blockchain technology, smart home application, ethereum

5.1 Introduction

Internet of Things, an internet technology promulgated to be the foremost key enablers of the next digital world revolution. The 'Thing' in IoT means any object or device with any built-in sensors with the potential to aggregate and fetch the facts through a network without any physical interposition. The IoT is a huge network where all devices are interconnected; sharing information like how they are used and where they are deployed and operated. Due to this global revolution, the cities and villages are transformed into smarter and more connected communities by integrating small sensors, wearable's, vehicles, and actuators to the internet to interconnect with the environment, as shown in Figure 5.1. The IoT network comprises 3 components, namely: IoT objects, communication networks, and destination nodes, where IoT objects are employed to perceive various substantial characteristics like temperature, humidity, pressure, or pollution level.

The perceived facts from the IoT devices are dispatched to the destination nodes through the communication network where they are fixed

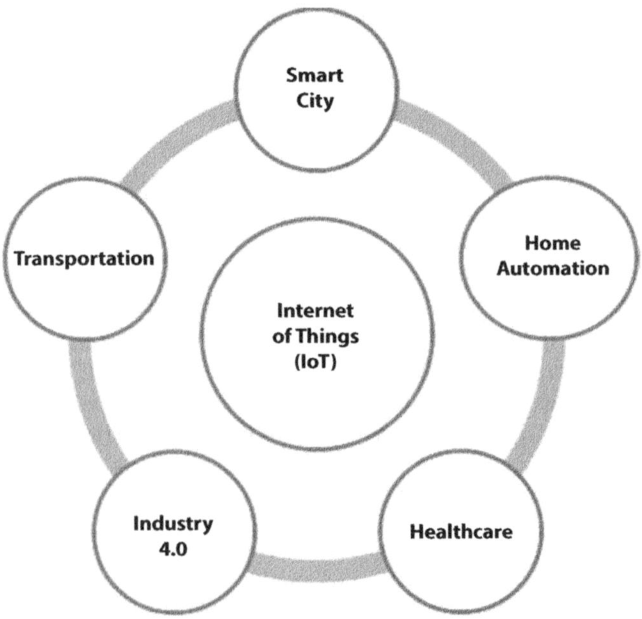

Figure 5.1 IoT- applications.

and extract valid information to assist in the prediction of taking important controllable output decisions. The embedded technology in the object makes them communicate with the external and internal states to help in the decision-making process. The accuracy of this predicted output decision influences the performance of the IoT-enabled applications, which is literally related to the originality of the facts collected from the IoT objects. Occasionally, the freshness of the desired data will depend on the application for which IoT is being used. For example, the freshness of the desired data will be considered relatively for a long extent if the temperature or moisture sensors were employed to sense the data even if it seems to be incredibly small for human safety applications [1].

IoT devices have many privileges for users and businesses by modernizing many actions. Still, they have some drawbacks like security and privacy, which are significant open issues in IoT as the end-user information is guarded from eavesdropping and interruption. For example, having personal data transferred between devices may have the possibility of losing a lot of our confidentiality. Because many mischievous hackers try to make use of the IoT object frailty to access our private details for their profit, so, the information of the end-user has to be authenticated, and the integrity of the information must be maintained for secure data transmission. For this purpose, various cryptographic computations are put forwarded for data authentication, but it requires more energy and bandwidth [2]. There are various security challenges in IoT that can be summarized in three-wide categories, namely IoT data, communication, and end applications associated with security.

Some of the methods to detect and prevent attacks on data are Security Auditing Module [3], an Attack detection unit, and Random Canaries Repository. In Security Auditing Module, both internal and external performance of security architecture [4], was monitored to evaluate the stability of the IoT devices to prevent them from device damage. If any malignant issues [5], are detected in the device, alarm the network to prevent the device from the security threat. By analyzing the monitored device [6], details the efficiency of the architecture [7], can be improved, and detection of threats can be done quickly. Secondly, the electrical signals from the controller are continuously monitored by the Attack Detection Unit [8], for the detection of threat, if any, it alerts the network to identify the abnormalities and prevent device damage. The Random Canaries Repository method [9], is an upgraded stack smash protector, which increases the difficulty to attack by generating Read only variables by exploiting the vulnerabilities of buffer overflow [10]. This book chapter describes a method of enhancing the security of the IoT network using the blockchain technology.

5.2 Literature Review

The internet of things (IoT) have become an inevitable technology and numerous novel methodologies have been introduced by the researchers and network scientists. Some of the notable research results providing IoT security is listed here for the study and analysis. This section identifies the challenges of the existing methods and assists in determining the objectives of this chapter.

W. Jing *et al.*, had proposed a high level security authentication scheme for IoT using the fingerprint based authentication. The author designed an Integrative Trust Model (ITM) framework [11], with the Radio Frequency Fingerprint (RFF) for performing authentication validation of the incoming user. The proposed work exhibited 99% of security against the potential risks of IoT network. P. Satyanarayana *et al.*, had introduced a Refined Adaptive Harris Hawks Optimization Algorithm (RAHHO) [12], and amalgamated with the Harris Hawks Optimization (HHO) algorithm for a speed and accuracy in the optimization process. The proposed work reveals the degree of security in IoT environment. The security analysis of the proposed work exhibited 73.33% less vulnerable when compared with the existing methodologies.

R. Yalda *et al.*, presented a cost effective approach of securing the IoT devices by implementing the IDS/IPS system on the Raspberry pi [13]. The implementation process determined the penetration testing of the attack to any network to make the system ineffective. The hacker tends to break the IDS/IPS system for the exploitation of the network, whereas the author intended to protect the network from various attacks using the IDS/IPS systems. P. William *et al.*, had contributed to enhance the level of security of the IoT network based on the Smart Grid ecosystem [14]. The smart grid ecosystem offers a reliable energy power supply by mitigating the security threats. The author employed cryptographic tools to perform encryption and decryption process, to provide validation of the incoming data and to provide security to the IoT environment. D. Sharma *et al.*, had integrated the IoT technology with the cloud computing using the livestock monitoring systems [15]. The proposed integrated method offered potential security against the security vulnerabilities by providing livestock monitoring, authentication, encryption and intrusion detection and prevention mechanisms.

K. Jeysuriya *et al.*, had examined the security aspect of the healthcare application by providing cryptographic algorithm [16], based security to the data. The system offered access control, authentication and intrusion detection system and is proved to be highly robust against the security vulnerabilities. F. T. Jaigirdar *et al.*, had designed a hypothetical IoT health care system [17], to restrict the unauthorized access to the data stored in the database. The author provides access control using the IDS/IPS method based on the identity of the incoming user. The network admin holds the sole right of providing access control and to modify the same, such that all the data were authenticated and are encrypted before being communicated. H. Wang *et al.*, had designed an Asymmetric Computing Key Exchange (ACKE) protocol [18], for the security of the IoT environment. The designed key exchange protocol was designed on the basis of the Diffie Hellman Key exchange protocol and the Subset Product Problem.

J. Zhou *et al.*, had designed a framework using the Swarm Intelligence algorithm based Task scheduling process [19], to enhance the security of the IoT devices. This system concentrated on providing security for the IoT devices from the vulnerabilities and to tackle the tradeoff between the devices. S. Kabir *et al.* [20], had utilized the design time system analysis for generating the network monitoring model with a proved security against the vulnerabilities. The appropriate actions of the system minimized the risk of the system, while operating in the unsafe environment. Based on the above literature review, the following challenges have been observed in the security aspect of the IoT environment.

- IoT devices come from various manufacturers, using different protocols and operating systems. This heterogeneity makes it difficult to enforce consistent security standards.
- IoT devices come with default credentials that are often easily guessable, providing attackers with a straightforward entry point.
- Data transmitted between IoT devices and the network is often unencrypted, making it susceptible to interception and tampering.
- Attackers can intercept and manipulate data transmitted over insecure channels.
- IoT devices can be easily turned into botnet members, which can be used to launch large-scale DDoS attacks.

The consensus mechanism of the blockchain technology consumes significant quantity of power thus restrains the life time of the IoT devices as they possess limited battery support. In addition to the power constrains, the blockchain in IoT also necessitates the excessive storage capacity to store the data in the form of registers. The limited storage of the IoT environment experiences a massive struck in storing the authentication data.

To overcome these challenges, it will be good to incorporate the contribution of the blockchain technology to provide enhanced level of security to the IoT devices and the network. This chapter illustrates the various protocols and blockchain models that shall be employed to strengthen the security level of IoT network.

5.3 Secured Protocols for IoT Environment

A framework is used to detect various threats, assaults, and anomalies, all of which are major IoT issues. For novel security solutions, the architecture is based on SD-IoT. The interface comprises an IoT passage that speaks with IoT hubs, just as an SDN-based security regulator [20], and IoT regulator. Group-based geography is utilized in IoT organizations, with each head hub in a bunch dealing with a group of IoT gadgets. The three layers that make up this framework is shown in Figure 5.2.

Different projects, for example, network the board applications, security applications, and other organization administrations offered to the customer/association, are designed to operate on top of the controller. Two applications are utilized to identify the assault in the SD-IoT organization. They are counter-based DDoS [21], assault recognition calculation and assault alleviation module or application. The control layer in the SDN worldview permits switch usefulness at the main issue and is powerfully programmable. The principal reason for this layer is to screen and deal with the IoT network in a dynamic, programmable, and customized way. The SDNWISE regulator and the IoT regulator are the two segments that make up this layer. The application layer, which is otherwise called an information sending plane, is only used to forward packets. As indicated by SDN ideal models, this layer involves non-intelligent sending gadgets,

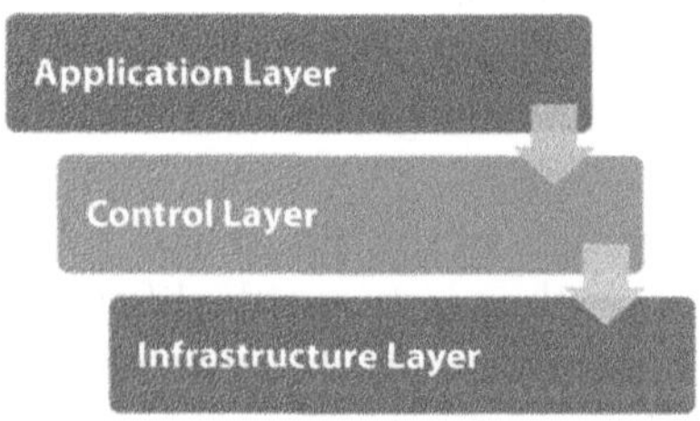

Figure 5.2 Layers of SD-IoT.

for example, Open Flow switches, which forward traffic based on the flow table entry. The three components make up the SSA architecture are:

- An ECG signal detection module
- A mechanized module for signal quality appraisal
- A transmitter module for signal quality assessment and an ECG analysis shown in Figure 5.3.

The sensor bit or IoT framework, the limit switch, and the web are the three segments that make up the SLCPS stage. Sensor motes are part of an internal network, while the internet is part of an external network. The proposed strategy is approved by the SLCPS structure's activity and system. In an IoT convention stack, sensor bits use CoAP at the device layer. In contrast, a line switch uses 6LoWPAN at the organization layer. The RPL boundary router connects the external IP network to the internal 6LoWPAN network shown in Figure 5.4. The motivation behind SLCPS is to interface CoAP-based sensor bits to the web through a 6LoWPAN-focused

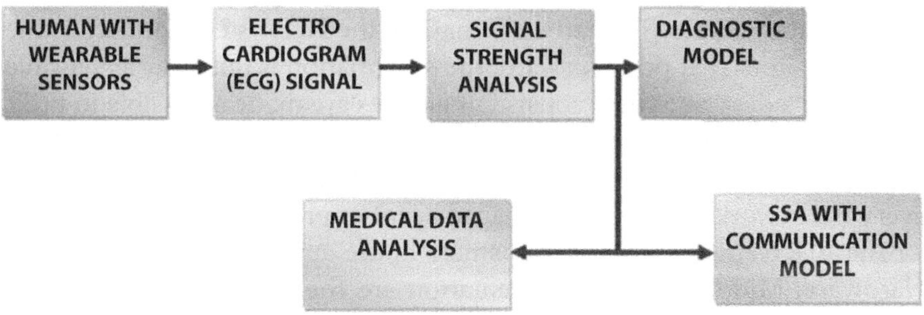

Figure 5.3 SSA framework structure.

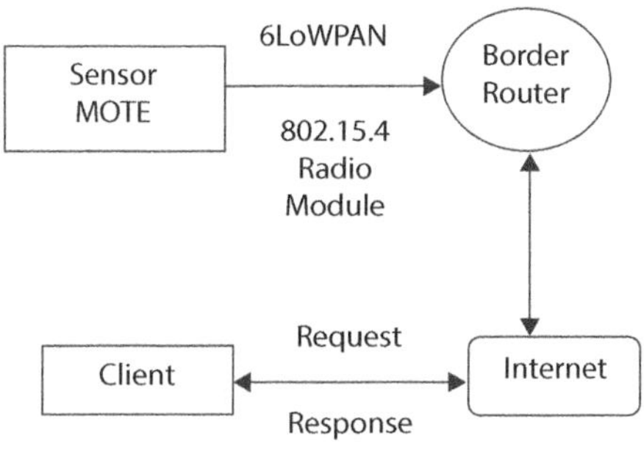

Figure 5.4 SCLPS framework structure.

line edge switch. For calculated purposes, sensor mote depends on an IEEE 802.15.4 radio module.

5.3.1 Secure Network for Smart Home Network

The HGW could dissect and channel information from the home organization based on the engineering's smart passage approach. The HGW will decide if a critical threshold has been crossed after analyzing results. If this is the case, the HGW may take measures to deal with the situation locally or notify the relevant manager. Empowering knowledge in an entryway settles both neighborhood and distant interoperability issues while reducing the number of changes expected to interface apparatuses. Maybe than requiring complete knowledge in every unit, the door should give immediate insight to both. A managed agent is assigned to each device. The controlled agent on the computer is in charge of configuring and collecting knowledge about the device. Indirectly operated computers are attached to the HGW and send and receive data or instructions from the HGW's resource information collector. Intelligent Applications (IAs) on the HGW cycle information from the resource information collector perform the executive's capacities. To share information, the HGW's IAs connect to the MP's IAs. From that point forward, the information is put away as sensible gadgets in a data set. These consistent gadgets are made accessible to projects or utilities to be utilized as web assets. The MP administers straightforwardly directed PCs as opposed to the HGW. To assemble framework data, every framework has its own managed agent as presented in Figure 5.5.

The IoT elements used in the smart home application are as follows. Hardware, Middleware and Presentation are the three categories of IoT elements.

1. **Hardware:** Sensors, actuators, and embedded processors are the prominently used components that are more important to build IoT enabled services.
2. **Middleware:** Middleware is software or collection of sub-layers inserted between the technological and application levels. Middleware disables the various technological complexities and leads the programmer to create advanced IoT enabled applications.
3. **Presentation:** As visualization needs user interaction with the environment, it has become quite critical, and hence it is important to make it simple to understand.

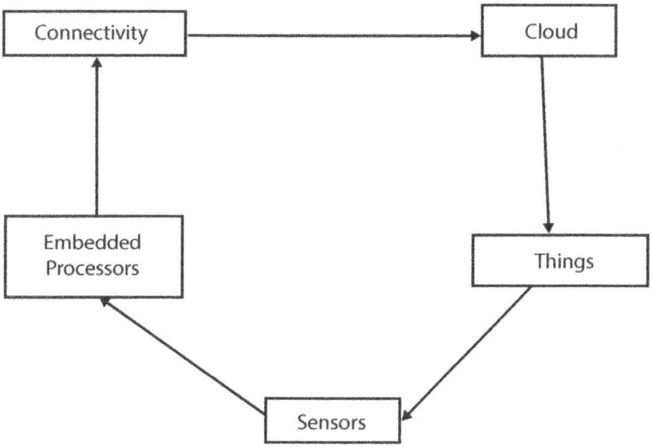

Figure 5.5 IoT elements for smart home application.

The IoT network in the smart home application is composed of seven layers as depicted in Figure 5.6. The seven layers are physical layer, connectivity layer, edge and fog computing at level 3, data collection at level 4, data abstraction in level 5, application and collaboration in level 6 and 7 respectively. The IoT model initiates with level 1. At this level, various end devices are used to send and receive the information. Nowadays, devices are maximum. As devices are concerned, there are no limitations for size, location, and origin. Few devices are smaller in size, few are much bigger, but the IoT has to support the entire range. IoT devices are capable of generating data, converting analog into digital data, and also it can be controlled over the net. In level 2, communication occurs between level 2 with level 1 and level 2 with level3. This connectivity level mainly concentrates on communication and processing with existing networks. Not all the devices are IP enabled; they require some communication gateways [22], to process the data. The functions of this connectivity level are reliable delivery in the network, Protocol implementation, translation, switching, and routing, provide network-level security. The major function of level 3 is to change the flow of data suitable for high level processing. This level 3 helps to analyze the large volume of data and transformation. Here, processing can be done packet by packet. This can be restricted due to the only knowledge of data, not on specific sessions. Data element analysis and transformation include filtering data, data aggregation, inspection on

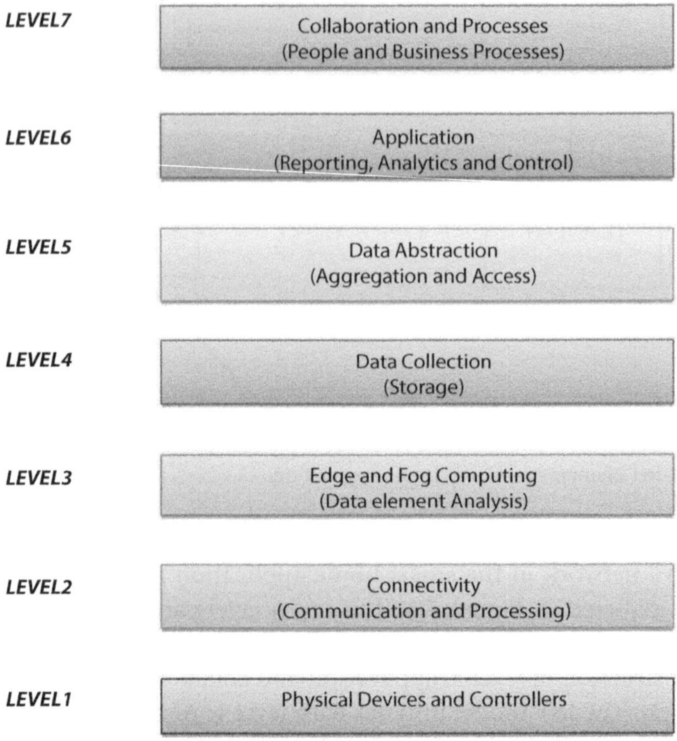

Figure 5.6 IoT network layers.

packet content, combining the network and data level analytics, and event generation. During the level 4, "data in motion" is converted to "data is at rest." Up to level 3, the data movement can be determined by the IoT devices that generate the data. Level 4 converts the network packets to relational databases, also achieves the event to query-based transition. These levels filter and store the selective data. As the data can be generated from multiple devices, data storage is not an easy task. Hence, multiple storage systems are required to accommodate the IoT device data and data from other systems. This level executes the following things: (i) Integrating different data formats from various sources, (ii) Ensure that the data is forwarded to the next level, (iii) Consolidate the data and providing access, and (iv) protect the data. IoT reference model does not restrict to specific applications. Some of the applications are device control, monitoring, etc. In some cases, both monitoring and control take place. If the first five levels are properly architected, the work in level 6 will be reduced. If level 6 is properly configured, users can perform well in their works. People can communicate and collaborate to make the IoT useful. People can use the application and the data for their requirements. Multiple people can use the same application for various purposes. Here, the focus is not an application, and it is to endow people with better work.

5.3.2 IoT Network- Protocols

The Data Link Protocols consists of physical and MAC layer protocols which are combination of commonly used IEEE wireless standards [23]. IEEE 802.15.4 is an IoT standard of MAC layer protocols which is evolved from the wireless protocol standards. This protocol provides communication between each node. The existing frame format which contains header and destination addresses can produce frame overhead which is not applicable for less power multi-hop networking. In order to consume low power, the version called IEEE802.15.4e has evolved. IEEE 802.11AH consumes very less power when compared to the traditional wireless standard protocols, in common which is called Wi-Fi, that are suitable for the digital devices such as smart phones, digital PC's, Smart TV's and tablets etc.. Even this standard also has frame overhead and high power utilization problem, and hence IEEE 802.11 AH version has been introduced to overcome all these common issues.

5.3.3 Routing Layer Protocols

The network layer is partitioned into couple of sub-layers. The first sub-layer that handles the transfer of data from source to destination is termed as routing layer and the second sub-layer which produces the packets is named as encapsulation layer.

- **RPL:** This Routing Protocol version is for minimum power and loss less Networks (RPL). It is a distance-vector protocol that can support a variety of data-link protocols such as IEEE 802.15.4, IEEE 802.15.AH etc. Destination Oriented Directed Acyclic Graph (DODAG) topology is used to do the routing.
- **CORPL:** For cognitive networks CORPL has been designed. It is an advanced version of RPL and uses DODAG topology generation with some novel changes in existing routing protocol.

- **CARP:** Channel-Aware Routing Protocol (CARP) routing protocol is proposed especially for deep-water communication. Due to its lightweight packets, it is used for IoT services.

Due to long addresses IPv6 is not suitable for smaller data link frames, hence IETF has developed few versions to encapsulate IPv6 datagram using various data link layer frames with IoT applications.

- 6LoWPAN (IPv6 over Low power Wireless Personal Area Network) is the standard which consumes less power, and efficiently encloses IPv6 wider headers into IEEE802.15.4 as small packets, that does not exceed the size of 128 bytes. It can support specifications such as cost effective, adaptable networks, mobile, unreliability and longer sleep time.
- 6TiSCH is developed to allowIPv6 to pass through TSCH (Time- Slotted Channel Hopping) mode of version IEEE 802.15.4e. Here the network scheduling operation is done by distribution of channels using available frequencies and time slots in matrix format. And these matrices are commonly known by all the nodes in the network as chunks. The negotiation between each node is done to transmit each chunk within its interference domain. The same scheduling operation will become complicated if it comes in terms of group of nodes that shares the same application.

Session layer protocol is designed for passing messages in the IoT systems. The integration of IP and IoT application uses transport protocols such as TCP and UDP. The few standards such as MQTT and SMQTT are discussed under this sub-topic.

- **MQTT:** It is designed to provide embedded connectivity between applications and middlewares on one end and networks and communications on the other end. Whereas subscribers are application part, waiting for a data collected by the sensors, and connected to brokers and gets information from the subscriber whenever a novel data is received. The brokers classify sensors' data based on topics and pass them to subscriber's interest.
- **SMQTT:** Secure MQTT is an encryption technique which uses broadcast encryption feature. Here, the original encrypted message is sent to the multiple neighboring nodes

which is usually followed in IoT applications. The different phases involved in SMQTT are setup, encryption, public, and decryption. Each of these phases mimics the characteristics of subscriber, broker, and publishers. In the first phase they get registered to the broker, and using the key generation algorithm they generate private key. Then, the data gets encrypted by the publishers and decrypted at the subscribers end.

5.4 Blockchain Technology in Smart Home Applications

Blockchain technology, known for its efficiency and security in IoT environment, had found vital positions in numerous smart applications. The major reasons for choosing the blockchain technology for smart applications is for its security, transparency in operation, trust, and decentralization nature. Some of the well suitable protocols of blockchain, which were suitable for smart home applications, are Ethereum, Hyperledger Fabric, IOTA, and Ripple protocols. This section describes the role of the blockchain protocols and the algorithm for smart home application.

Ethereum, characterized by its advanced smart contract functionalities and an extensive community of developers, represents a highly promising platform for the development of decentralized smart home applications. The working of the ethereum blockchain protocol is as follows.

- **Smart Contracts:** These self-executing agreements, with the stipulations embedded directly into code, possess the capacity to automate a variety of smart home operations. For example, a smart contract may be designed to modify thermostat settings in accordance with external temperature, time of day, or occupancy levels.
- **Tokenization:** The processes of tokenizing devices, energy consumption, or even access rights to the home, facilitate secure and transparent management practices.
- **Decentralization:** Through the utilization of Ethereum's decentralized architecture, smart home systems can enhance resilience against single points of failure while providing augmented data privacy.

The potential use cases of the ethereum protocol is illustrated as follows.

- **Peer-to-Peer Energy Trading:** Smart contracts can enable direct trading of energy between neighboring households, thereby optimizing grid utilization and potentially lowering expenses. Energy Consumption Tracking: Immutable records pertaining to energy consumption can be documented on the blockchain, thereby ensuring transparency and facilitating the implementation of energy efficiency strategies.
- **Home Security:** Access Control: Smart contracts may govern access permissions for various users and devices, thereby bolstering security measures. Insurance Claims: In the event of theft or property damage, blockchain-based documentation can expedite the insurance claims process.
- **Device Interoperability:** Ethereum has the potential to establish a standardized protocol for disparate smart home devices to communicate and operate in unison.
- **Remote Control:** Users can securely manage home appliances and systems from any location through the application of smart contracts.
- **Data Privacy:** Data Ownership: Individuals can retain authority over their data by employing blockchain technology for storage solutions.
- **Data Sharing:** Smart contracts can delineate the terms of data sharing with third-party services, thereby ensuring privacy protections.

The challenges and Considerations Scalability in the Ethereum protocol is the current limitations of Ethereum's scalability; presenting challenges for large-scale smart home applications that require frequent transactional activity.

- **Cost:** The transaction fees associated with the Ethereum network may be prohibitive, impacting the economic feasibility of certain applications.
- **Complexity:** The development of intricate smart contracts necessitates specialized expertise, which can escalate the costs of development.

To mitigate the Challenges in the layer-2, the implementation of scaling solutions such as Optimism or Polygon can substantially enhance the performance of Ethereum and mitigate costs.

- **Off-Chain Computations:** For tasks that require significant computational resources, off-chain computations may be executed, with only the outcomes being recorded on the blockchain.
- **Specialized Development Tools:** An expanding ecosystem of development tools and frameworks is simplifying the process of creating Ethereum-based smart home applications.

Hyperledger Fabric is an elite permissioned blockchain framework crafted for enterprises, positioning it as an ideal match for smart home innovations that demand robust security, privacy, and governance over network participants. Smart contracts articulate the business workflows you wish to automate, embedding self-executing stipulations within lines of code that bind the involved parties. The code and its contractual provisions flourish across a distributed, decentralized blockchain ecosystem. Each transaction is both traceable and immutable, fostering trust among organizations and empowering businesses to make swifter, well-informed decisions—ultimately conserving time while minimizing costs and risks.

- **Hyperledger Fabric:** Tailored for permissioned networks that prioritize stringent security and privacy protocols.
- **Hyperledger Sawtooth:** Delivers modularity and adaptability, perfect for distinct use cases. Hyperledger Indy: Concentrates on decentralized identity, advantageous for authenticating devices and users.

Hyperledger provides a dynamic platform for crafting secure and reliable smart home applications. By meticulously weighing the unique needs and obstacles, you can choose the most fitting Hyperledger platform and develop groundbreaking solutions for the interconnected home.

5.4.1 IOTA

IOTA represents an extraordinary distributed ledger technology (DLT) meticulously devised for the Internet of Things (IoT). Its innovative DAG (Directed Acyclic Graph) architecture, combined with feeless transactions and impressive scalability, positions it as an exciting option for smart home functionalities. Micropayments: Facilitating device-to-device transactions for shared assets (e.g., bandwidth, energy). Pay-per-use frameworks for smart home amenities. Data Exchange: Safeguards the sharing of sensor data among devices and applications. Establishes data marketplaces to capitalize on valuable insights. Device Authentication: Confirms the genuineness of smart devices. Thwarts unauthorized access. Home Automation: Empowers intricate automation scenarios involving a multitude of devices. Encourages peer-to-peer interactions among devices. The challenges in the IOTA protocol while implementing in the smart home application are as follows.

- **Maturity:** IOTA is a relatively nascent technology compared to well-established blockchains.
- **Adoption:** A broader acceptance is essential for cultivating a resilient ecosystem.
- **Complexity:** Employs IOTA solutions may necessitate specialized expertise.
- **Tangle Structure:** Grasps the complexities of the tangle for effective data governance.
- **Data Integrity:** Integrates mechanisms to uphold data integrity and authenticity.
- **Security:** Utilizes sophisticated cryptographic strategies to safeguard data and devices.
- **Performance Optimization:** Enhances data transmission and processing for instantaneous applications.
- **Interoperability:** Factor in integration with other IoT protocols and standards.

IOTA's distinctive attributes render it a captivating selection for smart home applications that necessitate high transaction throughput, rapidity, and fee-less operations. By tackling the challenges and harnessing its advantages, it can play a pivotal role in the evolution of innovative and efficient smart home solutions.

5.4.2 Ripple

Ripple is ingeniously crafted as a dynamic real-time gross settlement system (RTGS) tailored for currency exchange. Its foundational capabilities center around enabling swift, secure, and cost-effective international money transfers. Although Ripple's rapidity and effectiveness are remarkable, its principal attributes do not harmonize seamlessly with the distinct demands of smart home applications.

- **Absence of Smart Contract Functionality:** In contrast to Ethereum or Hyperledger Fabric, Ripple lacks a robust framework for crafting intricate smart contracts, which are vital for automating smart home operations.
- **Emphasis on Payments:** While the notion of micropayments could be theoretically pursued, Ripple's predominant focus on currency exchange may not serve as the most efficient remedy for this scenario.
- **Scalability for IoT Devices:** Though Ripple can accommodate a considerable volume of transactions, it is primarily tailored for financial dealings, not the myriads of small, frequent interactions that characterize IoT devices.

5.4.3 Blockchain Functions and Algorithm

The blockchain technology provides access control to the devices and the users, thus providing security against the vulnerabilities. The Access Based Control (ABC) scheme provides a specific control by providing the attribute based access control mechanism. Let's consider the attributes of the home environment as Attr(H); Attr(A) for access based attribute, Attr(D) for attributes for source devices and Attr(N) as the attributes of the network.

$$Attr(H) = HD_1 \times HD_2 \times \ldots \times HD_N \tag{5.1}$$

$$Attr(A) = AC_1 \times AC_2 \times \ldots \times AC_M \tag{5.2}$$

$$Attr(D) = D_1 \times D_2 \times \ldots \times D_I \tag{5.3}$$

$$Attr(N) = N_1 \times N_2 \times \ldots \times N_J \tag{5.4}$$

Where, $HD_N(1 \leq n \leq N)$; $AC_M(1 \leq m \leq M)$; $D_I(1 \leq i \leq I)$; and $N_J(1 \leq j \leq J)$

The protection policy of the home network using the blockchain network shall be defined in Equation 5.5.

$$SP(HN) \rightarrow f(HD_N; AC_M; D_I; N_J) \tag{5.5}$$

The device identity and the user identity act as the major source of the attribute based access control mechanism. The network refers to the home environment and the attribute based control strategy is described as defined in Equation 5.6.

$$SP(HN) \rightarrow f\big(Attr(H); Attr(A); Attr(D); Attr(N)\big)$$

$$\rightarrow \{Authorized\ Traffic : Access\ Granted\ Unauthorized\ Traffic :$$

$$Access\ Denied \tag{5.6}$$

The attributes of the devices and the network is treated with the hash functions namely Secure Hash Algorithm (SHA-1; SHA-2; SHA-256). The hash function operation is mathematically defined in Equation 5.7.

$$B_n \leftarrow H(HD_N; AC_M; D_I; N_J; B_{n-1}) \tag{5.7}$$

$$B_{n-1} \leftarrow H(HD_{N-1}; AC_{M-1}; D_{I-1}; N_{J-1}; B_{n-2}) \tag{5.8}$$

$$B_{n+1} \leftarrow H(HD_{N+1}; AC_{M+1}; D_{I+1}; N_{J+1}; B_n) \tag{5.9}$$

The chain of blocks keeps including new authorized devices, and access is created accordingly, thereby increasing the security level of the home network.

5.5 Security Analysis

As the realm of blockchain technology flourishes, a multitude of cyber threats has surfaced. Instances of digital currencies being pilfered and exchanges falling prey to attacks, among other incidents, are on the rise. BCSEC's analysis of blockchain-related breaches revealed a staggering 2.1 billion dollars lost to security failures in 2018. These figures represent merely a fraction of the existing vulnerabilities, and as the allure of blockchain escalates, so too will the frequency of these assaults. Currently, blockchain technology is still navigating its nascent phase of swift evolution, yet its security measures lag significantly behind developmental demands. Potential dangers may arise from both external aggressors and internal actors. The surge in blockchain adoption creates fresh imperatives for safeguarding security and preserving privacy concerning data storage, transmission, and application, alongside presenting novel obstacles to current security frameworks, authentication processes, data safeguarding, privacy preservation, and information governance. Given the ongoing spate of digital currency heists, exchange hacks, and account thefts, it has become imperative to devise one or more cooperative security strategies to bolster the security efficacy of blockchain systems.

The awareness of cyber security among manufacturers of mining devices is highly inconsistent, and due to their closed-source nature, the integrity of their code remains unchecked. When a breach is reported, the fallout can be catastrophic. Furthermore, whether the device manufacturers might embed back doors for remote control or siphon off mining outputs remains an open question for debate.

Zero day: Most mining systems are designed as general-purpose platforms. The moment an attack is discovered to possess a zero day vulnerability, its security fortifications can be breached in the blink of an eye. The attacker can exploit this vulnerability to gain modification privileges, subsequently altering the reward receiving address and hijacking the user's earnings. Possible Methods. It is unfeasible for any single entity to combat the myriad attacks that can occur. Developers must make sure their software is devoid of known vulnerabilities and undergoes rigorous testing. The performance of the proposed blockchain based secure IoT environment shall be performed on the basis of computational efficiency, latency, and success rate in threat detection. The performance of the proposed work is compared with the state of art security aspects of the IoT environment.

Table 5.1 Comparison of performance of proposed blockchain based secured IoT environment.

Parameters	ZTA [24]	FL-IoT [25]	FBMP-IDS [26]	OFDMA [27]	Proposed
Computational Efficiency (%)	69.36	70.59	71.33	72.15	82.16
Threat Detection (%)	61.54	63.02	70.31	71.14	83.04
Latency (ms)	83.21	83.06	81.65	79.47	65.21

The state of art methodologies includes, Zero Trust Authentication (ZTO) scheme, Fuzzy logic based IoT, FBMP based Intrusion Detection System (FBMP-IDS) and OFDMA. Table 5.1 presents the comparative analysis of the proposed blockchain based secured IoT environment with the traditional methods.

The comparison of the performance of the proposed blockchain technology is expressed with a better computational efficiency with 82.16%, 83.04% of successful threat detection and a minimal latency of 65.21ms.

5.6 Conclusion and Future Work

The Internet of Things has become more attractive technology due to the development of internet based access to the devices. This assists in numerous applications like smart home, smart city, health care applications etc. In this context, it is essential to maintain the level of security in all these applications, as the hacker tends act like passive or active in exposing the confidentiality of the information. To overcome this hazard, it is good to implement the blockchain technology in preserving the security aspect of the IoT network. This book chapter illustrates the basic security protocols along with the blockchain technology providing access based control to the IoT network. The security analysis proves that the blockchain technology stands ahead in proving its robustness against various attacks. This could further be enhanced by employing a proper IDS/IPS system to the network. The security of the proposed 6G based IoT environment shall further be enhanced with the incorporation of the quantum technology for securing the data communication.

AI disclosure statement: The author acknowledges the use of AI-based tools for minor language editing or grammatical correction. However, all intellectual contributions, analyses, and conclusions presented in this chapter are entirely the author's own.

References

1. Abd-Elmagid, M.A., Pappas, N., Dhillon, H.S., On the Role of Age of Information in the Internet of Things. *IEEE Communications Magazine*, 57, 12, Dec 2019.
2. Hussain, F., Hussain, R., Hassan, S., Hossain, E., Machine Learning in IoT Security: Current Solutions and Future Challenges, 2019.

3. Dean, A. and Agyeman, M.O., A Study of the Advances in IoT Security. ISCSIC '18. *Proceedings of the 2nd International Symposium on Computer Science and Intelligent*, September 2018.
4. Ding, J., Nemati, M., Ranaweera, C., Choi, J., IoT Connectivity Technologies and Applications:A Survey. *IEEE Access*, 8, 67646–67673, 2020.
5. Haseeb, S., Hashim, A.H.A., Khalifa, O.O., Ismail, A.F., Connectivity, Interoperability and Manageability Challenges in Internet of Things. *AIP Conference Proceedings*, vol. 1883, p. 020004, 2017.
6. Tolcha, Y., Kassahun, A., Montanaro, T., Conzon, D., Schwering, G., Maselyne, J., Kim, D., Towards Interoperability of Entity-Based and Event-Based IoT Platforms: The Case of NGSI and EPCIS Standards. *IEEE Access*, 9, 2021.
7. Samaila, M.G., Sequeiros, J.B.F., Simões, T., Freire, M.M., Inácio, P.R.M., IoT-HarPSecA: A Framework and Roadmap for Secure Design and Development of Devices and Applications in the IoT Space. *IEEE Access*, 8, 16462–16494, 2020, doi: 10.1109/ACCESS.2020.2965925.
8. Bhayo, J., Hameed, S., Shah, S.A., An Efficient Counter-Based DDoS Attack Detection Framework Leveraging Software Defined IoT (SD-IoT). *IEEE Access*, 8, 221612–221631, 2020, doi: 10.1109/ACCESS.2020.3043082.
9. Abbas, W. and Marwat, S.N.K., Scalable Emulated Framework for IoT Devices in Smart Logistics Based Cyber-Physical Systems: Bonded Coverage and Connectivity Analysis. *IEEE Access*, 8, 138350–138372, 2020, doi: 10.1109/ACCESS.2020.3012458.
10. Pham, C., Lim, Y., Tan, Y., Management architecture for heterogeneous IoT devices in home network. *2016 IEEE 5th Global Conference on Consumer Electronics*, pp. 1–5, 2016, doi: 10.1109/GCCE.2016.7800448.
11. Jing, W., Peng, L., Fu, H., Hu, A., An Authentication Mechanism Based on Zero Trust With Radio Frequency Fingerprint for Internet of Things Networks. *IEEE Internet Things J.*, 11, 13, 23683–23698, 1 July1, 2024.
12. Satyanarayana, P., Sofi, U.B., Ahmed, B.F., Saranya, N.N., Rao, G.V.S.P., Krishnan, V.G., Enhancement of Network Security in MANET Using Refined Adaptive Harris Hawks Optimization Algorithm (RAHHO) for IoT Applications. *2024 International Conference on Emerging Smart Computing and Informatics (ESCI)*, Pune, India, pp. 1–5, 2024.
13. Yalda, R., Nepal, N., El Hawari, T., Enhancing IoT Security Affordably with Raspberry Pi and Open-Source IDS/IPS. *2024 IEEE International Conference on Advanced Systems and Emergent Technologies (IC_ASET)*, Hammamet, Tunisia, pp. 1–6, 2024.
14. William, P., Chowdhury, S., Falah, A., Hussain, A., Kumar, R., Rao, A.L.N., Security Enhancement In Iot Based Smart Grid System Using Cryptographic Techniques. *2024 4th International Conference on Innovative Practices in Technology and Management (ICIPTM)*, Noida, India, 2024.

15. Sharma, D., Anawade, P., Gahane, S., Patil, Y., Security and Privacy Considerations in IoT-Based Livestock Monitoring Systems. *2024 International Conference on Innovations and Challenges in Emerging Technologies (ICICET)*, Nagpur, India, pp. 1–6, 2024.
16. Jeysuriya, K., MR-TBA – An improved Trust-based Security mechanism for IoT Networks. *2024 IEEE International Students' Conference on Electrical, Electronics and Computer Science (SCEECS)*, Bhopal, India, pp. 1–5, 2024.
17. Jaigirdar, F.T., Tan, B., Rudolph, C., Bain, C., Security-Aware Provenance for Transparency in IoT Data Propagation. *IEEE Access*, 11, 55677–55691, 2023.
18. Wang, H., Wen, J., Liu, J., Zhang, H., ACKE: Asymmetric Computing Key Exchange Protocol for IoT Environments. *IEEE Internet Things J.*, 10, 20, 18273–18281, 15 Oct.15, 2023.
19. Zhou, J., Shen, Y., Li, L., Zhuo, C., Chen, M., Swarm Intelligence-Based Task Scheduling for Enhancing Security for IoT Devices. *IEEE Trans. Comput. Aided Des. Integr. Circuits Syst.*, 42, 6, 1756–1769, June 2023.
20. Kabir, S., Gope, P., Mohanty, S.P., A Security-Enabled Safety Assurance Framework for IoT-Based Smart Homes. *IEEE Trans. Ind. Appl.*, 59, 1, 6–14, Jan.-Feb. 2023.
21. Ramachandran, S. and Prabakaran., D., A Novel Deep Reinforcement Learning (DRL) Method for Detecting Evasion Attack in Iot Environment. *2024 International Conference on Integrated Circuits and Communication Systems (ICICACS)*, Raichur, India, pp. 1–6, 2024.
22. Prabakaran., D., Praveena., N.G., Jackson, B., Varalakshmi, S., Maheswari, G.U., A Secure Multi-Factor Authentication System Using ElGamal Bakers Map Function in Virtual Private Network. *2024 Third International Conference on Distributed Computing and Electrical Circuits and Electronics (ICDCECE)*, Ballari, India, pp. 01–07, 2024.
23. Prabakaran, D. and Sathyapriya, H., A review on methodologies and performance analysis of device identity masking techniques. *Int. J. Sci. Technol. Res.*, 8, 12, 2018–2022, 2019.
24. Son, S., Kwon, D., Lee, S., Kwon, H., Park, Y., A Zero-Trust Authentication Scheme With Access Control for 6G-Enabled IoT Environments. *IEEE Access*, 12, 154066–154079, 2024.
25. Alghamedy, F.H., *et al.*, Unlocking a Promising Future: Integrating Blockchain Technology and FL-IoT in the Journey to 6G. *IEEE Access*, 115411–115447, 2024.
26. Sakraoui, S., Ahmim, A., Derdour, M., Ahmim, M., Namane, S., Ben Dhaou, I., FBMP-IDS: FL-Based Blockchain-Powered Lightweight MPC-Secured IDS for 6G Networks. *IEEE Access*, 12, 105887–105905, 2024.
27. Jha, S., *et al.*, Enabling Resilient Wireless Networks: OFDMA-Based Algorithm for Enhanced Survivability and Privacy in 6G IoT Environments. *IEEE Trans. Consum. Electron.*, 70, 1, 3810–3819, Feb. 2024.

6

Future Directions: The Evolving Landscape of Secure 6G IoT with Quantum and Blockchain

Muhammadu Sathik Raja[1]*, Swarnalatha A. P.[2], Sowparnika B.[3] and Karthikeyan M.[4]

[1]*Department of Biomedical Engineering, Dhanalakshimi Srinivasan University, Perambalur, Tamilnadu, India*
[2]*Department of Biomedical Engineering, VSB Engineering College, Karur, Tamilnadu, India*
[3]*Department of Biomedical Engineering, Nandha Engineering College, Perundurai, Tamilnadu, India*
[4]*Department of Information Technology, Sengunthar Engineering College, Tiruchengode, Tamilnadu, India*

Abstract

Although 6G networks will provide billions of IoT devices with hitherto unheard-of speed and connectivity, this networked society has serious security problems given the flaws in existing encryption systems. The development of quantum computing aggravates these risks and renders generally used encryption methods useless. The chapter investigates the utility of lattice-based and hash-based cryptosystems as well as the incorporation of quantum key distribution (QKD) in safe communication in the face of these challenges. Blockchain technology emerges as the foundation allowing safe 6G IoT networks. Its distributed and unchangeable architecture solves the problems of hyper-connected systems by allowing data integrity, identity management, and device authentication. The chapter shows how robust frameworks for preserving trust and security in IoT systems are created by quantum-resistant blockchain solutions when coupled with post-quantum cryptography techniques. Resilient network construction depends critically on methods including sophisticated consensus mechanisms and scalable topologies including sharding and Layer 2 solutions.

**Corresponding author*: scewsadik@gmail.com

T. Perarasi, M. Karthiga, S. Sountharrajan, E. Suganya and Balamurugan Balusamy (eds.) Secure Blockchain and Quantum Technologies for 6G-Enabled Internet of Things, (117–148) © 2026 Scrivener Publishing LLC

Examined are practical uses of these technologies, showing how they would impact sectors including health care, smart cities, autonomous systems, and vital infrastructure. The applications are aimed to show how operational efficiency, data security, and real-time decision-making may all be enhanced by using quantum-secure blockchain platforms. Finally, the chapter creates a strategic road plan for using quantum-secure blockchain in systems of 6G IoT. It emphasizes the need of industry standards, multidisciplinary teams, and regulatory frameworks in handling problems including scalability, energy economy, and interoperability. Based on the combined strengths of IoT, blockchain, and quantum computing, the chapter projects a future dominated by safe, scalable, and smart digital systems heading towards a strong and creative technological period.

Keywords: Quantum-safe cryptography, 6G IoT ecosystem, blockchain security, post-quantum challenges, decentralized trust, quantum-enhanced AI, interoperability standards

6.1 Introduction

6G networks, the Internet of Things (IoT), quantum computing, blockchain, and faster growth of communication technologies are opening the path for revolutionary innovation. In an ultra-connected digital environment, these technologies are revolutionizing the interaction between individuals, systems, and gadgets taken collectively. Promising ultra-low latency, great bandwidth, and unmatched device connectivity, the sixth generation of wireless networks (6G) helps unfettered communication and data exchange between different sectors. Concurrent with this is the IoT ecosystem, which is expanding with billions of networked devices offering the infrastructure for smart cities, healthcare networks, autonomous cars, and industrial purposes. Still, such hyper-connectivity presents major difficulties, especially with regard to security, privacy, and scalability.

As a breakthrough technology able to solve intractable problems tenfold more quickly than traditional computers, quantum computing offers potential and hazards combined. Although its great processing capacity can enhance predictive analysis and IoT operations optimization, it also poses a threat to make present cryptographic methods obsolete and susceptible to attack that could compromise IoT communications and blockchain networks security. The need of robust security systems and quantum-resistant cryptography is never more critical. With its distributed trust mechanisms, immutable ledgers, and consensus procedures, blockchain technology—whose trust is dispersed—has shown to be a major help for IoT system security. Blockchain addresses problems of device identification, data integrity, and trust management therefore safeguarding the integrity of 6G IoT networks. Blockchain combined with improved protocols and quantum-resistant technologies could help these ecosystems be strong against upcoming cyberattacks.

The complex dynamics among blockchain, 6G IoT, and quantum computing are covered in this chapter. It negotiates the quantum obstacles, quantum-safe innovations, and harmonic opportunities these technologies present for creating dependable, distributed, and intelligent systems. By emphasizing both possibilities and obstacles equally, this chapter offers a complete vision plan for realizing a guaranteed and trustworthy digital world in the age of 6G IoT.

6.1.1 The Convergence of 6G, IoT, Quantum, and Blockchain

6G, IoT, quantum computing, and blockchain taken together offer a creative technological environment able to meet growing demands for scalability, security, and speed. SixG's high-speed capabilities and ultra-low latency fit IoT's need for real-time data flow over billions of linked devices. While posing a threat to present encryption systems, quantum computing offers unthinkable computational capability, breaking difficult problems and improving IoT capability. Essential for IoT's linked character, blockchain provides a distributed framework for safe, transparent, unchangeable data management. These technologies used together provide strong and flexible systems across many industries, guaranteeing a safe and intelligent future [1, 2].

6.1.2 The Need for Advanced Security in 6G IoT

The exponential growth of 6G IoT networks raises serious security concerns needing innovative solutions. The great number of linked devices greatly increases the attack surface, hence increasing cyberattack risk [3]. From industrial measurements to healthcare information, sensitive data transfer emphasizes how urgently strong data privacy standards are needed. Critical technologies to help to reduce these vulnerabilities are blockchain, quantum-resistant cryptography, and AI-driven threat detection systems [4]. These advanced security elements ensures the dependability and dependability of 6G IoT ecosystems under ultra-connected environments.

6.1.3 Future 6G IoT Ecosystems Vision

6G IoT ecosystems will shape a world transformed by safe, smart, and distributed technology. Integrated systems of traffic, waste management, and energy will enable smart cities to grow, so optimizing sustainability and efficiency. Through safe, interoperable IoT devices, remote diagnostics and real-time monitoring will improve healthcare. To guarantee efficiency and safety, autonomous transportation systems will rely on intact communication between infrastructure and cars. This vision combines decentralization, quantum-resistant security, and AI-enabled flexibility to create a strong and globally interoperable framework equipped to solve problems of tomorrow.

6.2 Quantum Technology and Its Role in 6G IoT

Leading a revolutionary wave, quantum technology has the ability to alter many different sectors, particularly in relation to 6G IoT networks. Incorporation of quantum advances into 6G IoT offers hitherto unheard-of possibilities as the demand for faster, safer, and more efficient communication networks rises. Doing this also brings complex difficulties, especially in the domains of network infrastructure and cybersecurity. Integral components of this technology, quantum computing and quantum communication offer innovative solutions by using the ideas of quantum mechanics as in Figure 6.1.

6.2.1 Quantum Computing and Communication Understanding

Using the unique properties of quantum mechanics, quantum computing drastically alters the face of computation. Unlike conventional computers built on binary bits, quantum computers use qubits—quantum information units—that's because the superposition principle, can be in several states simultaneously. This enables exponential increase in computational capabilities and parallel processing. Quantum entanglement is another important factor since it lets qubits remain connected so that instantaneous information flow across large distances without any loss of information. The great promise of quantum systems is proven by the already demonstrated enormous speedup in the solution of some computer problems displayed by quantum algorithms such as Shor's and Grover's algorithms. Concurrently, quantum communication technology—including Quantum Key Distribution (QKD)—uses quantum mechanical ideas to generate quantumly safe channels. Together and separately, quantum computing and communications offer the building blocks required for IoT infrastructure development following the path toward an uncompromised 6G network.

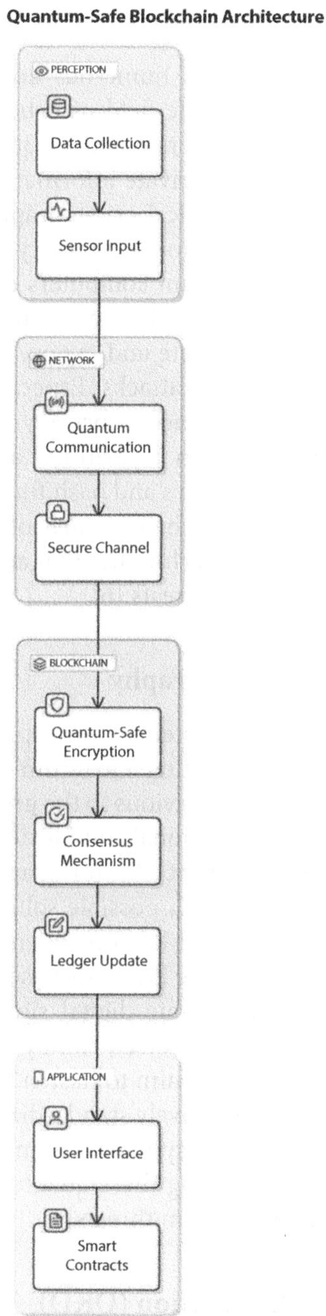

Figure 6.1 Quantum-safe blockchain architecture.

6.2.2 Quantum Threats to Traditional Security

While quantum technology offers numerous advantages, it also poses tremendous risk, particularly in the field of cybersecurity. The processing capability of quantum computers could be quite harmful for present cryptography systems protecting private information on IoT systems and blockchain architectures [5]. Classical cryptography methods such RSA, ECC, and SHA rely on computational difficulty of some mathematical problems—that kind which quantum computers can break far more rapidly than conventional computers. This capability would make most of the present security systems obsolete and expose IoT devices and blockchain networks to quantum-based attacks. Especially vulnerable to these risks are IoT systems, which depend on privacy, data integrity, and safe authentication. Similarly, quantum algorithms attacking cryptographic processes including digital signatures and hash functions can compromise the security aspects behind blockchain, which offer immutable transactions. Developing cryptographic techniques that are quantum decryption-resistant helps one counter these threats [6].

6.2.3 Quantum-Safe Cryptography

Quantum-safe cryptography has emerged as a top focus of research to offset the dangers of quantum computing. Quantum-safe cryptography seeks to create encryption methods impervious to the great strength of quantum computers. Based on the computational complexity of lattice problems—a challenge still computationally intractable for quantum computers [7], lattice-based cryptography is one such possible solution. While code-based encryption, best represented by the McEliece scheme, uses error-correcting codes to make communications safe [9], hash-based cryptography, like the SPHINCS+ algorithm [8], offers safe digital signatures. Efforts include the Post-Quantum Cryptography Project, run by the National Institute of Standards and Technology (NIST), aim to hasten the global acceptance of quantum-resistant protocols by actively standardizing these cryptographic approaches. IoT and blockchain systems can make their security and dependability feasible by combining these quantum-resistant techniques, even in face of approaching quantum threats.

6.2.4 Quantum Key Distribution (QKD)

Quantum Key Distribution (QKD) is among the most interesting uses for quantum communication. QKD warns the participants to the probable invasion by means of the secure transfer of encryption keys between two parties using the ideas of quantum mechanics, therefore disturbing the quantum states employed and warning them. This technique is fit for protecting private data in 6G IoT systems since it offers a hitherto unattainable degree of security. Although QKD offers a good instrument for safe key exchange, mass adoption of it is hampered by hardware limitations and environmental factors that could compromise quantum signal integrity. Researchers have been investigating hybrid security solutions that combine QKD with post-quantum cryptography to help reduce these risks and strengthen the security architecture for the future IoT networks.

Therefore, the junction of quantum technology and 6G IoT networks contains both exciting promise and terrible security consequences. The development of quantum-safe cryptography and safe communications protocols will be crucial to ensure the next iteration of the linked world as we keep discovering and using these technologies into our environment.

6.3 Blockchain as a Security Enabler for 6G IoT

The contribution of creative technologies to meet the growing needs of the internet of things (IoT) becomes more important as worldwide developments towards the creation of 6G networks advance towards their realization. Blockchain has shown itself among such technologies to be a basis mechanism guaranteeing the security, privacy, and scalability of linked networks. The demand for end-to--end and distributed security systems has been unparalleled as IoT devices are installed increasingly in many different sectors. With its distributed ledger architecture and fundamental characteristics including immutability, transparency, and decentralized control, blockchain offers an attractive way to overcome the growing difficulties of data integrity, authentication, and safe transactions in 6G IoT networks [10].

An amazing number of devices in communication will define 6G IoT networks and create an incredibly complex web of communication needing high-level security procedures. The particular difficulties of such a very dynamic, distributed system will not be able to be addressed by current security paradigms. Blockchain provides a distributed, tamper-evident system that lets IoT devices interact securely free from centralized brokers. Blockchain is a fundamental enabler of trust in 6G IoT systems since it allows safe and transparent data exchanges, hence lowering risks of data manipulation, illegal access, and cyberattacks [11]. Furthermore, blockchain technology's capacity to enable automated operations and safe smart contracts provides an extra degree of security, therefore enabling transactions among IoT devices to be more dependable and efficient. Blockchain will become increasingly important in keeping 6G IoT networks as strong, reliable, and secret as their complexity and scale keep rising. Blockchain integration into the 6G IoT architecture guarantees not only enhanced security but also long-term scalability and network sustainability, therefore ensuring the connected society.

Blockchain use here is an underlying technology enabling safe, distributed, and autonomous functioning of next-generation IoT networks, not only simple transaction tracking. Blockchain's special qualities make it a great weapon to combat most important security concerns about 6G IoT, therefore acting as a necessary enabler of next-generation linked systems.

6.3.1 Blockchain Fundamentals

Distributed ledgers—which ensure that every network participant has access to a shared, synchronized ledger of transactions—form the foundation of blockchain technology. Its most unique feature is immutability, which suggests that once data is entered onto the blockchain, it cannot be altered without network consent. Blockchain is quite safe for data storage and transfer since this characteristic maximizes trust and openness. Consensus methods, for example Proof of Work (PoW) and Proof of Stake (PoS), keep consistency among parties as to what is a genuine transaction, therefore preventing any illegal activity. Such inherent qualities make blockchain a highly good tool for safeguarding modern digital societies such as 6G IoT systems.

6.3.2 Blockchain's Role in IoT Security

Blockchain provides a distributed platform in Internet of Things to address most critical security concerns. It minimizes the risk of illegal access by creating tamper-proof digital IDs for IoT devices, therefore safeguarding device identities. By storing transactions in an unchangeable manner and hence preventing data modification and breaches, blockchain preserves data integrity [12]. Another crucial advantage is decentralized trust management since blockchain lessens single point of failure by removing reliance on central authorities. Blockchain makes IoT networks more overall robust by allowing safe and open communication between devices. This makes it clearly useful in the ultra-connected environment designed for 6G IoT [13].

6.3.3 Scalable Blockchain Solutions for 6G IoT

With billions of linked devices in 6G IoT systems, blockchain adoption suffers a significant challenge related to scalability. Payment channels and roll-ups among Layer 2 solutions permit off-chain transaction processing to reduce main blockchain congestion [14]. Another technique that increases throughput by breaking the blockchain into smaller pieces—shards—processes transactions in parallel. Running in parallel with the main blockchain, sidechains ensure compatibility and let individual transactions to be handled in isolation [15]. Scalable solutions ensure that blockchain can effectively meet low-latency needs of 6G IoT networks and support the high transaction volumes.

6.3.4 Smart Contracts for IoT Applications

Living on the blockchain, smart contracts are self-executing codes meant to automate and enforce contracts without middlemen. Smart contracts let devices in 6G IoT networks secure and in real time [16]. Once products have been delivered and checked by IoT sensors, a smart contract might automatically pay for them. Since these agreements demand particular criteria to be satisfied before making transactions, they reduce the possibility of fraud and further promote openness. Smart contracts help 6G IoT ecosystems to become more dependable, efficient, and safe in their running conditions.

6.4 Synergy of Quantum and Blockchain in 6G IoT

For the security and scalability of 6G IoT networks, the junction of blockchain with quantum technologies presents a fascinating new frontier. With 6G seeing a hyperconnected world, blockchain and quantum computing can assist address the complex issues of protecting vast networks, enabling real-time processing, and building trust in the running of the system. Although every technology independently offers revolutionary capabilities, their combined synergy has the ability to increase the security, performance, and robustness of 6G IoT systems to hitherto unheard-of heights as shown in Figure 6.2.

6.4.1 Quantum Computing and Blockchain: Complementary Forces

By using the ideas of quantum physics to process data at rates much beyond those of conventional computers, quantum computing helps to solve difficult problems with astonishing simplicity. Fields including data security, big data analysis, and IoT network device coordination could all

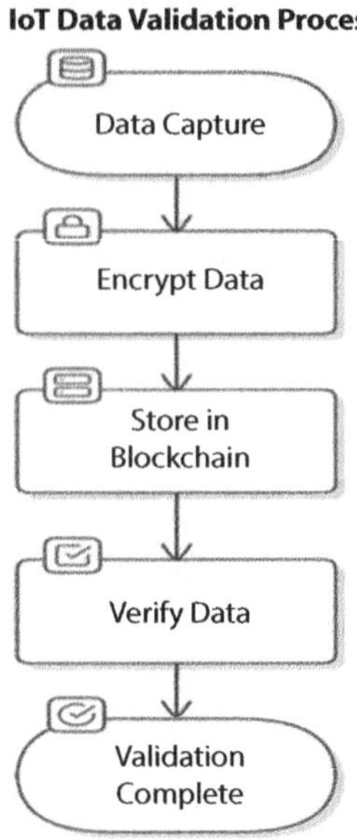

Figure 6.2 IoT data validation process.

be transformed by this technical development. But as quantum computing could perhaps destroy current encryption systems like RSA and ECC, its growing strength also presents major security issues. Fundamental for protecting blockchain transactions and guaranteeing safe communications inside IoT systems are these encryption techniques. Conversely, blockchain technology offers a distributed and safe structure for transaction integrity, device authentication, and data storage. Maintaining confidence in IoT systems depends on data being kept unaltered after it is recorded. Nonetheless, blockchain depends on conventional encryption techniques, hence the greater processing capacity of quantum computing could threaten its security.

6.4.2 Quantum-Blockchain Synergy for Enhanced Security

Blockchain combined with quantum technology could help reduce the security concerns that quantum attacks bring about. To maintain blockchain systems safe in a post-quantum age, experts might include lattice-based or code-based quantum-safe cryptography into them. By permitting the safe exchange of encryption keys such that any efforts to eavesdrop during key exchange are immediately seen, Quantum Key Distribution (QKD) can further improve blockchain security [17]. Joining quantum-safe cryptographic algorithms with blockchain's built-in decentralization and unchangeability would enable developers to create a powerful future-ready security framework for 6G IoT networks.

6.4.3 Optimized Performance and Scalability

Apart from increasing security, merging blockchain with quantum computing improves IoT network performance and expansion. By improving blockchain consensus methods using quantum algorithms, we could accelerate transaction checking and increase general blockchain network efficiency. The capacity of quantum computing to execute sophisticated math all at once could also assist to manage the enormous volumes of data that IoT devices produce, enabling us to process and make decisions immediately away without sacrificing security or dependability.

Furthermore, the distributed character of blockchain combines nicely with the capacity of quantum computing to operate with data across many systems. This implies that in 6G IoT configurations quantum-powered devices can and share data. With billions of devices talking to one another in 6G IoT systems, our collaboration helps to ensure that data flows across networks under robust security mechanisms.

6.4.4 A New Era of Trust and Transparency

Combining blockchain and quantum technologies would greatly increase openness and trust in 6G Internet of Things (IoT) networks. Quantum computing improves the efficiency of blockchain smart contracts, therefore enabling more sophisticated and safe automated procedures. By using quantum cryptography, these contracts let IoT devices operate depending on particular conditions without middlemen, therefore reducing mistakes and fraud. This degree of openness combined with the permanent character of blockchain guarantees a safe record of all IoT-related transactions and activities, therefore fostering user and device trust and responsibility. Blockchain and quantum technologies working together show great promise for producing scalable, safe, and effective 6G IoT systems. While blockchain provides a distributed and permanent framework for trustworthy data management, quantum computing presents enormous processing capability. These technologies together improve the performance and scalability of 6G IoT systems and address security issues presented by the quantum era. Maintaining the resilience and dependability of upcoming IoT ecosystems depends on the integration of quantum and blockchain as networks becoming more complicated and linked.

6.5 Advanced Use Cases and Applications

By means of the confluence of quantum technology and blockchain integration, which influences healthcare along with logistics and finance industries respectively, 6G IoT networks deliver revolutionary applications and use cases. These technologies provide extraordinary security measures together with efficiency and extendable powers to tackle modern IoT network flaws. Blockchain combined with quantum technologies will allow several significant developments to take place [18]:

6.5.1 Secure and Autonomous Healthcare Systems

Healthcare is essential, hence blockchain and quantum technologies taken together can have a significant influence. Vast amounts of sensitive data in 6G IoT healthcare originate from health monitoring systems, fitness trackers, and medical gadgets. Patient records are kept on a secure ledger made of blockchain, which maintains immutable and open data. Faster and more accurate diagnosis and treatment predictions follow from better data analysis enabled by quantum computers.

For example, fast processing medical data made possible by quantum technology enables real-time patient information analysis across several systems. Blockchain guarantees only authorized users may access or modify this data. Furthermore, applying safe techniques such as Quantum Key Distribution (QKD) and Quantum-safe cryptography can help to greatly guard sensitive medical data transmission, hence lowering the possibility of data leaks or cyberattacks [19].

6.5.2 Blockchain-Based Quantum-Secure Supply Chain Management

IoT devices are now increasingly important for supply chains tracking and managing asset, stock, and goods movement as they occur. With a transparent, permanent record of transactions, blockchain has shown value in safeguarding these processes. Working out complicated issues faster and better helps blockchain to improve supply chain procedures including routing, stock control, and demand prediction when coupled with quantum computing.

Applications: Use Case Quantum tech IoT sensors enable supply chains driven by them to monitor how products are performing—including their temperature and moisture—as they are being transported. Blockchain ensures that every stage of the journey is recorded and unchangeable, so holding everyone responsible. Quantum formulae might therefore improve supply chain paths and identify issues before they arise, so enabling a system that could react faster and operate more efficiently.

6.5.3 Smart Cities with Quantum-Blockchain Integration

Since its connected gadgets control traffic networks and energy systems among other functions, the 6G IoT vision mostly emphasizes smart cities. Blockchain's distributed and safe technology offers a great framework to manage a distributed device network; since it preserves anonymity and maintains data intact throughout the infrastructure of a whole city. Quantum computing processing of IoT sensor data makes the real-time decision-making procedures for smart city management feasible.

IoT devices help the smart city deployment of quantum-blockchain integration control its traffic system. The system continuously manages enormous traffic data using quantum algorithms to conduct traffic signal modifications that lower congestion and produce traffic prediction models. Blockchain, which records every action and transaction, would help the city government to become transparent and responsible. Quantum-safe encryption technologies taken together will safeguard personal data privacy in these platforms.

6.5.4 Decentralized Financial Systems and Quantum-Secure Cryptocurrencies

Blockchain has brought distributed finance (DeFi) and cryptocurrencies, therefore altering the financial scene. Quantum computers run the danger of violating the security now in place to guard transactions and digital wallets as they develop more sophisticated. Blockchain quantum-safe cryptography will help to safeguard cryptocurrencies against these upcoming dangers, therefore safeguarding the future of digital currencies.

For instance, quantum computers can greatly speed up banking system transaction processing, therefore enabling instantaneous cross-border payments. Long-term protection for distributed financial systems will come from quantum-safe methods keeping these transactions safe from the capabilities of upcoming quantum computers.

6.5.5 Quantum-Enhanced Privacy in Identity Management

Because of their increased connectedness in our digital environment, security of IoT devices and user privacy calls for effective identity management and authentication methods. Blockchain guarantees safe maintenance of identities by transparent procedures; quantum technology offers safe protection of privacy by means of its improved authentication techniques including quantum-secured biometric identification.

By means of blockchain ledger storage for users' personal data, the quantum-blockchain technology helps IoT devices to achieve distributed secure identity management. By use of encryption, quantum cryptography techniques can safeguard biometric data and grant authorized users only access to personal computer systems and devices. By assuring safe authentication techniques and thereby preventing possible identity theft, fraud attempts, and hacker operations, digital authentication systems reinforced with quantum technologies would guard IoT devices against illegal access.

6.5.6 Enhanced Cybersecurity for IoT Networks

Securing these networks from intrusions is becoming difficult as the internet of things (IoT) grows. Because of its distributed character, blockchain technology improves IoT networks' resistance against threats such distributed denial of service (DDoS). Blockchain can be enhanced with quantum-safe cryptography when combined with quantum computing, therefore strengthening its capacity to thwarting new cyber threats. Blockchain, *via* a distributed authentication scheme, might guarantee safe device-to-device communication in a 6G IoT security architecture. Effective real-time cyber threat detection and mitigation could be made possible in great part by quantum computing. Analyzing network traffic patterns and spotting odd behavior helps one to find indications of continuous attacks.

6.5.7 Quantum-Blockchain-Enabled Autonomous Vehicles

Blockchain and quantum computing taken together are also likely to revolutionize the growth of autonomous vehicles. Dependent on a network of IoT devices for navigation, communication, and decision-making, autonomous vehicles will require quick, dependable data processing capability. While quantum computers can improve real-time data processing and decision-making, blockchain guarantees safe and unchangeable communication between vehicles [20]. Utilization Case: Quantum algorithms might examine vast amounts of real-time sensor data from IoT devices in an autonomous car network, therefore enhancing route optimization and safety judgments. Blockchain would guarantee that no incorrect information or tampering is passed during the decision-making process, therefore securing vehicle-to-vehicle (V2V) and vehicle-to-infrastructure (V2I) connections. In 6G IoT systems, the synergy between quantum technology and blockchain allows the development of extremely safe, scalable, and efficient systems able to address the most difficult problems in many spheres. From improving supply chains and financial systems to privacy in healthcare and identity management, these technologies have many possible uses. The future of 6G IoT promises to be more secure, efficient, and resilient as we keep exploring their combined capabilities, therefore enabling businesses to innovate and grow in ways before unthinkable.

6.6 Challenges in Adoption

Although blockchain and quantum technologies could revolutionize 6G IoT networks, their acceptance presents a variety of technical, financial, and legal difficulties even if their possibilities are great. Including these cutting-edge technologies into current IoT systems calls for overcoming major obstacles to guarantee that they can be securely and successfully scaled. In the framework of 6G IoT, the following represent the main obstacles in the acceptance of quantum and blockchain technologies:

6.6.1 Complexity of Quantum Computing Integration

Though very exciting, quantum computing is still in its early years of research. One major challenge is the intricacy of incorporating quantum computers into current systems. Quantum computers are challenging to scale and fit into real-world IoT systems, since they depend on a highly regulated environment to run effectively—that is, ultra-low temperatures and isolation from outside noise.

Challenge: Large-scale IoT applications of quantum computing technologies call for notable developments in quantum hardware, error correction algorithms, and quantum programming methods. Overcoming these constraints calls for significant hardware and software development investment as well as research.

6.6.2 Quantum-Safe Cryptography Development

Classical encryption techniques applied in security of IoT devices and blockchain systems are seriously threatened by the development of quantum computers. Although quantum-safe cryptographic methods are still under development, some distance remains before they are generally adopted and standardized. These algorithms also have to be backward, compatible with current cryptographic systems and provide the same degree of security without adding inefficiencies.

Task: Turning now to quantum-resistant cryptography calls for significant modifications to current infrastructure, protocols, and applications. Furthermore, the race against quantum attacks depends much on making sure these new algorithms can resist the computational capability of quantum systems.

6.6.3 Scalability Issues with Blockchain

Well-known for its distributed and unchangeable ledger that guarantees security and openness is blockchain technology. But as IoT networks grow, the problem of blockchain scalability takes front stage. Every transaction kept on a distributed ledger could result in slower transaction speeds, more storage needs, and more energy use. Although blockchain offers IoT network security, its acceptance for major applications in 6G IoT systems calls for overcoming scalability issues like speedier consensus procedures and lowest energy consumption of blockchain nodes. To solve these problems, ideas such hybrid blockchain models, off-chain transactions, and sharding are being investigated; yet, they need further testing and development before they can be generally used.

6.6.4 Interoperability Between Quantum and Blockchain Systems

Blockchain's distributed character is one of its main advantages since it lets devices interact and transact without depending on a central control. Still, including quantum technologies into these distributed systems presents interoperability issues. Blockchain networks and quantum systems have somewhat different topologies, which makes it challenging to guarantee flawless communication between quantum devices and IoT applications. New protocols, interfaces, and standards must be created that allow interoperability between quantum-powered systems and conventional blockchain networks, if we are to effectively mix quantum and blockchain technology in 6G IoT. These solutions have to solve the particular difficulties presented by both blockchain and quantum settings, including consensus systems and quantum-specific cryptography techniques.

6.6.5 Cost and Resource Intensive Implementation

Blockchain technology as well as quantum computing call for large technical and financial resources for research and implementation. While blockchain architecture sometimes needs significant processing power and energy consumption, quantum hardware is costly to manufacture and maintain. The great expense of implementing these technologies might be a major obstacle to entrance for many IoT network operators, particularly in developing areas or smaller companies.

Challenge: Reducing the expenses connected with blockchain implementation and quantum computing is necessary for their general acceptance in 6G IoT. This covers hardware affordability, energy consumption reduction, and cost-effective quantum-safe cryptography and blockchain infrastructure models creation.

6.6.6 Regulatory and Standardization Issues

The scene of regulations surrounding blockchain and quantum computing is continually changing. Particularly with relation to data protection, privacy, and cybersecurity, many nations and areas have not yet set explicit rules on the application of quantum technologies. Furthermore, lacking is a worldwide consensus on how best to include quantum computing into blockchain-based architectures.

Challenge: Consistent and safe adoption depends on developing worldwide standards for quantum-safe cryptography, blockchain systems, and the interplay between quantum systems and Internet of Things devices. Particularly with regard to privacy and data security, regulatory authorities must work with industry players to build frameworks guaranteeing the ethical and safe use of these technologies.

6.6.7 Environmental and Energy Considerations

Particularly proof-of-work (PoW) blockchain systems, quantum computers and blockchain networks are sometimes resource-intensive and have a major environmental effect because of great energy consumption. Particularly quantum computers depend on a stable environment kept at very low temperatures, which calls for energy-intensive cooling equipment. Given their energy consumption—especially as they grow to handle more transactions—blockchain systems also draw criticism.

Challenge: Long-term acceptance of quantum and blockchain technologies depends on their being able to balance environmental sustainability with their energy needs. Minimizing the environmental impact of these advanced technologies depends on developing energy-efficient quantum processors and more sustainable blockchain models including proof-of-stake (PoS).

6.6.8 Security Risks in Transition Period

Quantum technology presents a major risk during the transition phase when both classical and quantum systems have to coexist. The systems depending on classical encryption techniques remain susceptible to quantum attacks even while quantum-safe cryptography is under development. This opens a window of opportunity for hostile players to take advantage of weaknesses in the transition from present encryption standards to quantum-resistant systems.

Challenge: Protecting IoT systems and blockchain networks during the shift to quantum-safe cryptography calls for deliberate design, testing, and execution. A major difficulty for developers and cybersecurity professionals is making sure both classical and quantum systems can run safely together.

6.6.9 Public Perception and Trust

Adoption of quantum and blockchain technology in important internet of things networks calls for public confidence development. The consequences of blockchain for privacy, security, and governance as well as quantum computing remain unknown to many people and companies. Particularly in sectors like surveillance, data privacy, and automation, ethical usage of these technologies could also give cause for questions.

Challenge: Fostering trust and support for adoption requires public and stakeholder education on the advantages, hazards, and ethical issues of quantum and blockchain technology. Ensuring that these technologies be applied in ways that fit society values and norms will depend on open communication and accountable government.

Although using quantum and blockchain technology in 6G IoT networks has great potential, certain obstacles have to be solved if we are to completely realize their possibilities. Dealing with these difficulties—from technological questions about scalability and integration to legal and financial concerns—will call for ongoing cooperation among academics, business leaders, and legislators. Ensuring that quantum and blockchain technologies can be central in forming the safe, efficient, and scalable networks of the future depends on overcoming these obstacles.

6.7 Future Research Directions in Quantum and Blockchain Technologies for 6G IoT

Several important research directions are developing to investigate how quantum technology and blockchain might be harmonized, maximized, and used at scale, since their combined incorporation into 6G IoT networks promises transforming possibilities. Overcoming the present difficulties, guaranteeing security, and allowing the flawless operation of 6G IoT ecosystems will depend critically on these fields of research. The main areas of research that might propel quantum and blockchain technologies for the 6G IoT to develop are shown below:

6.7.1 Quantum-Safe Cryptography Development and Standardization

Development and standardization of quantum-safe cryptographic algorithms is among the most pressing scientific subjects. Quantum computers endanger the security of current cryptographic algorithms used in IoT and blockchain systems as they develop. Ensuring the security of IoT and blockchain systems in the post-quantum future depends critically on the evolution of quantum-resistant encryption methods like lattice-based, hash-based, and code-based cryptography.

Research Focus:

- Examining the performance and resilience of newly developed quantum-safe algorithms in practical IoT settings.
- Working with standards groups such as NIST to propel quantum-safe cryptography's worldwide acceptance.
- Creating hybrid encryption models for a seamless transition that combine quantum-safe cryptography with current systems.

6.7.2 Quantum Blockchain Integration for IoT Applications

Unlocking their combined promise in 6G IoT systems depends on research on the integration of quantum computing and blockchain. This entails knowing how quantum algorithms might maximize scalability, transaction speed, and blockchain consensus processes. Furthermore, by means of more sophisticated cryptographic algorithms as Quantum Key Distribution (QKD), quantum approaches can be applied to guard blockchain networks.

Research Focus:

- Creating effective quantum algorithms for blockchain performance optimization (e.g., resource management, speedier consensus processes, scalability).
- Investigating in a quantum-safe environment the application of QKD for blockchain communication channel security.
- Developing hybrid quantum-classical blockchain models fit for current 6G IoT systems without interfering with operations.

6.7.3 Scalability and Energy Efficiency in Quantum and Blockchain Systems

Two main obstacles are quantum computing's and blockchain's energy consumption and scalability. Blockchain's storage and computational needs get more challenging to control as IoT networks expand exponentially. Although strong, quantum computing runs on large amounts of energy and calls for realizing the promise of these technologies at scale depending on thorough study on scalable blockchain models and energy-efficient quantum computing.

Research Focus:

- Creating quantum hardware and processors with low energy consumption that can run at scale, and hence lower environmental impact.
- Researching alternative blockchain consensus systems such hybrid models or Proof-of- Stake (PoS) will help blockchain networks to consume less energy.
- Investigating off-chain and sharding options can help blockchain networks to become more scalable and cut energy consumption.

6.7.4 Quantum-Blockchain Interoperability and Protocol Design

The smooth integration of quantum and blockchain technologies into 6G IoT systems depends on their being compatible. Key research areas are developing new communication protocols allowing quantum-powered devices to securely interface with blockchain networks and vice versa. To guarantee compatibility, this will need fresh ideas on blockchain protocol design as well as quantum communication.

Research Focus:

- Creating universal communication protocols that enable smooth interaction between IoT systems based on blockchains and quantum-powered gadgets.
- Especially for secure and effective transactions, protocols and procedures for the integration of quantum computing with current blockchain systems should be developed.
- Dealing with issues in real-time synchronizing quantum and blockchain processes, particularly in IoT networks with large data volumes.

6.7.5 Quantum-Enhanced Machine Learning for IoT Data Processing

In the realm of machine learning especially in relation to analyzing vast amounts of data produced by IoT devices, quantum computing's capacity to execute parallel calculations has major benefits. Faster, more effective processing of IoT data resulting from quantum-enhanced machine learning (QML) will enable real-time decision-making, anomaly detection, and predictive analytics.

Research Focus:

- Creating quantum machine learning models for IoT data application toward tasks including predictive maintenance, defect detection, and resource optimization.
- Examining quantum-inspired methods of machine learning for uses where completely quantum devices might not yet be practical.
- Combining blockchain systems with QML techniques to provide transparent and safe machine learning models and results in Internet of Things devices.

6.7.6 Privacy-Enhancing Technologies in Quantum and Blockchain Systems

Privacy will be a top issue since 6G IoT systems will rely on massive data collecting from personal devices. By means of safe, distributed networks for data storage and communication, quantum and blockchain technologies can be merged to improve privacy. Research in this field will concentrate on guaranteeing user privacy while allowing data sharing and processing in Internet of Things devices.

Research Focus:

- Developing privacy-preserving blockchain techniques (e.g., homomorphic encryption, zero-knowledge proofs) that let IoT devices safely exchange data without endangering privacy.
- Examining how quantum encryption methods might improve data privacy and guard against quantum-enabled monitoring.
- Developing privacy-enhancing systems for user authentication so IoT devices and users may interact safely without disclosing private data.

6.7.7 Quantum Blockchain for Secure Autonomous Systems

6G IoT will depend much on autonomous systems like robotics, drones, and cars. These systems depend on safe, real-time communication and decision-making; so, the combination of quantum and blockchain could offer improved security, openness, and decision-making capacity. To guarantee their safe and effective operation in dynamic surroundings, research on quantum blockchain applications for autonomous systems will be absolutely vital.

Research Focus:

- Examining blockchain application for safe autonomous decision-making guarantees that actions done by autonomous systems are open and tamper-proof.
- Creating quantum algorithms to process sensor data in autonomous cars or drones in real-time, thereby maximizing navigation, obstacle avoidance, and route planning by means of decision-making.
- Designing distributed autonomous networks—such as drone fleets or autonomous vehicle networks—that make use of blockchain and quantum computing for safe communication and collaboration.

6.7.8 Ethical, Regulatory, and Governance Frameworks for Quantum-Blockchain IoT

Comprehensive ethical, legal, and governance structures will be increasingly needed as quantum and blockchain technology get more included into IoT networks. Investigating the social and legal ramifications of quantum-blockchain integration will be crucial to guarantee responsible and moral application of these technologies.

Research Focus:

- Particularly in sectors like healthcare, banking, and transportation, developing ethical rules and legal frameworks for the application of quantum and blockchain technology in IoT is crucial.
- Dealing with issues in quantum-blockchain systems around digital autonomy, surveillance, and data privacy.
- Working with legislators to set global norms and rules guiding the acceptance of quantum-safe blockchain systems in important Internet of Things infrastructures.

For 6G IoT, the future developments in quantum and blockchain technology present fascinating chances for invention in many other fields. Unlocking the whole potential of these technologies depends on addressing issues with scalability, security, privacy, and integration. Pursuing these study topics will help us to establish the fundamental knowledge and infrastructure required to provide sustainable, efficient, and safe 6G IoT networks; so guaranteeing, they satisfy the needs of an ever linked society.

6.8 Roadmap for Implementation of Quantum and Blockchain Technologies in 6G IoT

From basic research and development to major deployment, the application of quantum and blockchain technologies in 6G IoT networks will call for a well-crafted roadmap spanning many phases. While guaranteeing a flawless transition to next-generation IoT networks as in Figure 6.3, this roadmap must solve the difficulties presented by these developing technologies like scalability, security, cost, and interoperability. This suggested road map shows the main stages and benchmarks for the effective application of blockchain and quantum technologies in the 6G IoT.

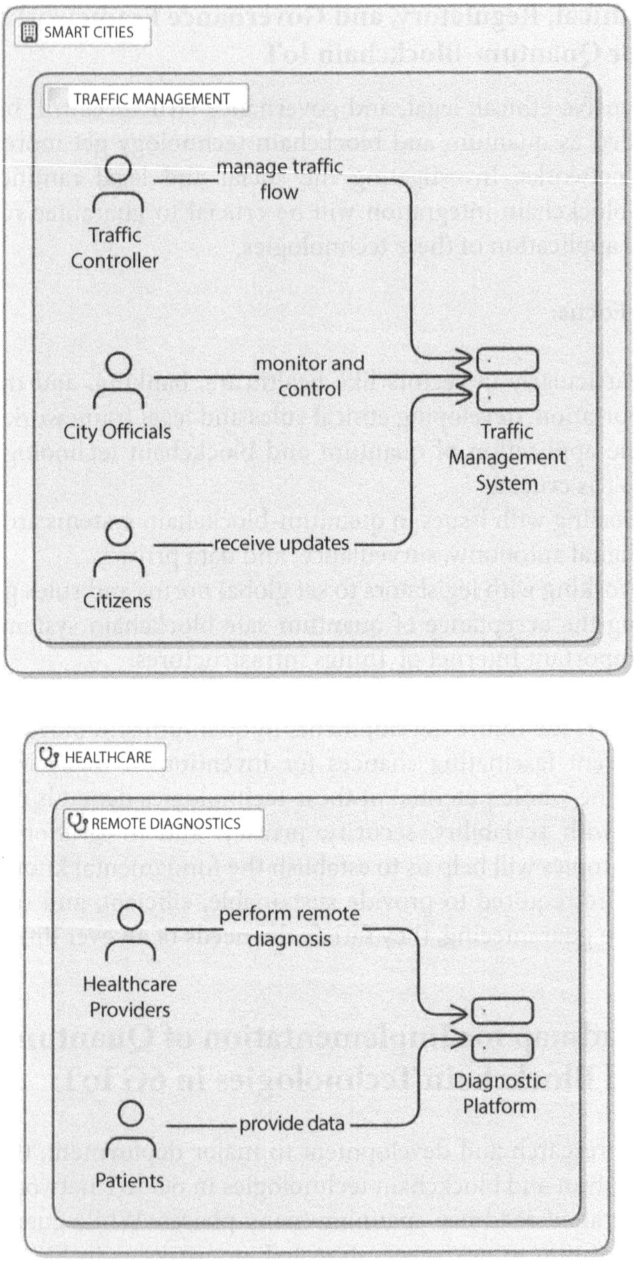

Figure 6.3 Use cases in smart cities and healthcare.

Phase 1: Foundational Research and Development (2025 - 2027)
Research and development (R&D) will be the main emphasis of the first phase in order to solve the technical and theoretical difficulties including blockchain and quantum technologies into IoT networks. Academic institutions, research institutes, and business players will cooperate in this phase.

Key activities:

- Quantum-Safe Cryptography Research: Create and evaluate quantum-safe cryptography systems able to resist the computational capability of quantum computers. This covers hash-based cryptography, code-based and lattice-based encryption.
- Blockchain Optimization: Research into more scalable, energy-efficient blockchain technologies—including substitutes for conventional consensus methods (e.g., Proof of Stake, sharding)—to enhance transaction speeds, scalability, and resource economy.
- Quantum-Blockchain Integration Models: Investigate how quantum computing may maximize blockchain systems, enhance security, and allow more effective consensus procedures in IoT settings.
- Quantum Machine Learning (QML) for IoT: Create quantum-enhanced machine learning algorithms able to process vast IoT data for predictive analytics and real-time decision-making.
- Standardization and Frameworks: Work with international organizations (e.g., NIST, ISO) to start the standardizing process for hybrid systems in IoT, blockchain interoperability, and quantum-safe cryptography.

Phase 2: Prototype Development and Testing (2027 - 2029)
This phase will see prototypes and proof-of-concept demonstrations, test of theoretical models, and algorithms. These prototypes will help to confirm if it is possible to include blockchain and quantum technologies into practical IoT projects.

Key activities:

- Prototype Development: Create modest-scale quantum-enhanced blockchain systems for IoT uses including distributed control, data integrity, and secure communication.
- Quantum Key Distribution (QKD) Trials: Trials of Quantum Key Distribution (QKD): Install QKD systems for safe communication inside IoT networks such that blockchain networks and IoT devices securely exchange encryption keys.
- Integration with IoT Devices: Create hardware and software interfaces to let quantum-enabled IoT devices interface with blockchain systems. This covers designing light-weight quantum sensors fit for IoT settings and processors. Blockchain Scalability Testing: Under reasonable IoT loads, test blockchain systems for scalability, with an eye toward transaction throughput, latency, and resource consumption.
- Simulated Environments: Create virtual environments for testing the interplay between IoT devices, blockchain networks, and quantum systems in many real-world settings (e.g., smart cities, autonomous vehicles, industrial IoT).
- Security Audits: Specifically with regard to possible quantum threats, do thorough security assessments to find weaknesses in the combination of quantum and blockchain technology.

Phase 3: Pilot Deployments and Optimization (2029 - 2031)
Following the validation of the prototypes, pilot implementations in controlled conditions will be conducted to evaluate the scalability, security, and performance of quantum-blockchain IoT systems in actual environments. Cooperation with industry partners for trial deployments in smart cities, healthcare, automotive, and other important IoT areas will define this phase.

Key activities:

- Pilot Deployment in Select IoT Sectors: One pilot deployment in a specific IoT sector is to install pilot projects in fields like transportation (autonomous vehicle communication), smart cities (decentralized traffic management), and healthcare (safe patient data management).

- Hybrid Quantum-Classical Systems: Create safe, scalable, and effective IoT networks by designing hybrid quantum-classical systems combining quantum computing with traditional blockchain architecture. For increased security, this can involve combining quantum key distribution with traditional blockchain systems.
- Interoperability Testing: Verify that blockchain systems and quantum-enabled IoT devices can easily interact and communicate across several platforms and protocols.
- Performance Optimization: Fine-tuning algorithms for quicker processing, lower latency, and reduced resource consumption will help quantum processors and blockchain networks to be optimized.
- Regulatory Compliance: Particularly in industries like healthcare, finance, and critical infrastructure, make sure pilot initiatives follow legal frameworks and data security rules [21].
- Public Awareness and Education: Start teaching developers, business leaders, legislators, and other participants on the advantages, drawbacks, and possibilities of quantum-blockchain IoT systems.

Phase 4: Full-Scale Deployment and Commercialization (2031 - 2035)
Following effective pilot installations and optimizations, the last phase will concentrate on the worldwide commercialization and deployment of quantum-blockchain IoT networks. This will entail building the ecosystem to enable general acceptance and increasing the infrastructure.

Key activities:

- Global Deployment: Scale up installations of quantum-blockchain IoT networks in important sectors including telecoms, healthcare, smart cities, and autonomous systems worldwide. This covers the building of blockchain infrastructure and specifically tailored quantum data centers.
- Standardization and Interoperability: Standardize hybrid systems, blockchain interoperability, and quantum-safe cryptography finalizing worldwide standards. Make sure these criteria are embraced worldwide to allow smooth integration across many sectors and areas.

- Commercial Products and Services: Launch ready for major commercial use quantum-powered IoT devices, blockchain solutions, and quantum-blockchain platforms. Providing safe, distributed IoT solutions, these devices will appeal to end consumers as well as business customers.
- Continuous Optimization: Quantum-blockchain IoT networks should be constantly optimized depending on user comments, new technology developments, and evolving industrial needs.
- Regulatory and Ethical Governance: Particularly with relation to privacy, security, and data sovereignty, engage with governments and international organizations to create ethical rules and legal frameworks for the use of quantum and blockchain technologies in IoT.
- Sustainability Focus: Incorporate sustainability initiatives in the implementation of quantum and blockchain technologies, such energy-efficient quantum processors and green blockchain models, to minimize the environmental impact of the technologies [22].

Phase 5: Evolution and Next-Generation Innovations (2035 and Beyond)
The last phase emphasizes on the ongoing development of quantum and blockchain technologies in response to changing needs of 6G IoT systems. Advances in quantum computing, blockchain, and IoT will inspire fresh use cases and applications developed in this phase.

Key activities:

- Quantum-Blockchain Convergence: Discover more developments in the confluence of quantum and blockchain technology, including the creation of totally quantum-blockchain ecosystems competent of supporting ultra-secure, high-performance IoT systems.
- Autonomous and Decentralized Systems: Research on totally autonomous and decentralized IoT systems driven by quantum and blockchain technologies—including self-managing smart cities, autonomous vehicles, and distributed supply chains—powered by autonomous and decentralized systems powered by quantum and blockchain technologies, including Autonomous.

- Quantum-Enhanced AI and IoT Integration: Investigate how IoT networks might be integrated with quantum-enhanced artificial intelligence to provide advanced decision-making, predictive analytics, and optimization in dynamic surroundings.
- Global Quantum-Blockchain Ecosystems: Encourage the development of worldwide ecosystems whereby transparent, safe, effective IoT systems spanning sectors and areas are built on quantum and blockchain technology as fundamental pillars.

From basic research and prototype development to major commercialization and worldwide deployment, the road map for using quantum and blockchain technologies in 6G IoT networks runs several phases. This staged approach guarantees that the required technical, legal, and infrastructure issues are resolved as well as that the advantages of these developing technologies will be completely realized in the IoT ecosystem going forward. Following this road map will enable stakeholders to drive the effective integration of quantum and blockchain technologies, hence forming the distributed, scalable, and secure networks that will run 6G IoT.

6.9 Conclusion

A revolutionary approach toward transforming the future of connection, security, and data management is the integration of quantum technologies and blockchain into 6G IoT networks. As this chapter has shown, many of the present difficulties experienced by IoT systems can be resolved by the unique but complimentary characteristics of quantum and blockchain technology. The great computational capability of quantum computing, together with its capacity to guarantee ultra-secure communication *via* ideas including superposition, entanglement, and Quantum Key Distribution (QKD), offers IoT security and performance of new opportunities. Conversely, blockchain provides distributed, tamper-proof systems that can improve IoT network data integrity, privacy, and trust by means of which change can happen. Realizing what this synergy does, however, present certain difficulties. Key challenges that need to be overcome by study, creativity, and cooperation are the possible hazards quantum computing presents to conventional cryptographic systems, the scalability of blockchain, and the need of quantum-safe cryptography. Dealing with these issues as we approach full-scale deployment calls for concentrated efforts in infrastructure modification, standardization, and algorithm development.

Beginning with basic research, the road plan described in this chapter guides the methodical integration of these technologies; first, through prototype development, then through pilot deployments and finally, through large-scale commercialization. The future of 6G IoT is set for hitherto unheard-of expansion and change as quantum-safe cryptographic protocols, quantum-enhanced blockchain systems, and hybrid model research continue to evolve. In the end, the synergy of quantum technology with blockchain has the power to open a new IoT age marked by hitherto unheard-of security, scalability, and performance. A safe, effective, and linked future will be shaped in great part by these technologies as they develop and their uses in the 6G IoT change. Ensuring the successful implementation of this vision depends critically on the continuous cooperation among researchers, business leaders, and legislators.

AI disclosure statement: The author acknowledges the use of AI-based tools for minor language editing or grammatical correction. However, all intellectual contributions, analyses, and conclusions presented in this chapter are entirely the author's own.

References

1. Stallings, W., *Cryptography and Network Security*, 5th ed, Pearson, London, England, UK, 2010.
2. Keshav, S., *Mathematical Foundations of Computer Networking*, Addison-Wesley, New Jersey, USA, 2012.
3. Tanenbaum, A.S., *Computer Networks*, 5th ed, Pearson Education, London, UK, 2013.
4. Liu, Y.-D., Hwang, R.-H., Baker, F., *Computer Networks: An Open Source Approach*, McGraw-Hill, New York, USA, 2011.
5. Shor, P.W., Algorithms for Quantum Computation, in: *Proceedings of the 35th Annual Symposium on Foundations of Computer Science*, pp. 124–134, 1994.
6. Grover, L.K., A Fast Quantum Mechanical Algorithm for Database Search, in: *Proceedings of the 28th Annual ACM Symposium on Theory of Computing*, pp. 212–219, 1996.
7. National Institute of Standards and Technology (NIST), "Kyber and Dilithium Specifications," 2022. [Online]. Available: https://csrc.nist.gov.
8. National Institute of Standards and Technology (NIST), "SPHINCS+ Specifications," 2022. [Online]. Available: https://csrc.nist.gov.

9. National Institute of Standards and Technology (NIST), "McEliece Cryptosystem Specifications," 2022. [Online]. Available: https://csrc.nist.gov.
10. IBM, "Quantum-Safe Cryptography Initiative," 2023. [Online]. Available: https://www.ibm.com.
11. European Commission, "EuroQCI Program on Quantum Communication," 2023. [Online]. Available: https://digital-strategy.ec.europa.eu.
12. Quantum Research Group, Applications of QKD in Blockchain Systems. *Quantum J.*, 18, 2, 45–60, 2023.
13. Smart Cities Alliance, "Case Studies in Smart Cities and Healthcare IoT," 2024. [Online]. Available: https://smartcities.org.
14. Horizon Europe, "Quantum-Enabled 6G Networks," 2023. [Online]. Available: https://horizon-europe.eu.
15. Menezes, A.J., van Oorschot, P.C., Vanstone, S.A., *Handbook of Applied Cryptography*, CRC Press, Boca Raton, Florida, USA, 1996.
16. Boneh, D. and Franklin, M., Identity-Based Encryption from the Weil Pairing, in: *Advances in Cryptology—CRYPTO 2001*, pp. 213–229, Springer, Berlin, Heidelberg, Germany, 2001.
17. Singh, A. and Alam, M.A., 6G-Enabled Quantum Cryptographic Systems. *IEEE Trans. Emerging Top. Comput.*, 9, 3, 1082–1090, 2023.
18. Autonomous Systems Lab, "Quantum-Safe Blockchain for Autonomous Vehicles," 2023. [Online]. Available: https://autonomouslab.org.
19. Cryptography Innovation Consortium, "Zero-Knowledge Proof Implementations," 2024. [Online]. Available: https://zkpconsortium.org.
20. European Telecommunications Standards Institute (ETSI), "Quantum-Safe Cryptography and Security," 2023. [Online]. Available: https://etsi.org.
21. Bank of Canada, "CBDC Quantum-Resilience Research," 2023. [Online]. Available: https://bankofcanada.ca.
22. Government of Estonia, "Estonian e-Residency Program," 2023. [Online]. Available: https://e-resident.gov.ee.

7

Challenges and Considerations: Ethical Implications and Regulatory Framework

Punniyakotti Varadharajan Gopirajan[1]*, Kaladevi Ramar[2], S. Naveen[3], Vel Murugesh Kumar. N.[4] and Jayaraj Ramasamy[5]

[1]*Department of Computational Intelligence, School of Computing, SRM Institute of Science and Technology, Kattankulathur, Chennai, Tamil Nadu, India*
[2]*Department of Artificial Intelligence and Data Science, Saveetha Engineering College, Thandalam, Chennai, Tamil Nadu, India*
[3]*Saveetha School of Engineering, Saveetha Institute of Medical and Technical Sciences, Chennai, Tamil Nadu, India*
[4]*Department of Computer Science and Engineering, RMK Engineering College, Kavarapettai, Tamil Nadu, India*
[5]*Department of Computing, De Montfort University, Almaty, Kazakhstan*

Abstract

Using secure blockchain, quantum technology, and 6G-enabled IoT presents remarkable advantages to the users by providing more opportunities. As opportunities grow, challenges related to individual privacy and security also grow. This chapter has outlined these issues and challenges and proposed the ethical concerns while using the recent technologies. Some parts of the laws are followed by many countries with respect to the regional, religious and other geographical significance. Slightly related to that, faster personal data collection is one of 6G and IoT implementation, which poses a major privacy concern. Despite the higher security promise in the application of the blockchain, the negative side is also advanced. The complex relationship between ethics, technology, and freedom can be only solved with a good balance strategy. The chapter covers issues like weaknesses of blockchain network in terms of scalability, compatibility of IoT devices, energy required for quantum computing and 6G networks. Cultivating the ethical use of technology begins with interactions of the stakeholders with the establishment of effective and efficient awareness strategies to educate the public on the privacy concerning digital use of available gadgets.

**Corresponding author*: gopirajp@srmist.edu.in

T. Perarasi, M. Karthiga, S. Sountharrajan, E. Suganya and Balamurugan Balusamy (eds.) Secure Blockchain and Quantum Technologies for 6G-Enabled Internet of Things, (149–176) © 2026 Scrivener Publishing LLC

Keywords: Blockchain, 6G, internet of things, technology integration, challenges

7.1 Overview of Secure Blockchain, Quantum Technologies, and 6G-Enabled IoT

The 6G-enabled internet of things (IoT) devices offer the feature of high-speed data transfer and performance. It is critically important to include secure blockchain solutions simultaneously with quantum technologies for IoT devices to have both data protection and high calculating potential [1, 2]. However, integrating these advanced technologies leads to challenges in ethical implications and needs a regulatory framework.

With the advent of 6G technology, a data transfer rate could be achieved up to approximately 1TB per second [3]. This high-speed internet connection when given to IoT devices creates seamless data transfer between the IoT devices and the computer systems. To achieve a very high security for transmission of personnel and confidential data, the two solutions that one can think of and apply are block chain and quantum innovations to give solidity to data and increase the intensity of the encryptions, and to guard against those attacks originating from classical and quantum domain.

Ethical considerations are crucial in implementing advanced technologies with highly sensitive users' information. Users' data should be fairly protected to maintain their privacy and misuse of data [4]. Addressing proper ethical concerns enables trust and potential positive impacts on the advanced technologies among the users.

Providing clear global standard guidelines is necessary for governing the integration of advanced technologies. The regulatory framework must be acceptable universally without any conflicts. Cybersecurity plays an important role in providing high security to users. Proper cyber security methods should be imposed by the government to avoid cybercrime [5].

7.2 Ethical Implications

7.2.1 Privacy Concerns

The convergence of blockchain, quantum technologies, and 6G-enabled IoT is leading to an increased focus on privacy problems. The widespread presence of networked devices and the vast quantities of data they produce pose new difficulties in protecting personal information. During this period of digital transformation, it is crucial to prioritize the protection of privacy for consumers as well as businesses to uphold reliability and safety [6].

The implementation of 6G networks would greatly enhance the ability to process and transfer data instantaneously; hence, facilitating the development of advanced applications such as remote healthcare, smart cities, and autonomous vehicles. Nevertheless, the enhanced interconnectivity and sharing of data amplify the possibility of unauthorized entry and improper utilization of confidential data. Despite its decentralized and irreversible ledgers that provide greater security, blockchain technology nevertheless encounters difficulties concerning data anonymity and transparency. Furthermore, quantum computing brings new challenges since its use relies on concepts that endanger the current protection of privacy [7].

The advent of high-speed 6G technologies enables the collection of a high volume of user's daily activity usage data from various IoT-enabled devices such as security cameras, refrigerators, wearable devices (smart watches and other health monitoring devices), medical monitoring devices, industrial devices and so on [8]. Each device generates different data types and formats. Real-time surveillance and close monitoring of these devices is crucial.

Maintaining anonymity and transparency in the ethical consideration of advanced technologies is a challenging task. Though anonymity protects users' privacy, there may be a chance of malicious activity also.

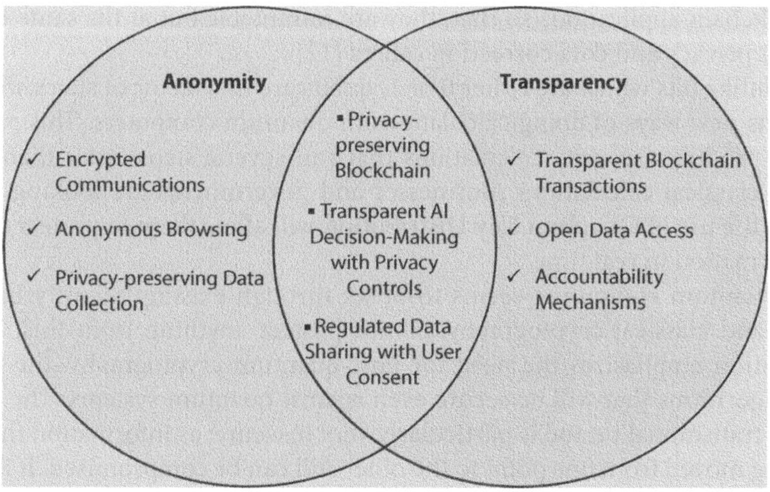

Figure 7.1 Anonymity vs transparency.

Conversely, transparency may lead to threat to the user's private data. Figure 7.1 shows the boundary of transparency and anonymity. Anonymity includes encrypted communications, anonymous browsing, and privacy-preserving data collection. Transparency includes transparent blockchain transactions, open data access, and accountability mechanisms. Privacy-preserving blockchain, transparent AI decision-making with privacy controls, and regulated data sharing with user consent combines both anonymity and transparency of data sharing and protection.

7.2.2 Data Security

Data security is a paramount problem in the era of technological change, particularly with the emergence of sophisticated technologies like blockchain, quantum computing, and 6G-enabled IoT. In today's world, where both organizations and individuals heavily depend on digital systems to store, process, and send large quantities of sensitive information, it is crucial to prioritize the security of this data by preventing unintentional access, dishonesty, and thievery [9, 10].

Securing data stored in anonymous clouds and servers is extremely fundamental. Blockchain technology has the benefit of unchangeable records, guaranteeing the confidentiality and openness of data [11]. Nevertheless, this lack of changeability might also present ethical quandaries. Data within a blockchain database is secured and once put into the blockchain, database cannot be altered or deleted. This may become a challenge to users who want to either retract or edit sensitive data. The issue is to design the blockchain applications so that, they are immutable but at the same time meet privacy and data correction callers [12].

Unlike bits which are either 0 or 1, qubits are in a factor of states which opens new ways of doing calculations in quantum computers. This property produces security calculations that run several steps faster than the best classical calculations. Businesses and governments are looking into how the use of Quantum Key Distribution will allow them to protect their information in real time.

Quantum computing seems to break through existing security barriers, and classical cryptography cannot protect anything from this. This situation emphasizes the need for post-quantum cryptography–the type of algorithms that will be secure even against quantum systems. The current transitional period is particularly very insecure, as information that is being moved from one point to the other still can be compromised. It is for these reasons that it is important that organizations ensure the security of data as they move across to this new method to protect information that is sensitive and to keep the public's trust in the internet secure [13, 14].

7.2.3 Ethical Use of AI in IoT

The major guidelines that must be maintained while using Artificial Intelligence in the IoT environment include the fairness, the disclosure and anonymity. Expectations on what AI systems should do in order for their activities to be neither totally opaque nor unbiased. Of these, anonymization, and obtaining users' consent with the use of sound algorithms are important. In the first place, the use of data in its proper form, and secondly, the work of an open AI algorithm, contribute to the emergence of trust. Like the two solutions, AI integrated IoT solutions are favorable for and have potential for all stakeholders besides solving societal vices such as unemployment and technology divide.

Decision-making capabilities exist in intelligent systems that are implemented in IoT devices, and their implication is significant to the users of the devices. The critical importance is to guarantee that such judgements are correct and, most importantly, ethical. This is important in assigning responsibility for AI results, since it allows for errors or offer biased results or even malice usage. Honesty in AI making decisions on procedures and systems, as well as where to seek remedy are critical to continue with ethical standards.

IoT when combined with 6G, blockchain, quantum computing has some critical implications for the society [15]. These technological advances can worsen the digital divide, resulting in unequal access and economic inequality. The proliferation of data collecting, and surveillance has led to heightened concerns regarding privacy and security [16]. As a result, the issue of automation in the employee market calls for retraining if the employees are to be of use to the new working world. Both telemedicine and remote monitoring add to the possibility of receiving medical help. Ideal or not, e-learning and the faculty's digital competence are inarguably important to the field of education.

Figure 7.2 depicts the societal consequences of emerging technologies on the IoT, emphasizing the main domains that are influenced and the factors to be considered within each domain.

The digital divide encompasses technological inequality, the progress of creating infrastructure, as well as strugglers of imitating economic inequalities made even worse by new technologies. Privacy and security challenges include issues to do with protecting information in the face of problems with surveillance, and potential cyber threats from connected devices. Measures for employment and the workforce include job loss, the need to retrain a workforce, and the creation of new opportunities due to an advancement in technology.

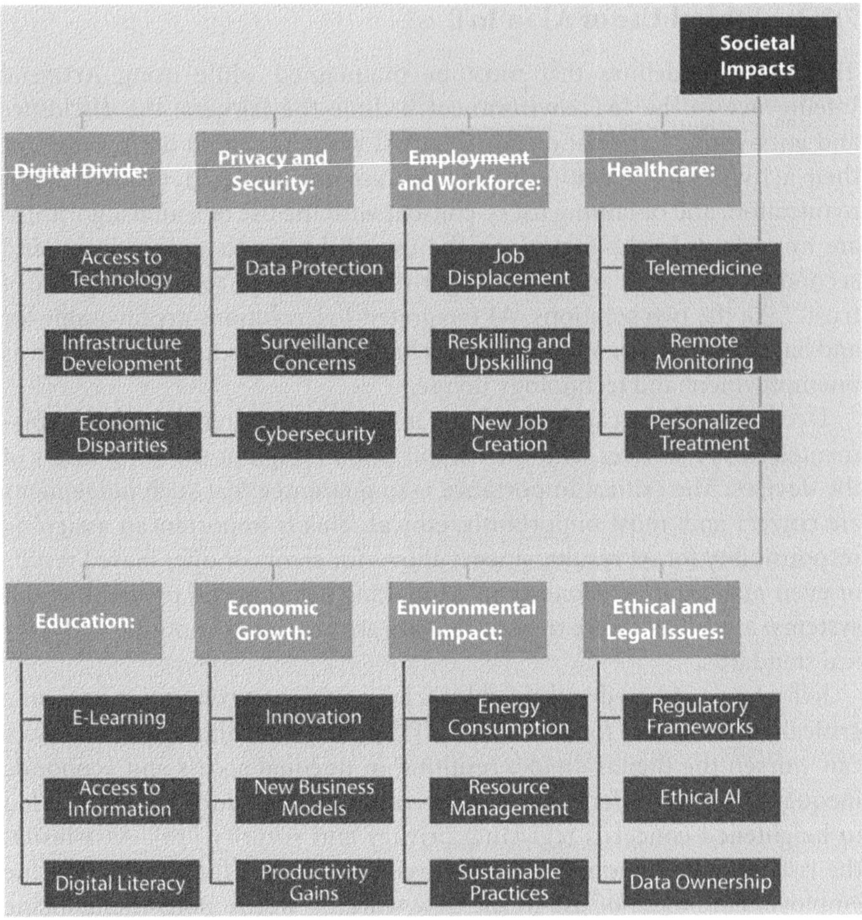

Figure 7.2 Societal impacts of implementing advanced technologies.

The healthcare sector experiences advancements and difficulties in telemedicine, remote monitoring, and personalized therapy facilitated by IoT technology. Education is improved by advancements in e-learning, increased access to information, and the promotion of digital literacy through the incorporation of technology in educational systems. Economic growth is driven by the contributions made to innovation, the advancement of new business models, and the increase in productivity facilitated by evolving technologies.

Environmental consequences encompass the evaluation of energy use, the management of resources, and the implementation of sustainable practices, all of which are influenced by IoT technologies. Finally, ethical and legal concerns emphasize the necessity of establishing regulatory frameworks, implementing ethical practices in AI, and formulating regulations on data ownership to effectively tackle the ethical consequences of technological progress.

Many blockchain networks, especially those using proof-of-work consensus mechanisms (like Bitcoin), consume significant amounts of energy due to the intensive computational power required for mining. Proof-of-stake or other energy-efficient consensus algorithms can reduce energy demands. Quantum computing systems require specialized environments (like ultra-low temperatures) that can be energy intensive. The deployment of 6G networks and associated IoT devices will increase overall energy usage due to the vast number of connected devices. Energy-efficient protocols and low-power technologies will be critical to managing this consumption.

Organizations should prioritize using renewable energy sources (solar, wind, hydro) to power data centers and network infrastructures. Developing and adopting energy-efficient hardware and software solutions can lower the overall energy demands of networks. Conducting lifecycle assessments for new technologies can help identify areas for improvement in sustainability, from production and operation to disposal. Sustainable sourcing and recycling initiatives can help mitigate these impacts. Implementing robust recycling programs and encouraging a circular economy can reduce e-waste's ecological footprint. Careful planning and impact assessments are necessary to minimize ecological harm.

7.3 Regulatory Frameworks

7.3.1 Existing Policies and Regulations

The current legislation and regulations regarding blockchain, quantum technologies, and 6G-enabled IoT varies greatly between different locations. One example of data protection regulations is the General Data Protection Regulation (GDPR) in Europe, which establishes stringent criteria for confidentiality and safety of your information. The Federal Trade Commission (FTC) in the United States is responsible for enforcing regulations about consumer protection and data privacy. Similarly, the California Consumer Privacy Act (CCPA) and other rules seek to safeguard users' personal information. Nevertheless, the swift progress of technical innovations frequently surpasses the setting up of legislative frameworks, resulting in gaps and contradictions that demand attention.

Table 7.1 denotes the regulatory focus of major countries. Table 7.2 denotes the International Regulatory Bodies for Emerging Technologies.

Table 7.1 Regulatory focus in major countries.

Country	Regulatory body	Key focus areas
United States	Federal Communications Commission (FCC)	Spectrum allocation, network security, privacy, innovation
China	Ministry of Industry and Information Technology (MIIT)	Spectrum allocation, technology leadership, domestic industry support, security
South Korea	Ministry of Science and ICT (MSIT)	5G and 6G technology development, spectrum allocation, network security
Japan	Ministry of Internal Affairs and Communications (MIC)	Spectrum management, network security, international cooperation
United Kingdom	Ofcom	Spectrum management, network security, consumer protection
Germany	Federal Network Agency (Bundesnetzagentur)	Spectrum allocation, network security, data privacy
France	Autorité de régulation des communications électroniques, des postes et de la distribution de la presse (ARCEP)	Spectrum management, network security, competition
India	Department of Telecommunications (DoT)	Spectrum allocation, licensing, infrastructure development
	Ministry of Electronics and Information Technology (MeitY)	Technology development, policy formulation, digital India initiative
	Telecom Regulatory Authority of India (TRAI)	Independent regulator, consumer protection, tariff regulation

Table 7.2 International regulatory bodies for emerging technologies.

Organization	Role
International Telecommunication Union (ITU)	Sets global standards for telecommunications, including spectrum allocation and network technologies.
International Organization for Standardization (ISO)	Develops and publishes international standards for various products and services, including information and communication technologies.
International Electrotechnical Commission (IEC)	Develops and publishes standards for all electrical, electronic, and related technologies.
3rd Generation Partnership Project (3GPP)	Develops global standards for mobile telephony.
European Telecommunications Standards Institute (ETSI)	Develops global standards for information and communication technologies.
European Union (EU)	Sets data protection standards (GDPR), influences telecom policies within member states.
Organisation for Economic Co-operation and Development (OECD)	Develops evidence-based policies on a wide range of issues, including digital economy and society.

7.3.2 Developing Robust Regulatory Frameworks

7.3.2.1 Data Privacy and Security

Effective legislative frameworks should provide high importance to safeguarding data privacy and security to shield users from breaches and unauthorized usage. Within the framework of 6G-enabled IoT, this entails guaranteeing end-to-end encryption and secure protocols for transmitting data. An adoption regulation for adopting blockchain technology should direct the use of cryptographic security methods in maintaining the transaction record's security and user privacy, as well as a guidance on the technology's vulnerabilities.

AES encryption is prevalent in IoT networks for the protection of their data transfer. It provides high level of security and fast rate of flow.

- Elliptic Curve Cryptography (ECC): ECC when incorporated with blockchain technology can provide suitable IoT device support with its easy small key access.
- Hash-based Cryptography: by applying advanced SHA-256 like algorithms with blockchain, can provide high integrity and security.
- Quantum technologies provide distinct difficulties, since they have the capability to render current encryption approaches ineffective.
- Lattice-based Cryptography: Utilizes the difficulty of solving lattice issues to provide robust protection against quantum assaults.
- Hash-based Signatures (e.g., Merkle Trees): Offering cryptographic techniques that are immune to quantum computing attacks for the purpose of creating digital signatures.
- Code-based Cryptography (e.g., McEliece Cryptosystem): Employing error-correcting codes to guarantee safe communication in a post-quantum environment.

7.3.2.2 Interoperability Standards

Communication guidelines are essential for the smooth integration and communication between diverse systems and technologies. For example, 6G networks will require seamless integration with current 4G and 5G infrastructures, IoT devices, and blockchain platforms. Regulatory frameworks should promote the use of open standards and protocols that enable compliance and data interchange across different platforms and devices.

7.3.3 Adaptive and Future-Proof Regulations

7.3.3.1 Dynamic Policy Making

Dynamic and easy adaptable regulatory frameworks is highly essential for agile policy-making processes. Since the technological change happens quickly, dynamic regulation making reduces the technology transfer problems. Due to the development of quantum computing, that calls for new regulations that address new safety measures and standards possible for preventing quantum attacks, policy makers should ensure that they involve professionals, researchers and stake holders to ensure that rules are up to date and effective.

7.3.3.2 Anticipatory Governance

The use of anticipatory governance is a preventive approach whereby thinking ahead about what the society is yet to encounter as the technologies emerge will assist in preventing the flops. Regulatory agencies could offer advanced collaborative planning for the opportunities and challenges associated with emerging technologies such as blockchain, quantum computing, and the 6G enabling IoT. Table 7.3 gives the details of novel regulatory frameworks for recent technologies.

Table 7.3 Novel regulatory frameworks for secure blockchain, quantum technologies, and 6G-enabled IoT.

Regulatory framework	Description
Risk-Based Regulatory Approach	Categorizes technologies based on risk level and applies appropriate regulations.
Data Governance and Privacy	Focuses on data ownership, control, privacy, and cross-border data flows.
Quantum Computing and Cybersecurity	Addresses the challenges posed by quantum computing, such as developing quantum-resistant cryptography and cybersecurity standards.
Blockchain Governance	Establishes regulations for smart contracts, token issuance, and decentralized autonomous organizations (DAOs).
6G Spectrum Management	Defines policies for spectrum allocation, sharing, and management to support 6G technologies.
Ethical Considerations	Develops frameworks for addressing algorithmic accountability, environmental impact, and digital divide issues.

7.4 Technical and Operational Challenges of IoT with Blockchain, 6G and Quantum Computers

7.4.1 Challenges in Quantum Computing with IoT

Technological integration has immense potential for revolutionizing various sectors, but integrating them presents unique technical and operational hurdles [17].

Technical Challenges are as follows:

- **Resource Limitations of IoT Devices:** Many IoT devices are battery-powered and have limited processing power. Running complex quantum algorithms or establishing secure communication with quantum computers could drain their resources or require additional hardware, creating a compatibility issue.
- **Qubit Communication and Entanglement:** Current IoT devices often communicate using classical bits. Quantum computers utilize qubits, which can be in multiple states simultaneously. To leverage this, data needs to be transferred in a way that preserves the qubit state, requiring specialized communication protocols. Maintaining entanglement, a crucial quantum phenomenon where linked qubits share information instantly, over long distances with resource-constrained IoT devices is another significant challenge. **Superposition** allows a single particle to be in

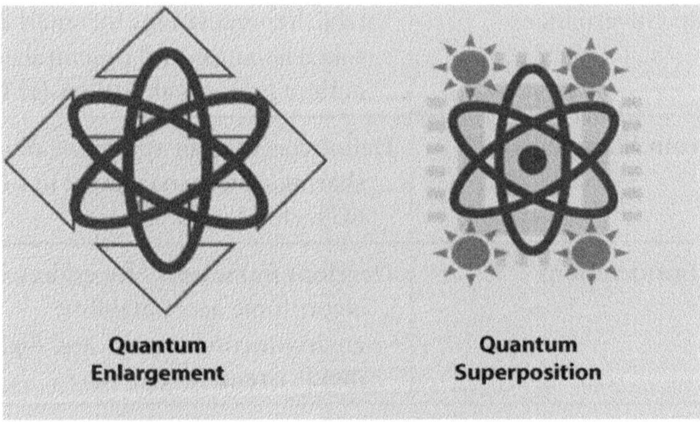

Figure 7.3 Quantum enlargement vs quantum superposition.

multiple states at once. **Entanglement** connects multiple particles, so their states are interdependent regardless of distance (Figure 7.3).

- **Error Correction:** Qubits can be erroneous due to the environmental factors. Error correction mechanisms in quantum requires high processing power as it is dealing with IoT devices.
- **Skill Gap:** The integration of quantum computing and IoT requires talented professionals who understand both and those with specialized knowledge on the handling. Strong skillset must be given to the professionals to fill the skill gap.

Operational Challenges are given as follows:

- **Standardization:** Standardization across both quantum computing and IoT is lacking. Developing common protocols for communication, data exchange, and security is crucial for ensuring interoperability between different devices and platforms.
- **Scalability:** Building and maintaining large-scale quantum computers and integrating them with a vast network of IoT devices is a significant challenge. Developing scalable solutions for communication, processing, and security will be crucial for widespread adoption.
- **Energy Consumption:** While quantum computers are generally more energy-efficient than classical supercomputers, the energy needs of running both the quantum computer and the vast network of IoT devices need careful consideration. Optimizing energy usage at both ends will be important.

7.4.2 Challenges in the Deployment of IoT in 6G Networks

6G promises a massive surge in data traffic due to the proliferation of IoT devices. Hence, few challenges should be considered before deployment. Building networks with sufficient capacity and scalability to handle this exponential growth is a major challenge [18]. Technical challenges and operational challenges in deployment of IoT in 6G networks is given in Table 7.4.

Table 7.4 Challenges in the deployment of IoT in 6G networks and their categories.

Challenges	Category	Description
Technical Challenges	Network Capacity	Handling exponential data growth from IoT devices with scalable and high-capacity networks.
	Latency & Reliability	Ensuring ultra-low latency and high reliability for critical applications like autonomous vehicles and surgery.
	Security & Privacy	Securing vulnerable IoT devices and protecting sensitive data and user privacy.
	Standardization	Addressing lack of universal protocols for seamless IoT and 6G integration.
	Energy Efficiency	Developing energy-efficient protocols for sustainable network operation.
	Spectrum Allocation	Allocating sufficient bandwidths and exploring new frequency bands for 6G.
Operational Challenges	Deployment & Management	Automating management of billions of IoT devices and vast network infrastructure.
	Cost & Investment	Addressing high costs of developing and deploying 6G infrastructure and IoT devices.
	Regulatory Landscape	Adapting regulations for data privacy, security standards, and spectrum allocation in a hyper-connected world.
	Skill Gap	Bridging gaps in specialized skills for 6G, IoT management, and advanced technologies like quantum computing.

7.4.3 Challenges in the Collaboration of Blockchain and IoT Technologies

It offers a powerful combination for enhanced security, transparency, and automation; integrating these technologies presents several technical and operational hurdles [19, 20]. The challenges are given in Table 7.5 in detail.

Table 7.5 Operational and technical challenges in collaboration of blockchain and IoT technologies comparison.

Challenges	Category	Description
Technical Challenges	Scalability	Blockchain ledgers grow large, challenging resource-constrained IoT devices with limited storage and processing power.
	Data Storage & Throughput	Managing high-volume IoT data efficiently without compromising security or transaction speed.
	Security & Privacy	Securing communication channels between IoT devices and blockchains while maintaining user privacy and transparency.
	Consensus Mechanisms	Traditional mechanisms (e.g., Proof-of-Work) are unsuitable for IoT due to energy and speed constraints, requiring lightweight alternatives.
	Energy Efficiency	Optimizing energy consumption in both IoT networks and blockchain infrastructures with efficient protocols.

(*Continued*)

Table 7.5 Operational and technical challenges in collaboration of blockchain and IoT technologies comparison. (*Continued*)

Challenges	**Category**	**Description**
Operational Challenges	Standardization	Lack of universal communication protocols and data formats between blockchain and IoT platforms.
	Interoperability	Ensuring compatibility between different blockchain networks and IoT ecosystems.
	Complexity & Management	Managing interconnected IoT devices and blockchain infrastructure with robust security and skilled personnel.
	Regulation	Adapting regulations and developing frameworks for blockchain-based IoT applications.
	Energy Efficiency	Addressing energy use challenges across IoT and blockchain systems.
	User Adoption	Encouraging adoption with user-friendly interfaces and clear value propositions showcasing security and transparency benefits.

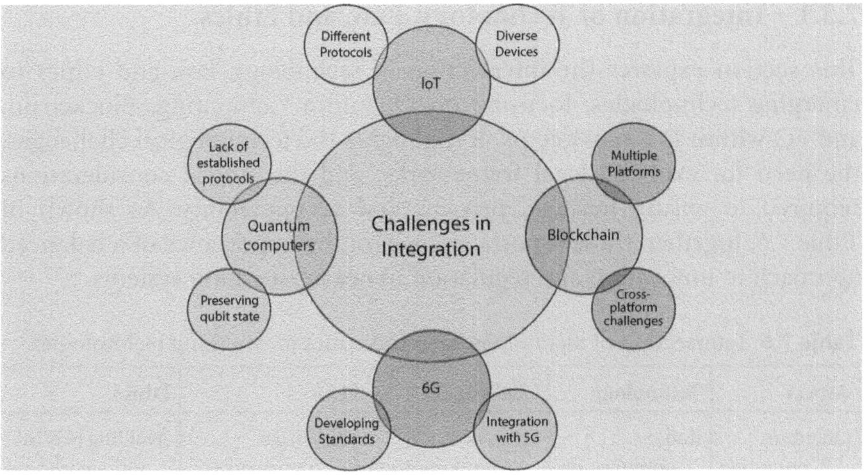

Figure 7.4 Challenges in technological integration.

7.4.4 Interoperability Challenges: IoT, Blockchain, 6G, and Quantum Computers

Integrating these exciting technologies presents a significant challenge mainly in interoperability [21]. Currently, there's no single, universal standard for communication protocols or data formats across all these technologies.

Each technology (IoT, blockchain, 6G) has its own evolving set of standards, making seamless communication and data exchange difficult. Figure 7.4 shows the interoperability challenges faced while integrating domains.

7.5 Considerations for Implementation

The implementation requirements for integrating quantum computing with IoT is discussed below in terms of technology, law and ethics. Table 7.6 denotes the integration of technical and other aspects in emerging technologies.

7.5.1 Integration of Technology, Law, and Ethics

This section explores the intersection of technology, law, and ethics in emerging technologies, focusing on Quantum Computing, Blockchain, and 6G within IoT ecosystems. It highlights the technological challenges, the need for evolving legal frameworks, and the ethical considerations required to ensure fairness, privacy, and accountability. As shown in Table 7.6, together, these aspects emphasize the importance of a balanced approach to innovation and regulation in next-generation systems.

Table 7.6 Intersection of technology, law, and ethics in emerging technologies.

Aspect	Technology	Challenges	Law	Ethics
Quantum Computing (QC)	Route optimization and anomaly detection in IoT logistics and sensor data.	Efficient communication protocols for resource-constrained IoT devices and powerful QCs.	New legal frameworks needed as QC might break current encryption standards. IP protection for QC algorithms with IoT data.	Avoiding bias in QC algorithms to prevent discriminatory outcomes. Addressing privacy concerns with IoT data usage.
Blockchain	Secure data exchange and automated processes between IoT devices.	Ensuring scalability with massive data influx from IoT devices.	Legal frameworks for smart contracts and liability. Clear definitions for data ownership.	Addressing privacy concerns with transparency. Monitoring bias in automated decisions.
6G	Faster speeds and lower latency for real-time IoT applications.	Energy-efficient solutions for 6G-connected IoT devices.	Revised spectrum allocation and robust data protection laws.	Clear regulations for data collection and usage. Ensuring transparency and user control over data.

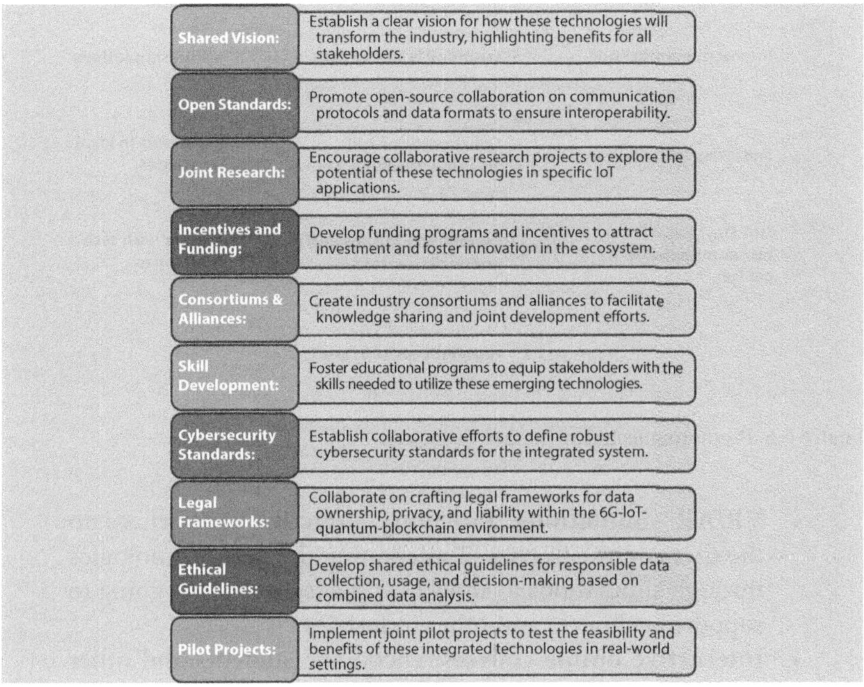

Figure 7.5 Different stakeholders' collaboration.

7.5.2 Collaboration among Stakeholders

It is the responsibility of the stakeholders to develop and implement the roles and responsibilities of each stakeholder involved in the task. Vision and mission of the work should be clear among the stakeholders. Figure 7.5 denotes the clear representation of duties of each stakeholder involved.

7.5.3 Public Awareness and Education

7.5.3.1 Promoting Technological Literacy

As shown in Figure 7.6, it is mandatory to enhance the skill set of the individuals involved in technological development.

- **Interactive workshops:** Hands-on sessions to explore connecting everyday objects and understanding data flow.
- **Gamified learning apps:** Interactive games that teach 6G speed, quantum computing basics, and blockchain security in a fun way.

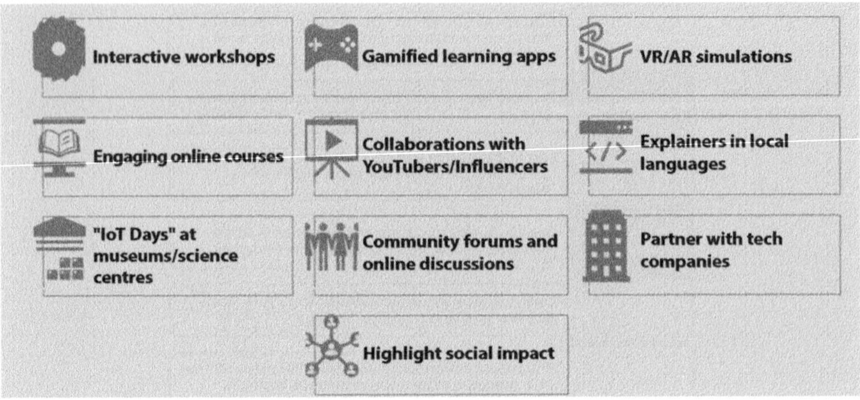

Figure 7.6 Promoting technical literacy in society.

- **VR/AR simulations:** Providing attractive experiences to the users on the impact of integrating the new technologies through simulations to show how the technology is going to support healthcare and other industries.
- **Interactive online courses:** encourage students and other participants to undergo certificate courses on the IoT foundations, 6G, and applications of blockchain, collaboration of these technologies.
- **Regional language support:** Translated resources guarantee accessibility to the stakeholders.
- **"IoT Days" at museums/science centers:** conducting formal exhibitions and road shows to create awareness.
- **Community forums and online discussions:** spreading awareness through faculty development programs, seminars and conferences.
- **Partner with tech companies:** live demonstration and workshops with technical support from companies.
- **Highlight social impact:** Illustrate how these technologies could be used to impact sustainably with positive effects to human beings.

7.5.3.2 Engaging with Society

- **Focus on real-world benefits:** Highlight how these technologies can improve everyday lives (e.g., smart cities, remote healthcare).

- **Transparency about data usage:** Clearly explain how data collected from IoT devices will be used and secured.
- **Address privacy concerns:** Proactively discuss measures to protect user privacy in this interconnected ecosystem.
- **Empowerment workshops:** Offer workshops on digital literacy and data privacy control mechanisms for citizens.
- **Partner with NGOs:** Collaborate with NGOs to ensure ethical considerations and social responsibility are prioritized.

7.5.4 Ongoing Research Challenges

Table 7.7 summarizes the research requirements in IoT with respect to Quantum computing, Blockchain and 6G networks [18, 22–25].

Table 7.7 Research problem and specific challenges in implementing 6G networks.

Problem	Major research areas	Specific challenges
Quantum Computing with IoT	Network Optimization	• Telecom • Logistics • Business • Healthcare • Finance
	Securing IoT with QC	• Quantum Steganography • Quantum Cryptography • Intrusion Detection • Access control • Privacy, integrity and Authentication
	Quantum Sensors for IoT	• Quantum Image Sensors • Gravitational Wave Detectors • Environment Monitoring • Quantum Chemical Sensors • Quantum clock for GPS and Navigation
	Quantum Digital Marketing	• Dynamic Price Strategies • Fraud detection • Quantum Content Optimization • Real time Ad Optimization

(Continued)

Table 7.7 Research problem and specific challenges in implementing 6G networks. (*Continued*)

Problem	Major research areas	Specific challenges
	Faster Computation at IoT endpoints	• Drug Discovery • Dynamic Pricing in Retail • Decision support • Simulation
	Quantum Secured Smart Locks	• Keyless Entry Technology • Electronic Door Locks • Mobile App Integration • High Tech Locker Systems • Access Security System
Blockchain with IoT	Consensus related	• Decreasing network broadcasting • Selection of primary nodes
	Interoperability	• Fitting the std features of eco system • Cost of multi signature and transparent eco system
	Smart contract	• Extraction of information from massive databases • Processing of huge data
	Security, legal and regulation	• Vulnerabilities detection and prevention • Legal and regulation for anonymization
	Identity management	• Uniqueness • Monitoring of possession
6G with IoT	Architecture	• Service based architecture • Non-Terrestrial Network (NTN) • AI functions • Service Level Agreement (SLA) and low latency
	Technological	• Area • Frequency • Radio wave usage
	Social	• Frequency utilization • Network security • Carbon free environment • Network and servers

Table 7.8 Applications of 6G network.

Application	Explanation
Holographic communications	Reality technology that initiates real time capturing, encoding, transporting and rendering of 3D objects
WBCI-Wireless Brain Computer Interfaces	neural signals generated in the human's mind with a certain number of electrodes, then translates these acquired signals into commands that a machine can understand
Five-sense communications	6G aims to remotely transfer data obtained from the five senses. Hearing, smell, taste, touch, sight
Fully autonomous driving	Equipped with multiple high-definition cameras and high-precision radar sensors and supported by 6G, fully autonomous driving can be achieved
Deep-sea communications	Internet services *via* seabed sensors, floating buoys, remotely and autonomous underwater vehicles
Space communications	Space station send signal through tracking and TDRS (Data Relay Satellites) to ground stations
Super smart verticals	Five different verticals: Health, Industry, Vehicular, Energy, and lastly, Defence & Security.

The specific applications of 6G network in accordance with IoT are discussed which is shown in Table 7.8.

7.6 Future Directions

7.6.1 Emerging Trends in Technology

The utilization of blockchain with quantum computing is anticipated to bring about a significant transformation across multiple industries. Progress in blockchain technology will bolster security, transparency, and efficiency in the interchange of data and automation of processes. Advancements in quantum computing will facilitate the ability to solve difficult problems, such as optimizing routes more quickly and improving anomaly detection in IoT systems. These technologies will facilitate the development of new scenarios and applications, promoting the expansion of a highly interconnected and smart environment [26].

Future IoT applications will utilize 6G connectivity, sophisticated sensors, and artificial intelligence to achieve unparalleled levels of automation, efficiency, and real-time data processing. Illustrations encompass intelligent urban areas, self-driving automobiles, and meticulous farming. Such applications will depend on strong integration with new technologies such as blockchain for safe data management and quantum computing for completing intricate analytical tasks.

7.6.2 Evolving Ethical Frameworks

7.6.2.1 Adaptive Ethical Guidelines

As technology advances, rules of ethics need to adjust to tackle emerging difficulties and guarantee responsible progress and implementation. This involves developing standards that proactively address possible ethical quandaries, such as issues related to privacy, biases in AI systems, and the fair allocation of technology advantages. Implementing adaptive ethical principles is essential for upholding public trust and guaranteeing that advances in technology have a good impact on society [27].

Establishing global ethical standards is crucial for achieving uniformity in ethical actions across diverse locations and cultures. These criteria ought to foster equity, clarity, and responsibility in the advancement and utilization of nascent technology. Globally ethical norms can play a crucial role in reducing ethical hazards and ensuring that technological advancements are in line with human values and social requirements [28–30].

7.6.3 Policy Recommendations

Government officials should be engaged in coming up with policies for the regulations that may suit the advanced pace of technology. This involves constant referring to the field practitioners, scholars as well as other relevant stakeholders to identify emerging trends and risks. Bringing effective legislative measures to the institutionalization of the mentioned policy types would help create a framework to encourage innovation in the IT industry while protecting the clients and the public [31].

The public private collaboration in policy making should consider collaboration frameworks (government, industry, academic bodies, civil society), advisory council (experts from various fields), pilot programs, feedback mechanism, Joint Standards Development (to ensure interoperability), global coordination, funding initiatives from both public and private sectors, comprehensive security policies, privacy regulations and stakeholder engagement forums.

It is vital that international collaboration is a key component of addressing the international nature of developing technology. There are possibilities of creating precisely regulated structures through international partnerships, the exchange of best practices and unified efforts to solve similar challenges. Strengthening the international collaboration will bring faster and more ethically proper integration of such innovations as, for example, blockchain, quantum computing, IoT [32].

7.7 Conclusion

Integrating blockchain and quantum technologies into secure 6G IoT brings opportunities for change across various industries in terms of security and added capabilities. However, this merging also carried out quite significant challenges and issues that are essential to overcome to attain these benefits fully.

Advancements and Challenges in Technology: The development in the field of blockchain guarantees high level of security and transparency for IoT data exchange, and KQCs enable complex calculations and optimizations. With 6G networks internet, IoT devices can enjoy high data transfer rates together with low latency, which is very essential in real-time IoT operations. However, the increased load on blockchain and quantum communication channels, the development of effective communication channels, and the use of energy-saving technologies in triangles that operate in 6G networks remain outstanding challenges.

Legal and Regulatory Factors to Consider: While these technologies are developing, the existing law must adopt and deal with new threats and opportunities. The threat, the same quantum computing poses to today's encryption standards requires the creation of new legal barriers, and the lack of clarity in approaches to the definition of ownership, rights, and the nature of smart contracts in relation to the blockchain also requires new legislation. Propagation characteristics and fierce protection regulations are crucial for controlling the enhanced connectivity and data flow arising from integrating new 6G IoT devices.

Ethical Considerations: Major innovations of such a kind must address the issue of ethical implications of their deployment. Due to the immense amount of information that IoT derived devices amass, there arise significant ethical issues concerning the privacy aspect. Bias is present in today's AI and quantum algorithms, so it is necessary to prevent biased results. Transparency and user control of the data should be maintained as a key to understanding people's expectations and to maintain trust in further developments.

Prospects for the Future: To create regulatory frameworks that are adaptable and resistant to future challenges, it is crucial to focus on proactive policy formulation and foster international collaboration. The development of ethical norms and global standards will assist in managing the intricacies of these emerging technologies, guaranteeing their beneficial impact on society. Tackling these difficulties with a thorough and visionary approach will create a foundation for a secure, ethical, and cutting-edge technological environment.

AI disclosure statement: The author acknowledges the use of AI-based tools for minor language editing or grammatical correction. However, all intellectual contributions, analyses, and conclusions presented in this chapter are entirely the author's own.

References

1. Ahad, A., Jiangbina, Z., Tahir, M., Shayea, I., Sheikh, M.A., Rasheed, F., 6G and intelligent healthcare: Taxonomy, technologies, open issues and future research directions. *Internet Things*, 25, 101068, Apr. 2024, doi: 10.1016/J.IOT.2024.101068.
2. Quy, V.K., Nguyen, D.C., Van Anh, D., Quy, N.M., Federated learning for green and sustainable 6G IIoT applications. *Internet Things*, 25, 101061, Apr. 2024, doi: 10.1016/J.IOT.2024.101061.
3. Abbas, G., Abbas, Z.H., Ali, Z., Asad, M.S., Ghosh, U., Bilal, M., Smart stochastic routing for 6G-enabled massive Internet of Things. *Comput. Commun.*, 180, 284–294, Dec. 2021, doi: 10.1016/J.COMCOM.2021.09.015.
4. Dao, N.N., Internet of wearable things: Advancements and benefits from 6G technologies. *Future Gener. Comput. Syst.*, 138, 172–184, Jan. 2023, doi: 10.1016/J.FUTURE.2022.07.006.
5. Javeed, D., Saeed, M.S., Ahmad, I., Adil, M., Kumar, P., Islam, A.K.M.N., Quantum-empowered federated learning and 6G wireless networks for IoT security: Concept, challenges and future directions. *Future Gener. Comput. Syst.*, 160, 577–597, Nov. 2024, doi: 10.1016/J.FUTURE.2024.06.023.
6. Ahammed, T.B., Patgiri, R., Nayak, S., A vision on the artificial intelligence for 6G communication. *ICT Express*, 9, 2, 197–210, Apr. 2023, doi: 10.1016/J.ICTE.2022.05.005.
7. Abbas, M.T., *et al.*, Towards zero-energy: Navigating the future with 6G in Cellular Internet of Things. *J. Network Comput. Appl.*, 230, 103945, Oct. 2024, doi: 10.1016/J.JNCA.2024.103945.

8. Alotaibi, A. and Barnawi, A., IDSoft: A federated and softwarized intrusion detection framework for massive internet of things in 6G network. *J. King Saud Univ. Comput. Inf. Sci.*, 35, 6, 101575, Jun. 2023, doi: 10.1016/J.JKSUCI.2023.101575.
9. Zhaofeng, M., Lingyun, W., Xiaochang, W., Zhen, W., Weizhe, Z., Blockchain-Enabled Decentralized Trust Management and Secure Usage Control of IoT Big Data. *IEEE Internet Things J.*, 7, 5, 4000–4015, 2020, doi: 10.1109/JIOT.2019.2960526.
10. Dimitriou, T., Efficient, Coercion-free and Universally Verifiable Blockchain-based Voting. *Comput. Networks*, 174, 107234, Apr. 2020, doi: 10.1016/j.comnet.2020.107234.
11. Mangia, M., Marchioni, A., Pareschi, F., Rovatti, R., Setti, G., Chained Compressed Sensing: A Blockchain-Inspired Approach for Low-Cost Security in IoT Sensing. *IEEE Internet Things J.*, 6, 4, 6465–6475, 2019, doi: 10.1109/JIOT.2019.2910402.
12. Miao, Q., Lin, H., Hu, J., Wang, X., An intelligent and privacy-enhanced data sharing strategy for blockchain-empowered Internet of Things. *Digital Commun. Networks*, Jan. 2022, doi: 10.1016/J.DCAN.2021.12.007.
13. Cai, X.Q., Wang, T.Y., Wei, C.Y., Gao, F., Cryptanalysis of quantum digital signature for the access control of sensitive data. *Physica A*, 593, 126949, May 2022, doi: 10.1016/J.PHYSA.2022.126949.
14. Visalaxi, G. and Muthukumaravel, A., IOT monitoring membrane computing based on quantum inspiration to enhance security in cloud network. *Meas.: Sens.*, 27, 100755, 2023, doi: https://doi.org/10.1016/j.measen.2023.100755.
15. Walsh, J.P., Social media and moral panics: Assessing the effects of technological change on societal reaction. *Int. J. Cult. Stud.*, PG-1367877920912257-1367877920912257, 1367877920912257–1367877920912257, 2020, doi: 10.1177/1367877920912257.
16. Bhuyan, S.S., *et al.*, Privacy and security issues in mobile health: Current research and future directions. *Health Policy Technol.*, 6, 2, 188–191, Jun. 2017, doi: 10.1016/J.HLPT.2017.01.004.
17. Chawla, D. and Mehra, P.S., A Survey on Quantum Computing for Internet of Things Security. *Procedia Comput. Sci.*, 218, 2191–2200, Jan. 2023, doi: 10.1016/J.PROCS.2023.01.195.
18. Qadir, Z., Le, K.N., Saeed, N., Munawar, H.S., Towards 6G Internet of Things: Recent advances, use cases, and open challenges. *ICT Express*, 9, 3, 296–312, Jun. 2023, doi: 10.1016/J.ICTE.2022.06.006.
19. Abbassi, Y. and Benlahmer, H., IoT and Blockchain combined: for decentralized security. *Procedia Comput. Sci.*, 191, 337–342, Jan. 2021, doi: 10.1016/J.PROCS.2021.07.045.
20. Adhikari, N. and Ramkumar, M., IoT and Blockchain Integration: Applications, Opportunities, and Challenges. *Network*, 3, 1, 115–141, 2023, doi: 10.3390/network3010006.

21. Jahid, A., Alsharif, M.H., Hall, T.J., The convergence of blockchain, IoT and 6G: Potential, opportunities, challenges and research roadmap. *J. Network Comput. Appl.*, 217, 103677, Aug. 2023, doi: 10.1016/J.JNCA.2023.103677.
22. Lu, Y., The blockchain: State-of-the-art and research challenges. *J. Ind. Inf. Integr.*, 15, 80–90, Sep. 2019, doi: 10.1016/J.JII.2019.04.002.
23. Reyna, A., Martín, C., Chen, J., Soler, E., Díaz, M., On blockchain and its integration with IoT. Challenges and opportunities. *Future Gener. Comput. Syst.*, 88, 173–190, Nov. 2018, doi: 10.1016/J.FUTURE.2018.05.046.
24. Abdelmaboud, A., *et al.*, Blockchain for IoT Applications: Taxonomy, Platforms, Recent Advances, Challenges and Future Research Directions. *Electronics (Basel)*, 2022. [Online]. Available: https://api.semanticscholar.org/CorpusID:247030613.
25. Peelam, M.S., Rout, A.A., Chamola, V., Quantum computing applications for Internet of Things. *IET Quantum Commun.*, 5, 2, 103–112, 2024, doi: https://doi.org/10.1049/qtc2.12079.
26. Stahl, B.C. and Eke, D., The ethics of ChatGPT – Exploring the ethical issues of an emerging technology. *Int. J. Inf. Manage.*, 74, 102700, Feb. 2024, doi: 10.1016/J.IJINFOMGT.2023.102700.
27. Harvey, C., Hajli, N., Hyman, M.R., Ethical issues in the application of new and emergent technologies of marketing. *J. Bus. Res.*, 141, 111–112, Mar. 2022, doi: 10.1016/J.JBUSRES.2021.12.010.
28. Stahl, B.C., Virtual suicide and other ethical issues of emerging information technologies. *Futures*, 50, 35–43, Jun. 2013, doi: 10.1016/J.FUTURES.2013.03.004.
29. Luxton, D.D., Anderson, S.L., Anderson, M., Ethical Issues and Artificial Intelligence Technologies in Behavioral and Mental Health Care. *Artif. Intell. Behav. Mental Health Care*, 255–276, Jan. 2016, doi: 10.1016/B978-0-12-420248-1.00011-8.
30. Cook, A.M., Polgar, J.M., Encarnação, P., Ethical Issues in Assistive Technology. *Assistive Technol.*, 71–86, Jan. 2020, doi: 10.1016/B978-0-323-52338-7.00005-6.
31. Liu, C. and Jayakar, K., The evolution of telecommunicationspolicy-making: Comparative analysis of China and India. *Telecomm. Policy*, 36, 1, 13–28, 2012, doi: 10.1016/j.telpol.2011.11.016.
32. Sridhar, V. and Prasad, R., Towards a new policy framework for spectrum management in India. *Telecomm Policy*, 35, 2, 172–184, 2011, doi: 10.1016/j.telpol.2010.12.004.

8

Quantum Secured 6G in Precision Healthcare: Future Challenges and Trends

J. Shanthalakshmi Revathy[1]* and J. Mangaiyarkkarasi[2]

[1]*University College of Engineering, Ramanathapuram, Tamilnadu, India*
[2]*Nadar Mahajana Sangam S. Vellaichamy Nadar College, Madurai, Tamilnadu, India*

Abstract

The advent of 6G technology, enhanced by quantum security, marks a transformative era in precision healthcare. This chapter provides a comprehensive overview of the potential, challenges, and emerging trends in integrating quantum-secured 6G networks into the healthcare sector, aimed at researchers, practitioners, and policymakers. With unprecedented data transmission speeds, ultra-low latency, and massive connectivity, 6G technology is essential for real-time processing and analysis of vast healthcare data. Integrating quantum security mechanisms, such as Quantum Key Distribution (QKD), ensures robust encryption and protection against cyber threats, safeguarding sensitive medical information. Precision healthcare, which focuses on personalized treatment plans based on individual patients' genetic profiles, lifestyle, and environmental factors, is significantly enhanced by 6G and quantum security. This convergence enables seamless, secure data exchange among healthcare providers, researchers, and patients, making advanced diagnostics, remote surgeries, and AI-driven treatment recommendations more feasible.

However, significant challenges remain. Implementing QKD at scale poses technical and logistical issues, including compatibility with existing healthcare IT infrastructure and real-time key distribution. The transition phase may also expose systems to vulnerabilities, and establishing a quantum-secured 6G network requires substantial investment, which could burden healthcare institutions, particularly in low-resource settings. Furthermore, deploying advanced technologies in healthcare must align with regulatory frameworks and ethical guidelines. Emerging trends indicate that 6G networks will facilitate early diagnosis

**Corresponding author*: revathyjeganathan@gmail.com

T. Perarasi, M. Karthiga, S. Sountharrajan, E. Suganya and Balamurugan Balusamy (eds.) Secure Blockchain and Quantum Technologies for 6G-Enabled Internet of Things, (177–202) © 2026 Scrivener Publishing LLC

and personalized treatment plans through real-time AI analysis of patient data, making healthcare more accessible to remote and underserved populations. By addressing these challenges and embracing these trends, the healthcare sector can fully leverage quantum-secured 6G for a more connected, secure, and personalized medical future.

Keywords: 6G technology, quantum security, precision healthcare, quantum key distribution (QKD), blockchain, personalized treatment

8.1 Introduction

The capabilities of 5G wireless technologies have been significantly surpassed by 6G, or sixth-generation, wireless technology. Although 5G established the foundation for improved connectivity, quicker data transmission, and the internet of things (IoT), 6G is set to completely transform the digital environment by bringing about previously unheard-of improvements in speed, latency, and network capacity. Up to 100 times faster data transfer rates than 5G are predicted for 6G technology, which will reach 1 terabit per second (Tbps) in speed. The massive volumes of data produced by cutting-edge technologies like artificial intelligence (AI), machine learning (ML), and advanced data analytics, especially in the healthcare industry, require this extremely fast connectivity [7].

Ultra-low latency, or the time it takes for data to travel from its source to its destination in just a few microseconds, is one of the key characteristics of 6G. This is especially important for applications like remote surgery, driverless cars, and industrial automation that need to process data and make decisions in real time [14]. Moreover, 6G is expected to support massive machine-type communications (mMTC), enabling billions of devices to connect simultaneously without degrading network performance. This level of connectivity is instrumental in creating smart cities, enhancing IoT ecosystems, and fostering seamless communication between devices in diverse environments.

With the concept of precision medicine, doctor's prescription are based on patient specific factors such as genetic makeup, lifestyle, and even surroundings. They are also friendly because it focuses on enhancing the degree of effectiveness through the provision of different care plans instead of the standardized treatments. The integration of cutting-edge technologies like terahertz (THz) frequency bands, which provide larger bandwidths and faster data rates than those utilized in earlier generations, is another important feature of 6G. This allows for more efficient and effective transmission of large datasets, making it ideal for applications in precision healthcare, where the timely and accurate transmission of medical data is critical [8]. Furthermore, 6G is designed to be more energy-efficient, addressing the growing concern over the environmental impact of expanding digital infrastructure. By optimizing energy use, 6G networks can support sustainable development goals while delivering enhanced performance.

8.1.1 The Role of Quantum Security in 6G

Quantum security employs mechanics from quantum physics to secure and encrypt information due to the fact that it is extremely hard for an external person to intercept or decode this data. It exploits certain features of the quantum world like entanglement to guarantee that the exchange is rather immune to hack attacks. The risks to data security and privacy are ever-changing along with the digital landscape. The amount of data being transferred across networks will rise dramatically with the introduction of 6G, making it a prime target for cyberattacks. Traditional encryption methods, while effective to some extent, are becoming increasingly vulnerable to sophisticated hacking techniques, especially with the rise of quantum computing [11]. The application of quantum mechanics to computers has made it possible for them to break traditional encryption schemes in a fraction of the time that classical computers take. This puts sensitive data integrity and confidentiality at serious risk, especially in industries like healthcare where data breaches can have disastrous repercussions.

Quantum security is being incorporated into 6G networks as a solution to these issues, providing an additional degree of defense against online attacks. Among the most promising quantum security techniques is quantum key distribution (QKD). Quantum Key Distribution or QKD is like sending a cipher that if someone tries to eavesdrop or change, both known mutually immediately. Imagine passing a sealed envelope with a lock through a clear tube: if anyone attempts to open or interfere with it the tube breaks and it indicates that someone attempted to pry. In QKD, the "envelope" is a stream of particles that will change if observed, meaning that any attempt of eavesdropping cannot occur without being known. Through the use of quantum bits (qubits) encoded in light particles like photons, QKD enables the safe exchange of encryption keys between two parties. The quantum states of the particles will collapse in the event of an attempt to intercept or eavesdrop on the key exchange process, thereby notifying both parties of the intrusion and rendering the intercepted data ineffective. This guarantees the security of the encryption keys even in the face of threats from quantum computing [5].

Quantum cryptography techniques are also being developed in addition to QKD to improve the security of data transferred over 6G networks. These algorithms use quantum mechanical concepts to generate encryption codes that are nearly hard to decipher with traditional computing techniques. Sensitive medical data can be protected from unwanted access by incorporating these quantum security techniques into 6G networks, guaranteeing patient privacy and data integrity.

8.1.2 Importance of Precision Healthcare in the Modern Era

The delivery of medical care is changing dramatically with precision healthcare; as a more targeted and individualized approach, it replaces the conventional "one-size-fits-all" method. To create treatment regimens that are more efficient and cause fewer side effects, this method considers the genetic profiles, lifestyles, environmental factors, and other distinctive features of each patient [20]. The field of precision healthcare has gained momentum due to developments in genomics, bioinformatics, and data analytics. These advances have made it possible for medical professionals to identify the root causes of illnesses and create more targeted treatments.

In the modern era, precision healthcare is becoming increasingly important due to the growing demand for personalized medicine and the need to improve patient outcomes. Chronic illnesses, like diabetes, cancer, and heart problems, are complicated and frequently call for individualized treatment regimens for each patient. Precision healthcare is able to analyze enormous amounts of patient data to find patterns and correlations that would be impossible to find manually by utilizing the power of big data, artificial intelligence, and machine learning. This makes it possible to diagnose patients earlier, predict the course of their diseases more accurately, and create individualized treatment regimens that are best suited to their individual profiles [12].

Precision healthcare's capabilities are further enhanced by the integration of 6G technology, which makes it possible to process and analyze huge datasets in real-time. Healthcare providers can access and analyze patient data in real time with 6G's ultra-fast data transfer speeds and low latency, enabling them to make instant treatment plan adjustments based on the most recent information. In critical care settings, where prompt interventions can mean the difference between life and death, this is especially valuable [22]. Moreover, 6G's massive connectivity allows for seamless communication between healthcare providers, researchers, and patients, facilitating collaboration and the sharing of insights across the healthcare ecosystem. Because it facilitates the integration of various data sources and the creation of thorough, data-driven treatment plans, this degree of connectivity is critical to the successful implementation of precision healthcare on a global scale.

8.2 Quantum Technologies for Securing 6G Networks

8.2.1 Quantum Key Distribution (QKD) in 6G

A key element of 6G networks is quantum key distribution (QKD), a ground-breaking technology that provides unmatched security for data transmission. QKD uses the ideas of quantum mechanics to safely exchange encryption keys between two parties, in contrast to traditional encryption techniques. Quantum bits, or qubits, are used in QKD to store keys. Qubits are capable of existing in multiple states at once. The most common implementation of QKD involves encoding these qubits in photons. Any attempt to intercept the key results in a detectable disturbance in the quantum state, alerting both parties to the potential security breach, and ensuring that the compromised key is discarded [2].

Especially in the healthcare industry, where patient confidentiality is crucial, QKD is crucial for safeguarding the enormous volumes of sensitive data transferred over the network in the context of 6G. QKD guarantees that encryption keys stay safe even against the powerful computing capabilities of quantum computers, while 6G technology allows real-time data transmission and processing. This makes QKD a foundational element of the quantum-secured 6G infrastructure, safeguarding data against eavesdropping and cyber-attacks. Figure 8.1 illustrates an SDN-based QKD framework, showcasing the APP layer, SDN Controller, QKD layer, and data layer with interconnected nodes and optical cross-connects.

To enable secure communication in 6G, quantum key distribution, or QKD, makes use of the concepts of quantum mechanics. The QKD key equation has to do with the BB84 protocol. This formula guarantees the detection of any attempt at eavesdropping [26]. The mutual information between two $I(A;B)$ communicating parties, I(A;B) and the mutual information between an eavesdropper and one of $I(A;E)$ the parties, I(A;E) must satisfy Equation (8.1).

$$I(A;B) > I(A;E)I(A;B) > I(A;E) \tag{8.1}$$

This inequality ensures that legitimate users (A and B) can communicate securely and detect eavesdropping attempts. The system modifies the

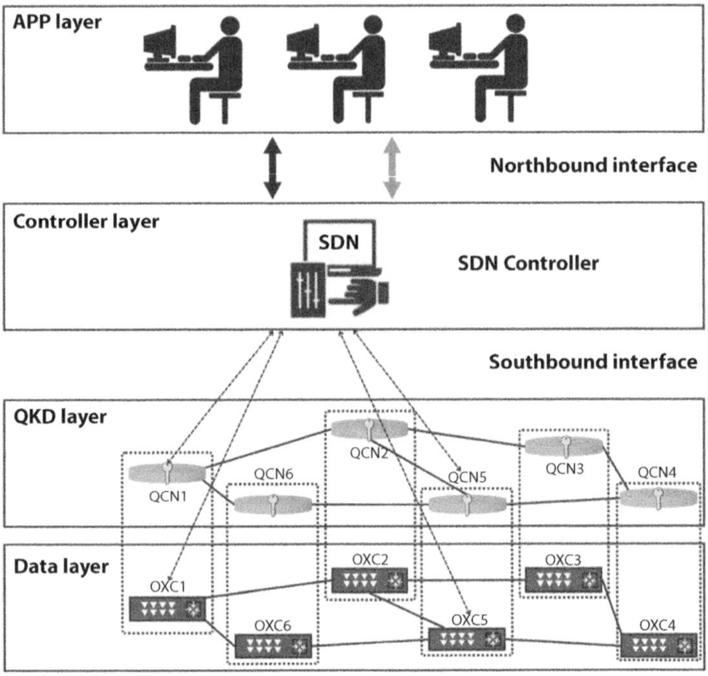

Figure 8.1 Quantum key distribution (QKD) integrated with software defined networking (SDN) architecture.

protocol to stop the transmission of the key in the event that an eavesdropper obtains additional information. The mutual information between Alice (A) and Bob (B) is represented by the symbol I(A;B), which shows how much information they share. The mutual information between Alice (A) and the eavesdropper (E) is represented by the symbol I(A;E), which indicates how much the eavesdropper knows about Alice's key.

8.2.2 Quantum Encryption Algorithms for Healthcare Data

The inequality ensures that Bob receives more accurate information from Alice than the eavesdropper. If eavesdropping is detected, the key exchange is aborted. This ensures that the quantum cryptographic system used in 6G is robust against attacks.

Quantum encryption algorithms are another key aspect of securing 6G networks, particularly in healthcare applications. These algorithms, which make use of quantum principles, go beyond conventional encryption techniques to produce extremely secure encryption schemes that fend off attacks from both classical and quantum computers. The creation of algorithms that maintain security in the face of potent quantum computers that are able to crack traditional encryption schemes is one such method known as quantum-resistant cryptography.

Quantum encryption algorithms offer additional security in the healthcare industry, where data privacy and security are critical considerations. Sensitive medical data, including genetic information, diagnostic results, and patient records, can be encrypted using these algorithms to keep it private and unreadable by unauthorized parties. Quantum encryption and 6G networks work together to securely transfer medical data between various platforms and devices, enabling smooth and safe communication throughout the healthcare ecosystem.

Quantum encryption algorithms are at the forefront of secure communication, especially crucial in sectors like healthcare where data privacy is paramount. With the rise of quantum computing, traditional encryption methods are increasingly vulnerable, making quantum encryption algorithms vital for ensuring long-term data security. Utilizing the concepts of quantum mechanics, these algorithms offer unmatched security features like eavesdropping detection, encrypted computations, and resistance against quantum-based attacks. These algorithms, which range from quantum-safe cryptography to quantum key distribution (QKD), are made to safeguard sensitive medical data in the 6G era and beyond.

8.2.2.1 Quantum Key Distribution (QKD) Algorithms

Secure communication requires the use of Quantum Key Distribution (QKD) algorithms, especially in the healthcare industry where private information must be kept private. Among the first and most extensively used QKD algorithms is the BB84 protocol. By utilizing photons' quantum states, it guarantees the safe transfer of encryption keys. An unmatched level of security is provided by the ability to identify any attempts at eavesdropping during the key transmission. Quantum entanglement is also used by the E91 protocol, which enables secure communication by measuring entangled particles. Additionally, by ensuring that any eavesdropper interference can be quickly detected, this protocol preserves the integrity of the exchanged key [21].

8.2.2.2 Quantum Homomorphic Encryption (QHE)

A breakthrough in safe healthcare data processing is provided by Quantum Homomorphic Encryption (QHE), which allows calculations to be done on encrypted data without the need for decryption. This capability is critical in healthcare, where patient data privacy is paramount, yet computation on this data—such as analyzing medical records for diagnosis—must still occur [19]. QHE ensures that the data remains confidential throughout the computational process, providing a robust solution for preserving data security while allowing healthcare providers to utilize the data effectively for decision-making and research.

8.2.2.3 Quantum-Safe Cryptography Algorithms

Secure Cryptography in Quantum: Since many conventional encryption schemes are expected to be broken by quantum computers, algorithms are built to withstand such attacks. Lattice-based cryptography is a leading quantum-resistant algorithm that relies on complex lattice problems, which are computationally infeasible for both classical and quantum computers to solve. This makes it ideal for protecting sensitive healthcare data. Another method, Multivariate Polynomial Cryptography, involves solving sets of multivariate equations, which is similarly resistant to quantum attacks. Both approaches offer a promising defense against future threats posed by quantum computing to healthcare systems [27].

8.2.2.4 Post-Quantum RSA and ECC

Elliptic Curve Cryptography (ECC) and Post-quantum RSA are modifications of classical encryption techniques that withstand quantum attacks. These algorithms are critical for ensuring backward compatibility and future-proofing existing healthcare data systems that currently rely on RSA or ECC for security. Post-Quantum RSA strengthens the classical RSA algorithm to resist attacks from quantum computers, while Post-Quantum ECC improves the security of Elliptic Curve Cryptography [4]. Healthcare providers can guarantee the long-term security of sensitive medical data in a world powered by quantum computing by implementing these tried-and-true encryption techniques.

8.2.3 Challenges in Implementing Quantum Security in 6G Networks

Quantum security has many advantages for 6G networks, but there are many obstacles to overcome before these technologies can be widely used.

The integration of quantum encryption algorithms and QKD with the current network infrastructure is one of the main challenges. Healthcare IT systems are intricate and frequently depend on antiquated technologies that might not be entirely harmonious with quantum security measures. Upgrading these systems to support quantum-secured 6G networks requires substantial investment and technical expertise, which may be a barrier for many healthcare institutions, especially those in low-resource settings [30].

Another challenge lies in the real-time management of quantum keys and encryption processes. The dynamic nature of 6G networks, with their massive connectivity and high data transmission rates, necessitates efficient and scalable quantum key management systems. Ensuring the secure distribution and management of quantum keys in such an environment is a complex task that requires advanced algorithms and robust network architectures.

Additionally, the transition to quantum-secured 6G networks introduces potential vulnerabilities during the implementation phase. As organizations migrate to new quantum technologies, there may be temporary gaps in security that could be exploited by cyber attackers. Therefore, a carefully planned and phased approach to implementation is crucial to minimize risks.

8.3 Integration of 6G in Precision Healthcare

A major development in the medical field, the integration of 6G technology into precision healthcare holds the potential to completely transform the way healthcare is provided and tailored to each patient. Customizing medical care to each patient's distinct genetic composition, way of life, and environmental circumstances is the core of precision healthcare, necessitating the processing and analysis of enormous volumes of data. To provide prompt and precise medical interventions, real-time data transmission and analysis are essential, and 6G's ultra-fast, low-latency connectivity is well-positioned to meet these demands. The deployment of 6G in healthcare not only enhances the speed and efficiency of data processing but also enables new possibilities for patient care, such as continuous monitoring, advanced telemedicine, and data-driven personalized treatment plans. As 6G networks become more prevalent, healthcare providers will have the tools to offer more precise, effective, and patient-centered care, ultimately improving health outcomes and patient satisfaction [25].

8.3.1 Benefits of 6G for Real-Time Patient Monitoring

Real-time patient monitoring is one of the biggest advantages of incorporating 6G technology into precision medicine. Patient monitoring in conventional healthcare settings frequently entails routine examinations and the gathering of data at predetermined intervals. But with the introduction of 6G, continuous, real-time monitoring is now possible, enabling medical professionals to keep tabs on a patient's vital signs, symptoms, and other health indicators at all times.

Healthcare providers can respond promptly to any changes in a patient's condition—thanks to 6G's ultra-low latency and high data transmission speeds. For instance, in critical care scenarios, like monitoring patients with chronic illnesses or those recovering from surgery, 6G-enabled devices can transmit data continuously to healthcare professionals, allowing them to make timely decisions to modify treatment plans, give medication, or intervene in emergencies.

This level of responsiveness is essential for preventing complications and improving patient outcomes. Moreover, real-time monitoring facilitated by 6G technology can be extended to remote and underserved areas [13]. Patients who live far from healthcare facilities can benefit from the same level of care as those in urban centers, as 6G's expansive network coverage and reliability ensure that data transmission remains uninterrupted, even in geographically challenging locations. This accessibility democratizes healthcare, reducing disparities and ensuring that all patients, regardless of location, receive the best possible care.

8.3.2 Enhancing Telemedicine through 6G Connectivity

Additionally, after the COVID-19 pandemic underlined the need for remote healthcare services, telemedicine has become an essential part of contemporary healthcare. However, the effectiveness of telemedicine is often limited by the quality of the underlying communication networks. The integration of 6G into telemedicine holds the potential to overcome these limitations, offering significantly enhanced connectivity that can transform the way remote healthcare is delivered.

Telemedicine services can offer patients and healthcare providers more immersive and interactive experiences—thanks to 6G's high data rates and extremely low latency. For instance, high-definition video consultations become more seamless, with no lag or buffering, enabling healthcare providers to conduct thorough examinations and assessments remotely. This is especially helpful for patients who have trouble moving around or who live in remote places and might find it difficult to get in-person medical care.

Furthermore, 6G's capabilities make it possible to incorporate cutting-edge telemedicine technologies like virtual reality (VR) and augmented reality (AR). With the help of these technologies, it will be possible to establish virtual clinics where patients and medical professionals can communicate in a more engaging and realistic setting. For example, a surgeon could use AR to guide a remote colleague through a complex procedure, or a patient could receive rehabilitation exercises through a VR platform tailored to their specific needs [9].

Furthermore, 6G's massive connectivity supports the simultaneous use of multiple devices and sensors during telemedicine sessions. This improves the precision of diagnosis and efficacy of treatment plans by enabling extensive monitoring and data collection. For example, during a telemedicine visit, a patient could wear several biometric sensors that track their vital signs in real-time, giving the medical professional a comprehensive picture of their health.

8.3.3 Data-Driven Personalized Medicine with 6G

Precision healthcare's cornerstone is personalized medicine, which aims to customize medical interventions and treatments to each patient's specific needs. The ability to evaluate sizable datasets, such as genetic data, medical histories, and lifestyle factors, in order to spot trends and generate precise health predictions for a patient, is critical to the success of personalized medicine. The capabilities of data-driven personalized medicine are greatly expanded by the incorporation of 6G technology into healthcare systems.

Healthcare providers can now process and analyze patient data in real-time, allowing them to make more informed treatment decisions—thanks to 6G's capacity to handle massive amounts of data at high speeds. For instance, it is possible to rapidly analyze a patient's genomic data to pinpoint particular genetic markers linked to particular diseases, which enables early diagnosis and the creation of tailored treatments. Because therapies can be customized based on the patient's genetic profile, this not only increases treatment effectiveness but also lowers the chance of adverse reactions.

Furthermore, 6G's sophisticated data processing powers make it easier to incorporate AI and machine learning algorithms into customized treatment plans. These algorithms are capable of sorting through enormous datasets to find insights that are impossible to find through manual means. Examples of such insights include potential health risks based on lifestyle and genetic data, or anticipating a patient's reaction to a specific treatment.

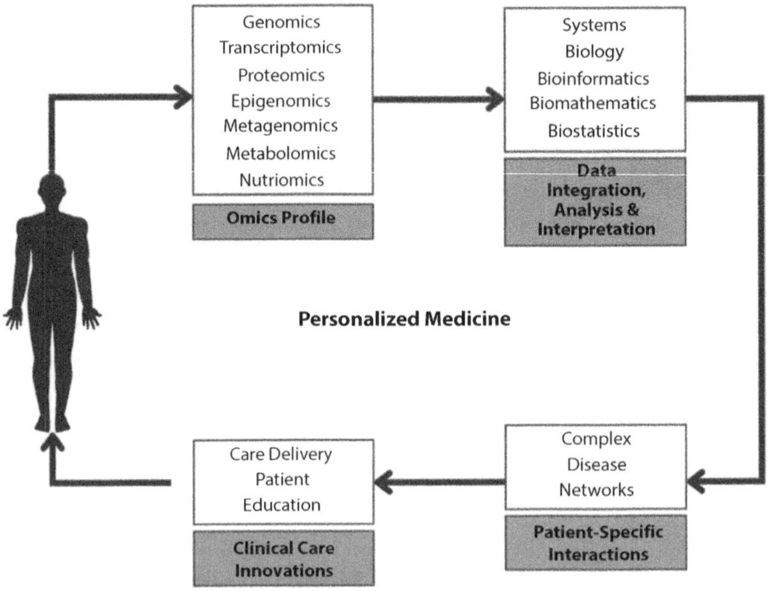

Figure 8.2 Personalized medicine framework.

This level of precision and customization ensures that patients receive the most effective treatments, improving outcomes and reducing the overall cost of healthcare [16]. Figure 8.2 shows the process of personalized medicine, beginning with an individual's omics profile (genomics, proteomics, etc.). This data is integrated and analyzed using bioinformatics and systems biology. Insights are applied to patient-specific disease networks, leading to clinical care innovations in patient education and care delivery.

Furthermore, even outside of clinical settings, the continuous collection and analysis of patient data is made possible by 6G's seamless connectivity. Real-time patient health monitoring is made possible by wearable technology and sensors, which send data to medical professionals so they can modify treatment plans as necessary. This continuous data-driven approach to personalized medicine guarantees that patients receive care that adjusts to their changing conditions in addition to being specifically tailored to meet their needs.

8.4 Challenges in Quantum Secured 6G Networks

The integration of quantum-secured 6G networks into the healthcare sector promises enhanced security and efficiency, but it also introduces a series of challenges. These challenges stem from the complexities of implementing quantum technologies at scale, ensuring data integrity in the face of quantum threats, and navigating the regulatory and compliance landscape. To fully explore the potential of quantum-secured 6G networks in precision healthcare, it is imperative to address these challenges.

8.4.1 Scalability Issues in Quantum Networks

Scalability is one of the main obstacles to the deployment of quantum-secured 6G networks. While quantum security protocols like Quantum Key Distribution (QKD) are very good at securing communications between two points, it is very challenging to scale these systems to cover large, intricate healthcare networks. The infrastructure required to support widespread QKD involves the deployment of quantum repeaters, specialized hardware, and dedicated communication channels, all of which are currently expensive and technically demanding to implement [18].

As healthcare institutions often operate vast networks with numerous interconnected devices and systems, ensuring that all nodes are secured through quantum technologies is a formidable task. This challenge is further compounded in low-resource settings, where the financial and technical barriers to adopting quantum-secured networks are even higher. Without significant advances in the scalability of quantum technologies, the full benefits of quantum-secured 6G networks may be out of reach for many healthcare providers. Many resource demands coupled with the manner in which data is transmitted, make scalability a challenge in quantum networks. These are quantum repeaters to increase the distance covered by the network, error control code to enhance the accuracy of data transmitted and routing protocols. Most research activities are to transport entanglement efficiently and explore the topology of the net as it is to build the quantum communication infrastructure for the near term and big scale.

8.4.2 Quantum Threats to Healthcare Data Integrity

Although quantum technologies provide increased security, they also present fresh risks to the integrity of data, especially when it comes to the medical field. When quantum computing is fully developed, it might be able to defeat the encryption systems in use today, endangering private medical information. This includes patient records, genomic data, and other critical information that, if compromised, could lead to severe privacy violations and potentially harmful outcomes for patients.

Moreover, the transition period during which healthcare institutions are adopting quantum-secured networks could be particularly vulnerable. As organizations update their systems to integrate quantum technologies, there may be temporary gaps in security, exposing data to threats from both classical and quantum attackers [3]. Ensuring that healthcare data remains secure throughout this transition requires robust strategies for managing encryption keys, updating cryptographic protocols, and continuously monitoring for vulnerabilities. Should there be any vulnerability in the established quantum computing, then RSA and ECC that is widely used to secure health information could be threatened. These systems are based on mathematical computations which are hard for quantum algorithm, thus posing serious threats to data credibility. Mitigating this risk is important as to avoid such a leakage of identification data in the future.

8.4.3 Regulatory and Compliance Challenges

Healthcare organizations will confront formidable regulatory and compliance obstacles when implementing 6G networks that are quantum-secured. Healthcare is a heavily regulated sector that is subject to stringent regulations protecting patient privacy and security. The advent of quantum technologies complicates these laws further because the particularities of quantum security may not be sufficiently addressed by the frameworks that are currently in place [6].

Since quantum-secured communications involve certain unique features, such as managing quantum keys and integrating quantum encryption algorithms, regulators must create new rules and regulations [17]. Compliance with these new regulations could be particularly challenging for healthcare providers, who must navigate a rapidly evolving landscape while ensuring that they continue to meet existing legal requirements.

Moreover, there's a chance that oversight gaps could result from regulatory bodies' inability to keep up with the lightning-fast developments in quantum technology. Healthcare providers must be proactive in working with regulators to ensure that their quantum-secured 6G networks meet all necessary compliance requirements while also advocating for regulatory frameworks that support innovation and the safe adoption of quantum technologies. Quantum technology brings innovation to healthcare data privacy and security but regulation. For example, quite common now existing restrictions such as HIPAA in the United States or GDPR in European countries may require adjustments regarding changes in quantum threats to encryption. In the meantime, new forms may appear to address quantum-safe data management and security in countries and healthcare systems around the globe.

8.5 Future Trends in Quantum Secured 6G Healthcare Systems

Some major themes are anticipated to propel the development of these technologies as quantum-secured 6G networks start to influence the direction of precision healthcare. Realizing the full potential of quantum-secured 6G healthcare systems is contingent upon the continuous development of quantum communication protocols, the incorporation of artificial intelligence and machine learning into 6G healthcare, and the imperative of international collaboration.

8.5.1 Evolution of Quantum Communication Protocols

The ongoing development of quantum communication protocols will be crucial to the development of quantum-secured 6G healthcare systems in the future. Although quantum technologies like Quantum Key Distribution (QKD) are already improving data transmission security, more developments are expected to improve these protocols and make them more effective, scalable, and suitable for a wider range of healthcare scenarios.

New quantum communication protocols are likely to emerge, addressing the limitations of current systems, such as the need for quantum repeaters over long distances or in complex healthcare environments. By strengthening the resilience of quantum-secured networks, these protocols will facilitate smooth integration between a variety of healthcare-related platforms and devices. Furthermore, advances in quantum fault tolerance and error correction will increase the dependability of quantum communications, guaranteeing the security of medical data even in the face of quantum-level noise and disruptions [28].

As these protocols evolve, they will become more accessible and easier to implement, making it feasible for a broader range of healthcare institutions to adopt quantum-secured 6G networks. This evolution will be critical in moving from niche applications to widespread, industry-wide adoption of quantum-secured communications in healthcare. Table 8.1 outlines the developmental stages of quantum communication and computing networks. It progresses from establishing fundamental networks like repeaters and entanglement distribution to creating fault-tolerant quantum networks, culminating in full quantum computing networks.

Table 8.1 Evolution of quantum communication and computing networks.

Stages	Description
Stage 1	Establishment of reliable repeater networks
Stage 2	Development of preparation and measurement networks
Stage 3	Construction of entanglement distribution networks
Stage 4	Construction of quantum memory networks
Stage 5	Creation of few-qubit fault-tolerant networks
Stage 6	Establishment of quantum computing networks

8.5.2 AI and Machine Learning Integration in 6G Healthcare

A key development that will fundamentally alter the provision of healthcare services is the incorporation of artificial intelligence (AI) and machine learning (ML) into quantum-secured 6G healthcare networks. When combined with 6G's lightning-fast data processing speeds, AI and ML algorithms can analyze enormous volumes of medical data in real time, producing predictive analytics, individualized treatment plans, and more accurate diagnoses.

AI-driven healthcare applications and devices will be able to securely share real-time data—thanks to quantum-secured 6G networks, which will speed up the creation of more advanced and adaptable healthcare solutions. For instance, AI algorithms could use real-time data from wearables to identify illness early on, suggest treatments, or modify treatment regimens at any time, all while guaranteeing that patient data is secure due to quantum encryption [15].

Furthermore, the combination of AI, ML, and quantum-secured 6G networks will open the door for cutting-edge telemedicine platforms that use predictive analytics to improve patient outcomes, AI-driven remote surgeries, and autonomous medical robots. Precision healthcare will be greatly impacted by the integration of AI and ML technologies with quantum-secured 6G networks as these technologies develop.

8.5.3 Global Collaboration for Quantum-Secured 6G Healthcare Solutions

Developing and deploying quantum-secured 6G healthcare systems will necessitate unprecedented degrees of international cooperation. Given the complexity and cost of quantum technologies, as well as the global nature of healthcare challenges, international cooperation among governments, research institutions, healthcare providers, and technology companies will be essential.

Global collaboration will be necessary to establish international standards for quantum-secured communications in healthcare, ensuring interoperability and security across borders. Additionally, shared research and development efforts will accelerate the advancement of quantum technologies, making them more accessible and affordable for healthcare institutions worldwide. Figure 8.3 highlights six critical healthcare applications that demand high Quality of Experience (QoE) and rely on 6G technologies: Wireless Brain-Computer Interface (BCI), Telesurgery, Wireless Body Area Networks (WBAN), Augmented/Virtual Reality (AR/VR)/ Holograms, Remote Health Monitoring, Five Senses Communication, and Intelligent Ambulance Services, enabling advanced healthcare solutions.

To solve the moral and legal issues raised by quantum-secured 6G networks in the healthcare industry, cooperation will be essential. Stakeholders can collaborate to create a harmonized framework that balances innovation, patient privacy, data security, and fair access to cutting-edge medical technology. The development of quantum communication protocols, the fusion of AI and ML, and international cooperation will all influence the future of quantum-secured 6G healthcare systems. These developments will propel the creation of healthcare solutions that are safer, more effective, and easier to access, ultimately leading to better patient outcomes and

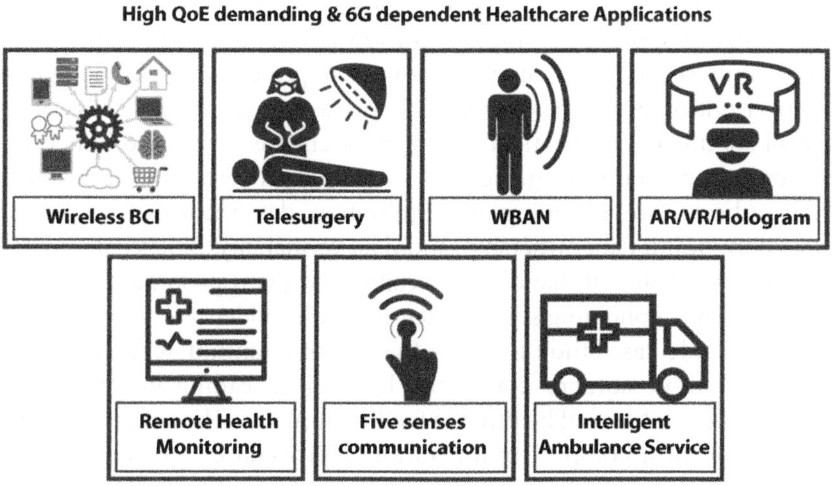

Figure 8.3 High QoE demanding and 6G dependent healthcare applications.

a revolution in precision medicine [10]. AI and ML are capable of providing significant improvement to quantum-secured 6G healthcare systems through the recognition of satisfactory threats, improving efficiency of data distributing and real-time caring for patients. Quantum security could enable the protection of important AI-driven health information insights, while AI can regularly scan data patterns encrypted through quantum for potential breaches. This synergy provides reliable and flexible support of the healthcare data protection in real time.

8.6 Case Studies and Applications

The healthcare industry can benefit greatly from the revolutionary solutions that quantum-secured 6G networks can provide for a wide range of medical applications. By examining specific case studies and applications, we can better understand how these advanced technologies are being implemented in real-world scenarios. This section examines the integration of quantum-secured 6G in healthcare data management and security, precision drug delivery systems, and remote surgery, outlining the advantages and difficulties specific to each application.

8.6.1 Quantum Secured 6G in Remote Surgery

Telesurgery, or remote surgery, is one of the most exciting uses of quantum-secured 6G networks. With robotic instruments controlled in real-time, surgeons can perform complex procedures on patients thousands of miles away—thanks to 6G technology's ultra-low latency and high bandwidth.

Quantum security adds an essential layer of protection, ensuring that the data transmitted during these surgeries—such as real-time video feeds, robotic control commands, and patient vital signs—remains secure and impervious to interception or tampering. Figure 8.4 highlights key aspects of using blockchain in healthcare, including decentralization, data security, transparency, availability, health data ownership, and data verifiability. Blockchain guarantees transparent and safe handling of health data, giving people authority over their data while upholding system integrity and confidence.

One notable case study involves the use of quantum-secured 6G networks in remote surgery conducted between a leading hospital in the United States and a rural healthcare facility in Africa. The surgery involved the removal of a complex brain tumor, a procedure that required precise control and real-time feedback. The 6G network facilitated seamless communication between the surgical team and the robotic instruments,

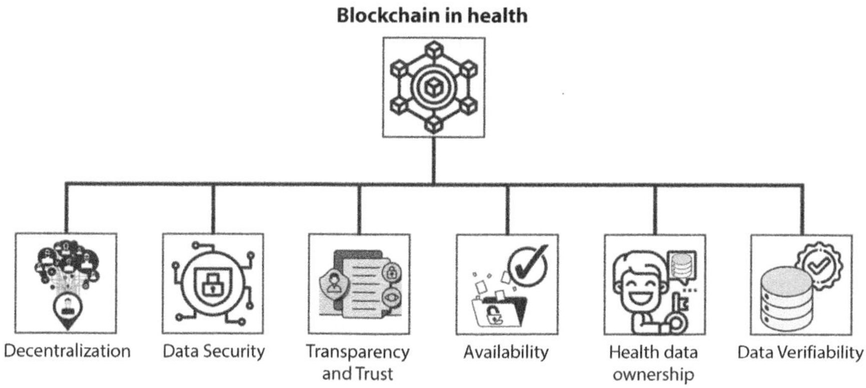

Figure 8.4 Blockchain in healthcare.

while quantum encryption ensured that the sensitive data remained secure throughout the operation.

This case study shows how access to top-notch medical knowledge in underserved areas could revolutionize remote surgery through quantum-secured 6G networks. However, challenges remain, such as the need for significant investment in infrastructure and the development of standardized protocols for quantum-secured remote surgery. Additionally, ensuring the availability of quantum-secured 6G networks in remote or low-resource settings poses a logistical challenge that must be addressed for widespread adoption [23].

8.6.2 Precision Drug Delivery Systems

Precision drug delivery systems represent another critical application of quantum-secured 6G networks. These systems are made to precisely deliver therapeutic agents to targeted areas of the body, reducing side effects and enhancing treatment effectiveness. The ability to monitor and analyze patient data in real-time is critical to the success of these systems, and 6G networks' high-speed, low-latency communication capabilities make this possible.

Precision drug delivery systems rely heavily on quantum security to preserve the confidentiality and integrity of their data. For example, quantum-encrypted 6G networks can securely transmit patient vital signs, drug levels in the bloodstream, and other pertinent biomarkers to healthcare providers. This guarantees that private patient data is shielded from online attacks and allows medical professionals to instantly modify the drug delivery process based on data [29].

Benefits of this approach are demonstrated by a case study involving the use of quantum-secured 6G networks in the treatment of chronic conditions like diabetes. In this case, an advanced precision drug delivery system was employed to manage insulin levels in diabetic patients. The system utilized real-time glucose monitoring data, which was securely transmitted over a quantum-secured 6G network to a cloud-based AI platform. The AI platform analyzed the data and made real-time adjustments to the insulin delivery rate, ensuring optimal blood sugar control. Figure 8.5 illustrates the cloud-based connectivity between different industries—manufacturing, healthcare, and supply chain—*via* gateway nodes. The Internet (cloud infrastructure) acts as the central hub, enabling seamless communication between industries and users, enhancing operational efficiency and information flow in a distributed system.

Precision drug delivery systems could greatly benefit from the integration of quantum-secured 6G networks since it would make interventions more precise and timely. However, the implementation of these systems requires overcoming challenges such as the high cost of quantum

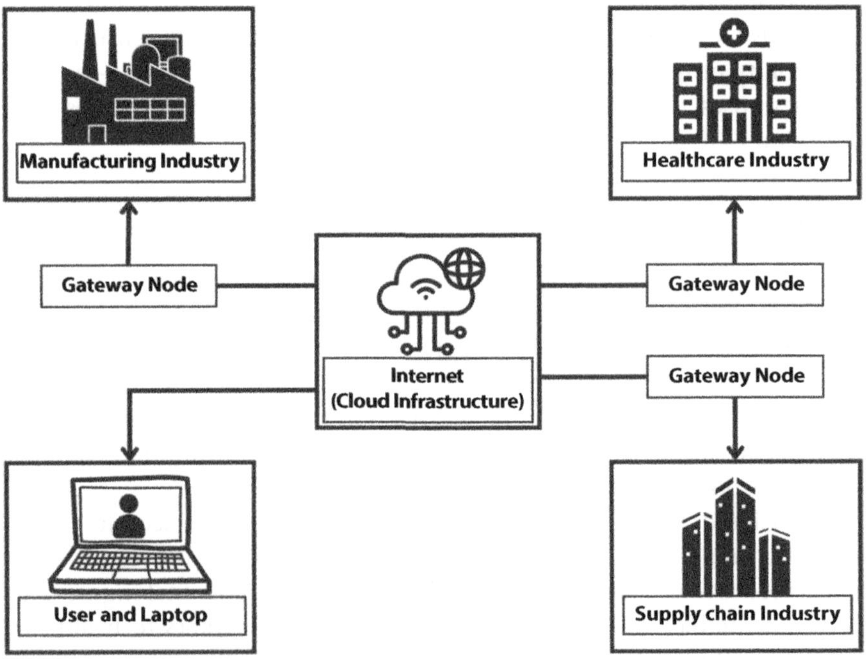

Figure 8.5 Cloud infrastructure integration in healthcare industries.

infrastructure and the need for robust regulatory frameworks to ensure patient safety and data privacy.

8.6.3 Healthcare Data Management and Security

Healthcare data management and security are critical areas where quantum-secured 6G networks can make a substantial impact. On a regular basis, the healthcare industry produces enormous volumes of data, including genomic information, electronic health records (EHRs), and medical imaging. Managing and securing this data is crucial to maintaining patient privacy, ensuring compliance with regulatory requirements, and enabling effective clinical decision-making.

Quantum-secured 6G networks offer a solution to the growing challenge of healthcare data security. These networks can offer unmatched protection against cyber threats, including those posed by future quantum computers that are capable of cracking classical encryption algorithms, by utilizing quantum encryption techniques like Quantum Key Distribution (QKD). Furthermore, 6G networks' fast data transmission speeds make it possible for healthcare data to be shared securely and quickly between various platforms and organizations, promoting more effective and team-based care.

A notable case study in this area involves a large healthcare system that implemented a quantum-secured 6G network to manage and protect its vast repository of patient data. The network was used to secure data transmission between hospitals, research institutions, and third-party service providers, ensuring that sensitive information remained protected throughout the entire data lifecycle. This included the use of quantum encryption for securing patient consent forms, genomic data used in precision medicine, and medical imaging files shared for diagnostic purposes [24].

The case study illustrated how well 6G networks with quantum security can protect medical data from new threats. However, it also highlighted challenges such as the need for continuous monitoring and updating of quantum security protocols to keep pace with advances in quantum computing. Furthermore, the implementation of quantum-secured 6G networks in the management of healthcare data necessitates a large financial outlay and close collaboration between multiple stakeholders, such as technology firms, regulatory agencies, and healthcare providers [1].

These case studies and applications underscore the transformative potential of quantum-secured 6G networks in healthcare. The security, effectiveness, and accessibility of healthcare services are expected to be improved by these technologies, which range from data management and precision medication delivery to remote surgery. But to fully enjoy these advantages, the technological, practical, and legal issues surrounding the deployment of quantum-secured 6G networks must be resolved. Ongoing research and cooperation will be crucial to guaranteeing these technologies' successful integration into the healthcare industry as they develop.

8.7 Conclusion

Precision healthcare could undergo a complete transformation if quantum-secured 6G technology is integrated, as it would allow for faster, more secure, and individualized treatment. We looked at the fundamentals of 6G technology, the importance of quantum security, and its uses in precision medicine delivery, remote surgery, and healthcare data management in this chapter. These developments are expected to protect private medical data from new cyberattacks, improve patient outcomes, and increase the effectiveness of healthcare delivery.

Future developments in quantum communication protocols and the application of AI and machine learning to the healthcare industry will be crucial. But overcoming obstacles with regard to scalability, regulatory compliance, and infrastructure development is necessary to achieve widespread adoption. To fully realize the promise of quantum-secured 6G networks, cooperation between governments, healthcare providers, and technology companies on a global scale is imperative. In order to move forward, all parties involved must work together to embrace and invest in these cutting-edge technologies and make sure they are used to build a more equitable, safe, and connected healthcare system for all.

AI disclosure statement: The author acknowledges the use of AI-based tools for minor language editing or grammatical correction. However, all intellectual contributions, analyses, and conclusions presented in this chapter are entirely the author's own.

References

1. Almalawi, A., *et al.*, Managing Security of Healthcare Data for a Modern Healthcare System. *Sensors*, 23, 7, 3612, 2023, [Online]. Available: https://www.mdpi.com/1424-8220/23/7/3612.

2. Amer, O., Garg, V., Krawec, W.O., An Introduction to Practical Quantum Key Distribution. *IEEE Aerosp. Electron. Syst. Mag.*, 36, 3, 30–55, 2021, [Online]. Available: https://ieeexplore.ieee.org/document/9374032/.
3. Barker, E. and Roginsky, A., *Transitioning the Use of Cryptographic Algorithms and Key Lengths*, NIST, Gaithersburg, MD, 2019, [Online]. Available: https://nvlpubs.nist.gov/nistpubs/SpecialPublications/NIST.SP.800-131Ar2.pdf.
4. Barker, W., Polk, W., Souppaya, M., *Getting Ready for Post-Quantum Cryptography: Exploring Challenges Associated with Adopting and Using Post-Quantum Cryptographic Algorithms*, NIST, Gaithersburg, MD, 2021, [Online]. Available: https://nvlpubs.nist.gov/nistpubs/CSWP/NIST.CSWP.04282021.pdf.
5. Chan, A., *et al.*, Quantum Encryption in Phase Space for Coherent Optical Communications, *arXiv preprint*, 2023, [Online]. Available: http://arxiv.org/abs/2301.06113.
6. Chenthara, S., *et al.*, Healthchain: A Novel Framework on Privacy Preservation of Electronic Health Records Using Blockchain Technology. *PLoS One*, 15, 12, e0243043, 2020.
7. Chowdhury, M.Z., Shahjalal, M., Ahmed, S., Jang, Y.M., 6G Wireless Communication Systems: Applications, Requirements, Technologies, Challenges, and Research Directions, *arXiv preprint*, 2019, [Online]. Available: http://arxiv.org/abs/1909.11315.
8. Cisotto, G., Casarin, E., Tomasin, S., Requirements and Enablers of Advanced Healthcare Services over Future Cellular Systems. *IEEE Commun. Mag.*, 58, 3, 76–81, 2020, [Online]. Available: https://ieeexplore.ieee.org/document/9040267/.
9. Cui, M., Baek, S.-S., Crespo, R.G., Premalatha, R., Internet of Things-Based Cloud Computing Platform for Analyzing the Physical Health Condition. *Technol. Health Care*, 29, 6, 1233–1247, 2021, [Online]. Available: https://www.medra.org/servlet/aliasResolver?alias=iospress&doi=10.3233/THC-213003.
10. Dave, M. and Patel, N., Artificial Intelligence in Healthcare and Education. *Br. Dent. J.*, 234, 10, 761–764, 2023, [Online]. Available: https://www.nature.com/articles/s41415-023-5845-2.
11. Gupta, D.S., Mazumdar, N., Nag, A., Singh, J.P., Secure Data Authentication and Access Control Protocol for Industrial Healthcare System. *J. Ambient Intell. Humaniz. Comput.*, 14, 5, 4853–4864, 2023, [Online]. Available: https://link.springer.com/10.1007/s12652-022-04370-2.
12. Hope, A., *et al.*, Artificial Intelligence Applications to Improve the Treatment of Locally Advanced Non-Small Cell Lung Cancers. *Cancers*, 13, 10, 2382, 2021, [Online]. Available: https://www.mdpi.com/2072-6694/13/10/2382.
13. Jiang, W., Han, B., Habibi, M.A., Schotten, H.D., The Road Towards 6G: A Comprehensive Survey. *IEEE Open J. Commun. Soc.*, 2, 334–366, 2021, [Online]. Available: https://ieeexplore.ieee.org/document/9349624/.

14. Jun, S., Kang, Y., Kim, J., Kim, C., Ultra-low-latency Services in 5G Systems: A Perspective from 3GPP Standards. *ETRI J.*, 42, 5, 721–733, 2020, [Online]. Available: https://onlinelibrary.wiley.com/doi/10.4218/etrij.2020-0200.
15. Khalifa, M., Albadawy, M., Iqbal, U., Advancing Clinical Decision Support: The Role of Artificial Intelligence across Six Domains. *Comput. Methods Programs Biomed. Update*, 5, 100142, 2024, [Online]. Available: https://linkinghub.elsevier.com/retrieve/pii/S2666990024000090.
16. Kim, W.-J., Knowledge-Based Diagnosis and Prediction Using Big Data and Deep Learning in Precision Medicine. *Investig. Clin. Urol.*, 59, 2, 69, 2018, [Online]. Available: https://icurology.org/DOIx.php?id=10.4111/icu.2018.59.2.69.
17. Mashatan, A. and Heintzman, D., The Complex Path to Quantum Resistance. *Queue*, 19, 2, 65–92, 2021, [Online]. Available: https://dl.acm.org/doi/10.1145/3466132.3466779.
18. Mohsan, S.A.H. and Li, Y., A Contemporary Survey on 6G Wireless Networks: Potentials, Recent Advances, Technical Challenges and Future Trends, *arXiv preprint*, 2023, [Online]. Available: http://arxiv.org/abs/2306.08265.
19. Munjal, K. and Bhatia, R., A Systematic Review of Homomorphic Encryption and Its Contributions in Healthcare Industry. *Complex Intell. Syst.*, 9, 4, 3759–3786, 2023, [Online]. Available: https://link.springer.com/10.1007/s40747-022-00756-z.
20. Naithani, N., *et al.*, Precision Medicine: Concept and Tools. *Med. J. Armed Forces India*, 77, 3, 249–257, 2021, [Online]. Available: https://linkinghub.elsevier.com/retrieve/pii/S0377123721001672.
21. Pahalı, M., Durak, K., Tefek, U., Optimal Photon Budget Allocation in E91 Protocol, *arXiv preprint*, 2022, [Online]. Available: http://arxiv.org/abs/2212.13837.
22. Pandey, M., Agarwal, R., Shukla, S.K., Verma, N.K., . Security of Healthcare Data Using Blockchains: A Survey, *arXiv preprint*, 2021, [Online]. Available: http://arxiv.org/abs/2103.12326.
23. Prateek, K., Ojha, N.K., Altaf, F., Maity, S., Quantum Secured 6G Technology-Based Applications in Internet of Everything. *Telecommun. Syst.*, 82, 2, 315–344,2023,[Online].Available:https://link.springer.com/10.1007/s11235-022-00979-y.
24. Puppala, M., *et al.*, Data Security and Privacy Management in Healthcare Applications and Clinical Data Warehouse Environment, in: *2016 IEEE-EMBS Int. Conf. Biomed. Health Inform. (BHI)*, pp. 5–8, 2016, [Online]. Available: http://ieeexplore.ieee.org/document/7455821/.
25. Qureshi, H.N., *et al.*, Communication Requirements in 5G-Enabled Healthcare Applications: Review and Considerations. *Healthcare*, 10, 2, 293, 2022, [Online]. Available: https://www.mdpi.com/2227-9032/10/2/293.
26. Rozenman, G.G., *et al.*, The Quantum Internet: A Synergy of Quantum Information Technologies and 6G Networks. *IET Quantum Commun.*, 4, 4,

147–166, 2023, [Online]. Available: https://ietresearch.onlinelibrary.wiley.com/doi/10.1049/qtc2.12069.

27. Srikanth, P. and Kumar, A., Secure Quantum Computing for Healthcare Sector: A Short Analysis, *arXiv preprint*, 2022, [Online]. Available: http://arxiv.org/abs/2211.10027.
28. Ur Rasool, R., *et al.*, Quantum Computing for Healthcare: A Review. *Future Internet*, 15, 3, 94, 2023, [Online]. Available: https://www.mdpi.com/1999-5903/15/3/94.
29. Yih, T.C. and Al-Fandi, M., Engineered Nanoparticles as Precise Drug Delivery Systems. *J. Cell. Biochem.*, 97, 6, 1184–1190, 2006, [Online]. Available: https://onlinelibrary.wiley.com/doi/10.1002/jcb.20796.
30. Yunakovsky, S.E., *et al.*, Towards Security Recommendations for Public-Key Infrastructures for Production Environments in the Post-Quantum Era. *EPJ Quantum Technol.*, 8, 1, 14, 2021, [Online]. Available: https://epjquantum-technology.springeropen.com/articles/10.1140/epjqt/s40507-021-00104-z.

9

An Efficient Net-B0 Deep Learning Model for the Detection of Breast Tumor from Histopathological Images

Monika S.[1*], Nagarajan. G.[1] and Perarasi T.[2]

[1]*Department of ECE, Puducherry Technological University, Puducherry, India*
[2]*Department of ECE, Bannari Amman Institute of Technology, Sathyamangalam, India*

Abstract

Biomedical Image Processing is an awfully developing field in the contemporary world. Its demand is increasing in various growth of several applications. Research into these medical technologies has many features and applications. Those features extracted from suspect regions of the images will help them find the place where the tumor is present in real time and is useful for speeding up the treatment process. This work deals with the detection methodologies of breast tumors from histopathological images.

The main motivation for selecting a histopathological image over a tomographic image is that a tomographic image is a preoperative diagnosis, whereas a histopathological image provides both a preoperative diagnosis and a predictive assessment of post-disease treatment (surgery) for effective decision-making regarding further treatment. Moreover, deep learning algorithms in artificial intelligence have become the successors of pathology image analysis for tumor area segmentation, identification, metastasis detection and patient prediction. As opposed to numerous current methods that employ single instance-level annotations, the original methodology just needs bag-level annotations. An EfficientNet-B0 Deep Learning Model is employed in this study to extract tumor images using Break-His databases. A whole slide image is roughly 40,000 × 40.000 pixels in size. During the proposed research, an improved framework accustomed to categorize massive digitally scanned tissue slides utilizing data used as training from slides that have

**Corresponding author*: monika.s@pec.edu

T. Perarasi, M. Karthiga, S. Sountharrajan, E. Suganya and Balamurugan Balusamy (eds.) Secure Blockchain and Quantum Technologies for 6G-Enabled Internet of Things, (203–224) © 2026 Scrivener Publishing LLC

weak labels. The approach that was suggested outperforms previous work, according to the results.

Keywords: Breast tumor, convolutional neural network, deep learning, efficientnet-B0, histopathological images, image classification, tumor detection, whole slide image analysis

9.1 Introduction

The medical envisioning intends to accomplish and extract useful information and accurate findings from those images with no errors. The main objective of "medical envisioning," is to come up with non-invasive well aimed diagnosis, treatment planning, and disease monitoring. Accurate Diagnosis, Real-Time Visualization for Biopsies and Surgical and monitoring the disease Progression. Over the previous decade, there is a rapid growth in computational power and also the image is enhanced and analyzed. Algorithms are used to improve computational methods for abnormal data. Full-slide digitized scanning along with computerized histopathological samples are currently recorded as digital images [1]. Significance of CAD algorithms enhance diagnostic accuracy by automatically analyzing medical images and identifying future deformity. These algorithms can detect small problems, improving diagnostic sensitivity and specificity. CAD algorithms are the rising—ones designed for disease detection, diagnosis and prognosis to improve pathologist awareness about diseases [2]. The importance of imaging technology for pathology is that the Pathologists rely heavily on imaging because it complements histopathological examination by providing spatial and structural context that enhances understanding of tissue anomalies, tumor boundaries, and vascular involvement. Histopathology is the study of diseased tissues under a microscope to diagnose and understand the nature of diseases at the cellular and tissue levels. It combines "histo-" (relating to tissue) and "pathology" (the study of disease). This discipline is fundamental in modern medicine, as it allows doctors to examine samples of cells and tissues to detect abnormalities and determine the exact cause and stage of diseases, especially cancers. The role of histopathology in Modern Medicine Histopathology is critical for diagnosing various conditions, particularly cancers, autoimmune diseases, infections, and inflammatory conditions. And also Diagnosis, Staging, Grading of Cancer, Monitoring Treatment Effectiveness, Research and Understanding of Disease Mechanisms. Histopathology is the study of diseased cells and tissues using a microscope. Histopathology slides provide a more complete picture of the disease and also its reaction on tissue [3]. A tumor will develop when the cells start to reproduce too quickly in our body. An unusual bunch of substances reverberation at the same time another bunch of substances fractionates further. At present assorted tumors start from a minute nodule or to a huge one, and they can appear more or less in any place on the body. Examples include Carcinoma, Sarcoma, Germ cell tumors, Blastoma and Meningiomas. We're not sure about the growth of cells, whether it will become good or bad. It is always better to check any growth that starts as benign and that benign becomes premalignant and that premalignant turns into a malignant tumor. A benign tumor is a non-cancerous growth of cells that generally rests in the body and certainly doesn't invade the surrounding tissues or spread to other parts of the body. While they can be significant due to their size or location, benign tumors generally do not pose the same health risks as malignant tumors (cancers). A malignant tumor is a cancerous growth that has the potential to invade the surrounding tissues and spread to other parts of the body. Unlike benign tumors, malignant tumors are aggressive, can disrupt normal body functions, and may lead to serious health complications. A benign and malignant image of a solitary fibrous tumor is cited in Figure 9.1.

The development of a tumor for a person will depend upon its stage. Most of the time benign tumors did not bring health risks [4]. But it's better to remove benign stages earlier. If the benign stage develops into premalignant or malignant, it may be more challenging to treat severe stages in the future. So, it is advisable to give treatment in the early stage [5]. Digital recording of pathology offers massive graphic information within the easy reach for computerized diagnosis [6]. It has tissue regions in high-resolution information [7]. This helps in imaging data such as stages and

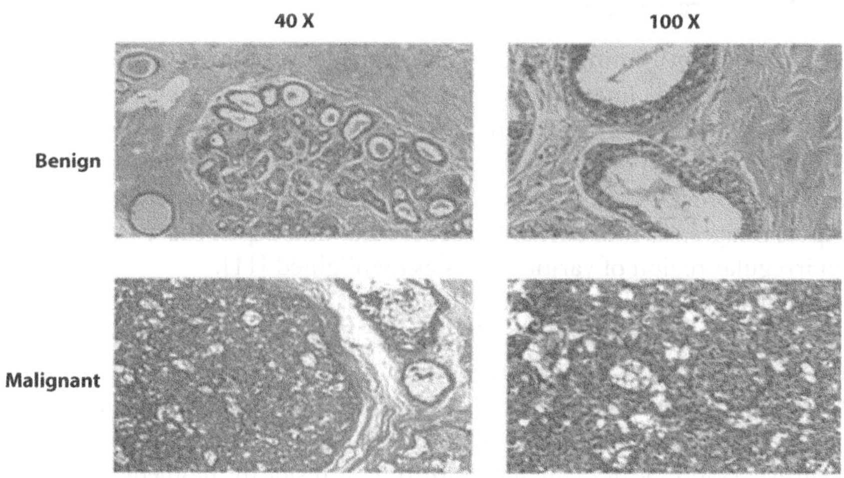

Figure 9.1 Solitary fibrous tumor [45].

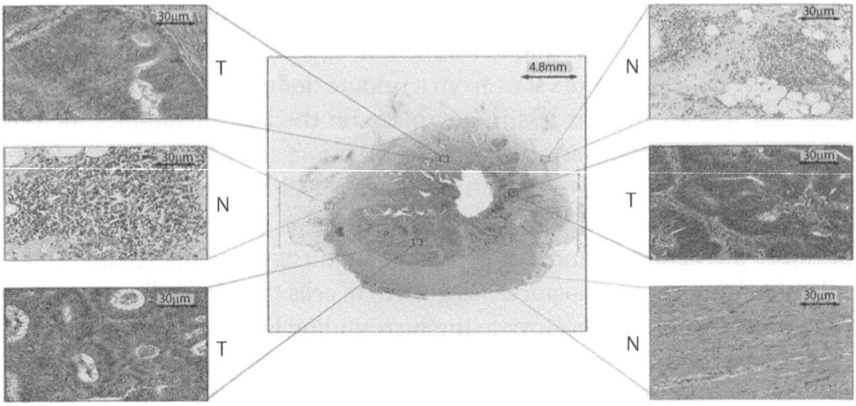

Figure 9.2 Nodules and tumor region split-up [46].

grades with a useful quantity of feature imaging [8]. Nowadays, whole slide imaging (WSI) shows better performance. The WSI can be divided into different forms as shown in Figure 9.2.

9.2 Related Works

The present segment displays the techniques used in the pre-existent technique and the dataset and framework of convolutional neural networks.

9.2.1 Literature Survey

Countless identification and categorization algorithms of the previous tissues in pathologic images are considered for the research development [9]. The well-performing algorithms for pathologic function and biomedical image scanning are used for preserving knowledge with an artificial intelligence approach [10]. A view of various methods will provide pathology report images, their details of the set of rules that depict those images have an irregular region of various types as highlighted [11].

In artificial intelligence, deep learning is a part that trains computer systems to carry out human intelligence. It is the greatest point in history in the rear of driverless cars, allowing them to understand a forestall signal or to differentiate a pedestrian from a lamp post. It is one of the rising fields in scientific imaging [12]. It also achieves reputation accuracy at better stages than ever before. So, it's a higher desire to apply inside the biomedical imaging subject for the detection of sicknesses and enhance the overall performance of scientific subjects [13]. In healthcare, cancer researchers are utilizing Deep Learning to automatically detect cancer cells [14]. Deep studying fashions are educated with the aid of using the massive units of labeled statistics and neural community architectures that analyze functions without delay from the statistics without the want for guide characteristic extraction [15]. Convolutional Neural Networks are solitary involved in a notable role in deep learning models [16]. By using CNN, purposeless is a guide for the extraction of features [17]. The computerized feature extraction will make the learning models more perfect for tasks of object detection [18]. Machine learning has unrelated techniques and frameworks used for extracting the issues that will be addressed. Comparing the artificial intelligence, a high-performance GPU and more labeled data are present. Machine learning techniques can be pre-owned so long as there exist scanty resources. Therefore, accurate and timely results are required [19]. In the existing works, a large number of datasets are used. This proposed framework simply needs bag-level annotations methods whereas the previous system uses individual instance-level annotations. Compared to the previous method, the algorithm employed in this case is defined below. For example, Kausik Das *et al.*, described a framework that has achieved an accuracy of a maximum of 93.06% [20].

9.2.2 Dataset Used

Breast cancer datasets are easily accessible in histopathology images. The BreakHis dataset is the one used in the following paper. A pathologist executes a surgical open biopsy to remove those breast tissue samples. The samples are then produced using the usual paraffin method, which incorporates test piece intrusion and insertion in paraffin and blemished with the Haematoxylin and Eosin dye. A high-resolution lens is habituated to capture images along with a microscopic system that has a disclosed lens and a magnifying lens [21]. There are 39,545 images in total within this database. Images have been taken at magnification levels of 40x. Table 9.1 summarizes the distribution of the images and Figure 9.3 shows the bar diagram.

Table 9.1 Distribution of image in dataset.

Magnification	Benign	Malignant	Total
40x	12400	27145	39545

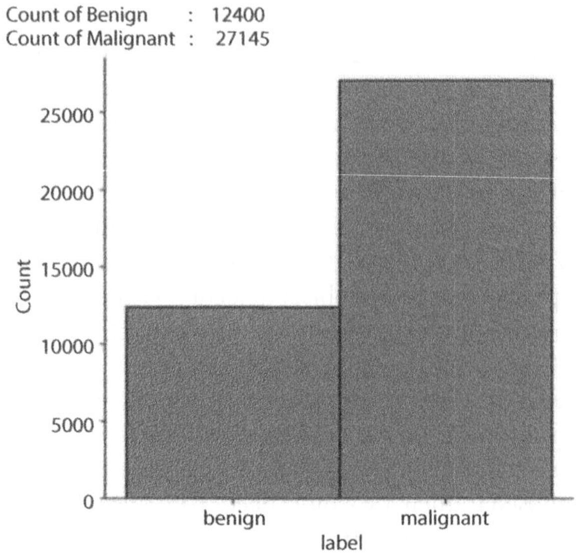

Figure 9.3 Bar diagram representation of benign and malignant tumor.

9.2.3 Convolutional Neural Network

Artificial intelligence algorithms may discover patterns and resolve common issues because networks of neurons reflect the mission of the human brain. A layout for whole story optimization that draws inspiration from biological nerve systems is the neural network model (ANN) [22]. It incorporates numerous, extensively interconnected processing cells called neurons that proclaim with one another through links in different layers of networks in order to alter data before classifying it as an output. The network is provided with information on a moment as part of a continuous process of learning, and weights related to the values provided for input are changed every time. During this learning phase, the network trains itself by adjusting the weights to speculate the correct class labels of the testimony samples. CNN is a pattern of deep neural network capable of recognizing and classifying specific features from images and is widely used for visual image analysis [17].

Applications include speech processing, classification of images, video and image evaluation for medical purposes, and image and video recognition. CNNs are effective in image recognition because they focus on patterns in small areas, making them highly effective for identifying shapes and structures. They down sample data with pooling, making it processable without losing key information. They can learn from complex data, building layers that recognize increasingly complex patterns from raw image pixels to specific objects. CNNs are highly effective at classifying and recognizing images, and they don't need human oversight to find key details. Transferring weights is also another key benefit of CNNs. In comparison to a conventional neural network, convolutional neural networks additionally simplify computation. The process of convolution is a mathematical procedure that involves multiplying two functions to create an extra function that depicts how the form of one of the functions is altered by the other. The term "convolution" is used in CNN to refer to this mathematical activity. For wrenching out the features from an image, two images that are capable of being described using a matrix are added together to generate an output. Three main operations–Convolution, pooling, and fully linked layer make up the establishment of this system. In the backdrop of a ConvNet, the main goal of convolution is to gather specific characteristics from the image entity used [23–25]. Filters function like detection devices for attributes belonging to the initial source image; it is vital to remember that.

In the additional filters applied, a greater number of visual features are recovered, and the network's ability to spot similarities in hidden images improves. The phrase "Fully Connected" suggests that each neuron in the anterior layer is connected to every neuron in the layer below. It features that the source images are represented within the result obtained which includes the pooling and convolution layers. The Fully connected layer's goal was to employ the aforementioned characteristics to divide the input image into different classes. The convolved feature's spatial size is decreased by the pooling layer. The highest value possible from the zone of the image that the Kernel has covered is returned by Max Pooling. According to filter size and strides, Max Pooling gives the most possible value from the feature map. Figure 9.4 indicates the architecture of the convolutional neural

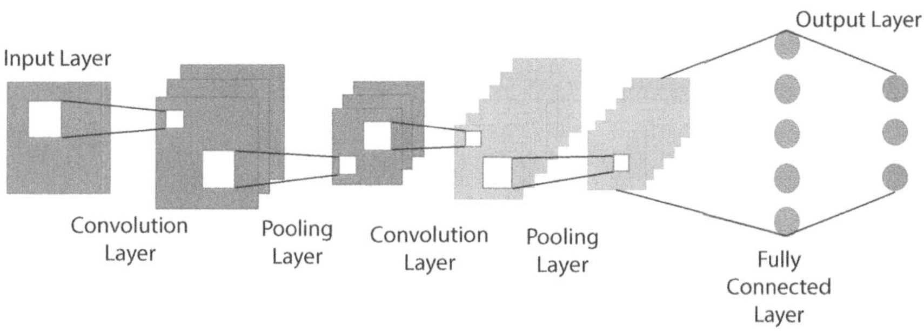

Figure 9.4 CNN architecture.

network; the result might be provided into a layer that is fully connected for effective classification following the use of a combined pooling and convolution layer combination.

9.3 Proposed Work

The present work for diagnosing breast cancer integrates ideas from the EfficientNet-B0 image classification system. It has discussed the topologies of deep neural networks, designed to process image data, including convolutional neural networks. This method uses a tagged (benign/malignant) input image of unprocessed images to emphasize the appearance of sequences, which is followed by a classification model to tell the difference between tissue that isn't carcinogenic and cells that contain cancer [26]. The corresponding RGB coloring dataset of 12400 benign and 27145 malignant models are under training the CNN's algorithms. Figure 9.5 illustrates the proposed method, which offers a useful framework for categorizing tissue from the breast as benign or cancerous. The H&E-stained biopsy specimens taken from female breast tumor tissues make up a breast cancer histopathological data set. It processes the datasets. It has 39,545 specimens in total. Then, it undergoes training, testing, and validation. And Table 9.2 contains a summary of the datasets. Then, helpers are created for scaling the image's height and breadth and absorbing the image's features [27].

Design and training are done on a convolution neural network architecture. The neural network's performance is then evaluated and a set of rules is generated. The EfficientNet-B0 algorithm deeply observes

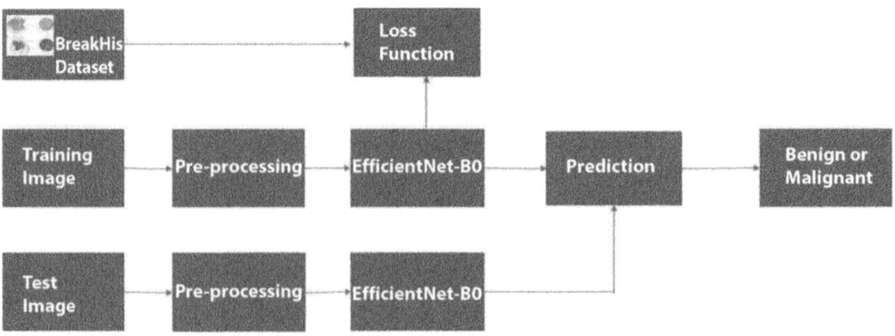

Figure 9.5 Block diagram of the proposed work.

Table 9.2 Break-his datasets for training, testing and validation.

Datasets	Training	Testing	Validation
Benign	9698	300	2402
Malignant	21458	300	5387

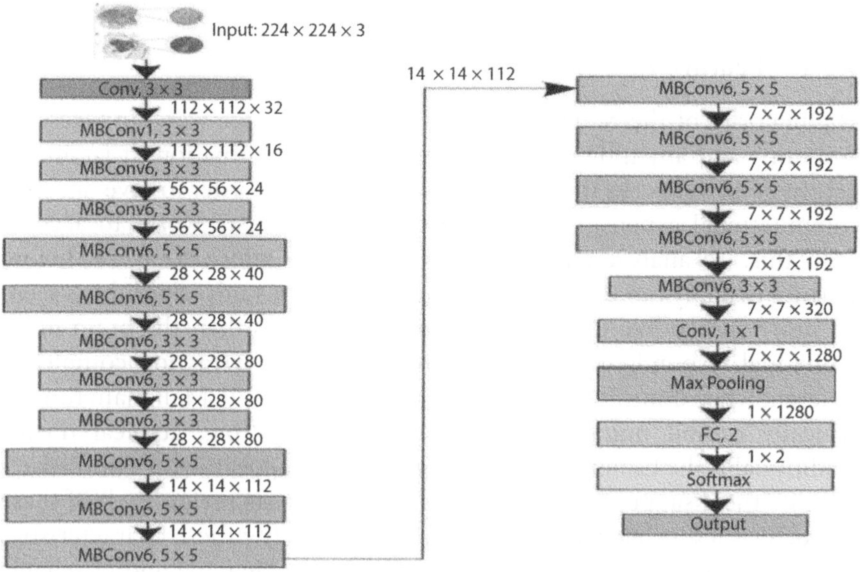

Figure 9.6 EfficienNet-B0 architecture.

the pixel of tumor images into benign and malignant. The architecture of EfficienNet-B0 is shown in Figure 9.6. Test the network on the test data. Then a loss function is defined. During the training phase, the CNN is fed with the training data. For training, the Break-His Dataset is given. The output is compared with the actual output to calculate the loss. The weights are updated using backpropagation. After training the model continues until the loss function reaches a minimum or the validation accuracy stops improving. Testing in a convolutional neural network (CNN) involves evaluating the performance of the trained model including the data that it has not seen before, called the test set [28].

The goal of testing is to size up in what way the CNN can generalize to state-of-the-art and make accurate predictions. To test a CNN, the following steps are carried out:

Step 1: Load the trained model
Step 2: Load the test data
Step 3: Evaluate the model
Step 4: Look over the results.

9.3.1 Feature Extraction

The majority of the remaining pixels within an image were unnecessary and don't add anything to the image's intrinsic information. It is vital to get rid of AI networks that get to grips with them in order to save needless computational expenses. The compression mechanism works to accomplish this. To analyze all the images within the information, set before starting to apply our deep network. According to a study, algorithms seem far more susceptible to patterns as well as textures than the brain of an individual responds to forms. This makes feature extraction completely different when done manually versus automatically [29]. Malignant tumors typically exhibit numerous nuclear structures or big, atypical nuclei. Additionally, the tumor alters, causing either the appearance of new structures or the disappearance of existing ones. Analysts review each of these characteristics, or algorithms are created to quantify these characteristics and automated detection [22]. This method is challenging and unreliable since choice and enumeration involve a number of difficult-to-address unknown flaws. Images are delivered to a CNN structure in this case, coupled with an identification number identifying the image kind (benign or malignant) [30].

9.3.2 Classification

The final pooling layer's deflated weight map of features is one input put to use in the classification process. The fully interconnected network of things uses these inputs to calculate the loss and adjust the corresponding weights for the inner nodes that are concealed accordingly [10]. Table 9.3 contains the setting parameters of these layers. The pre-processing is finished and then these layers are layered. As is typical, the final result of the very last layer is chosen. A fold in the framework of deep learning is a

Table 9.3 Fully connected layer.

Layer attribute	FC 1	FC 2
No of nodes	112	112
Activation used	ReLU	Softmax

Table 9.4 Results of folds.

Fold	Train (+Ve, -Ve)	Test (+Ve, -Ve)	Validation (+Ve, -Ve)
0	(9759,21397)	(300,300)	(2341,5448)
1	(9759,21397)	(300,300)	(2341,5448)
2	(9759,21397)	(300,300)	(2341,5448)

group of data in a set of values used to get the measure of pattern competence to provide more information. The fold's consequences are displayed in Table 9.4.

9.4 Results and Discussion

The framework that is suggested has an accuracy rate for the training of 98.03% when using the current method. The proposed work's assessment metrics are in the following Table 9.6 where they are described. The unit that belongs to a particular category that depicts the true response is called support. Table 9.5 provides a concise of the Network Performance.

Python has been evaluated as a coding language in this project *via* the Colab at Google platform, having an acquisition rate of 0.01. A total of 237 layers have been implemented in the design and 12 epochs of training and validation [31].

The standard explanation for accuracy applies as follows: For calculating accuracy, The sum of the number of correct predictions divided by the overall amount of predictions is computed. The number of both positive and negative outcomes for binary classification can also be used for assessing accuracy, as seen below:

$$\text{Accuracy} = (\text{True Positives} + \text{True Negatives})/(\text{True Positives} + \text{True Negatives} + \text{False Positives} + \text{False Negatives}) \quad (9.1)$$

Table 9.5 Analysis of network performance.

	Precision	Recall	F1-score	Support
Benign	0.98	0.98	0.98	63
Malignant	0.97	0.97	0.97	39
Accuracy	-	-	0.98	102
Macro Avg	0.98	0.98	0.98	102
Weighted Avg	0.98	0.98	0.98	102

For medical professionals, high accuracy means that the model is generally reliable in diagnosing patients.

A loss function analyzes how effectively the models of neural networks handle the training data by comparing the target value and the predicted value of the output. Training in between predicted versus actual outputs reduced this loss.

The recall is determined as the ratio of the total number of the positive samples that were correctly identified as 'positives' to the total number of the positive samples between those two positive samples. For clinicians, recall indicates how effective the model is at capturing all cases of a condition. High recall is particularly important in early disease detection, such as catching cancer at its early stages, as missing a true positive (false negative) could delay critical treatment. A high recall rate reassures healthcare providers that the model is likely to identify most patients who genuinely have the condition.

$$\text{Recall} = \text{True Positives}/(\text{True Positives} + \text{False Negatives}) \quad (9.2)$$

Specificity measures the proportion of true negatives that are correctly identified by the model.

$$\text{Specificity} = \text{True Negatives}/(\text{True Negatives} + \text{False Positives}) \quad (9.3)$$

Precision is the number of true positives divided by the total number of positive predictions. In a clinical context, precision tells healthcare providers how confident they can be when the model diagnoses a patient with a particular condition and high precision in cancer screening means that most patients are flagged as "positive".

$$\text{Precision} = \text{True Positives}/(\text{True Positives} + \text{False Positives}) \tag{9.4}$$

The geometric mean of precision and recall provides the F1 score.

$$\text{F1} = 2\ (\text{Precision} * \text{Recall})/(\text{Precision} + \text{Recall}) \tag{9.5}$$

Figure 9.7 illustrates the confusion matrix of this experiment. The numbers for the values of True Positive, True Negative, False Positive and False Negative are 62, 38, 1 and 1, respectively according to Figure 9.7. This model uses 39545 biopsy-images of both normal and cancerous breast tissue in training and testing to produce the desired outcome. Figure 9.8 shows the testing set's output for benign and cancerous images that can be predicted. Figures 9.9 and 9.10 show the accuracy and loss curves for training and validation generated during the training procedure.

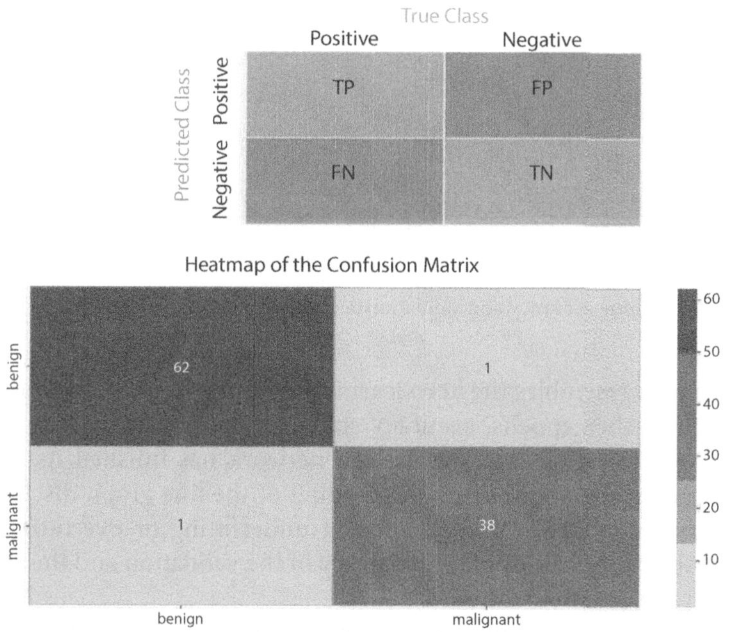

Figure 9.7 Confusion matrix.

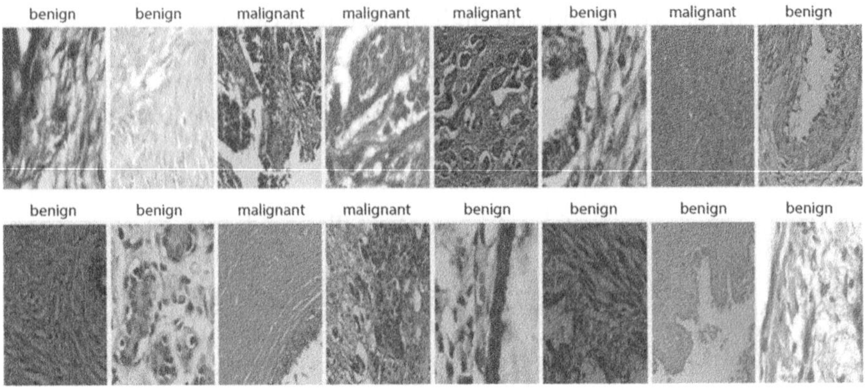

Figure 9.8 Proposed work of benign and malignant tumor.

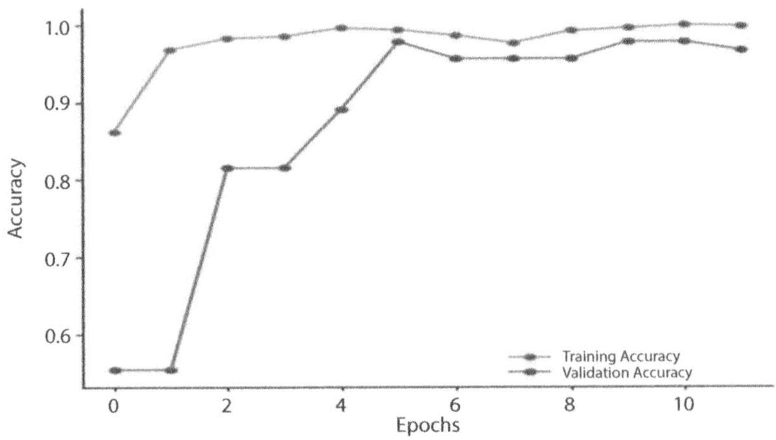

Figure 9.9 Training accuracy and validation accuracy.

This behavior resembles the deep learning training process as a whole [32–34]. With further epochs, accuracy starts to rise and eventually reaches saturation, indicating that the desired network has finished its training on the dataset. Furthermore, a key finding of the line graph disclose that the network's model is trained without underfitting or overfitting traits because the distributions of the accuracy of the validation and the training efficiency curves are identical.

The model described above offers a significant improvement in accuracy over the experimental designs used in numerous research studies [35–37]. In Table 9.6, numerous published research on the work's validation accuracy

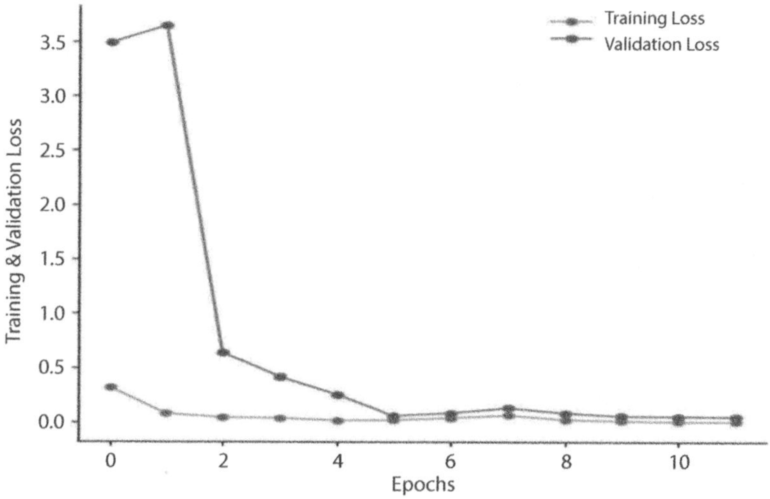

Figure 9.10 Training loss and validation loss.

Table 9.6 Comparison of existing and proposed work.

References/proposed work	Accuracy	Recall	Specificity	Precision
B. Babenka *et al.* [49]	49.64	48.15	55.56	-
Z.-H. Zhou *et al.* [50]	67.81	77.78	38.89	-
Q. Zhang *et al.* [51]	70.83	83.33	33.33	-
S. Andrews *et al.* [52]	77.42	79.30	72.22	-
J. Wang *et al.* [53]	78.86	94.44	33.33	-
Y. Rubner *et al.* [54]	80.43	88.89	55.56	-
C. Huang *et al.* [55]	88.81	94.43	77.78	-
Kausik Das *et al.* [20]	93.06	94.44	88.89	-
Proposed Work	**98.03**	**98.41**	**97.43**	**98.41**

result of 98.03% were recorded with the testing. There has been a substantial rise in recall, specificity, and precision in addition to an enhancement in accuracy. Additionally, the suggested model has undergone ROC AUC curve testing. The model has a rating of 0.9841 utilizing the ROC AUC measurements, indicating the model was very good. The outcome of more than one is compared using the ROC curve to test the overall diagnostic performance. Clinicians use ROC AUC to evaluate diagnostic tests or models because it provides a single, interpretable measure of accuracy. For instance, an AUC of 0.90 implies that there's a 90% probability the model will correctly rank a randomly chosen positive instance higher than a randomly chosen negative one. Impact on clinical decision-making of AUC-ROC is balancing sensitivity and specificity. In clinical settings, the threshold chosen affects patient outcomes directly. For instance, a high-sensitivity threshold is vital in infectious disease screening to avoid missing any positive cases, while a high-specificity threshold might be critical in non-invasive procedures to reduce patient anxiety and resource use.

While AUC compares the two models and offers an overall measure of performance throughout every possible classification of thresholds, accuracy determines how well one model is performing. AUC is a significantly more accurate measure of model performance. The True Positive Rate (TPR) and False Positive Rate (FPR) are compared using the ROC AUC, whereas Accuracy simply indicates the proportion of accurate predictions. Figure 9.11 shows the model performance using the ROC curve. The choice of threshold is often a balance between potential clinical risks and the benefits of early detection. The choice of thresholds on the ROC curve determines sensitivity and specificity. For example, in high-risk scenarios like cancer detection, a lower threshold may be chosen to increase sensitivity, ensuring fewer cases are missed.

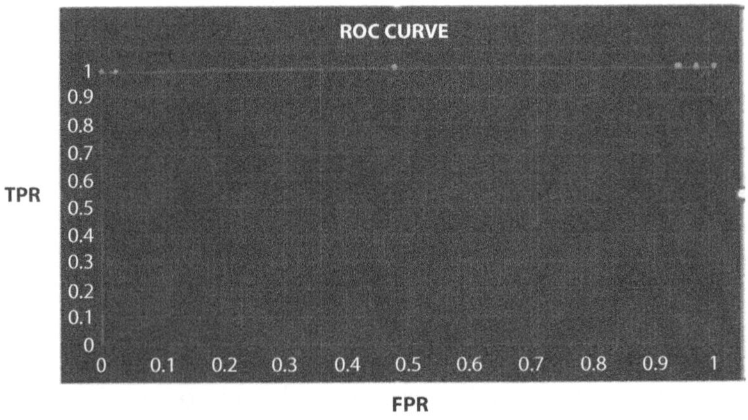

Figure 9.11 AUC ROC curve.

AUC ROC is Sensitivity Vs (1-Specificity). It can be concluded that proposed technique is better at classifying both the positive and the negative classes with a greater area under the curve (AUC), and it has achieved a good value of 0.9841 as illustrated in Figure 9.11.

$$\text{True Positive Rate} = \text{True Positive}/(\text{True Positive} + \text{False Negative}) \tag{9.6}$$

$$\text{False Positive Rate} = \text{False Positive}/(\text{False Positive} + \text{True Negative}) \tag{9.7}$$

9.5 Conclusion

In conclusion, the research highlights the vital role of performance metrics, including accuracy, precision and recall in assessing diagnostic models for clinical use. A high level of accuracy indicates a model's overall reliability, whereas precision and recall provide detailed perspectives on the model's effectiveness for identifying patients with a specific condition while minimizing false positives.

Finally, the contemplated method of EfficienNet-B0 Deep Learning algorithm for a Whole Slide Image classification using CNN architecture has been proposed and simulated. Results show that as compared to the previous existing frameworks, the proposed CNN framework achieved better achievement for the classification of images on WSI images [38–42]. The suggested method of working grasp with large sets of WSI imaging-based breast cancer detection tasks [43, 44]. The total work was carried out and was assessed using the Break-His breast cancer dataset with 98.03% accuracy, 98.41% recall, 97.43% specificity, and 98.41% precision was obtained respectively—as well as to estimate the performance of the model on different thresholds using the ROC curve AUC, obtaining an excellent value of 0.9841 [47, 48].

AI disclosure statement: The author acknowledges the use of AI-based tools for minor language editing or grammatical correction. However, all intellectual contributions, analyses, and conclusions presented in this chapter are entirely the author's own.

References

1. Ehteshami Bejnordi, B., *et al.*, Automated Detection of DCIS in Whole-Slide H&E Stained Breast Histopathology Images. *IEEE Trans. Med. Imaging*, 35, 9, 2141–2150, 2016, doi: 10.1109/TMI.2016.2550620.
2. Fauzan, D.F., Fauzi, R., Pratiwi, O.N., Ferreira Machado, J.M., Breast Cancer Detection on Histopathology Images Using Pre-Trained Computer Vision Models. *2023 International Conference on Advancement in Data Science, E-Learning and Information System (ICADEIS)*, Bali, Indonesia, pp. 1–6, 2023, doi: 10.1109/ICADEIS58666.2023.10270900.
3. Xu, W., Xu, L., Liu, N., *et al.*, Histological Image Diagnosis of Breast Cancer Based on Multi-Attention Convolution Neural Network. *J. Shanghai Jiaotong Univ. (Sci.)*, 2024, doi.org/10.1007/s12204-024-2705-4.
4. Bándi, P., *et al.*, From Detection of Individual Metastases to Classification of Lymph Node Status at the Patient Level: The CAMELYON17 Challenge. *IEEE Trans. Med. Imaging*, 38, 2, 550–560, 2019, doi: 10.1109/TMI.2018.2867350.
5. Fauzi, M.F.A., Chen, W., Knight, D., Hampel, H., Frankel, W.L., Gurcan, M.N., Tumor Budding Detection System in Whole Slide Pathology Images. *J. Med. Syst.*, 44, 2, 2020, doi: 10.1007/s10916-019-1515-y.
6. Veta, M., Pluim, J.P.W., Van Diest, P.J., Viergever, M.A., Breast cancer histopathology image analysis: A review. *IEEE Trans. Biomed. Eng.*, 61, 5, 1400–1411, 2014, doi: 10.1109/TBME.2014.2303852.
7. Ke, J., Shen, Y., Guo, Y., Liang, X., Fast Tumor Detector in Whole-Slide Image with Dynamic Programing Based Monte Carlo Sampling. *Proc. - Int. Conf. Image Process. ICIP*, vol. 2020-October, pp. 2471–2475, 2020, doi: 10.1109/ICIP40778.2020.9190987.
8. Zhang, X., Liu, W., Zhang, S., Mining histopathological images *via* hashing-based scalable image retrieval. *2014 IEEE 11th Int. Symp. Biomed. Imaging, ISBI 2014*, pp. 1111–1114, 2014, doi: 10.1109/isbi.2014.6868069.
9. Dabass, M., Vig, R., Vashisth, S., Review of histopathological image segmentation *via* current deep learning approaches. *2018 4th Int. Conf. Comput. Commun. Autom. ICCCA 2018*, pp. 1–6, 2018, doi: 10.1109/CCAA.2018.8777616.
10. Gündüz, K., Albayrak, A., Bilgin, G., Karslıgil, M.E., Histopatolojik Görüntülerde Tümörlü Bölgelerin Evri, simsel Sinir A ˘ glarıyla Sınıflandırılması Classification of Tumor Regions in Histopathological Images Using Convolutional Neural Networks.
11. Richardson, M.J. and Wiltshire, J.D., Processing Techniques. *Hologram*, 117–151, 2017, doi: 10.1002/9781119088929.ch6.
12. Kushwaha, S., Adil, M., Abuzar, M., Nazeer, A., Singh, S.K., Deep learning-based model for breast cancer histopathology image classification. *2021 2nd International Conference on Intelligent Engineering and Management (ICIEM)*, London, United Kingdom, pp. 539–543, 2021, doi: 10.1109/ICIEM51511.2021.9445319.

13. Jahromi, S.A.F., Khani, A.A., Shahreza, H.O., Baghshah, M.S., Behroozi, H., A Deep Learning Framework for Viable Tumor Burden Estimation. *6th Iran. Conf. Signal Process. Intell. Syst. ICSPIS 2020*, 2020, doi: 10.1109/ICSPIS51611.2020.9349569.
14. Jamaluddin, M.F., Fauzi, M.F.A., Abas, F.S., Tumor detection and whole slide classification of H&E lymph node images using convolutional neural network. *Proc. 2017 IEEE Int. Conf. Signal Image Process. Appl. ICSIPA 2017*, pp. 90–95, 2017, doi: 10.1109/ICSIPA.2017.8120585.
15. Corredor, G., Garcia-Arteaga, J.D., Arias, V., Romero, E., Learning basal cell carcinoma patterns by fusing pathologists' wsi navigations and graph-based centrality features. *Proc. - Int. Symp. Biomed. Imaging*, vol. 2019, pp. 910–913, doi: 10.1109/ISBI.2019.8759570.
16. Kanavos, A., Kolovos, E., Papadimitriou, O., Maragoudakis, M., Breast Cancer Classification of Histopathological Images using Deep Convolutional Neural Networks. *2022 7th South-East Europe Design Automation, Computer Engineering, Computer Networks and Social Media Conference (SEEDA-CECNSM)*, Ioannina, Greece, pp. 1–6, 2022, doi: 10.1109/SEEDA-CECNSM57760.2022.9932898.
17. Saric, M., Russo, M., Stella, M., Sikora, M., CNN-based Method for Lung Cancer Detection in Whole Slide Histopathology Images. *2019 4th Int. Conf. Smart Sustain. Technol. Split. 2019*, pp. 14–17, 2019, doi: 10.23919/SpliTech.2019.8783041.
18. Naylor, P., Laé, M., Reyal, F., Walter, T., Segmentation of Nuclei in Histopathology Images by Deep Regression of the Distance Map. *IEEE Trans. Med. Imaging*, 38, 2, 448–459, 2019, doi: 10.1109/TMI.2018.2865709.
19. Vu, Q.D., Kim, K., Kwak, J.T., Unsupervised Tumor Characterization *via* Conditional Generative Adversarial Networks. *IEEE J. Biomed. Heal. Inf.*, 25, 2, 348–357, 2021, doi: 10.1109/JBHI.2020.2993560.
20. Das, K., Conjeti, S., Chatterjee, J., Sheet, D., Detection of Breast Cancer from Whole Slide Histopathological Images Using Deep Multiple Instance CNN. *IEEE Access*, 8, 213502–213511, 2020, doi: 10.1109/ACCESS.2020.3040106.
21. Razavi, S., *et al.*, An Automated and Accurate Methodology to Assess Ki-67 Labeling Index of Immunohistochemical Staining Images of Breast Cancer Tissues. *Int. Conf. Syst. Signals Image Process.*, 2018-June, 2018, doi: 10.1109/IWSSIP.2018.8439184.
22. Yadav, A., Verma, V.K., Pal, V., Jain, V., Garg, V., Automated Detection and Classification of Breast Cancer Tumour Cells using Machine Learning and Deep Learning on Histopathological Images. *2021 6th Int. Conf. Converg. Technol. I2CT 2021*, vol. 1–6, 2021, doi: 10.1109/I2CT51068.2021.9417996.
23. Abdelli, A., Saouli, R., Djemal, K., Youkana, I., Combined Datasets for Breast Cancer Grading Based on Multi-CNN Architectures. *2020 10th Int. Conf. Image Process. Theory, Tools Appl. IPTA 2020*, 2020, doi: 10.1109/IPTA50016.2020.9286653.

24. Sun, Y., *et al.*, Detection of Breast Tumour Tissue Regions in Histopathological Images using Convolutional Neural Networks. *IEEE 3rd Int. Conf. Image Process. Appl. Syst. IPAS 2018*, pp. 98–103, 2018, doi: 10.1109/IPAS.2018.8708869.
25. Shen, Y. and Ke, J., Sampling Based Tumor Recognition in Whole-Slide Histology Image with Deep Learning Approaches. *IEEE/ACM Trans. Comput. Biol. Bioinforma.*, 19, 4, 2431–2441, 2022, doi: 10.1109/TCBB.2021.3062230.
26. Wang, S., Yang, D.M., Rong, R., Zhan, X., Xiao, G., Pathology Image Analysis Using Segmentation Deep Learning Algorithms. *Am. J. Pathol.*, 189, 9, 1686–1698, 2019, doi: 10.1016/j.ajpath.2019.05.007.
27. Qidwai, U. and Sadia, M., Color-based Fuzzy Classifier for automated detection of cancerous cells in histopathological analysis. *IECBES 2014, Conf. Proc. - 2014 IEEE Conf. Biomed. Eng. Sci. "Miri, Where Eng. Med. Biol. Humanit. Meet*, pp. 103–108, 2014, doi: 10.1109/IECBES.2014.7047464.
28. Jannesari, M., *et al.*, Breast Cancer Histopathological Image Classification: A Deep Learning Approach. *Proc. - 2018 IEEE Int. Conf. Bioinforma. Biomed. BIBM 2018*, pp. 2405–2412, 2019, doi: 10.1109/BIBM.2018.8621307.
29. Fukuma, K., Surya Prasath, V.B., Kawanaka, H., Aronow, B.J., Takase, H., A study on feature extraction and disease stage classification for glioma pathology images. *2016 IEEE Int. Conf. Fuzzy Syst. FUZZ-IEEE 2016*, pp. 2150–2156, 2016, doi: 10.1109/FUZZ-IEEE.2016.7737958.
30. Mercan, C., Aksoy, S., Mercan, E., Shapiro, L.G., Weaver, D.L., Elmore, J.G., Multi-Instance Multi-Label Learning for Multi-Class Classification of Whole Slide Breast Histopathology Images. *IEEE Trans. Med. Imaging*, 37, 1, 316–325, 2018, doi: 10.1109/TMI.2017.2758580.
31. Sharma, H., Zerbe, N., Boger, C., Wienert, S., Hellwich, O., Hufnagl, P., A Comparative Study of Cell Nuclei Attributed Relational Graphs for Knowledge Description and Categorization in Histopathological Gastric Cancer Whole Slide Images, 2017-June, 61–66, 2017, doi: 10.1109/CBMS.2017.25.
32. Noorbakhsh, J., *et al.*, Deep learning-based cross-classifications reveal conserved spatial behaviors within tumor histological images. *Nat. Commun.*, 11, 1, 1–14, 2020, doi: 10.1038/s41467-020-20030-5.
33. Krijgsman, D., *et al.*, Quantitative Whole Slide Assessment of Tumor-Infiltrating CD8-Positive Lymphocytes in ER-Positive Breast Cancer in Relation to Clinical Outcome. *IEEE J. Biomed. Heal. Inf.*, 25, 2, 381–392, 2021, doi: 10.1109/JBHI.2020.3003475.
34. Stenman, S., *et al.*, Antibody Supervised Training of a Deep Learning Based Algorithm for Leukocyte Segmentation in Papillary Thyroid Carcinoma. *IEEE J. Biomed. Heal. Inf.*, 25, 2, 422–428, 2021, doi: 10.1109/JBHI.2020.2994970.
35. Ling, M., Lv, G., Wang, J., Hao, X., Shi, J., An, H., Fast whole slide image analysis of cervical cancer using weak annotation. *Proc. - Int. Symp. Biomed. Imaging*, vol. 2021-April, pp. 1037–1041, 2021, doi: 10.1109/ISBI48211.2021.9433964.

36. Siddiqui, F., Gupta, S., Dubey, S., Murtuza, S., Jain, A., Classification and diagnosis of invasive ductal carcinoma using deep learning. *Proc. Conflu. 2020 - 10th Int. Conf. Cloud Comput. Data Sci. Eng*, vol. 242–247, 2020, doi: 10.1109/Confluence47617.2020.9058077.
37. Banaeeyan, R., *et al.*, Tumor budding detection in HE-stained images using deep semantic learning. *IEEE Reg. 10 Annu. Int. Conf. Proceedings/ TENCON*, vol. 2020-November, pp. 52–56, 2020, doi: 10.1109/TENCON 50793.2020.9293732.
38. Sathish Kumar, B.S. and Nagarajan, G., Tomographic Image Reconstruction Using SART Algorithm. *Inderscience Int. J. Med. Eng. Inf.*, 8, 3, 239–248, 2016.
39. Sathish Kumar, B.S. and Nagarajan, G., Image Reconstruction for Tomographic Using Wavelet Transform. *Int. J. Sci. Eng. Res.*, 7, 6, June 2016.
40. Sathish Kumar, B.S. and Nagarajan, G., Performance of Landweber Iteration Algorithm in Tomography Image Reconstruction. *Inderscience Int. J. Image Min.*, 2, 3/4, June 2017.
41. Sathish Kumar, B.S., Nagarajan, G., Elavarasan, P., Image Reconstruction Algorithms for Computer Tomography on Different Projections. *Int. J. Res. Advent Technol. (Special Issue) E-ISSN 2321-9637*, 7, 6, 66–70, October 2018.
42. Sathish Kumar, B.S. and Nagarajan, G., An Efficient Algorithm for Computer Tomography in Low Radiation Images. *Adv. Modell. Anal. B*, 61, 4, 189–197, December 2018.
43. Monika, S. and Nagarajan, G., An exploration of state of art on various tumor detection in histopathological image using deep learning techniques, in: *International Conference on Advances in Engineering and Web of Things-ICAEWoT*, National Institute of Computing, Bangalore, 4th December 2022.
44. Monika, S., Nagarajan, G., Sathish Kumar, B.S., An Extensive Survey on Various Tumor Detection in Histopathological Images using Deep Learning Techniques. *2nd International Conference on Emerging Trends in Engineering (ICETE 2023)*, University College of Engineering, Osmania University, Hyderabad, India, 2023.
45. DeVito, N., Henderson, E., Han, G., Reed, D., Bui, M.M., Clinical Characteristics and Outcomes for Solitary Fibrous Tumor (SFT): A Single Centre Experience. *PLoS One*, Public Library of Science, San Francisco, USA, 2015.
46. Qaiser, T., Tsang, Y.W., Taniyama, D., Sakamoto, N., Nakane, K., Epstein, D., Rajpoot, N., Fast and Accurate Segmentation of Histology Images Using Persistent Homology and Deep Convolutional Features. *Med. Image Anal.*, Elsevier, Amsterdam, Netherlands, 2019.
47. Subramanian, M., Bagwari, A., Ganesan, N., Detection of Breast Tumour from Histopathological Images using Recurrent Neural Network. *2nd International Conference on Wireless Technologies, Networks and Science-2024 (ICWTNS-2024)*, National University Mayor de San Marcos, Peru and

Advanced and Innovative Research Laboratory, Dehradun, India, 11th -12th MAY 2024.

48. Monika, S., Nagarajan, G., Sathish Kumar, B.S., An Extensive Survey on Various Tumor Detection in Histopathological Images using Deep Learning Techniques, in: *Advances in Engineering Research*, vol. AER 223, pp. 105–118, Journal, Springer Nature ICETE 2023, Hyderabad, 2023, ISSN 2352-5401, ISBN 978-94-6463-252-1, https://doi.org/10.2991/978-94-6463-252-1_13.
49. Babenko, B., Dollár, P., Tu, Z., Belongie, S., Simultaneous learning and alignment: Multi-instance and multi-pose learning, in: *Proc. Workshop Faces Real-Life Images, Detection, Alignment, Recognit*, pp. 1–15, 2008.
50. Zhou, Z.-H., Sun, Y.-Y., Li, Y.-F., Multi-instance learning by treating instances as non-I.I.D. samples, in: *Proc. 26th Annu. Int. Conf. Mach. Learn. (ICML)*, pp. 1249–1256, 2009.
51. Zhang, Q. and Goldman, S.A., EM-DD: An improved multiple-instance learning technique, in: *Proc. Adv. Neural Inf. Process. Syst.*, pp. 1073–1080, 2002.
52. Andrews, S., Tsochantaridis, I., Hofmann, T., Support vector machines for multiple-instance learning, in: *Proc. Adv. Neural Inf. Process. Syst.*, pp. 577–584, 2003.
53. Wang, J. and Zucker, J.-D., Solving multiple-instance problem: A lazy learning approach, in: *Proc. 17th Int. Conf. Mach. Learn.*, Morgan Kaufmann, San Francisco, CA, USA, pp. 1119–1125, 2000.
54. Rubner, Y., Tomasi, C., Guibas, L.J., The earth mover's distance as a metric for image retrieval. *Int. J. Comput. Vis.*, 40, 2, 99–121, Nov. 2000.
55. Wu, J., Yu, Y., Huang, C., Yu, K., Deep multiple instance learning for image classification and auto-annotation, in: *Proc. IEEE Conf. Comput. Vis. Pattern Recognit. (CVPR)*, pp. 3460–3469, Jun. 2015.

10

Compact MIMO Patch Antenna Design for 6G-Enabled Internet of Medical Things Operating within the IoT Ecosystem

Janani P.* and Koushick Venkatesh

Vel Tech Rangarajan Dr. Sagunthala R & D Institute of Science and Tehchnology, Chennai, Tamil Nadu, India

Abstract

In the upcoming era of IoT, the Internet of Medical Things (IoMT) is bringing about a transformation in the medical technology industry by connecting various medical devices, wearables, and health applications. The use of this innovation makes it possible to perform continuous health monitoring, instantaneous data transfer, and individualized patient treatment, which ultimately leads to improved outcomes and an increase in the effectiveness of healthcare delivery. The Internet of Medical Things (IoMT) has an impact on a variety of fields, including hospitals, clinics, home healthcare, and medical research, which helps to create a healthcare environment that is more interconnected and responsive. The relevance of IoMT in modern healthcare is emphasized in this essay, which also provides an illustration of how connection encourages innovation and improves patient care. Key areas like remote patient monitoring and advanced diagnostics benefit from IoMT, offering practical insights on incorporating IoMT solutions into healthcare practices. The rapid adoption of 6G networks necessitates the use of 6G antennas for wearable and wireless communication in IoMT and other medical technologies. Integrating 6G antennas with the Internet of Medical Things (IoMT) necessitates the development of a communication system that utilizes the high-speed, low-latency, and extensive connectivity attributes of 6G to improve medical device networking. This research introduces a MIMO antenna designed to operate within the 6 GHz to 12 GHz frequency range. The proposed antenna is compact (20x20x0.8 mm) with a return loss below -10 dB and a VSWR below 2 dB across

**Corresponding author*: jananisasikumar2701@gmail.com

T. Perarasi, M. Karthiga, S. Sountharrajan, E. Suganya and Balamurugan Balusamy (eds.) Secure Blockchain and Quantum Technologies for 6G-Enabled Internet of Things, (225–256) © 2026 Scrivener Publishing LLC

most of the band. With a 5 dBi gain and consistent omnidirectional radiation patterns, it ensures reliable wireless coverage both indoors and outdoors enabling a high impact in remote patient monitoring. The design is highly suitable for wearable and wireless IoMT devices.

Keywords: IoMT, healthcare, 6G, short-range communication, MIMO antenna, wireless IoMT, ECC

10.1 Introduction

Over the course of the last few decades, the development of wireless communication has been regularly regarded as one of the most successful technological achievements in the history of the world. At this same moment, there are five distinct wireless communication networks that have been put into operation. Since its introduction in 1980, a new generation has developed practically every decade since then. Its initial appearance was in 1980. When wireless devices were first introduced, they were a monopoly (1G), then they became a successful attractiveness spectacle (2G), and then they became popular with 3G. When it comes to services, 1G and 2G were only capable of providing phone service, and they gradually increased the amount of data they contained (on 3G, they were unsuccessful, but on 4G, they were successful). Applications like multimedia, services for multiplayer play, and streaming video in high definition are included in this category. As a direct result of this, there has been a significant increase in both the number of people using wireless devices and the amount of data traffic [1]. At the commencement of 2020, the total number of individuals subscribed to cellular devices reached 7.75 billion, with each user averaging a request of 10 gigabytes of data annually with their membership. Data traffic per user per year is projected to reach 82 gigabytes due to unprecedented demand for streaming video content. This augmentation will represent almost fifty percent of the global wireless data flow. The extensive use of (IoT) Internet of Things will eventually elevate network traffic volume. A remarkable increase in the volume of traffic results in a significant expansion of the capabilities of wireless networks. The development of 5G wireless networks is being helped along by these issues, which are major motivators.

ITU, which is an acronym that stands for the International Telecommmunication Union, is the institution that is responsible for developing the standards and its vision. It is expected that 5G would be able to meet eight key performance indicators (KPI) as well as three common situations [2]. Massive machine challenge technology is examined in three situations involving air interface delays of milliseconds (ms), enhanced mobile broadband (eMBB) data speeds of gigabits per second (Gb/s), and massive machine-type communication (mMTC). These key performance indicators (KPIs) have been accomplished through the development of a wide variety of enabling technologies, which have been reviewed during the standardization process and put into practice in technical trials [3]. Among the various types of wireless technology, some examples are millimeter-wave communications and ultra-dense networks (UDNs), flexible frame structures, dual connectivity designs, non-orthogonal multiple access, simple coding and modulation, and huge multiple input multiple output (MIMO) [4, 5].

Conversely, the proliferation of interconnected devices—which may reach hundreds of devices per cubic meter—may be associated with the exponential expansion of data traffic. The exponential growth of data transmission can be attributed to this factor. Data will be required to provide lower and higher latency than 5G networks, in addition to an increasing number of creative applications like integrated three-dimensional communications, self-driving cars, virtual reality (VR), and augmented reality (AR) [6]. The utilization of virtual reality (VR) and augmented reality (AR) exemplifies such applications. Many feel that the advancement of 6G communication technology has been motivated by the necessity to resolve these difficulties, with implementation expected in 2030 [7, 8]. With that being said, these enhancements and additions are going to be implemented to achieve these objectives through the provision of assistance for the Internet of Things, as well as through the provision of complete assistance for the proliferation of smart life and the industrial ubiquitous smart society.

Wireless communication technology has progressed dramatically over the years. The 4G infrastructure must evolve to accommodate the growing demands of users, advancing to a 5G system. The implementation of additional frequency bands greatly exceeds the Microwave frequency bands utilized for 3G and 4G. This study focusses on the advancement of 6G antennas for millimeter-wave frequency ranges. Considering 24 GHz and 100 G, researchers specializing in mm-wave 6G antennas frequently design antennas for 5G devices or base stations/access points. The subsequent antennas are meticulously designed to function independently without human oversight. When it comes to mm-wave 5G applications, the massive MIMO and beamforming antenna arrangement is considered to be the most preferred antenna structure. Several factors contribute to this, including the low cost, the ease of production, the simplicity of integration, and the lightweight properties. To the greatest possible extent, regardless of whether or not dual-band technology exists, designs are categorized as either circularly polarized or dual polarized; the critical edges of the antenna typically determine the bandwidth of the antenna, and the gain value is quite modest in single-element designs. Through the utilization of a MIMO antenna that achieves a return loss of less than -10dB over the frequency range of 6GHz to 12GHz, this study tackles the problems that were previously described. Furthermore, this surpasses the current state-of-the-art requirements by achieving a broad bandwidth that is greater than 6.5GHz. In addition to that, the gain can range anywhere from 5 to 8.6 dBi. A tiny antenna like this one is suited for use in healthcare equipment, especially wearables. Specifically, [9], connecting various medical equipment to create the Internet of Medical Things (IoMT) is one of the ways that the Internet of Things (IoT) is revolutionizing the healthcare industry.

Among the many applications that may be found in the field of healthcare, the Internet of Medical Things (IoMT) include health and wellness, remote patient monitoring, telemedicine, diagnostics, robotics, diabetes control, and drug delivery. Significant progress has been made in wireless communication across a variety of domains with the introduction of 6G technology. It provides enhanced speeds relative to existing wireless networks in hospitals, enabling real-time patient monitoring. The platform supports several users and enables swift downloads, allowing for the quick transfer of huge image files and the performance of data analytics. Moreover, remote and robot-assisted operations will have less latency, hence improving their accessibility. The desire for technologies that are portable and wearable, in addition to those that are equipped with remote patient monitoring equipment linked to the(IoT), has surged notably, particularly during the outbreak of the COVID-19 virus. It makes it possible to monitor patients indirectly and minimizes the amount of direct interaction that occurs between healthcare workers and patients, which in turn helps to reduce the spread of viruses. The rapid growth of remote therapy is causing a great deal of concern because it will lead to a rise in the utilization of wearable medical equipment, in particular for patients who are afflicted with chronic disorders such as diabetes and cardiovascular illnesses. Within the context of the internet of medical things (IoMT) sector, wireless wearables are now being developed [10].

In medical devices, sensors are used in vast cases such as glucose sensors, which are used to monitor and control the levels of glucose in the blood of diabetic patients. Individuals make use of electrocardiogram (ECG) sensors in conjunction with blood pressure monitoring devices to record the electrical activity of the heart for the purpose of identifying any cardiac rhythms that are not typical. The use of optical sensors is another

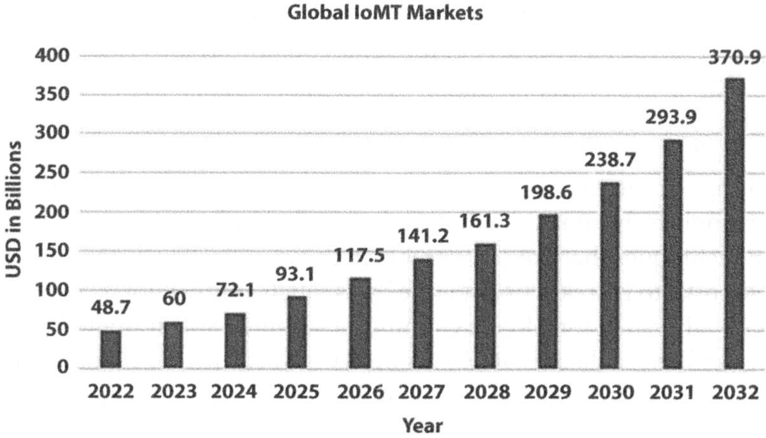

Figure 10.1 Growth stages of IoMT in global market.

option for determining the amount of oxygen present in the environment. Infrared (IR) sensors, piezo film sensors, ultrasonic sensors, and haptic sensors are all examples of sensors, and a number of other types of sensors are included in the category of temperature sensors that monitor blood saturation (SpO2).These gadgets provide healthcare professionals with signals that are vital to their work. Despite the fact that this technology is accessible through 4G networks, it comes with limits in terms of both the speed and capacity of the network. As a consequence of this, there is a growing need for 5G and the next 6G technologies, which are intended to improve and progress devices within the Internet of Things and machines industry. The projected aim here is to acquire recommendations that are appropriate, accurate, and succinct by doing an in-depth examination of disputed research subjects across a number of subfields. Figure 10.1 illustrates the current growth of IoMT in the global markets.

10.2 Evolution Stages of 1G to 6G

First-generation wireless communications were released in the 1970s.1G technology is an analogue system that can carry data at 2.4 kbps. It was made for voice communication. The thirty-kilohertz system uses FM and FDMA to communicate On the other hand, there are a number of challenges that are connected to 1G, including the following: i) The utilization of analogue modulation, signifying inadequate encryption, inferior quality, and compromised security; ii) The implementation of FDMA technology, leading to a restricted user base; iii) The use of base station power radiation that is not secure and the lack of transmission protocols; iv) The restriction of services to voice applications alone, and v) the presence of heterogeneous systems resulting from the lack of standardized international protocols [11–13]. It is considered to be 2.5G for GPRS. The technologies of packet switching and circuit switching that are made available by GSM are utilized to accomplish this goal. Furthermore, it utilizes transmission and modulation techniques that are comparable to those utilized by GSM, which has the potential to increase its data rate by as much as fifty kilobits per second. The Global System for Mobile Communications (GSM) framework, which enables enhanced data (EDGE), begins with GPRS. Before 3G data transfer, EDGE radio technology was invented. Users can transmit data at 200 kbps. This is the top speed. Gaussian Minimum Shift Keying (GMSK) and eight phase-shift keying (8PSK) modulate EDGE instead of GSM. This contradicts the GSM standard. The GSM standard underpins EDGE, which uses the same transmission mechanism and bandwidth. GMSK is reliable and has wide coverage, while 8PSK can achieve a faster data rate but has less coverage. GMSK is a robust model that provides comprehensive coverage all over the world. The purpose of developing this method was to enhance the services of packet switching and to make it easier to implement future applications, such as multimedia, utilizing high-speed data [14].

The third-generation (3G) system makes use of technologies such as wideband code division multiple access (WCDMA) and high-speed packet access (HSPA) to provide customers with a speedy internet connection and significantly improved capabilities for the transmission of audio and video over the internet. Within the HSPA framework, there are two mobile protocols that are part of the package. Both high-speed downlink packet access (HSDPA) and high-speed uplink packet access (HSUPA) are examples of these types of protocols. Using the WCDMA protocol, the objective of High-Speed Packet Access (HSPA) is to enhance the performance of third-generation (3G) networks. The High-Speed Internet Protocol (HSP) standard, which is often referred to as HSPA+, is another version of the third generation partnership project (3GPP) standard that is considered to be among the most sophisticated variants. The year 2008 came to a close with its introduction, and the year 2010 marked the beginning of its implementation in every region of the world. Furthermore, 3.9G long-term evolution (LTE) offers characteristics that are superior to those that are observed in traditional 3G communications [15]. These features are going to be discussed in further depth in the following section, which can be found here. The organization known as the International Telecommunication Union (ITU) and the Third Generation Partnership Project (3GPP) came to the conclusion that the technology known as LTE is capable of meeting the requirements for 4G technology [16].

LTE also known as 4G (Fourth generation), is the name given to the technology that was developed to make wireless access possible. OFDM, which stands for orthogonal frequency division multiplexing, is the foundation upon which this technique is built. Optical frequency division multiplexing (OFDM) offers complex multi-antenna transmission and allows for transmission bandwidths that can be extended up to 20 MHz. Enhanced data rates and simultaneous stream delivery are both made possible by the Multiple MIMO is a significant system technique. It allows simultaneous transmission of many streams, which optimizes spectrum efficiency, the quality of the connection, as well as the radiation patterns for the purpose of signal transmission and reduction. The antenna creates the interference array using adaptive beamforming. LTE technology can transfer data at 100 Mbps. In response to the growing annual demand for gigabits per second broadband communication capacity, the wireless technology roadmap now includes LTE Advanced (LTEA).This was executed to meet the increasing demand for capacity. LTEA may theoretically attain a peak throughput rate exceeding one gigabit per second upon implementation. The 4G system enhances the current communication network by providing a solution that is both comprehensive and reliable. This is achieved by providing information. The Internet Protocol (IP) is the method through which this is achieved. The wireless community has conducted a comprehensive examination of three principal research issues to enhance the capabilities of 4G networks [17].

This method increases network density in crowded places like public arenas and retail malls stadiums, concerts, and other public venues. This technique makes use of cells that are compact, low-power, and inexpensive in order to accomplish the goal of shortening the distance that separates terminals and base stations (BS). Because of this, there will be an increase in the quantity of spectrum that is reused, as well as an increase in the amount of network coverage. Both the conservation of energy and the signal interference plus noise ratio (SINR) are improved as a result of the tiny base station's coverage radius, which ranges from fifty to one hundred and fifty meters, and its broadcasting power, which is only 0.110 watts. A coverage radius is provided by the base station as a result of low-loss routing. When it comes to small base stations, operators want to make them plug-and-play so that they can adjust all of the critical parameters without having to perform maintenance [18]. Recent years have seen tremendous advancements in wireless communications. Improving spectral efficiency can be accomplished by the implementation of coordinated transmit/

receive technologies and solutions that lessen the amount of interference seen between cells. Co-channel interference can be reduced and spectrum efficiency can be increased by the utilization of these approaches and solutions, which make use of recent developments in signal processing and spatial variety. Within the Long-Term Evolution (LTE), carrier aggregation is employed to assist the expansion of bandwidth (up to 100 MHz) by aggregating individual component carriers. These carriers might be of varying sizes and are located in a spectrum that is not contiguous. Although the combined implementation of these technologies has the potential to theoretically supply fixed clients with data rates that are higher than one gigabit per second, further expansion is restricted due to the limited number of frequencies that are available [19]. The standardization of communication for 5G networks has been finalized, and the global implementation of these networks is presently underway [20]. The International Telecommunication Union (ITU) is tasked for establishing the vision and requirements for 5G. 5G is anticipated to fulfil eight essential performance indicators (KPIs) and three prevalent scenarios [21]. Significant machine challenge technology is investigated in three separate scenarios: improved Mobile Broadband (eMBB) with gigabit per second (Gb/s) data rates, URLLC with millisecond (ms) air interface delays, and comprehensive machine challenge technology in any one of these three diverse settings. For the purpose of communication indication, the mMTC service must be utilized. Under three distinct circumstances, technological advancements come into contact with enormous pieces of machinery. To accomplish these key performance indicators (KPIs), a large number of enabling technologies have been developed, taken into consideration throughout the process of standardization, and implemented during the phase of technical testing. Microwave communications, non-orthogonal multiple access, dual connection architecture, massive MIMO, universal domain network (UDN), advanced coding and modulation, millimeter-wave communications, and flexible frame structure are all examples of technologies that fall under the category of wireless technologies. The fundamental structure that underpins the 5G network is made up of a number of components that are dispersed across a wide area. All around the region, these components can be found in various locations. There are three components that are included in this group. These components are the next generation core (NGC), the multi-access edge computing (MEC) data center, and the 5G NR active antenna system (AAS) [22].

The 5G Advanced Access System (AAS) provider provides the telecommunication network. Edge computing needs cohesive technology integration. NGPON, CWDM, DWDM, and eCPRI are examples of these technologies It is necessary to have a fiber optic infrastructure that is compatible with the techniques in order to put any of these strategies into action. To meet the infrastructure requirements for 5G networks [23], which demand a substantial amount of capacity and speed, it is required to install fiber optic cable to the antenna. This is a requirement that must be met. Because of this, it is important to create the 5G network at a site that is as close to the antennas of the fiber infrastructure as is practically practicable. Additionally, in order to accommodate extra antennas during times when capacity is insufficient, it is necessary to install new infrastructure that is comprised of fiber optic cables [24]. Furthermore, as a consequence of the significant rise in the number of things that are associated with one another, the data flow has expanded exponentially, which can cause the number of devices per cubic meter to increase to hundreds. Data rates will still be necessary for these newly developed applications [25]. On the other hand, in comparison to 5G networks, it will have latency that is both higher and lower. There is a widespread belief that these challenges are the key driving forces that will ultimately result in the commercialization of 6G communication technologies. There have been efforts made by research institutes, academic institutions, and businesses to identify and describe the major qualifying technologies that can define 6G. These efforts have been made. Sixth-generation wireless technology is expected to be operational by the year 2030 [26].

10.3 6G Medical Improvements that 5G Wouldn't be Able to Do!

6G technology has the potential to significantly improve the way in which healthcare providers are able to perform their jobs. This is due to the fact that it will enable a larger range than the 5G technology that is currently available. The introduction of holographic interactions between medical experts and patients is one example of how 6G technology can be used to take telemedical consultations to the next level. In addition to this, it could make it possible for surgeons to carry out surgeries either in person or remotely, with the assistance of holographic reconstructions of the patient's anatomy. Secondly, the high-speed data transfer and low-latency characteristics of 6G can make it easier to establish personalized treatment plans that are tailored to the specific genetic makeup of the patient. This can be accomplished through the rapid analysis of enormous datasets. Advanced sensing and imaging technologies that are available on 6G networks could be of assistance in the early diagnosis of malignant growths through the use of increased, high-resolution 3D imaging that is performed in real time. On the other hand, this may increase the likelihood that a patient would respond favorably to treatment. Additionally, the technology will make it possible for surgeons to carry out delicate treatments with complete precision, with the assistance of high-definition pictures that are displayed in real time. This will result in improved outcomes and a reduction in the dangers that are connected with conventional surgical procedures. It is anticipated that 6G antennas will operate in a wider range of frequency bands than 5G antennas, and they will also have fewer delays in network transmission. This will be beneficial for the healthcare industry. Considering that the existing capability of data sharing with 5G is only effective for short ranges, the possibility of 6G could expand this range, making it possible for surgeons to perform remote procedures from a wider distance and allowing them to operate more efficiently. In this manner, 6G could make it possible to achieve better outcomes for patients, improve the capabilities of remote healthcare, and user in a new era of digital health technologies. The most important areas of expansion that could be made possible by 6G technologies are those that concern the enhancement of communication and collaboration. The combination of artificial intelligence with sixth-generation wireless networks could make it possible for medical personnel, including researchers, to communicate ideas and information more quickly and efficiently, regardless of their location. This would involve the accessing of patient data as well as the sharing of research findings and any other significant information may be available. As was noted, the ability of 6G to examine vast volumes of data, when combined with artificial intelligence, might free up valuable time for medical experts. This would enable them to recognize trends and anticipate potential health problems and consequences. In addition to this, it will enable the sharing of data in real time, which will enable staff members to make critical decisions in a timely and secure manner.

The implementation of 6G antennas in the medical business holds the potential to bring about major improvements in the processes of providing medical care and managing patients. Data Transmission at High Speed: Allow for the interchange of vast amounts of data, such as high-resolution imaging (for example, MRI and CT scans) or real-time video streaming for the purpose of remote diagnostics and surgical procedures. Enable real-time control for applications such as robot-assisted surgeries and emergency telemedicine consultations by utilizing low-latency communication. Connecting thousands of internet of medical things (IoMT) devices in hospitals, such as patient monitoring, smart beds, and wearables, in a seamless manner offers massive connectivity. Utilizing the centimeter- or millimeter-level positioning capabilities of 6G, precise localization can be utilized for the purpose of tracking assets (such as medical equipment) and monitoring patients in real time. Energy Efficiency and Miniaturization: Encourage the development of designs that are energy-efficient for wearables, implants, and portable diagnostic instruments.

10.4 Future Holds for Wireless Communication Networks with 6G Capability

Building upon the visualization and extension of 5G, 6G will be enhanced to provide data speeds up to 100 times faster, increased system space, diminished suspension, enhanced use of radio spectrum, and expanded more comprehensive scope. The realization of these objectives will occur through the achievement of improved spectrum efficiency. The implementation of 5G will enable the achievement of these significant breakthroughs. This project aims to accomplish the following objectives: enhancing rapid mobility; advancing the Internet of Everything (IoE); and thoroughly fostering the evolution of intelligent living and a ubiquitous intelligent mobile society inside the industry. The sixth-generation wireless network is anticipated. (G6) will be an all-encompassing network that spans a wider range of coverage. This network will include terrestrial, satellite, and short-distance communication between devices. As a result of the fact that 6G is capable of covering a wide range of scenarios, such as those involving aircraft, land, and sea, it has the potential to become the first broadband communication system that is omnipresent across the whole world [27].

6G, is expected to function at elevated frequencies, including millimeter-wave, terahertz, and visible light frequencies, to achieve enhanced bandwidth. Consequently, this would make it possible to achieve the highest potential data rate of one terabit per second (Tb/s), as well as a data rate of ten gigabits per second (Gb/s) for the user experience. Additionally, 6G is able to make use of flexible frequency-sharing technology, which can enable an even bigger increase in the efficiency of frequency reuse [28]. This capacity is a significant advantage of 6G.

The 6G network is a sophisticated architecture that can be adapted to meet the specific needs of individual users according to their preferences. It is anticipated that this network would transition from a conventional centralized architecture to a brand new type 3 centralized network that places an emphasis on the requirements of users, data, and is exclusively centered on centralized content. This transition will take place shortly. The amalgamation of artificial intelligence technologies with 6G will facilitate the virtualization of communication. The 6G network will utilize either a native security solution or an integrated functional security architecture to guarantee its safety and convenience. The 6G infrastructure comprises various features. These talents include self-awareness, real-time dynamic evaluation, risk adjustment, and confidence appraisal. You will facilitate cybersecurity by executing trust and security protocols [29].

A platform that integrates computational, navigational, and detection functionalities is termed 6G. A diverse array of products will be incorporated into the sixth generation of wireless technology. Examples of these things include radar detection systems, positioning systems, satellite navigation, and satellite communication systems. It will accomplish rapid autonomous intelligent development in conjunction with the rapid and dynamic deployment of network capabilities. A core network that makes use of software-defined algorithms will be incorporated into the design of 6G, which will also include a wireless access network that has a more open architecture. Due to the fact that this is the case, these goals will be attainable. There is a possibility that the Internet of Things will generate a significant amount of data, and 6G can be integrated with other developing technologies such as edge computing, cloud computing, artificial intelligence, and blockchain. All of these ideas are feasible. In addition to facilitating group intelligence, the sixth-generation wireless network is also capable of attaining numerous forms of intelligence [30].

10.5 IoMT vs IoT in Healthcare

Internet of Medical Things (IoMT) technologies represent a specific category within Internet of Things (IoT) technology. These technologies encompass applications and devices that are interconnected and utilized in the domain of medical and healthcare information technology. IoMT devices facilitate connections among patients, healthcare workers, and medical equipment by transmitting data *via* a secure network. This encompasses diagnostic instruments, medical apparatus, and wearable technologies [31]. Similar to conventional IoT, the IoMT, or Healthcare IoT, employs automation, sensors, and machine intelligence to diminish dependence on human intervention in standard healthcare procedures and monitoring activities. The IoMT diminishes the necessity for superfluous medical consultations by improving access to healthcare information. This is achieved by furnishing patients and professionals with more accurate information. The IoMT assists consumers and healthcare providers in reducing their expenses [32].

Telehealth and telemedicine will continue to revolutionize healthcare as the Internet of Medical Things (IoMT) business continues to develop. These technologies will make it possible for consumers and providers to receive more thorough and accurate diagnoses, receive care more quickly, and save money. The implementation of IoMT requires overcoming a number of challenges, the most prominent of which are concerns around privacy and security. Because of the tight controls that are placed on medical data, in particular, in compliance with the Health Insurance Portability and Accountability Act (HIPAA), providers are under a significant obligation to safeguard the privacy and authenticity of the data. The introduction of Internet of Medical Things (IoMT) devices into the environment raises a variety of concerns with regard to their potential impact, most of which are caused by the considerable amount of data that is transferred between patients and clinicians [33]. Interoperability and standards represent additional challenges encountered by IoMT suppliers. In an optimal scenario, healthcare IoT devices from a single vendor would integrate flawlessly with the infrastructure of another vendor; however, this has not occurred, and consistent standards have remained elusive [34]. Despite the emergence of certain certification systems, the industry remains far distant from achieving universal compatibility.

10.6 Challenges in Implementing IoMT

A persistent challenge — may be the most complex to address — is the incapacity to upgrade IoMT devices. Although IoMT devices are cutting-edge upon debut, upgrading or updating them with new capabilities might prove challenging once they are deployed in the field. Consumers are disinclined to annually upgrade their wearable or connected gadgets, and hospitals typically exhibit a sluggishness in deploying costly new technology, leading to a heterogeneous array of products with varying functionalities in the market. Upgrades provide a greater issue with implanted devices, such as surgically inserted pacemakers [35]. IoT has developed into a large category that encompasses approximately 7 billion different items. Some examples of these items are connected thermostats, smart refrigerators, robotic factory equipment, and smart autos. Because it is a subset of, IoMT is quite similar to the latter category in many respects. Although many IoMT technologies in the healthcare industry are solely medical in nature, such as robotic surgical assistants, many IoMT devices can also be categorized under the more general category of Internet of Things (IoT) [36]. The ability of a smartwatch to assess blood oxygen levels and pulse rate, which is obviously an Internet of Medical Things feature, also allows it to act as a standard consumer gadget that can receive text messages, provide navigational instructions, and perform other similar duties. The quantity of interconnected medical gadgets is anticipated to persist in its growth [37].

As IoT technology progresses, providers will incorporate these enhancements into IoMT devices and networks. Sensor technology is anticipated to progress, yielding enhanced and superior real-time data. Simultaneously, AI-driven data analytics and machine learning will enhance predictive healthcare [38]. Healthcare data created by IoMT will facilitate enhanced research and foster opportunities for novel treatments. IoMT devices possess the capability to streamline medical management, save expenses, and enhance data sharing and collaboration among healthcare entities [39].

10.7 Importance of IoMT in Antenna

The Internet of Things (IoMT) would be unable to communicate and share data if it did not have antennae. Both in the field of biomedical applications and in the field of medical devices, antennas play an essential role because they are responsible for conveying vital information that is obtained from within a living species. High-functioning antennas make it possible for carers and parents to monitor the blood sugar levels of younger diabetic children. Additionally, a Telehealth booth may communicate a patient's vitals to a doctor located hundreds of miles away. All of these things are made possible by satellite technology. In the worlds of the Internet of Medical Things (IoMT) and the Internet of Things (IoT), on-body MIMO antennas have found important applications [40]. These antennas are essential for applications ranging from wireless communication to continuous health monitoring in a variety of disciplines. In particular, wearable antennas that are connected with Internet of Medical Things-based Wireless Body Area Networks (WBANs) make it possible to maintain uninterrupted on/off-body communication connection. Furthermore, flexible MIMO antennas that are built for Internet of Things applications have a strong performance in bending and on-body situations, which makes them acceptable for wearable devices . Furthermore, MIMO antenna arrays that are based on metasurface technology are utilized in wireless body area networks and biomedical telemetry devices. These arrays offer increased isolation between radiators and enhanced radiation characteristics. The importance of on-body MIMO antennas in developing healthcare monitoring and

Internet of Things connectivity is highlighted by the variety of applications used for these antennas [41].

10.7.1 Why MIMO Antenna for IoMT Applications

Particularly as we progress beyond the 5G network, recent advancements in Increasing the use of MIMO antenna technology, which stands for multiple input multiple outputs, is essential to the development of wireless communication. Specifically, this is due to the fact that MIMO antennas enable simultaneous inputs and outputs from various sources [42]. These are among the most significant developments. These innovations promise to bring about considerable increases in data rates, reliability, and traffic management [43].

10.7.2 Importance of MIMO Technologies

Cell-Free Massive MIMO: This technique does away with the requirement for conventional cell structures, which enables uniform coverage and enhanced spectral efficiency across extremely vast areas. This technique, known as Beamspace Massive MIMO, takes advantage of spatial multiplexing to steer beams toward users, thereby increasing capacity and decreasing interference, particularly in densely populated metropolitan locations. These are: Surfaces that are capable of manipulating wireless signals in order to maximize coverage and capacity—referred to as intelligent reflecting surfaces. These surfaces function as programmable reflectors to improve signal quality [44].

Printed Multi-Band MIMO Antennas: Recent designs have begun to concentrate on compact multi-band systems that are able to sustain performance across a wide range of frequencies. This is done to address size limits in current devices.

Isolation Structures: Recent advancements in antenna design, including as proximity-coupled and slot antennas, have improved isolation and performance. These advancements have enabled high port isolation and good impedance matching to be achieved.

To revolutionize wireless communication, advancements in MIMO antenna technology have been made. These advancements have improved overall performance, increased capacity, and increased data transfer rates. Multi-input multiple-output (MIMO) systems make use of numerous antennas located at both the giving and receiving ends of the transmission, which results in a significant increase in both efficiency and throughput. Researchers have been concentrating their efforts on enhancing the design of MIMO antennas to attain better gains, lower error rates, and stable radiation characteristics. This enhancement has resulted in enhanced data rates and improved channel capacity. To improve isolation in MIMO antennas, which is essential for optimizing data speed and transmission channel capacity, various strategies have been developed. One of these strategies involves the utilization of metal strips to install stubs in the ground. The development of high-speed broadband wireless networks has been made possible by these developments in MIMO antenna technology, which have made them an essential component in the progression towards 5G and beyond [45].

10.8 Proposed Design Considerations of the Antenna

The proposed configuration was modeled utilizing ADS EM Simulator 2020. Figure 10.2 illustrates the proposed 6G antenna, characterized as a dual-band, highly decoupled, and compact microstrip patch co-planar waveguide (CPW)-fed MIMO antenna. The quad-element circular printed antenna, built on a widely used FR4 substrate of dimensions 20×20 mm^2, features a ground plane on the upper side of the substrate, measuring $P2 \times Q2$ mm^2, to aid in antenna fabrication [33]. The proposed antenna is situated above the altered circular radius R1 and consists of a feeding element with dimensions $P4 \times Q4$ mm^2 and a truncated rectangular element measuring $P3 \times Q3$ mm^2. To attain optimal isolation and a diverse array of patterns, each antenna is intentionally located in one of the four corners of the substrate; the exact construction specs, encompassing dimensions. These measurements are fixed and immutable, determined through parametric analysis utilizing the ADS EM-simulator.

The reflection and transmission coefficients for antennas one to four—each antenna component in the MIMO system encompasses a dual-band frequency spectrum, with each band covering frequencies from 6.25 GHz to 11.8 GHz as shown in the Figure 10.3. To attain isolation of up to 12.5 dB across antenna systems, it is necessary to position each antenna orthogonally. The primary significant aspect is that it does not require the decoupling operation, which is an additional advantage of orthogonal placement [46].

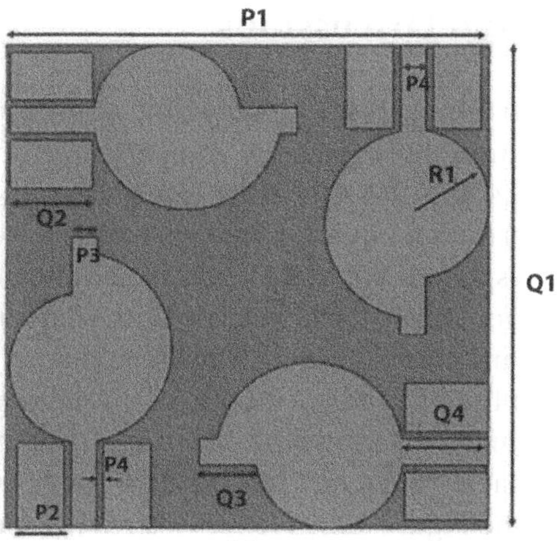

(a)

Parameters	P1	Q1	P2	Q2	P3	Q3	P4	Q4
Values (mm)	20	20	1.98	3.47	1.05	2.35	1.05	3.58

(b)

Figure 10.2 (a) The proposed antenna's structure and dimensions are described. (b) The parameters of the proposed antenna are measured.

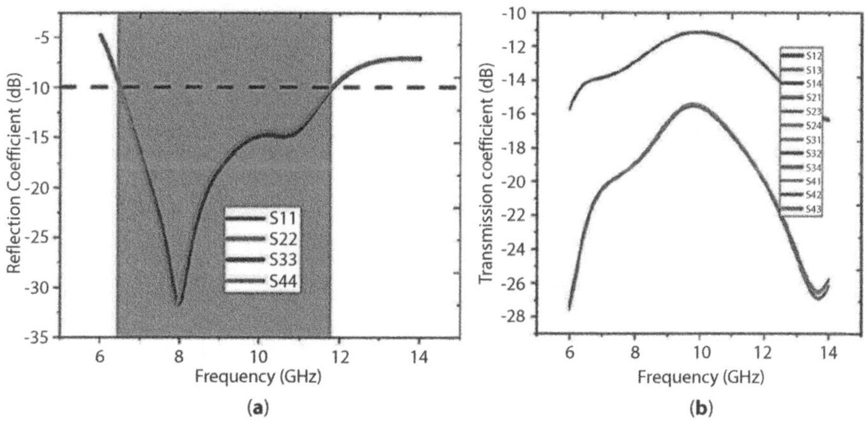

Figure 10.3 (a) Reflection coefficient. (b) Transmission coefficient of the proposed antenna.

10.9 Results and Discussions

To improve the performance the bandwidth and impedance matching marks the strip of dimesions (P4XQ4) mm which is designed at the top measuirng 1.97 to 3.47mm as showin the Figure 10.4. The Figures 10.4 (a), 10.4 (b) and 10.4 (c) are said to be altered where the lower band responses and higher band responses are mainly restrained. Figure 10.5 where the surface current demonstrates the behaviour of the antenna at 5.5 GHz and 6.5 GHz while the antenna is excited. Thus resulting in enhanced performance. The Figures 10.6 (a) and (b) illustrates the antennas cross polarization which is less than 30 dB across the operating frequency bands. Overall which every acceptable frequency has an ECC value which is less than 0.035 as shown in the Figure 10.7. Hence this results conclude the overall performance is good enough for the IoMT applications providing a MIMO

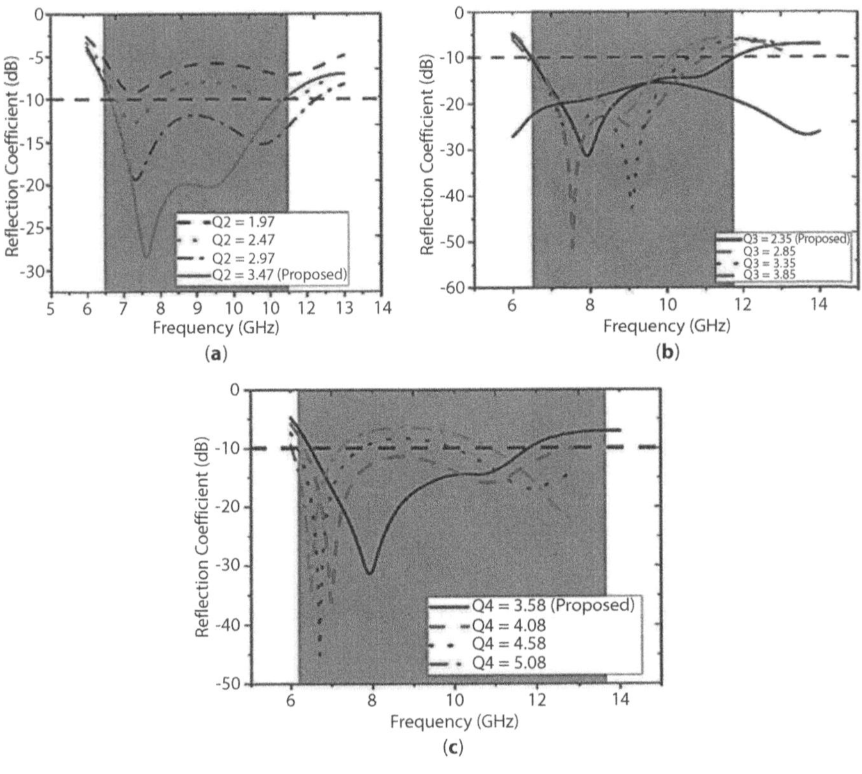

Figure 10.4 Study of the proposed antenna from a parametric perspective when it is changed (a) Q2, (b) Q3, (c) Q4.

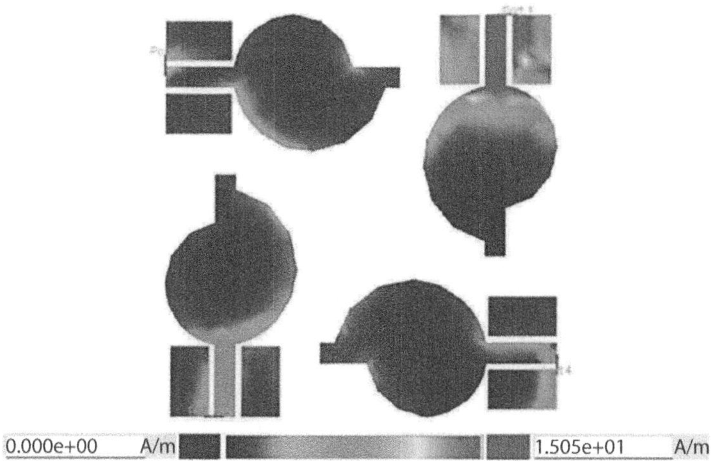

Figure 10.5 Distribution of Surface current of Antenna 1 at (a) 5.5 GHz, (b) 6.5 GHz.

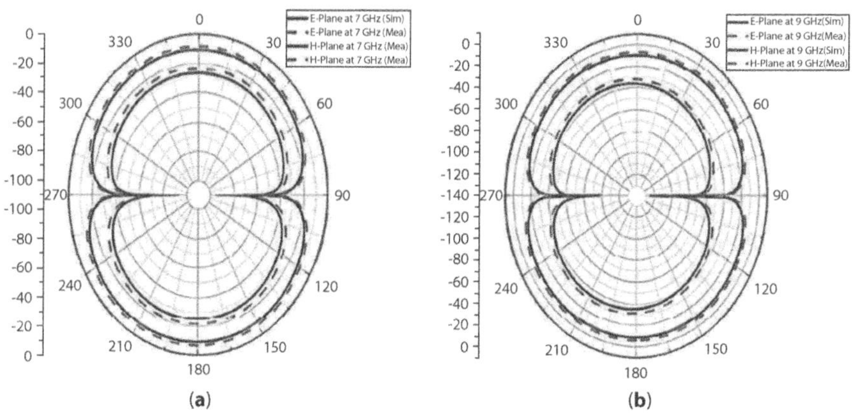

Figure 10.6 Two-dimensional pattern of radiation of Antenna 1.

antenna that can help improve the signal-to-noise ration (SNR) of the system for the given single antenna system.

10.10 Conclusion

A unique 6G MIMO antenna was developed and tested for use in the IoMT for the purpose of wireless communication and wearable medical devices using wireless technology. It has been demonstrated that the suggested

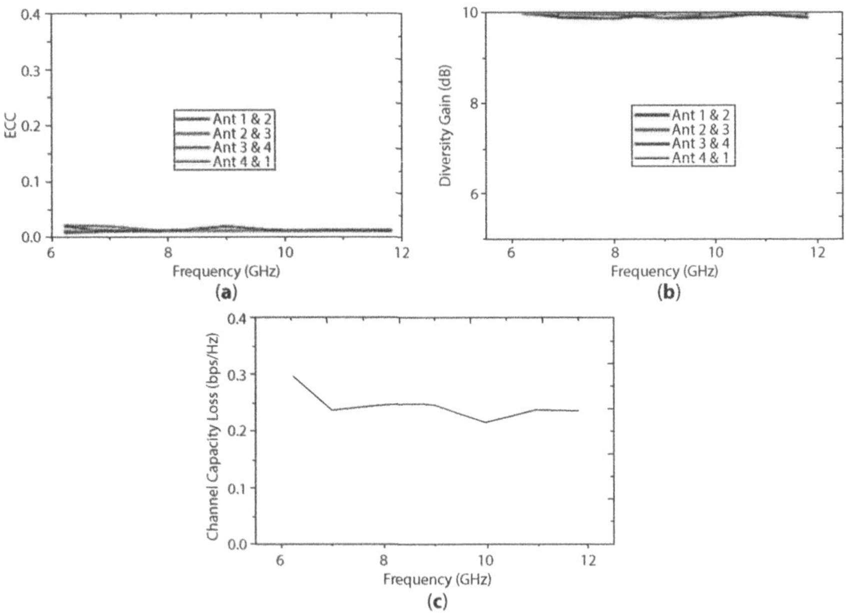

Figure 10.7 MIMO parameters (a) ECC, (b) diversity gain, (c) CCL.

antenna is extraordinarily broad, with a return loss of less than -10dB spanning the frequency range of 6GHz to 12GHz. Additionally, the antenna is exceptionally compact. This particular band is the one that is most suitable for the antenna that is used in applications that take advantage of 6G. It was established that the value increased with frequency, and this was followed by slight changes in the pattern of the far-field radiation. There is no doubt that these features are appealing for proposals in IoMT sector and wireless communication in general. IoMT is a significant improvement in the technology of medical devices that has the potential to completely alter the landscape of healthcare. As a result of technology improvements and an increasing level of acceptance, improving patient care, operational efficiency, and medical research are all areas that will benefit from IoMT. A healthcare ecosystem that is more interconnected, efficient, and centered on the patient will be made possible as a result of this. There is cause to be positive about the future of IoMT, which will usher in a new era of healthcare that is more intelligent, sensitive, and individualized than it has ever been before. This is a significant advancement in the field of healthcare.

10.10.1 6G Implementation in Rural Areas

There is a growing digital divide as a result of the fact that rural and remote locations in many parts of the world do not have enough connectivity. These regions may have low population density, a low average income, challenging terrain, or non-existent infrastructure, such as a power grid, which makes them less desirable locations for investment and for the operation of connectivity networks. It is possible that the sixth generation of mobile radio was the first generation to fully try to close the digital divide. However, in order to accomplish this, it is necessary to take into consideration the unique requirements and difficulties that arise from the very beginning of the design process. Because fifty percent of the world's population still does not have access to the internet or does not have adequate internet connectivity, connecting those who are not connected is a tremendous task. A low level of wealth, a low population density in the living region, or a lack of infrastructure such as roads or electrical grids are some of the causes for this. As a result of these features, as well as others, network, infrastructure, and service providers are less interested in investing in these locations because the revenues that are anticipated to be generated are relatively low. The digital divide, which is at the heart of our 6G network, is a problem that is always growing, and 6G will be a part of the solution that is needed to fix it. We are of the opinion that 6G has the potential to be the first data-driven standard in which the unconnected are taken into consideration from the very beginning. Moreover, this concept must be applied to places that are geographically isolated and rural as well. When spectrum is distributed across the country, it is not always utilized in an effective manner at the local level. This mismatch is especially problematic for rural and remote areas, which are more susceptible to its negative effects. It appears that a separate rural/remote mode is required to ensure that adequate services can be provided while maintaining the solutions' economic viability. Additionally, in many locations, it is necessary to have a low energy consumption in local relay and base stations in order to enable operations that are powered by solar panels. In addition, the installation and maintenance duties that are primarily autonomous are also another key component. These possibilities include terrestrial, air, space, power grid, optical, and other options. They require the addition of terrestrial fiber networks and maritime cables in order to be improved. It is also important to remember that air and sea routes, which also require connectivity in remote areas, should not be forgotten.

It is necessary for the many parties to work together in order to efficiently address the 6G complex connection issue. Those who make decisions at the political level are required to make adjustments and provide direction to regulations and rules, in addition to providing the necessary financial assistance. On the other side, regulators play a crucial part in ensuring that spectrum is used in a reasonable manner, while 6G network connection providers are able to deliver the essential infrastructure and services. The residents of the area need to be seamlessly integrated in order to not only communicate their connectivity requirements but also to acquire and implement new technology of 6G. Moreover, the provision of the digital services that are so desperately required in the future 6G systems requires the participation of local governance, healthcare, and suitable education. This will result in an increase in the value of better connectivity of 6G.In addition to this, it is essential to have an understanding of the local culture and to make certain that the community is participating and has faith in those who provide 6G connectivity services in the society of the future. It is especially true in the developing world that this is the case. The design of a 6G network should therefore take into consideration new key performance indicators (KPIs) that reflect the increase in economic growth, education, health, gender equality, digital literacy, happiness index, and other factors in unserved or under-served remote and rural areas. These KPIs should be considered in addition to the technology KPIs such as bandwidth, latency, jitter, security, and resilience.

10.10.2 Support of AI towards 6G in the Era of Healthcare

The junction of artificial intelligence and sixth-generation wireless networks symbolizes two cutting-edge technologies that are going to completely transform the landscape of wireless communication. The ability of artificial intelligence to do data analysis and decision-making in real time is a useful complement to the high-speed, low-latency network that 6G offers. This complementation enables connectivity that is not only more intelligent but also more efficient. To improve network speed, reliability, and energy efficiency, artificial intelligence makes it possible for 6G networks to optimize themselves in real time.

It makes it possible to do predictive maintenance, intelligent resource allocation, and tailored user experiences, thereby establishing the framework for a communication ecology that is highly flexible. Furthermore, artificial intelligence has the ability to enable a feature that would fundamentally revolutionize the game, and that feature is virtualization. This process has already begun with 5G, with certain components of the radio, like base stations, going to the cloud. It is true that this particular trend has already begun. The virtualization of additional components of the network, such as power amplifiers and antennas, will necessitate a significantly higher amount of power and artificial intelligence capabilities. Increases in virtualization will allow us to unleash the full potential of future 6G networks, allowing us to make more efficient use of spectrum while simultaneously reducing costs. In the future, the virtualization of a significant portion of base band processing is currently taking place. Consequently, this results in the dis-aggregation of the base station, which in turn leads to the requirement for common architectural boundaries and standardized interfaces across the base stations. When it comes to ensuring that 6G is flexible, this trend will increase. By automating and improving network operations and management, the use of artificial intelligence into 6G technology considerably accelerates the implementation of this technology. This synergy makes it possible for predictive analytics to detect and fix network problems before they create a disruption in service, which ultimately results in an improvement in the dependability and performance of 6G networks. On the other hand, the intricacy of combining AI with 6G presents a number of significant obstacles. To guarantee that these technologies are able to work together without any problems, it is necessary to make a significant investment in research and development. Additionally, it is necessary to adhere to security and privacy requirements in order to safeguard user information. The incorporation of artificial intelligence is a double-edged sword that highlights the importance of developing creative solutions and exercising careful control in the development of 6G. It is anticipated that the introduction of 6G technology, which will be supported by artificial intelligence (AI), would bring in a new wave of apps and services, thereby expanding the boundaries of what is possible in the category of digital connectivity. Sixth-generation, will develop new solutions across a wide range of industries, ranging from the improvement of everyday comforts to the resolution of complex industrial challenges. Let's have a look at some of the cutting-edge applications and services that artificial intelligence, which will be enabled by 6G technology, will be able to sustain, which will represent a big leap forward in our technical capabilities:

The Concept of Autonomous Systems

By processing huge volumes of data in real time, 6G networks that are powered by artificial intelligence will make it possible for more advanced autonomous cars and drones to operate. These networks will also make navigation and operation safer and more reliable. How are they going to accomplish this? The capacities of decision-making will be considerably improved by artificial intelligence, which will also enable real-time data processing and further improve operational efficiency. The use of artificial intelligence enables these systems to learn and adapt to their surroundings through the use of sophisticated algorithms and machine learning. This ultimately results in autonomous vehicles and drones that are safer and more reliable. It will be essential to undergo this change in order to successfully navigate complicated scenarios and optimize performance across various applications.

Cities that are Smart

Through the optimization of infrastructure management, the enhancement of public services, and the improvement of sustainability, artificial intelligence will revolutionize smart cities. These capabilities are achieved through the analysis of huge data sets. The result is that urban living becomes more efficient, the impact on the environment is decreased, and the quality of life for people is better. This is because cities become more sensitive to the demands and challenges of their residents.

The Provision of Healthcare

With the assistance of 6G, artificial intelligence will revolutionize the delivery of healthcare, including tele-medicine, by making it possible to conduct more precise tests, develop individualized treatment plans, and monitor patients in real time. The precision, minimal latency, and sensing capabilities of this technology make it possible to perform surgery remotely. The predictive analytic capabilities of AI can help anticipate health problems before they become critical, which enables preventative care to be administered. Consequently, it is hoped that this integration would make healthcare more accessible, efficient, and personalized to the specific requirements of individual patients. This will result in a significant improvement in both the outcomes and the experiences of patients.

Automation of Industrial Processes

The incorporation of artificial intelligence and sixth-generation wireless networks into industrial automation will usher in a substantial revolution in factories that are intelligent. The utilization of real-time data analysis will be utilized by this combination to enhance the efficiency of manufacturing and carry out predictive maintenance, which will ultimately result in a reduction in downtime and an increase in output. The capacity of artificial intelligence to handle large volumes of data in a short amount of time, in conjunction with the high-speed communication capabilities of 6G, will make it possible for factories to quickly adapt to changes, optimize operations, and anticipate breakdowns in machinery.

Realities that are AR & VR

The integration of artificial intelligence with sixth-generation wireless networks will yield significant improvements in virtual and augmented reality (VR and AR), therefore enhancing the impressiveness and interactivity of experiences. This technology will facilitate the possibility to generate high-definition, complicated virtual environments in real time without experiencing any lag, which will help improve applications in the gaming industry, as well as education and professional training.

In the Direction of a Future that Incorporates Both 6G and AI

Imagine a future in which artificial intelligence and wireless technology of the sixth generation are seamlessly merged, resulting in an environment in which digital connectivity is as natural and vital as the oxygen that we breathe. There has been progress made in every facet of our day-to-day existence in this globe, from the manner in which we work and learn the manner in which we take care of our health and navigate the streets of urban areas. Industry is attaining levels of automation and productivity that have never been seen before; intelligent cities are becoming more effective and responsive, healthcare is undergoing a change with tailored and easily available services, and industries are achieving levels of automation and productivity that have never been recorded before. Through the use of virtual and augmented realities, our experiences are elevated to a higher level of immersion, which in turn makes them more interesting to us. It is projected that this future, which will be powered by the combination of 6G and AI, would bring about a jump towards a society that is more connected, intelligent, and innovative. This is according to the predictions that have been made.

Case Study: Antennas in Wireless Capsule Endoscopy (WCE)

In the beginning within the field of Gastroenterology, the non-invasive diagnostic technology known as wireless capsule endoscopy (WCE) is utilized frequently. Through the process of swallowing a small capsule that contains a camera, sensors, and antennae for wireless connection, the experiment is carried out. The detection of illnesses that affect the gastrointestinal (GI) tract has been completely transformed by the technology.

Attributes of the Antenna Design in WCE that are Key

A capsule with dimensions of around 11 millimeters by 26 millimeters necessitates an antenna design that is extremely small in size. A few examples of common antenna designs are the mono-pole, patch, and helical design. Frequency Band: Operates in the Industrial, Scientific, and Medical (ISM) band, often 433 MHz, 868 MHz, or 2.4 GHz for the purpose of transmitting data with minimal power consumption and great efficiency. Impedance matching is a technique that is designed to ensure that signals are transferred effectively between the capsule and the receiver. Taking into account the material: In order to avoid any unfavorable responses within the human body, antennas are constructed using materials that are bio compatible.

Implementations in the Medical Field
The diagnostic system has real-time imaging capabilities, enabling the detection of ulcers, polyps, bleeding, and tumor. In contrast to conventional endoscopies, this method is non-invasive and does not require the patient to undergo anaesthesia. One of the capabilities of monitoring is the ability to incorporate physiological sensors, such as temperature, pH, and pressure.

The Obstacles
Attenuation of the Signal: The human body is capable of both absorbing and scattering transmissions, particularly in the GHz range. The positioning and orientation of the antenna are optimized to overcome this issue.
Efficient use of power: Low-power antennas ensure that the capsule's battery can continue to supply power for an extended period of time.
Reliability of the Data: It is necessary to have a reliable transmission to a worn receiver, regardless of any movement or interference.

The Influence on Healthcare
Improved accessibility allows for the early diagnosis of gastrointestinal (GI) disorders without the need for hospital stay. Improvements in outcomes include the provision of comprehensive imaging, which enhances diagnostic accuracy. Efficiency in terms of cost is achieved by reducing the need for repeated intrusive operations. This particular scenario illustrates how antenna technology has greatly improved the delivery of healthcare, notably in the diagnostics sector. Integration of artificial intelligence for data processing and multi-frequency antennas for increased resolution and usefulness are two examples of future technological breakthroughs.

10.11 Strengthening Cybersecurity over 6G Antenna

Building and maintaining a strong cyber security infrastructure is of utmost importance in the current digital environment, where cyber-attacks are becoming more complex. The implementation of MIMO antennas can considerably improve network security, in contrast to the usual security techniques that concentrate on software and encryption. As a result of its potential to improve the speed and reliability of wireless communication, MIMO technology is a key component for the protection of digital transactions. This technology makes use of multiple antennas to send and receive data through wireless networks. To improve the efficiency of communication, MIMO technology deploys multiple antennas at both the transmitter and receiver ends of the communication chain. By simultaneously delivering several data streams, MIMO reduces the number of mistakes that occur, maximizes the speed at which data is transmitted, and increases the capacity of radio transmission. In order to improve throughput and reliability, this technology makes use of spatial multiplexing and diversity techniques. As a result, it has become an essential component of contemporary wireless communication systems, including Wi-Fi networks, 4G and 5G cellular systems, and smart home devices.

The Contribution of MIMO to the Improvement of Cyber security

By incorporating MIMO technology into your network, you may greatly improve the rates at which data is transmitted and the reliability of the network. MIMO makes a contribution to cyber security in the following ways:

Increased Data Throughput: several Input Multiple Output (MIMO) increases the amount of data that can be broadcast and received simultaneously by utilizing several antennas that operate together. This leads in communication that is both quicker and more efficient, even in contexts that have a high level of interference or high levels of signal degradation.

Enhanced Encryption Capabilities: The higher data throughput that is made possible by MIMO makes it possible to use encryption algorithms that are more complicated, which makes it more difficult for cyber criminals to break into your network. A more robust encryption method results in a more secure delivery of data.

Techniques Used for Beamforming: The beamforming capabilities of MIMO direct the signal directly towards the receiver that is intended to receive it, thereby reducing the likelihood of signal interception and eavesdropping. These focused approaches make it substantially more difficult for unauthorized individuals to gain access.

The Advantages of MIMO for Information Security

1. ***Improved Network Performance:*** MIMO technology enhances the performance of networks and increases their speed by simultaneously managing numerous data streams.

Communication is improved in terms of clarity and dependability as a result of its ability to reduce the impact of noise and interference.

2. ***Robust Signal Processing:*** MIMO systems are able to discern between interference and relevant information, which improves the clarity of communication. In overcrowded areas, where signal interference is widespread, this is very helpful because it eliminates the problem.
3. ***Advanced Monitoring Capabilities:*** The capability of MIMO to analyze various data streams and patterns enables the detection of malicious activity to occur more quickly and with greater precision. This is a significant improvement to the system's capability of recognizing and responding to possible dangers. It is essential to use MIMO technology to maintain a solid cyber security profile. This technology improves data transmission, lowers the risk of signal interception, and offers comprehensive protection for a variety of applications. Maintaining an awareness of the latest developments in MIMO technology and proactively incorporating these solutions into your network architecture can considerably strengthen your defense against cyber-attacks. It is necessary to make use of MIMO technology in order to improve network security in this day and age, when data breaches and cyber-attacks are becoming more sophisticated. There is a significant contribution that MIMO makes to the protection of digital transactions. It does this by enhancing the efficiency of data transmission, the capacities of encryption, and the general performance of the network. Maintain a competitive advantage by gaining a grasp of the advantages and difficulties associated with MIMO technology and using it into your overall cyber security plan.

10.12 Future Scope of IoMT Applications

AI and ML Integration: When it comes to the future of the internet of medical things (IoMT), artificial intelligence (AI) and machine learning (ML) enhance predictive analytics, implement personalized patient care, and automate decision-making procedures. Artificial intelligence will make it possible to make more precise diagnoses, monitor patients' health in real time, and preemptively maintain innovative medical equipment.

Advanced wearables and implantables: In the future generation of wearable and implantable technology, the accuracy will be even higher, the battery life will be longer, and the usefulness will be increased. Not only will these devices monitor fundamental vital signs, but they will also monitor complex biomarkers and provide feedback in real time to both patients and medical professionals.
Statistical AI: The analysis of large volumes of data, often known as big data otherwise called as Statistical AI that are produced by (IoT) devices will be exploited through the application of advanced big data analytics. Consequently, this will provide essential insights on the changes in population health, sickness patterns, and treatment outcomes, paving the way for future advancements in healthcare systems.
Cross-industry collaboration: IoMT will continue to develop, which will result in increased collaboration between insurance firms, healthcare providers, technology companies, and regulatory authorities which are all included in this category. Due to these relationships, innovation will be sparked, interoperability will be promoted, and it will be ensured that solutions for the Internet of Medical Things are safe, effective, and widely accepted.

AI disclosure statement: The author acknowledges the use of AI-based tools for minor language editing or grammatical correction. However, all intellectual contributions, analyses, and conclusions presented in this chapter are entirely the author's own.

References

1. Blika, A., *et al.*, Federated Learning For Enhanced Cybersecurity and Trustworthiness in 5G and 6G Networks: A Comprehensive Survey. *IEEE (OJ-COMS)*, 2024.
2. Yin, S., *et al.*, An anomaly detection model based on deep auto-encoder and capsule graph convolution *via* sparrow search algorithm in 6G internet-of-everything. *IEEE Internet Things J.*, 2024.
3. Marasco, I., *et al.*, Design and fabrication of a plastic-free antenna on a sustainable chitosan substrate. *IEEE Electron. Device Lett.*, 44, 2, 341–344, 2022.
4. Ji, B., *et al.*, IRS-driven cybersecurity of healthcare cyber physical systems. *IEEE Trans. Netw. Sci. Eng.*, 10, 5, 2564–2573, 2022.
5. Wagih, M., *et al.*, Guest Editorial: *Antenna-Enabled Sensors and Systems, the New Frontier in Sustainable Wireless Systems. IEEE Open J. Antennas Propag.*, 5, 5, 1136–1139, 2024.
6. Falcone, F., *et al.*, Editorial Special Article Collection on Antennas and Propagation for Emerging 5G/6G Communications. *IEEE Trans. Antennas Propag.*, 72, 8, 6173–6176, 2024.

7. Dash, S.P., *et al.*, A cybertwin-based 6G cooperative IoE communication network: Secrecy outage analysis. *IEEE Trans. Ind. Inf.*, 18, 7, 4922–4932, 2022.
8. Dhiman, G., *et al.*, Cybertwin-driven 6G for Internet of Everything: Architectures, challenges, and industrial applications. *IEEE Trans. Ind. Inf.*, 18, 7, 4846–4849, 2022.
9. Ishteyaq, I., *et al.*, Unleashing the Power of Tomorrow: Exploration of Next Frontier with 6G Networks and Cutting Edge Technologies. *IEEE Access*, 2024.
10. Giuliano, R., From 5G-Advanced to 6G in 2030: New Services, 3GPP Advances and Enabling Technologies. *IEEE Access*, 2024.
11. Tyagi, V., *et al.*, Load Balancing in SDN-Enabled WSNs Toward 6G IoE: Partial Cluster Migration Approach. *IEEE Internet Things J.*, 2024.
12. Gopikrishnan, *et al.*, CyTFS: Cyber-Twin Fog System for Delay Efficient Task Offloading in 6G Mobile Networks. *IEEE Internet Things J.*, 2024.
13. Xu, X., *et al.*, Exploration of the principle of 6G communication technology and its development prospect, in: *2022 (ICEDCS)*, 2022, September, IEEE, pp. 100–103.
14. Xia, X., 6G Satellite Communication: Key Technologies, Challenges and Trends. *2024 (IWCMC)*, pp. 703–705, 2024.
15. Anitha, C., *et al.*, Recent developments, application cases, and lingering issues on the path to a 6G IoT, in: *2023 (RMKMATE)*, 2023, November, IEEE, pp. 1–10.
16. Bhatia, S., *et al.*, The Future IoT: The current generation 5G and next generation 6G and 7G technologies, in: *2023, (DICCT)*, 2023, March, IEEE, pp. 212–217.
17. Shakhatreh, H., *et al.*, Utilizing Partial Non-Orthogonal Multiple Access (P-NOMA) in Drone-enabled Internet-of-Things Wireless Networks. *IEEE OJVT*, 2024.
18. Kohli, P., *et al.*, Secured authentication schemes of 6G driven vehicular communication network in industry 5.0 Internet-of-Everything (IoE) applications: Challenges and opportunities, in: *2022 (ICMNWC)*, 2022, December, IEEE, pp. 1–5.
19. Saxena, A., *et al.*, Navigating of 6G Network into the Latest AI Technology for the Fastest Communication Without Loosing the Data, in: *2024 (ICACITE)*, 2024, May, IEEE, pp. 145–150.
20. Kohli, P., *et al.*, Secured privacy preserving techniques analysis of 6G driven vehicular communication network in industry 5.0 Internet-of-Everything (IoE) applications, in: *2022 (SMART GENCON)*, 2022, December, IEEE, pp. 1–8.
21. Sasikumar, J. and Koushick, V., Performance analysis of complementary split ring resonator with improved four element antenna for X band wireless applications. *Prog. Electromagn. Res. M.*, 130, 95–102, 2024.

22. Kong, D., *et al.*, Advancing Towards 6G: Challenges, Key Technologies, and Applications of the Internet-of-Intelligent-Things, in: *2023 (ICCC)*, 2023, December, IEEE, pp. 1059–1065.
23. Kitanov, S. and Nikolikj, V., The Role of Edge Artificial Intelligence in 6G Networks, in: *2022 57th (ICEST)*, 2022, June, IEEE, pp. 1–4.
24. Nassa, V.K., *et al.*, Sensor-Based Networks and the Internet of an Everything Solutions and Difficulties, in: *2023 IEEE (ICTBIG)*, 2023, December, IEEE, pp. 1–6.
25. Brahmi, R., *et al.*, Elaboration of Innovative Digital Twin Models for Healthcare Monitoring With 6G Functionalities. *IEEE Access*, 2024.
26. Mahmood, A., *et al.*, Analysis of Terahertz (THz) Frequency Propagation and Link Design for Federated Learning in 6G Wireless Systems. *IEEE Access*, 2024.
27. Sharma, B., *et al.*, Integration of AI, Digital Twin and Internet of Medical Things (IoMT) For Healthcare 5.0: A Bibliometric Analysis, in: *2023 (ICAICCIT)*, 2023, November, IEEE, pp. 1313–1318.
28. Mallick, S.R., *et al.*, Adoption of blockchain-fog-iomt framework in healthcare 4.0 digital revolution, in: *2022 (OCIT)*, 2022, December, IEEE, pp. 603–608.
29. Sachin, D.N., *et al.*, Fedcure: A heterogeneity-aware personalized federated learning framework for intelligent healthcare applications in iomt environments. *IEEE Access*, 2024.
30. Alawadhi, A., *et al.*, Towards edge computing for 6G Internet of everything: challenges and opportunities, in: *2023 1st (ICAISC)*, 2023, January, IEEE, pp. 1–6.
31. Shivagangatharani, B. and Rabiya, M.S., Enabling Technologies in IoMT Smart Healthcare: A Survey, in: *2024 10th (ICCSP)*, 2024, April, IEEE, pp. 665–670.
32. Goel, A. and Neduncheliyan, S., Health Monitoring and Diagnostic Platform Based on AI and IoMT Sensors: An Overview of Methodologies and Challenges, in: *2024 1st (ICTEST)*, 2024, April, IEEE, pp. 1–5.
33. Yuan, X., *et al.*, A DQN-based frame aggregation and task offloading approach for edge-enabled IoMT. *IEEE Trans. Netw. Sci. Eng.*, 10, 3, 1339–1351, 2022.
34. Jiang, F., *et al.*, Double DQN Based Associative Tasks Computing Offloading Scheme for Internet of Medical Things, in: *2023 IEEE 34th Annual International Symposium on Personal, Indoor and Mobile Radio Communications (PIMRC)*, 2023, September, IEEE, pp. 1–6.
35. Alawadhi, A., *et al.*, Deep learning techniques in mobile edge computing for Internet of medical things, in: *2023 3rd International Conference on Emerging Smart Technologies and Applications (eSmarTA)*, 2023, October, IEEE, pp. 1–6.
36. Omkar, J., *et al.*, The Use of 6G Communication Technology in Healthcare Applications for the Accurate and Better Transmission, in: *2024 4th*

International Conference on Advance Computing and Innovative Technologies in Engineering (ICACITE), 2024, May, IEEE, pp. 1993–1999.

37. William, M., *et al.*, Enabling communication and networking technologies for 6G in healthcare sector, in: *2023 Second International Conference On Smart Technologies For Smart Nation (SmartTechCon)*, 2023, August, IEEE, pp. 699–704.
38. Karak, A., *et al.*, 6G: Enabling the Future of Healthcare Delivery, in: *2024 IEEE International Conference on Information Technology, Electronics and Intelligent Communication Systems (ICITEICS)*, 2024, June, IEEE, pp. 1–7.
39. Jebri, S., *et al.*, Data Security and Anonymous Mutual Authentication in 6G/ IoT Healthcare System: Emergency Case, in: *2023 International Wireless Communications and Mobile Computing (IWCMC)*, 2023, June, IEEE, pp. 1082–1087.
40. Segun, A. and Telukdarie, A., Revolutionizing healthcare delivery through wireless wearable antenna frameworks: Current trends and future prospects. *IEEE Access*, 11, 80327–80347, 2023.
41. Zhang, C., *et al.*, A Miniaturized Wearable Annular Slot Antenna based on Designer LSPs for Telemedicine Communication. *IEEE Trans. Antennas Propag.*, 2024.
42. Nour-El Aine, Y. and Leghris, C., IoMT based Embedded Systems for healthcare: A Confidentiality and Privacy Approach throught Key Generation and Steganography, in: *2024 (ICCSC)*, 2024, June, IEEE, pp. 1–6.
43. Ni, W., Ao, *et al.*, FedSL: Federated Split Learning for Collaborative Healthcare Analytics on Resource-Constrained Wearable IoMT Devices. *IEEE Internet Things J.*, 2024.
44. Matre, P.V., *et al.*, 6G Enabled Smart IoT in Healthcare System: Prospect, Issues and Study Areas, in: *2023 International Conference on Artificial Intelligence for Innovations in Healthcare Industries (ICAIIHI)*, 2023, December, vol. 1, IEEE, pp. 1–6.
45. Kaliwo, A. and Nyirenda, C., Enhancing Digital Health in 6G Networks: A Cybertwin-driven Fuzzy Approach to Medical Traffic Identification and Classification, in: *2023 International Conference on Electrical, Communication and Computer Engineering (ICECCE)*, 2023, December, IEEE, pp. 1–8.
46. Majeed, F., *et al.*, ISA: Internet of Medical Things (IoMT) in Smart Healthcare and its Applications: A Review, in: *2023 3rd (ICAI)*, 2023, February, IEEE, pp. 129–135.

11

Quantum-Secure Blockchain: Revolutionizing Security for the 6G IoT

Parthasarathi P.[1]*, Nivedha S.[2], Krishnamoorthy V.[3] and Priyanga M. A.[1]

[1]*Department of Computer Science and Engineering, Bannari Amman Institute of Technology, Sathyamangalam, Tamilnadu, India*

[2]*Department of Information Technology, Bannari Amman Institute of Technology, Sathyamangalam, Tamilnadu, India*

[3]*Department of CSE, Sri Venkateswara College of Engineering, Sriperumbudur, Chennai, Tamilnadu, India*

Abstract

Combining blockchain technologies and quantum computing gives a transforming power to enhance security and scalability in 6G IoT systems. It is, therefore, imperative for large IoT device networks to take immediate security measures on the progression towards the next generation of linked systems. Today, existing blockchain implementations are insecure since cryptographic methods that rely on inverting difficult mathematical problems are easily solvable with the help of quantum computers. This chapter considers the subject of security challenges and directions in handling them with quantum-safe encryption and blockchain technology in our new quantum environment. In a manner based on the quantum mechanics, quantum computing performs calculations unimaginable for the conventional computers with references to superposition and entanglement. Classical cryptographic systems used in blockchain are at risk as the world moves toward quantum technology; hence, demand for quantum-safe cryptographic algorithms is realized. Blockchain is defined as a distributed, transparent, and most importantly, immutable-characterized framework that could provide a good foundation for IoTs network security. But if it is to last for the coming quantum age there is more to it; that is, it should be using quantum-safe encryption. It covers field of quantum-safe cryptography which includes hash-based cryptography, code-based cryptography and lattice-based cryptography. The chapter also explores the

**Corresponding author*: parthasarathip@bitsathy.ac.in

T. Perarasi, M. Karthiga, S. Sountharrajan, E. Suganya and Balamurugan Balusamy (eds.) Secure Blockchain and Quantum Technologies for 6G-Enabled Internet of Things, (257–298) © 2026 Scrivener Publishing LLC

use of QKD in enhancing secure communication among the blockchain systems. In addition, the chapter describes the pathway to enhance the research, prototype development, pilot adoption and widespread deployment of quantum-safe blockchain solutions. This chapter offers an adequate understanding of the current security scenario of the 6G IoT networks, which highlights the paramount role of the quantum-secure blockchain systems through the integration of quantum computing and blockchain. This might also be the case in a day where IoT devices and transactions on them will be virtually at scale and secure under quantum-susceptible solutions.

***Keywords*:** Quantum computing, blockchain, quantum-safe cryptography, 6G IoT, quantum key distribution (QKD), lattice-based cryptography, secure communication

11.1 Introduction

11.1.1 Overview of 6G and IoT

As wireless technology continues to revolutionize, the sixth generation (6G) of communication networks begins to be readied, expected to provide transforming capabilities much over what is achievable with 5G. The 6G will be designed to deliver ultra-fast data throughput, near zero latency and zero distance connectivity across an enormous diversity of devices, and will become an indispensable element for next generation applications such as holographic communications, the real time digital twin and AI enabled automation across industries [1]. At the core of this revolution is the internet of things (IoT), an ecosystem of linked devices that create, exchange, and process significant, real time generated data [2]. The spread of IoT presents businesses in smart cities, transportation, manufacturing, and healthcare with great possibilities, but also introduces some new security problems. IoT networks are massive in size and connected in their nature, and they are very vulnerable to cyberattacks; and therefore, very strong systems are required to protect the privacy, data integrity, and device authentication [3].

One of the most urgent issues of the 6G enabled IoT systems development is the development of quantum computing, that can compromise traditional cryptographic techniques used for protecting sensitive transactions and communications. Today's encryption methods, from RSA to ECC, rely on problems that have no solution today, using conventional computers. However, if the penetration of quantum computers deep into the network occurs, with sufficiently strong quantum computers, it will make current encryption techniques useless and open IoT networks and blockchain transactions to hitherto unheard hazards [4].

11.1.2 Challenges in Securing 6G IoT Networks

Some new business security challenges came from the combination of the IoT and 6G.

- For doorways – there are just six, but for connectivity – one, virtually limitless number of doors to access connectivity on 6G. There are many avenues that the outsiders can claim control of. Since IoT devices are often limited in resources, they can be taken advantage of. They are less likely to leave themselves exposed than mainframes and big machines, and also function as faucets through which a consistent stream of viruses can flow into the network, able to do more than bring down servers, but entire networks [5].
- As the IoT devices generate increasing amounts of data, it becomes even more critical to protect sensitive information from those who are unauthorized to access and modify it. What a network running in real time needs is not what conventional security systems are able to provide.
- Apart from the great burden 6G causes on system latency and processing speed to provide quick response from the network, these heights may be considered as excellent spots for pickup by hackers [6]. The communication can be a safety threat in real time.
- 6G networks are promiscuous—think of a network slicing and edge computing—that introduces additional intricate security needs that change network topologies. It takes a very long time to build up these multi-layered defenses and future minutes will consist an hour or more [7].

11.1.3 Role of Blockchain in Enhancing IoT Security

The blockchain technology has grown really fast to be one of the pillar answers to many security concerns of internet of things (IoT) systems. Some unique qualities make it sure that the IoT networks do not get into a compromised state of integrity, confidentiality and availability:

- Decentralization: One of the distinguished virtues of blockchain is the distributed character/decentralization. The great thing about Blockchain is that it slashes (almost out) the risk of data lying at a single point, as the data gets segregated across networks of node thereby making a central authority obsolete. This is especially important in IoT systems in which chassis is more likely to bottleneck, system fail over, and cyber-attack [1]. Each node in a distributed blockchain has a copy of the ledger; hence, if a node gets hacked or fails, the data stays up and robust.
- Immutability: Being naturally immutable, data entered in blockchain cannot be either changed or deleted. It means that for those who need to have data integrity, such as where data kept on the blockchain must not be tampered or changed, there are assurances that the channels will prevent that from occurring. The use of IoT in supply chain management, for instance, where tracking the origin of commodities is essential (or health data management, where precision and dependability are dominating) [2], which immutability can assist to keep the faith on confidence and openness of the data [8, 9].
- Trusted Data Management: Blockchain provides IoT device interactions a safe and open approach for data management. Smart contracts are self-executing contracts with the terms of the agreement being written into code through which it's managed, and through which these trustless and automated transactions can occur using Blockchain. If these smart contracts conform to other standards by which devices and systems talk to each other to a predefined criteria, then the middle man is no longer required. This openness is due to the fact that every action is logged and auditable on the blockchain, making players put their trust unto one another [3].

Blockchain in conjunction with IoT particularly with regard to 6G networks can assist in building more robust network infrastructure, safer sharing of data, and stronger authentication procedures. The use of blockchain technology can deal with a number of security issues that arise in massive IoT systems and makes use of decentralization, immutability and automated trust systems. However, like most things, blockchain is not completely immune to future hazards, particularly as quantum computing is developed. A Blockchain system has the prospective to become susceptible to quantum attacks as recognized cryptographic techniques of the conventional blockchain systems are susceptible to suffer from these quantum attacks [4]. This will risk the security of the IoT device as well as the blockchain network.

11.1.4 The Emerging Threat of Quantum Computing

Quantum computing is expected to transform many different sectors from issue solving to development of artificial intelligence. Nevertheless, along with great promise, there is a big obstacle: disrupt present cryptographic methods. RSA and Elliptic Curve Cryptography (ECC), cryptographical methods widely used in protecting IoT devices and blockchain networks, may in fact become serious vulnerabilities in the presence of quantum developments. Quantum algorithms including Shor's algorithm can solve particular types of mathematical problems that classical computers cannot—as particularly those related with breaking public-key cryptosystems. As quantum computing becomes practical the existing encryption techniques that protect IoT communications and blockchain transactions will be vulnerable, so there is a tremendous need for quantum resistant substitutes. This chapter firstly investigates the vulnerabilities of conventional cryptography systems, and on the other hand the necessity of quantum safe solutions for IoT and blockchain in the quantum age. Since the first days of quantum computing, it will prove to be able to solve some very complex mathematical problems beyond the traditional computer means, making the existing cryptography way no longer adequate for use. RSA, ECC, and Secure Hash Algorithms (SHA) are widely used encryption techniques that are based on problems that are well known to be difficult for classical computers but easy for quantum machines [1].

- **Quantum Dangers to Cryptography:** The key to the developing quantum danger is quantum algorithms, e.g. Grover's and Shor's algorithms. Exponential speed up is also available for applications such as integer factorization, which can in turn be used in creation of 'public key' cryptographic systems like RSA and ECC. Current encryption techniques would practically make themselves available to be quantum attacked, such that quantum computers would be able to read out data that would take classical computers centuries to get at [2]. On the other hand, while less powerful, Grover's method has the ability to halve the security of such widely used encryption systems as AES [3], which could render the force of symmetric key cryptography useless. As a result, sensitive data and transaction in our IoT systems and blockchain technologies can be compromised when there is a quantum computing threat that undermines the two fundamental security mechanisms of these systems.

- **Effect on Blockchain Systems:** Furthermore, depending on the cryptographic methods, blockchain systems allow participants to ensure data is immutable, that safe transactions take place, and that trust can be built among the participants. Some cryptographic methods require that once data is entered into the blockchain it cannot be changed or tampered with include digital signatures and hash functions. Most systems of blockchain security and integrity are built on these. However, as quantum computing gets the floor up, the potency of these encryption techniques begins to take a hit. Quantum algorithms can break these cryptographic methods and so compromise the integrity and immutability of blockchain and by implication, destroying trust and immutability and possibly empowering evil actors to change transaction records and messing up consensus mechanisms or start double spend attacks [4].
- **Implications for IoT Security:** Finally, the implications of quantum computing for IoT security are more important because in IoT where operational success rely on real time data interchange and data integrity are at risk by quantum computers. As 6G IoT networks become the backbone of everything from driverless cars to smart cities data has to stay safe and unmodified, so safety and privacy depend on it. If quantum attacks affect the authentication methods, (or) communication protocols, or (or) data storage mechanisms of IoT devices, it would have a very damaging effect to industries that rely on the secure, real time transfer of reliable data. If we undertake to protect IoT devices against future quantum-enabled attacks, even in the near future, we will have to develop and integrate quantum-resistant cryptographic techniques to existing systems [5].

The looming quantum computing vulnerability is made bigger in view of the merging of 6G networks, IoT technology, and the physics of overwhelming connectivity and automation that are leading us into an age where pervasive connectivity and automation coexist. Despite the security and trust owed to the blockchain's distributed and immutable character, the security measures used in the blockchain will have to develop to combine quantum safe cryptography. Similarly, solutions of post-quantum cryptography are required to ensure robustness in the real time data exchange and critical connections of the whole IoT ecosystem which is the base of 6G. As quantum computing grows, quantum resistance security will have to be introduced into blockchain and IoT systems to preserve the integrity and safety of future generation networks [6].

11.2 Foundations of Quantum Computing and Blockchain

To use the ideas from quantum mechanics to say something about problems that a classical computer can't find the answer too quickly at all is such a change in view about computation. As quantum computing progresses, so blockchain technology does, and it has additional hurdles to overcome. Blockchain is undoubtedly a solid option for data security and privacy for digital transaction, but upcoming quantum devices can pose serious issues in getting the blockchain algorithms and cryptographic methods working. This part investigates the basic ideas of quantum computing contradiction to the basic values of blockchain and how it affects the data integrity, the consensus and the privacy of both blockchain and the IoT networks.

11.2.1 Basics of Quantum Computing

As a way of completing some calculations a thousand million times faster than the orthodox computer, quantum computing breaks the tradition of classical computing by applying the principles of quantum mechanics. The following conceptual foundations can be mentioned as the key ideas underlying such a change:

- Quantum bits, or qubits: Qubits correspond to their classical counterparts in the form of bits but can occupy more than one state at the same time contrary to the bits which occupies state 0 or state 1. Superposition this ability enhances programming capability of qubits in a way that they represent several values at once. Quantum computers use several physical entities to implement qubits, for example trapped ions, superconducting circuits and photons [1]. This is followed by adding another dimension of parallelism that is not available to other forms of computers.

- Superposition: Just like in classical computing, superposition is a characteristic of quantum systems in which they can occupy more than one state. This can, for example, be true for a qubit which can have values of both 0 and 1 at the same time which enables parallel computation. Quantum algorithms can, therefore, apply parallel many attempts at the solutions to a problem for a faster computation of problems such as factoring large numbers or searching through rather large databases.
- Another essential quantic interaction is entanglement whereby a number of qubits couple in pairs (or groups) in a way that the state of one is dependent on the state of the other despite a vast distance apart. High-k Quality interaction of qubits in this way also makes quantum speedup possible; which is the capability of quantum computers to operate faster than classical systems on certain problems.
- Quantum speedup: Thus, quantum computers may have a strong speed advantage for specific types of problems. For example, Shor's algorithm lets quantum computers break the big numbers which are needed to perform in public key cryptosystems like RSA and ECC [2]. Grover's algorithm also improves the rate of search in unarranged database, thus increasing the speed to some types of cryptographical processes. These findings in quantum algorithms reveal the possibility of quantum systems potentially threatening the security strategies in IoT and blockchain technologies as is evidenced by the following discoveries.

These ideas taken together make the quantum computing not only technology but also a shift that is capable of affecting multi- domains in areas of material science, artificial intelligence & cryptography; thus, turning the quantum computing into the technical revolution. Even though these potential benefits can be quite vast, quantum computing poses significant challenges, particularly to the modern info structure using conventional encryption methods.

11.2.2 Blockchain: Key Principles

It refers to a distributed, secure data table that can be used in various industries such as finance, manufacturing, health and banking, but more popularly known as Bitcoin, Ethereum, etc.; blockchain is a decentralized and incorruptible database that can be useful across a broad range of applications. The strengths of the base concepts of the book are what gives blockchain its strength to ensure data protection and reliability [11]. These basic ideas include:

Distributed Ledgers

- Each participant that is in the blockchain network or the nodes have a record of the transaction history in the chain since it is a distributed ledger. This decentralizing eliminates the need to have a central authority, hence gives the following advantages:
- There is more transparency: a person cannot verify the record of transaction with the help of the third party.
- Sustaining attacks: Of most attacks, it becomes very hard for the attacker to invade the system as there are no central access point [13].

11.2.3 Consensus Mechanisms

Consensus algorithms tend to be at the core of blockchain systems in order to ensure that every member has an agreed view of the state of the blockchain as well as the transactions that are taking place. These are made to ensure that the ledger only gets additions of legal operations taking place in the organization. Common consensus systems consist of:

- Proof of Work (PoW): The members of the network-or the miners have to solve complex mathematical problems. A complaint is also concluded, and the particular transaction is recorded on the blockchain every time a problem is solved. Despite its security, PoW consumes a lot of energy and also requires a high computational power [14].
- Proof of Stake (PoS) : PoS also selects the nodes based on the number of cryptocurrency and the proportion of these coins that are willing to risk, or "stake" for the chance at becoming a validator. This is not very demanding in terms of computing as it requires, and therefore consumes more energy than PoW.
- Delegated Proof of Stake (DPoS) and other variants: For specific application, these consensus types offer deviations concerning participants' choices and network decision-making.

11.2.4 Cryptographic Underpinnings

In a nutshell, information security as well as accountability in block-chain derive from its exclusive dependence on a mere cryptography. It is provided mainly by two cryptography techniques,

- Hashing: As is common with blockchain, data is transformed into an identical number of characters by the use of cryptographic hash functions such as SHA-256. Each block in the block chain is represented by this output making the data storage rather immutable, and it is referred to as hash. Should even a minor modification take place in the data of the block, then hash will change to signal manipulation and maintains blocks' purity [15].
- Digital Signatures: Moreover, the use of public key cryptography, RSA or ECC is used to secure a transaction done on blockchain. After that, to prove their authenticity and ownership of the transaction, the users sign these with their private key. This assures that any transaction begins with the legal proprietor of an item or coin.

Indeed, blockchain is an operational, credible means of managing data as a result of decentralization, non-changeability, and availability. Hence, relying so much in conventional encryption techniques such as RSA and ECC counters such as: This indicates that there is potential for future development in quantum computing that could potentially threaten current cryptographic systems to some extent, which emphasizes the need for quantum-resistant blockchain solutions [16].

11.2.5 Intersection of Quantum Computing and Blockchain

In areas such as public-key cryptography and hash functions, quantum computing opens up new and large classes of vulnerabilities to blockchain systems. These cryptographic methods are crucial to ensure the security and nonsuitability of smart contracts along with the blockchain transactions. Implementation of Shor's method can threaten well-known public-key cryptography such as RSA and Elliptic Curve Cryptography (ECC), which is applied for signing operations and cryptographic keys, for instance, in cryptocurrency. In addition, it is postulated that cryptographic hash algorithms securing the blocks into the blockchain, like SHA-256, are at a risk of being broken by quantum computing. Especially for IoT devices and sensitive data, this part examines the vulnerabilities due to quantum computing and what these threats imply to the assurance and security that blockchain currently provides.

The security of such systems tends to be endangered even more as quantum computing progress advances rapidly. As for the major vulnerability points of convergence of these two technologies, the following can be highlighted:

1. **Challenges with Public-Key Cryptography:** Since most of Blockchain security rely on public-key cryptography especially for identity authentication and transactions, there are the following challenges that are associated with public-key cryptography. To protect data, generation of digital signatures and cryptography is based mainly on what is known as RSA and ECC. While Shor has provided means of factoring big numbers and solutions to discrete logarithm problems, which take the classical computers years to solve, thus his quantum algorithm poses a direct threat to the current encryption methods. This makes blockchain security vulnerable since the public-key infrastructure that essentially relies on it is vulnerable to QS-enabled attacks [10].
2. **Vulnerabilities in Hashing:** The true SHA-256 is a secured form of hashing where Blockchain uses hashing to link blocks and to ensure data integrity. Despite this, quantum computing has risks, though in an indirect manner it does not affect the one-way character of hash functions. It means that Grover's method could reduce the time required to find a hash collision, thus increasing the rate of brute force attacks on hash functions. Thus, despite the fact that today's significant loads for their computations still keep modern hash functions such as SHA-256 reasonably safe, quantum advancements may require the use of quantum-safe equivalents in the future [12].
3. **Consensus Mechanisms and Quantum Computing:** The consensus algorithms of blockchain guarantee transparent, safe addition of blocks and validation of transactions. However, quantum computing posed a threat to these systems:
   - Proof of Work (PoW): PoW is a type of consensus algorithms in which miners solve a number of complicated puzzles in order to affirm transactions. This being the

case, attackers would be able to solve PoW problems far much faster than traditional miners, thus gaining a relatively higher mining power. This may compromise the network's security and decentralization since the attackers could flood the network with malicious activities [14].
- Proof of Stake (PoS): While enhancing the risks posed by quantum computers is not as direct as in the case of PoW, it also has them. Quantum attacks could threaten the cryptographic methods that are used for stake and transaction authentication in PoS systems, and therefore, it is mandatory to integrate the quantum-safe cryptographic solutions for protection of these processes [19].

4. **Long-Term Impact on Blockchain Security:** Influence on Blockchain Security in the Long Term: Further Consequences for Blockchain Security is in significant danger in the long term due to quantum computers.
   - Rewriting History: The idea of rewriting the past transactions through the quantum power is one of the scariest ideas. Through digital signatures, and due to the fact that block manipulation is already possible with the help of quantum computers, the above-mentioned individuals can tamper with the identity of blockchain history. This would be doing away with the credibility of the entire system; and hence, eradicating the immutability, which is a key aspect of the blockchain.
   - Smart Contracts: Also, other blockchain-based smart contracts may be susceptible to quantum threats that employ cryptographic techniques. If the quantum computers shall be capable of breaking the cryptographic procedures protecting such contracts, then breaches can occur, and the strength that smart contract brought in enforcing deals as envisioned, shall be negated.
5. **Post Quantum Blockchain Initiatives:** The quantum threat is gradually becoming a concern and researchers as well as the blockchain builders are already developing post-quantum blockchains. These projects hold on development and implementation of cryptography approaches which are immune to quantum attacks. New consensus solutions are also currently being looked into to address the problem that quantum computing poses to the current systems. One interesting field is Quantum Key Distribution (QKD),

a technology that meets this need since it is based on quantum physics to securely transmit encryption keys, and therefore enhance the security of blockchain systems.

Quantum computing's interaction is necessary to start building the strong systems that are capable of withstanding all the threats in the future while keeping the security and trust intact in their primary forms. Blockchain has to adapt as quantum technologies emerge to ensure that it fulfills its role as a reliable and secure IoT platform in the future and beyond.

11.3 Quantum Threats to Blockchain and IoT Security

The applications of Blockchain and IoT have reached the advanced level in terms of security; however, the advancement of quantum computing unravel catastrophic threats to the cryptographic foundations of these systems. Blockchain security and IoT ecosystem security are most affected as the quantum computing progresses with the ability to solve complex mathematical problems within a short span of time and thus, undermining conventional cryptosystems. As a result of errors in current cryptographic technology approaches, this section explains how quantum computing threaten the security of IoT and blockchain.

11.3.1 Traditional Cryptographic System Vulnerabilities

Issues, which could hardly be solved by the mathematical systems of traditional computers, serve as the basis of present days encryptions. Actually, quantum computers are thought to be capable of making an effective use of these structures which means that the encryption methods that is in widespread use is actually quite secure.

1. **Rivaest-Shamir-Adleman, RSA**
   - The need to factor big composite numbers into their prime factors is the main driving force behind RSA encryption [16].
   - When large scale quantum computers are built by Shor's algorithm, quantum computers can factor such numbers exponentially faster than classically, which means that RSA encryption is under threat of decryption.

RSA communication will therefore always be at the mercy of quantum computers as soon as the latter attains a level that makes it capable of cracking cryptographic systems.

Also, due to its efficiency, smaller key size in comparison with RSA although its implementation is in the business of growth, elliptic curve cryptography (ECC) is used more and more for safe communications. Off course, this depends on how hard it is to solve the elliptic curve discrete logarithm problem (ECDLP). Due to the fact that Shor's method can solve ECDLP, the ECC-based systems are vulnerable. This is quite concerning since IoT device authentication and blockchain digital signatures widely use ECC [17].

2. **SHA—Secure Hash Algorithms**
    - Instead, one has to be assured that one is dealing with a consistent and reliable system that has functionalities such as hash algorithms like SHA-256. They are resistant to pre-image and collision; Grover's technique, which utilize the strength in quantum computation, allows performing of brute force against hash functions at a faster manner.
    - This would not completely compromise SHA-256, but it would certainly downgrade the security; so, longer hash sizes are required to provide the same level of security [18].

These weaknesses highlight the necessity for using post-quantum cryptography (PQC) –cryptographic procedures designed in an approach that they can ward off capabilities of quantum computers.

11.3.2 Risks to Blockchain Security

Essentially, the security of blockchains is anchored on cryptography such as signing, hash and consensus techniques. All these parts are subject to integrity threats from quantum computers in one way or the other:

- **Hashing:** With respect to hash and Grover's method a result could weaken proof-of-work (PoW) systems; nevertheless, the effect will not come very early and quickly in the near run. In fact, hash functions are the foundation of the blockchain since they connect both the blocks and warrant the reliability of the data regarding the transaction. However, these characteristics may eventually vanish after some time; and thus, the security of the systems is likely to be compromised too [12].

- **Digital Signatures:** Blockchain uses solutions based on public-key cryptography like RSA and ECC to create digital signatures, which check transactions and identities. Digital signatures to be created with a quantum computer can grant the attacker a possibility to impersonate the user or modify the transaction or even the blockchain history. Blockchain systems' openness and transparency would therefore be severely threatened [21].
- **Consensus Method:** In one way or another, all the consensus methods including the popular PoW and proof of Stake (PoS) ensure consensus about the state of the blockchain all across the network. In PoW, quantum computers could bring accurate solutions to computation algorithms much faster than their classical counterparts, which in turn gives a leeway to the side with destructive intentions. This could allow 51% attacks through which one party makes most of the decision making through possession of most hash power, hence compromising the decentralized nature of the network [14]. Thus, PoS relies on cryptographic techniques vulnerable to quantum attacks even though quantum computing seems to have a lesser impact on it. The weaknesses in such staking and validation systems mean that quantum threats could pose serious issues in PoS-based blockchains for both security and confidence.

Based on these pitfalls, it is now essential to research on quantum-safe blockchain method that possesses more efficient consensus mechanisms and quantum-secure cryptography.

11.3.3 Challenges in IoT Security

The Internet of Things is a collection of many devices interconnected by a data link and the number is growing rapidly. The security issues in a post-quantum perspective are worth noticing how the new 6G networks expand the IoT networks and their complexity. Important questions include:

1. Device Authentication: About the IoT devices, the lightweight cryptographic protocols ensued for authentication and safe communication at times with the help of ECC, which gets vulnerable to quantum hacking; Although in the

presence of quantum computers, there could be easy impersonation of devices that can lead to severe attacks on the IoT authentication process and the infrastructure.

2. Data Integrity: This kind of data is often very large and is in most cases sent in real-time by IoT devices. It is particularly so when it comes to crucial applications such as in healthcare, autonomous cars or smart cities, where data is sacrosanct and has to remain untampered. Quantum computing poses a great danger to cryptographic hash functions for example SHA-256 on which the IoT devices rely on to ensure that the data is secure and has not been tampered with. In the case where quantum assaults impact the hash functions, then the integrity of IoT data would be affected thus affecting the integrity of mainly essential systems and providing out wrong information and wrong decisions [20].
3. Scalability: Because IoT networks have been devised to interconnect tens of millions, if not billions of connected devices, their scalability requires non-resource-intensive yet good security solution. The use of post-quantum cryptography sometimes involves a higher computational capacity which presents a significant constrain for IoT devices with limited computational ability that may have to provide the added processing power required for the execution of quantum-resistant algorithms [20].
4. Real-Time Connection: Low latency connection is critical in multiple IoT applications like industrial control and auto-pilot to allow for almost immediate decision making to be made. One of the challenges with implementing quantum resistant security to IoT systems that require fast and seamless connectivity is that it is rather difficult to do so without creating the formation of a bottleneck.
5. Life Cycle Management: While IoT devices naturally have long lifetimes, these devices can be provisioned with little thought as to quantum-safe cryptography. In particular, transforming such devices to quantum-safe cryptography may be cumbersome and time-consuming for large-scale networks. Following requirements are addressed by quantum-safe IoT systems, which include quantum-resistant encryption, QKD, and safe firmware upgrade to protect IoT devices from future quantum threats.

Using quantum computing yields a quantum leap forward in computational power but results in significant issue to solve cryptographic protocols that secure IoT and blockchain technologies. Quantum computing poses fundamental threats to the very fundamental elements of blockchain and IoT ranging from signatures to data and consensus. Some of the risks may include; to overcome them, using quantum-resistant cryptographic technique and developing secure block chain technology, as well as setting higher security bar for the IoT networks. The IT juniors realize that the lifespan of digital ecosystems defined by quantum technologies is a result of these initiatives [27].

11.4 Quantum-Resistant Blockchain Technology

It is highly alarming that the advancement in quantum computing is quickly threatening the cryptographic foundations of blockchains. This is answered by post-quantum cryptography (PQC) which develops cryptographic methods which cannot be vulnerable to both classical and quantum computers. In being able to provide secure tradings and other forms of data, even in the presence of quantum threats, PQC aims to protect blockchains. This section considers the specific cryptographic algorithms, consensus algorithms, secure communication protocols, and other advanced technologies that can be used in the context of blockchain to reduce the likelihood of quantum attacks.

11.4.1 Post-Quantum Cryptography (PQC)

Post-quantum cryptography is the kind of cryptography that aims to counter quantum attacks and is generally deployed especially after the discovery of quantum computing. These depend on the problems solved mathematically that even the quantum computers' latest generations cannot solve them fully, including Grover's and Shor's algorithms.

1. **Lattice-Based Cryptography**
   - Lattice-based systems employ the difficulty of problems such as LWE and the shortest vector problem in a lattice.
   - Kyber and Dilithium which are two of the NIST finalists have the capability to protect the blockchain network against the quantum threat; they are useful for quantum-resistant encryption as well as digital signatures [22–24].

Some of the applications include key exchange systems, digital signatures, safe multiparty computations and so on.

2. **Code-Based Cyphers**
   The fact that decoding random linear codes is a problem that becomes more difficult with increased length, and cannot be attacked by quantum computers is the basis of this encryption method.
   - The first and probably the most famous quantum-safe technique is McEliece encryption method, which can be referred to as an ideal example of this approach.
   - Applications: Especially when backward compatibility is desirable to previous systems, the secure encryption is the long-term solution for data security.

3. **Cryptography Based on Hashes**
   - Merkle Tree Signatures and other schemes such as SPHINCS+, both of which had expressed special suitability in providing quantum-resistant digital signatures; hash-based cryptographic methodology depends on hash functions for signatures and immunity to attacks such as the pre-image and collision attacks.
   - Applications: Blockchain transactions, in which immutability and data integrity rule most importantly.
   - Whereas isogeny-based cryptography relies on isogeny to both an elliptic curve and another isogeny, the multivariate and isogeny- based cryptography involves solving nonlinear polynomial equations [25]. These developing areas present potential in providing such solution for lightweight cryptographic system designed for IoT devises.

The integration of these PQC techniques into blockchain systems will assist in ensuring that in the post-quantum security digital signatures, encryption, and even transaction verifications are achieved safely.

11.4.2 Quantum-Safe Consensus Mechanisms

These methods are used to ensure that each of the parties that is using the blockchain maintains a multiple number of nodes have synchronized blockchain states. These systems have to adapt to be protected against such attacks because of the existence of quantum computers.

1. Traditional Proof of Work (PoW): They are generally feeble to the quantum speedup using Grover's algorithm; Quantum-Resistant Proof of Work (PoW): It is capable of using more immense challenging computations or post-quantum hash functions like SHA-3 in spite of enhanced quantum threats.
2. Quantum-Safe PoS: Due to the growing vulnerability of the existing cryptographic techniques in PoS for staking and validation of stakeholders, quantum-safe PoS can provide better security and protection to the process and identification of bona fide validators.
3. Hybrid Consensus Mechanisms: The classical consensus algorithms are partially combined with quantum resistant consensus algorithms. For example, while post-quantum cryptography is used for transaction validation, quantum key distribution (QKD) can safeguard the validator's communication.
4. Leader Election Protocols: It can be concluded that, quantum-safe cryptography can be used in leader election protocols, thus providing safe and objective election of leaders in both the public and permissioned block chains.

Employment of these quantum-safe consensus systems ensure that no matter the level of quantum capability of the adversary, the blockchain networks of that network will remain both secure and distributed.

11.4.3 Secure Communication Channels

If blockchain and IoT devices are to have safe communication in quantum era networks, Quantum Key Distribution (QKD) is a viable answer. The method is based on quantum mechanical ideas to detect eavesdropping and disseminates cryptographic keys safely.

1. Quantum Key Distribution (QKD) gives cryptographic keys to producing and distributing them using quantum physics. The quantum state is disturbed by any effort at listening in and signals to the participants that there has been a breach. The protocols like BB84 and E91 are the basis of QKD technology. The applications of 6G networks include IoT data transmission, inter device communication and securing the communication between the blockchain nodes.

2. QKD can be integrated with IoT networks designed for 6G to ensure data confidentiality and integrity by securing the communication between IoT devices and blockchain nodes. Hybrid methods that mix QKD with post quantum cryptography systems are investigated to provide more scalable and economical implementations.
3. Quantum communication requires a specific hardware such as photonic devices and quantum repeaters, QKD. Scalability is one of main issues, particularly for large scale IoT networks that require a considerable infrastructure to support quantum communication.

By combining QKD with cutting edge cryptographic methods, one can construct safe communication channels that can handle efficiently the quantum issues in IoT and blockchain applications.

11.4.4 Role of Zero-Knowledge Proofs (ZKPs)

Cryptographic systems of zero knowledge proofs (ZKPs) are such that one party can validate a statement without revealing the underlying data. ZKPs are critical to improvement of privacy and quantum resistance in blockchain systems.

Boosting Blockchain Transaction Privacy

- ZKPs provide a means by which blockchain transactions can be discreetly executed while still validating their validity by masking sensitive transaction data.
- For use of such protocols as zero knowledge Succinct Non Interactive Arguments of Knowledge (zk-SNARKs) and zero knowledge Scalable Transparent Arguments of Knowledge (zk-STARKs), privacy oriented blockchain initiatives like Zcash make extensive use of.

Quantum Resistant ZKP Protocols:
There are many existing ZKPs that are based on classical assumptions of cryptography, which may be vulnerable to quantum attacks. Quantum resistant ZKPs use postquantum cryptographic methods such as lattice cryptography to keep security against such threats.

Blockchain and IoT Applications

- Authentication: Privacy and security are improved with ZKPs, through authentication of IoT devices without revealing private data.
- Data Integrity: For making safe decisions in sectors like healthcare and driverless cars, ZKPs can prove the integrity of IoT data without revealing the data itself.
- Compliance: ZKPs help in preserving the privacy, but may provide official evidence of compliance with regulatory standards.

11.4.5 Prospective Difficulties and Challenges

For all these reasons, computational overhead and scalability in particular, represent significant challenges that ZKPs face, especially in the context of resource constrained IoT environments; however, ZKPs are becoming more practical in quantum resistant form to be used in the real world to ensure the privacy, efficiency and quantum resistance of blockchains.

Special difficulties in the development of quantum computing are posed by cryptographic systems that support security of IoT and integrity of blockchain. However, the promising answers are given by Post-Quantum Cryptography (PQC), quantum-safe consensus algorithms, Quantum Key Distribution (QKD) and Zero-Knowledge Proofs (ZKPs) developments. These technologies collectively enable quantum resistance in blockchain systems that will survive the attacks of a quantum. Therefore, the incorporation of these technologies will lead blockchain and IoT ecosystems to high security and trustworthiness towards the quantum age, capturing the assurances for continuous dependability and resilience of digital infrastructures.

11.5 Integrating Quantum-Secure Blockchain with 6G IoT

With the arrival of 6G networks coming up with the ultra-low latency, massive device connection, and AI driven automation, guaranteeing the security of IoT communication becomes almost crucial. With quantum computing in place, the encryption techniques applied to protect the IoT ecosystem and the blockchain transactions would become extinct. If we are to solve this, quantum secure blockchain has to be included into 6G IoT systems since it offers quantum resistant cryptographic protections to protect data exchanges and distributed, transparent, immutable transaction records. This part then provides a detailed investigation of how quantum secure blockchain may be included in 6G enabled IoT networks, emphasizing important topics such as data authentication, decentralized identity management, quantum resistant smart contracts, and safe real time data visualization through Augmented Reality (AR). As 6G and IoT continue to grow, it becomes a must to grow secure, scalable and efficient infrastructures. The following section discusses the layered method of merging quantum secure blockchain with IoT, and therefore ensuring a robust framework for next generation networks.

11.5.1 Quantum-Secure IoT Network Architecture

To lessen quantum facilitated cyber threats, a quantum secure IoT network enabled the use of matching blockchain technology, post quantum cryptography (PQC), and quantum communication protocol. The design has several layers, all of which contain security systems that resist quantum physics.

1. **Layered Design**
   Quantum safe technologies are integrated into IoT network through multi layered security systems.
   - Comprising IoT sensors and equipment in charge of data collecting and transfer, the perception layer
   - The device authentication and data integrity is assured by including the quantum resistant cryptographic system (hash based signatures or lattice based cryptography) [22].
   - Network Layer: Utilizes 6G communication networks' ultra-low latency and high speed data transfer. A couple techniques such as quantum key distribution (QKD) and post quantum cryptography help strengthen security and avoid interception and man in the middle data [23].
   - Blockchain Layer: It allows values data exchanges in IoT networks and records unchangeable transactional records on a distributed ledger. It uses quantum resistant consensus systems like hybrid PoW/PoS system [24], under post quantum cryptographic algorithm security.
   - Application Layer: There is Application Layer which supports dApps for different IoT driven use case (smart cities, autonomous vehicles, supply chain management, and

healthcare), at application layer itself. It combines several privacy enhancing technologies namely Zero Knowledge Proofs (ZKPs) to ensure safe and secure confidential transactions by not disclosing any private information [25].

2. **Combining Quantum Safety**
   - To protect IoT data, authentication systems, and communication channels, quantum-safe security solutions need to be included in IoT-blockchain networks.
   - Post quantum encryption ensures that data generated from IoT remains secure even if quantum computers attempt to crack it.
   - Lattice based, hash based, code based cryptography systems have strong security against quantum attacks.
   - The blockchain technology ensures tamper proof record of IoT transactions and thus, establishes data authentication and transparency, and the smart contract provides post quantum cryptography to ensure safe and automated IoT interactions.
   - Quantum Key Distribution (QKD) for Secure Communication: QKD systems generate unbreakable encryption keys for such nodes of a blockchain and IoT devices to interconnect safely. It ensures end to end encryption for critical IoT transactions, thus no eavesdropping and man in the middle attacks.
3. **Scalability and Effectiveness**
   Quantum secure blockchain with 6G IoT brings in problems of scalability, performance and resource economy. The architecture has to include:
   - Optimized Quantum Safe Protocols: Lowest energy consumption is guaranteed by using the best in class optimized quantum-safe protocols that run on the smallest footprint while preserving the security. Blockchain based decentralized identification solutions enable IoT devices to have their own safe decentralized identities without the need to be dependent on a central authority. Real time anomaly detection and cyber-attack prevention are done using AI algorithms which are inducted in blockchain smart contracts.
   - Adaptability to Interoperate with Emerging Technologies: The design should be flexible so that it can easily integrate with AI, AR, cloud-based IoT systems and cross-chain connectivity.

11.5.2 Quantum-Secure Smart Contracts and AR Integration

IoT-blockchain networks also include quantum-decipherable smart contracts and augmented reality (AR) interfaces to enhance automation at further pace and in real-time manner than ever:

- Quantum-Safe Smart Contracts: Classical cryptographic primitives, i.e. smart contracts, are open to quantum attacks, thus Quantum-Safe Smart Contracts are needed. Safe contract execution can be guaranteed when using lattice-based encryption as well as hash-based signatures even in the presence of quantum adversaries. Automated decision making, safe IoT transactions and IoT analytics with artificial intelligence use cases are among them.
- Basis for AR: In Secure Data Visualization: Augmented Reality (AR) makes IoT system real-time monitoring possible, and therefore helps stakeholders see the blockchain safe data on real time. The use cases belong to the smart factories, autonomous car diagnostics, and medical IoT applications where quick access to secured blockchain data is essential.

To defend the 6G networks, which enable a faster and smarter hyper connected IoT environment, it is important to integrate quantum secure blockchain technology. Long term security is assured by layering security post quantum cryptography, blockchain openness, and quantum safe authentication on top of each other in a layered security architecture. Secure smart contracts, distributed identity management, and AR driven display of real time data can help next generation IoT-blockchain networks to attain scalability, efficiency as well as quantum resistance. The ongoing development of quantum secure IoT designs will shape in a great part a safe, distributed, and intelligent digital infrastructure capable to solve the security problems of the quantum age.

11.5.3 Data Authentication and Integrity

Since data authentication and integrity are very important to ensure that data gathered from devices are tamper proof and trustworthy, IoT applications rely on them mostly. Figure 11.1 details about the integration of blockchain with IoT applications. The unchangeable character of the Blockchain along with the cryptographic security creates a great basis for protection of the data generated by IoT from cyber-attacks. A quantum

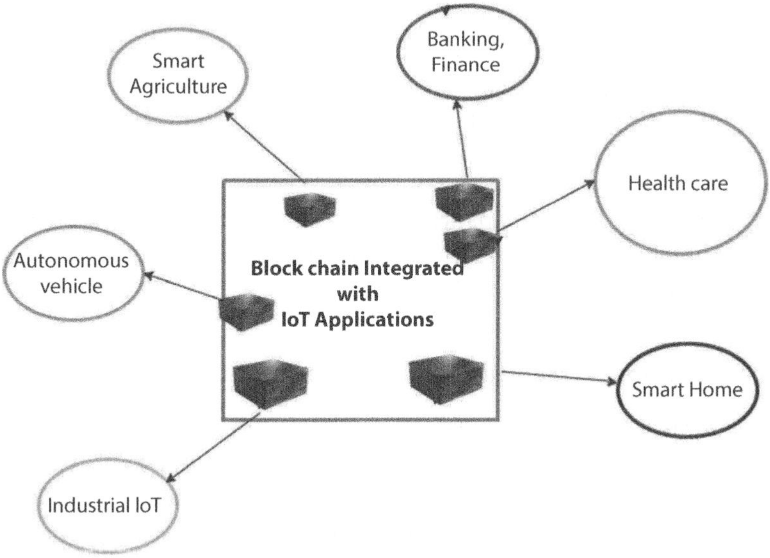

Figure 11.1 Block chain integrated with IoT.

secure IoT system has a distributed trust layer provided by blockchain; the data security is further improved by post-quantum cryptography methods.

1. **Blockchain to Verify Data**
   - IoT devices register their public keys on the blockchain, and thus create their validity in a distributed and tamper-proof way.
   - Device to device transactions can be protected from illegal access and impersonation assaults by using quantum resistant digital signatures [13].
2. **Ensuring Information Integrity**
   - The blockchain keeps the IoT data hashed so it is not easily manipulated. A hash mismatch would be produced by any effort at data modification, signaling possible manipulation.
   - Quantum-resistant hash functions such as those based on the lattice based cryptography [17], bring about the requisite strength against the quantum computing assaults.
3. **Uses in Critical Sector**
   - Privacy: Assuring the veracity of data collected by wearable devices from patients and the privacy of patients.

- o Smart Cities: Valuing sensor-generated data for smart infrastructure management, air quality monitoring, and traffic control, smart cities.
- o Supply Chain Management: Assurance to the integrity of commodities as they move across the logistics chain.

Incorporating blockchain with post quantum cryptography maintains the integrity and authenticity of data even in quantum computing environment.

11.5.4 Decentralized Identity Management (DID)

With billions of IoT devices expected to run in 6G enabled ecosystems, device authentication has to be secure and scalable and that depends on Decentralized Identity Management (DID). Blockchain and quantum resistant encryption improves DID by providing them with tamper proof identity records and thereby removing their dependency on centralized authentication mechanisms.

1. **Quantum-Safe DID Structures**
   - o Each IoT gadget is given a distinct distributed identity (DID) stored safely on the blockchain.
   - o This verification is safe with respect to post quantum cryptography, including lattice-based digital signatures, and they are blockchain-based DID solutions [26].
2. **Authorize and Verify Devices**
   - o Techniques of post quantum cryptography allow IoT devices to verify themselves, ensuring the resilience against attacks enabled by quantum computers.
   - o Smart contracts based on blockchain enforce access control policies, hence safe and automatic permission of the device interactions [13].
3. **Benefits of Blockchain-Based DID**
   - o Decentralization: Removing the need to rely on centralized identity authorities makes the danger of single points of failure disappear.
   - o Immutable: Identity records are secure for the long term as they cannot be changed or created.
   - o Scalability would be designed to fit billions of Internet of Things devices across a given network.

4. **IoT Use: Applications**
   - Smart Homes: Safely managing sensor, security system, and connected appliance identity [17].
   - Industrial Internet of Things (IIoT): Manufacturing automation systems and machine authentication.
   - The vehicle-to-vehicle (V2V) and vehicle-to-infrastructure (V2I) vehicle interactions are examined to prevent malicious cyberattacks.

Quantum safe blockchain-based DID solutions can be included into IoT ecosystems to improve security and trust in order to ensure seamless and tamper proof device interactions.

11.5.5 Smart Contracts for IoT

Because of this, smart contracts make it possible to have safe, self-executing agreements between devices, adding automation and efficiency to IoT enabled blockchain ecosystems. Thus, the change to quantum-resistant smart contracts is required, since conventional smart contract systems are vulnerable to quantum enabled attacks.

1. **Quantum-Resensitive Smart Contract Design**
   - Post quantum cryptographic primitives allow to build smart contracts, and thus assure that their execution is safe against quantum risks.
   - The QSA enables authentication and triggering of smart contract transactions based on quantum-safe digital signatures (lattice-based and hash-based being the most relevant).
2. **IoT Applications**
   Energy management is about automating real time redistribution of energy in smart grids based on the sensor data.
   - Shipments: Tracking shipments, and automating payments once the items arrive to the target.
   - Healthcare: Safe automation of patient privacy guaranteeing data sharing between IoT medical devices and healthcare providers.
3. **Privacy and Security Improvements**
   - Zero knowledge proofs (ZKP) supports better privacy by having the ability to execute a transaction wherein the

authenticity of the data is established without revealing private data.
  - Immutability of blockchain ensures that every smart contract execution is open and tamper proof.
4. **Difficulties and Remedies**
  - Quantum-safe cryptographic methods are designed to minimize processing and storage requirements for IoT devices with limited resources.
  - The creation of cross platform compatibility rules ensures that quantum secure smart contracts are implemented flawlessly over IoT systems.
  - Quantum resistant smart contracts can help in implementing IoT ecosystems to safe, automated, and effective transactions across businesses like healthcare, logistics and energy management etc.

At the end of the day, by integrating quantum secure blockchain with 6G IoT systems, a robust security architecture can be created to protect the distributed identities, data integrity, and device communications against the quantum empowered cyber-attacks. Thus, ensuring the scalability and dependability over the IoT environments, data authentication, distributed identity management and quantum resistant smart contracts are combined in a layered architecture. As quantum computing progresses, the use of these quantum safe solutions is necessary to future proof IoT security and blockchain based automation. By implementing this method, IoT networks are ensured to be scalable, quantum resistant, and efficient while permitting a secure digital future for all sectors around.

11.6 Advancements in 6G and Quantum-Resistant IoT Applications

As 6G networks become more developed, integrating IoT technologies and quantum resistant blockchain presents new opportunities to use it in a scalable, safe, and effective manner. Post quantum cybersecurity, AI driven optimization and interoperable framework based 6G IoT ecosystems can be secured from the fast emerging quantum threats with low latency and high security. These advances employ cutting edge tools like artificial intelligence (AI) to make real time, energy efficient and cross domain solutions as in Figure 11.2.

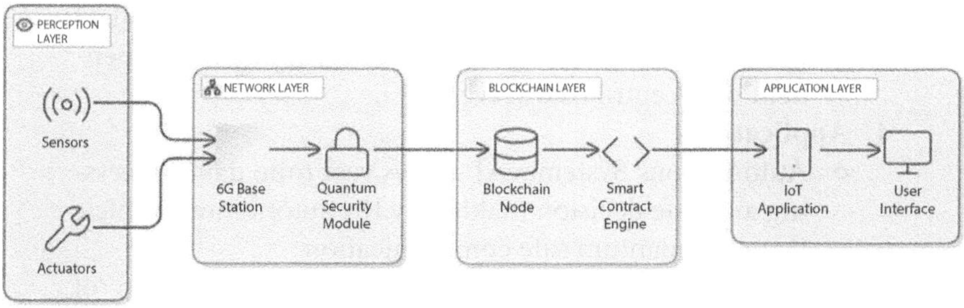

Figure 11.2 Architecture of quantum-secure 6G IoT.

11.6.1 AI-Driven 6G IoT Networks

AI is necessary in controlling and securing the complexity of 6G IoT networks to ensure the same performance, and to thwart quantum attacks. Through AI solutions, network intelligence, security, as well as scalability, are improved and IoT interaction become more adaptive and more resilient.

1. **Role of AI in Network Management**
   - AI models drive the optimal decentralized IoT operation in terms of resource, bandwidth, hence maximize the minimization of the latency.
   - Machine learning (ML) algorithms can be used for prediction, detection and neutralization of security threats and support development of quantum-resistant blockchain frameworks [28].
2. **AI-Powered Security Enhancements**
   - It constantly observes the IoT traffic behavior, and becomes able to detect anomalies and possible cyber threats in real-time.
   - By having AI integrated with post quantum cryptographic algorithms in networks, they can respond dynamically to identify emerging quantum-enabled attacks and updating the already available framework in the network to counter them dynamically.
3. **Enhancing Scalability and Decentralization**
   - AI based decision making models allow the scalability of blockchain network to support billions of interconnected IoT devices.
   - Through the use of decentralized AI frameworks, we can access a decentralized option that processes the data

locally on the IoT devices, thereby improving upon data privacy as well as trust, while rendering us less dependent on a centralized server.

4. **Applications**
   - Autonomous Systems: AI allows real time data processing and safe decision making by the autonomous vehicle through quantum safe communication.
   - AI optimizes (Smart Cities): Intelligent operation of smart infrastructure with the purpose of performance of secure real-time operations in IoT based smart urban management systems.

Incorporating AI powered intelligence, 6G IoT networks can be made to operate in a secure, adaptive and highly responsive manner in quantum-threatened environments.

11.6.2 Real-Time Applications

When quantum-resistant blockchain combined with 6G comes into play, it gives rise to revolutionary real time applications—especially in autonomous vehicles, smart cities, and in the healthcare industry. They are security sensitive, low latency, real time data validation.

1. **Autonomous Vehicles**
   - Vehicles also gain secure communication as it's utilizing quantum-safe blockchain protocol for communication of data while the protocol protects it from cyber threats and unauthorized access.
   - Using 6G's ultra-low latency, AI powered navigation and collision-avoidance systems employ real-time decision making with fast fidelity situational awareness allowing for fast response.
2. **Smart Cities**
   - IoT sensors gather real-time data in traffic flow, energy distribution and environmental conditions using blockchain secured for data integrity [28].
   - AI based surveillance integrated with Secure IoT empowers surveillance with public safety and improves emergency response and security in the cities.

3. **Healthcare**
   - Remote Patient Monitoring: In using quantum-secure blockchain, the real-time health data is sent to the healthcare provider through the medical IoT devices which guarantee privacy and data integrity [29].
   - AI Driven Diagnostics: Real-time patient data will be monitored by an AI engine that provides insights into the personalized treatment to the most possible extent; blockchain is to maintain the accuracy of the data and would not allow it to be tampered.

The real time applications above show how Quantum Secure 6G IoT has the ability to impact the critical industries with the speed, security, and reliability that these industries should have.

11.6.3 Energy-Efficient IoT Systems

In the rapid growth of IoT, energy consumption is becoming a major issue. It is necessary to optimize quantum resistant security solutions to support sustainable and energy efficient operations.

1. **Energy Optimization in 6G IoT**
   - Dynamically, AI powered resource management adjusts the power usage according to the network demand; hence, increasing the energy efficiency.
   - Quantum resistant cryptographic protocols are optimized to minimize computational overhead, so as to enable IoT devices to be operated efficiently with minimal energy consumption.
2. **Green Blockchain Technologies**
   - Proof-of-Stake (PoS) and Delegated PoS are in place of energy intensive Proof-of-Work (PoW) consensus mechanism, making blockchains reduce their environmental impact.
   - Layer 2 scaling solutions handle transactions off chain, using minimal energy as compared to the conventional blockchain, but maintaining highly secured and high speed blockchain verification.

3. **Applications in Sustainable IoT**
   - IoT enabled smart grids increase efficiency in captive energy distribution and storage avoiding any sort of waste and inefficiency.
   - Low-power IoT Sensors that are used for environmental monitoring to track air pollution, climate patterns and utilization of resources in the process of supporting sustainability initiatives.

Energy efficient blockchain technologies enable IoT networks to scale properly and sustainably for the long term with respect to the environment.

11.6.4 Cross-Domain Applications

The ability to connect and integrate with other quantum-secure IoT networks across multiple industries is the key to realizing the full potential of quantum-secure IoT networks in any given industry.

1. **Finance**
   - Secure API: Use plustx API for quick and secure API development.
   - AI for fraud detection: AI identifies unusual transaction patterns to support businesses in fraud prevention, digital banking and fintech.
2. **Supply Chain Management**
   - Transparency End-to-End: Blockchain provides an ability to record every stage of the supply chain, such as verifying authenticity, compliance, avoiding fraud etc. [30].
   - Real time IoT sensor data adds into tracking and monitoring capability and thus provides a better visibility of the supply chain.
3. **Critical Infrastructure**
   - Utility Management: IoT secure networks are used to monitor and optimize water, energy, and transportation system for efficiency purposes.
   - Quantum resistant blockchain solutions assure high security Blockchain that blocks cyberattacks on the infrastructure and ensures network resilience.
4. **Interoperability Challenges and Solutions**
   - Standardized quantum resistant protocols allow communication between different IoT ecosystems without any problem.

- Decentralized data sharing comes in the form of enabling secure collaborations between organizations while preserving data privacy and trust.
- Quantum secure 6G IoT applications in various domains show how 6G IoT can reshape the respective corporates from efficient, transparency, and secure perspective.

While many of the 6G and quantum resistant IoT applications grab the limelight, 6G and quantum resistant IoT applications significantly benefit from the benefits of automated AI security, blockchain security, and sustainable operations. Industry future proves digital ecosystem with real time decision making, energy efficient frameworks, and cross domain interoperability. With quantum-resistant cryptographic solutions becoming a standard, the 6G IoT networks would rapidly become the most secure, scalable, and AI powered network and would redefine the connectivity, trust and efficiency of the future in digital age. These developments open up a future of completing quantum secure, and presents new opportunities for advancing the use of innovation and security in an environmentally sustainable way.

11.7 Challenges in Implementing Quantum-Secure Blockchain for IoT

The integration of quantum-secure blockchain into IoT networks is in line with a secure, scalable, and efficient systems path, but there are several technical and operational obstacles needed to be sorted out before its widespread adoption. The challenges facing central bank digital currencies are derived from various factors; among them—scalability problems, computational overhead, interoperability, standardization, and regulatory challenges. Energy efficiency is also a key concern for the IoT especially in the case of resource constrained IoT devices.

Next part of this section dwells into the critical challenges of implementation, and puts forward the possible solutions that can boost security on the blockchain. It remains the best and at the same time maintain the efficiency in IoT-blockchain ecosystem using off-chain computations, sidechains, and energy efficient quantum secure protocols.

11.7.1 Scalability Challenges

The wide-scale implementation of quantum-secure blockchain technology within IoT systems needs to manage massive numbers of networked devices while processing their substantial amounts of data. The challenge lies in achieving decentralization alongside security and performance while maintaining speed levels [31, 32].

Managing High Volume of IoT Devices:

- Extensive IoT systems accommodate billions of devices which produce ongoing real-time data production.
- The growth of blockchain-based storage together with processing power creates an escalating amount of strain on network infrastructure.

Consensus Mechanism Bottlenecks

- The proof-of-work and proof-of-stake systems used by the combined network constitute scalability obstacles in extensive IoT environments.
- Scalability experiences more negative impacts because quantum-resistant consensus mechanisms demand extra processing power from the system.

Latency Concerns

- Real-time operational systems including automated vehicles and smart grids need data processing times to be less than an instant.
- A quantum-secure distributed system should provide prompt operation along with absolute security features.

Potential Solutions

- The implementation of sharding techniques splits blockchain networks into smaller segments that help maintain its operations.
- Off-chain processing through layer-2 solutions decreases the congestion in main blockchain networks.
- Devices used for IoT require quantum-resistant lightweight cryptographic protocols that work efficiently with their minimal power capability.

11.7.2 Computational Overheads

Post-quantum cryptographic methods require great computing power hence development for resource-limited IoT devices proves difficult as reported in [33, 34].

Resource Constraints in IoT Devices

- The computational intensity of post-quantum cryptographic operations makes it difficult to run them successfully on IoT devices because most of these devices have minimal power availability and restricted memory capacities as well as short battery life.
- The additional computational weight of these techniques shortens device operational time and requires users to change batteries more often.

Increased Bandwidth Requirements

- Post-quantum algorithms require increased key sizes together with signature sizes which consume more network bandwidth.
- The processing of data becomes slower and transaction times grow longer when these technologies are used.

Potential Solutions

- Hardware accelerators serve as a solution to transfer cryptographic computations outside of IoT devices for better operational efficiency.
- Two types of algorithms exist for low-power IoT environments: optimized lattice-based and hash-based algorithms.
- The processing of IoT device data through Edge computing solutions enables local data management to reduce the amount of work required from IoT devices.

11.7.3 Standardization and Interoperability

The adoption of quantum-secure blockchain for IoT remains limited because different platforms face operational standards and interoperability problems [35, 36].

Heterogeneous IoT Ecosystems

- Various IoT device manufacturers create products with their own communication methods and cryptographic approaches.
- The integration of quantum-resistant security standards faces difficulties because devices cannot easily communicate with each other.

Absence of Universal Standards

- The evaluation process of post-quantum cryptographic algorithms continues because researchers have not yet settled on one standard that receives universal recognition.
- Differences during implementation may result in separated encryption systems which may decrease the ability of different platforms to communicate.

Potential Solutions

- Post-quantum security standards should be established by working together with standardization organizations NIST, ISO and ITU.
- Compatible technological structures allow IoT devices to interact with blockchain systems for smooth system integration.
- The adoption of post-quantum security solutions becomes faster through established cooperative groups between industries while they work together to harmonize regulatory requirements.

11.7.4 Regulatory and Ethical Considerations

The implementation of quantum-secure blockchain for IoT systems raises multiple concerns about both privacy and compliance needs and ethical requirements [37].

Data Privacy and Compliance

- Neutral blockchain documentation violates GDPR rules by preventing authorities from permanently removing personal information.
- The management of privacy against transparency presents a complicated problem for international IoT implementations.

Ethical Implications

- The deployment of IoT surveillance networks generates privacy and data collection risks that affect large-scale data management.
- Topics concerning AI-based monitoring and data-sharing systems need to be handled from an ethical perspective.

Potential Solutions

- ZKPs enable users to conduct private blockchain transactions which respect regulatory requirements [38].

- Standards for policy adaptation should be created through joint work between governments and industrial groups together with regulatory bodies.
- The adoption of guidelines by industries serves two purposes: it establishes responsible methods to use AI and blockchain while reducing possible risks of misuses.

11.8 Future Directions

Further research is required to establish quantum-secure blockchain as a revolutionary security solution for 6G IoT systems. The main focus for future development should target scalability and efficiency improvements and connection standards regarding 5G/6G technology.

11.8.1 Innovations in Post-Quantum Cryptography

Bluetooth and Fourth Generation (4G) technology will determine the security of IoT systems through post-quantum cryptography development as quantum computing capacity advances.

Novel Cryptographic Methods

- Internet of Things systems benefit from lattice-based cryptography because it delivers safe and efficient execution of key exchange and authentication methods.
- The scalability of code-based cryptography depends on efficient computational cost optimization of McEliece techniques and optimized implementation.
- Quantum security is delivered through digital signature systems which include XMSS and SPHINCS+ under Hash-Based Cryptography.

Strategies for Optimizing Performance

- Creation of low-power Internet of Things lightweight PQC algorithms.
- Hardware accelerators reduce computational expenses and strengthen cryptography execution speed.

11.8.2 Evolution of 6G IoT Standards

Future-generation IoT ecosystems need quantum security methods incorporated into 6G communication standards for their development.

1. **Quantum-Resistant 6G Protocols**
   - Post-quantum security solutions will protect 6G IoT data streams from end to end.
   - Low-latency authentication systems provide real-time security protection for different applications.
2. **Global Standardization Projects**
   - The creation of quantum-secure communication systems requires collaboration between government agencies and 3GPP and ITU.
   - The inclusion of AI security concepts must become part of 6G IoT standard requirements.

11.8.3 Convergence of Emerging Technologies

These three technologies combined will transform how IoT works.

1. **AI for Quantum Safety**
   - Predictive artificial intelligence systems use their capabilities to detect cyberattacks that quantum computers make possible.
   - The implementation of PQC algorithms adjusted for AI processing results in faster cryptographic operation.
2. **Blockchain: Layer of Security**
   - Decentralized identity management system combines with trustful data-sharing features under quantum-resistant protocols for security.
   - The security protocol called Zero-Knowledge Proofs (ZKPs) allows users to create private transactions when transacting.
   - The creation of a quantum-secure digital ecosystem demands sustained creative development as well as strongest cooperation among everyone alongside ethical responsibility.

Future developments have to guarantee:

- The framework needs to adjust to advancing quantum-computing security threats while maintaining scalability options.
- Every government, industry and research institution must unite for speeding up the deployment of post-quantum security infrastructure.

- The energy savings and sustainability of cryptographic solutions for IoT networks should maintain low computational requirements.
- A solution to these issues will create the basis for resilient distributed secure digital infrastructure in the upcoming quantum-secure IoT networks generation.

11.9 Conclusion

The requirement to merge quantum-secure blockchain with 6G IoT systems becomes more essential because quantum computing is advancing to secure data privacy and integrity and trust within the rapidly transforming digital environment. Post-quantum cryptography represents the key solution to protect blockchain-based IoT systems from quantum-enabled attacks because it strengthens their security. Organizations need to protect themselves from upcoming threats through quantum-resistant encryption protocols and new consensus-procedure evaluation, so they can maintain productive IoT operation. Ongoing research is vital to develop quantum-safe frameworks because scalability limitations together with legal hurdles and computational overheads need standardized efforts between companies. The advancement of quantum-incompliant security features with automated communication systems and artificial intelligence capabilities will build a secure digital network framework that can overcome quantum-threats to define upcoming IoT infrastructure. Quantum-resistant technologies show their worth by securing healthcare and banking operations and autonomous systems and smart cities which establish their ability to transform information technology. An AI-enhanced blockchain distributed platform uses quantum computing security measures for adaptive protection of next-generation services and future interoperability and operability capabilities.

AI disclosure statement: The author acknowledges the use of AI-based tools for minor language editing or grammatical correction. However, all intellectual contributions, analyses, and conclusions presented in this chapter are entirely the author's own.

References

1. Stallings, W., *Cryptography and Network Security*, 5th, Pearson, London, UK, 2010.
2. Keshav, S., *Mathematical Foundations of Computer Networking*, Addison-Wesley, New Jersey, USA, 2012.
3. Tanenbaum, A.S., *Computer Networks*, 5th, Pearson Education, London, 2013.
4. Liu, Y.-D., Hwang, R.-H., Baker, F., *Computer Networks: An Open Source Approach*, McGraw-Hill, New York, USA, 2011.
5. Shor, P.W., Algorithms for Quantum Computation, in: *Proceedings of the 35th Annual Symposium on Foundations of Computer Science*, pp. 124–134, 1994.
6. Grover, L.K., A Fast Quantum Mechanical Algorithm for Database Search, in: *Proceedings of the 28th Annual ACM Symposium on Theory of Computing*, pp. 212–219, 1996.
7. National Institute of Standards and Technology (NIST), Kyber and Dilithium Specifications, 2022, [Online]. Available: https://csrc.nist.gov.
8. National Institute of Standards and Technology (NIST), SPHINCS+ Specifications, 2022, [Online]. Available: https://csrc.nist.gov.
9. National Institute of Standards and Technology (NIST), McEliece Cryptosystem Specifications, 2022, [Online]. Available: https://csrc.nist.gov.
10. IBM, Quantum-Safe Cryptography Initiative, 2023, [Online]. Available: https://www.ibm.com.
11. European Commission, EuroQCI Program on Quantum Communication, 2023, [Online]. Available: https://digital-strategy.ec.europa.eu.
12. European Commission, Horizon Europe Program on Quantum Security, 2023, [Online]. Available: https://ec.europa.eu.
13. AI Research Institute, AI-driven Quantum-Resistant IoT Models, 2023, [Online]. Available: https://ai-institute.org.
14. Quantum Research Group, Applications of QKD in Blockchain Systems. *Quantum J.*, 18, 2, 45–60, 2023.
15. Smart Cities Alliance, Case Studies in Smart Cities and Healthcare IoT, 2024, [Online]. Available: https://smartcities.org.
16. Autonomous Systems Lab, Quantum-Safe Blockchain for Autonomous Vehicles, 2023, [Online]. Available: https://autonomouslab.org.
17. Cryptography Innovation Consortium, Zero-Knowledge Proof Implementations, 2024, [Online]. Available: https://zkpconsortium.org.
18. National Institute of Standards and Technology (NIST), Post-Quantum Cryptography Standardization Project, 2023, [Online]. Available: https://csrc.nist.gov.
19. Bank of Canada, CBDC Quantum-Resilience Research, 2023, [Online]. Available: https://bankofcanada.ca.
20. Government of Estonia, Estonian e-Residency Program, 2023, [Online]. Available: https://e-resident.gov.ee.

21. Horizon Europe, Quantum-Enabled 6G Networks, 2023, [Online]. Available: https://horizon-europe.eu.
22. Menezes, A.J., van Oorschot, P.C., Vanstone, S.A., *Handbook of Applied Cryptography*, CRC Press, Florida, USA, 1996.
23. Calderbank, A.R. and Shor, P.W., Good Quantum Error-Correcting Codes Exist. *Phys. Rev. A*, 54, 2, 1098–1105, 1996.
24. Boneh, D. and Franklin, M., Identity-Based Encryption from the Weil Pairing, in: *Advances in Cryptology—CRYPTO 2001*, pp. 213–229, Springer, Berlin, Heidelberg, Germany, 2001.
25. Katz, J. and Lindell, Y., *Introduction to Modern Cryptography*, 2nd, CRC Press, Florida, USA, 2014.
26. Singh, A. and Alam, M.A., 6G-Enabled Quantum Cryptographic Systems. *IEEE Trans. Emerg. Top. Comput.*, 9, 3, 1082–1090, Sep. 2023.
27. Braunstein, S.L. and Van Loock, P., Quantum Information with Continuous Variables. *Rev. Mod. Phys.*, 77, 2, 513–577, 2005.
28. van Meter, R., *Quantum Networking*, Wiley-IEEE Press, New Jersey, USA, 2014.
29. Schneier, B., *Applied Cryptography: Protocols, Algorithms, and Source Code in C*, 2nd, Wiley, New Jersey, USA, 1996.
30. Biham, E. and Shamir, A., Differential Cryptanalysis of DES-like Cryptosystems. *J. Cryptology*, 4, 1, 3–72, 1991.
31. European Telecommunications Standards Institute (ETSI), Quantum-Safe Cryptography and Security, 2023, [Online]. Available: https://etsi.org.
32. Zheng, Y., Digital Signcryption for Confidential and Authentic Communications, in: *Proceedings of the 15th Annual International Cryptology Conference (CRYPTO '95)*, pp. 378–393, Springer, Berlin, Heidelberg, Germany, 1995.
33. Mosca, M., Cybersecurity in an Era with Quantum Computers: Will We Be Ready? *IEEE Secur. Privacy*, 16, 5, 38–41, 2018.
34. Kumar, V.S., Lightweight Cryptography for IoT Applications, in: *Proceedings of the IEEE International Conference on IoT and Applications (ICIOTA 2022)*, pp. 145–150, 2022.
35. Rivest, R.L., Shamir, A., Adleman, L., A Method for Obtaining Digital Signatures and Public-Key Cryptosystems. *Commun. ACM*, 21, 2, 120–126, 1978.
36. ElGamal, T., A Public-Key Cryptosystem and a Signature Scheme Based on Discrete Logarithms. *IEEE Trans. Inf. Theory*, 31, 4, 469–472, 1985.
37. Bennett, C.H. and Brassard, G., Quantum Cryptography: Public Key Distribution and Coin Tossing, in: *Proceedings of the IEEE International Conference on Computers, Systems, and Signal Processing (ICCSSP)*, pp. 175–179, 1984.
38. National Institute of Standards and Technology (NIST), Digital Signature Standard (DSS), 2013, FIPS PUB 186-4.

12

From Sci-Fi to Reality: Making Secure 6G IoT Applications a Reality

Muhammadu Sathik Raja[1], Karthikeyan M.[2*], K. Syed Ali Fathima[2] and Manoj R.[3]

[1]*Department of Biomedical Engineering, Dhanalakshimi Srinivasan University, Perambalur, Tamilnadu, India*
[2]*Department of Information Technology, Sengunthar Engineering College, Tiruchengode, Tamilnadu, India*
[3]*Department of Electronics and Communication Engineering, Bannari Amman Institute of Technology, Sathyamangalam, Erode, Tamilnadu, India*

Abstract
The vision of a world interconnected by 6G IoT applications is now closer than ever. As we approach the deployment of 6G networks, the need for secure, efficient, and scalable solutions becomes increasingly critical. This chapter addresses the challenges and technological innovations that are transforming science fiction into tangible 6G IoT solutions. The chapter focuses on the key technologies driving the development of 6G IoT, with an emphasis on advanced security solutions essential for protecting large networks of connected devices. As 6G IoT is expected to link billions of devices across various applications, from autonomous vehicles to healthcare systems, securing these devices and the data they produce is vital. Traditional security models are no longer enough, and more advanced methods, like quantum-safe cryptography and decentralized trust models such as blockchain, are essential for ensuring data integrity and privacy. Additionally, the chapter highlights the role of AI and machine learning (ML) in enhancing the security and performance of 6G IoT applications. These technologies enable real-time monitoring, threat detection, and autonomous decision-making, ensuring that security systems can adapt to new risks as they emerge. The chapter concludes with a roadmap for integrating these technologies into practical, secure 6G IoT systems, with an emphasis on ongoing research, pilot projects, and international cooperation. Through the strategic use

**Corresponding author*: karthickamsec@gmail.com

T. Perarasi, M. Karthiga, S. Sountharrajan, E. Suganya and Balamurugan Balusamy (eds.) Secure Blockchain and Quantum Technologies for 6G-Enabled Internet of Things, (299–332) © 2026 Scrivener Publishing LLC

of cutting-edge technologies, this chapter demonstrates how the once speculative ideas surrounding 6G IoT are being transformed into secure, scalable, and efficient solutions, paving the way for a new era of connectivity.

Keywords: 6G IoT, secure applications, quantum-safe cryptography, blockchain, artificial intelligence, machine learning, data privacy

12.1 Introduction

The Internet of Things (IoT) and communication technologies have rapidly evolved over the past few decades, revolutionizing how devices interact and enabling smart systems across various industries. As we transition from 5G to 6G, the IoT landscape is set to experience unprecedented advancements, characterized by faster data rates, ultra-low latency, and massive connectivity. This section explores IoT's evolution, the transformative potential of 6G, the growing need for security, and the groundbreaking applications that 6G will enable.

12.1.1 Evolution of IoT and Communication Technologies

IoT began with the idea of connecting devices to enable remote monitoring and control. Early IoT systems were built on basic communication technologies such as Wi-Fi, Bluetooth, and 2G/3G cellular networks, supporting applications in logistics, healthcare, and home automation.

The arrival of 4G sparked significant growth in mobile IoT applications, driving innovations such as connected cars, wearables, and smart cities [1]. The introduction of 5G further boosted IoT by offering higher data rates, lower latency, and network slicing, opening the door to industrial IoT (IIoT) and large-scale deployments like autonomous vehicles and telemedicine.

Looking ahead, 6G envisions a hyper-connected world where billions of devices communicate seamlessly, with advanced technologies like terahertz (THz) communication, quantum computing, and edge AI becoming integral to IoT [2]. This marks a transition from simply interconnected devices to a fully intelligent and automated IoT ecosystem.

12.1.2 6G: The Next Frontier

6G, the sixth generation of wireless communication, promises to redefine connectivity and IoT applications by addressing the limitations of previous generations. Key features of 6G include:

1. **Ultra-Low Latency:** Achieving latency under 1 millisecond, enabling real-time applications such as remote surgery, augmented reality (AR), and virtual reality (VR) [3].
2. **High Reliability:** Ensuring secure, robust communication for mission-critical systems like autonomous vehicles and smart grids.
3. **Massive Connectivity:** Supporting up to 10 million devices per square kilometer, enabling seamless IoT integration in urban environments.
4. **Advanced Spectrum Utilization:** Leveraging THz frequencies to achieve data rates up to 1 terabit per second (Tbps) [4].
5. **AI-Driven Networks:** Using machine learning and AI for dynamic resource allocation, predictive analytics, and improved network management [5].
6. **Energy Efficiency:** Designing sustainable communication systems to minimize power consumption for IoT devices [6].

These features will open new possibilities, including tactile internet, holographic communications, and smarter environments.

12.1.3 Need for Security in 6G IoT Applications

The introduction of 6G technology delivers new innovations that establish complex security risks for IoT systems in particular.

- Vulnerable security networks occur from the widespread amount of IoT devices because they present extensive opportunities for Distributed Denial of Service (DDoS) attacks and unauthorized data breaches and access attempts.
- The most critical operations must be positioned within protected IoT systems that require real-time communication and secure protected data exchange between healthcare facilities and financial corporations and safety networks. All systems demonstrate catastrophic effects following the discovery of any security vulnerability [7].
- The high level of detail available in 6G technology requires user privacy to be a priority since systems can manage data in real time.
- A protective solution for HetIO architecture depends heavily on robust authentication systems that also use encryption and anomaly detection methods.

- Traditional cryptographic systems face serious threats from quantum threats because quantum computing will become mature resulting in the requirement for quantum-resistant security protocols [8].

The solution requires an integration of three core elements that use AI threat detection along with blockchain communication to protect privacy while performing calculations.

12.1.4 Sci-Fi to Reality: Vision for 6G IoT

The 6G technology will make possible what today seems like imaginary future.

- The upcoming technology of holographic telepresence will transform into usable solutions—thanks to 6G development.
- 6G technology will make digital entity replication possible through digital twin applications which enhance predictive maintenance for manufacturing plants and urban systems.
- 6G technology used in smart transportation systems will allow vehicles to communicate through V2X protocols which will produce efficient and secure mobility systems.
- The healthcare field will undergo a revolution because remote surgery and health monitoring systems together with AI-assisted diagnostics will depend on ultra-reliable 6G IoT systems with low latency.
- The sustainable environment goals will achieve better results through 6G IoT as it promotes innovative environmental management practices and conducts sustainable waste reduction programs and performs smart environmental monitoring activities.

The implementation of 6G IoT technology will close the divide between imaginary concepts and real-world implementations, thus creating a new era of human-digital physical world interaction which uses smart connected systems for fast and protected communication.

12.2 Fundamentals of 6G and IoT

6G technology works as the upcoming wireless communication standard by opening new possibilities for IoT applications. Modern IoT networks based on 6G technology use terahertz (THz) communication together with artificial intelligence (AI) and quantum computing to create exceptional speed and capacity along with extraordinary intelligence capabilities [9]. This part outlines an extensive analysis about 6G fundamental elements along with their consequences on IoT systems [10].

12.2.1 What Defines 6G Technology?

The main transformative features of 6G technology separate it from earlier generations of communications infrastructure.

Terahertz (THz) Communication:

- 6G technologies access THz spectrum frequencies from 0.1 to 10 THz which allows data transfer rates of one terabit per second (Tbps) according to [11].
- Very short wavelengths of THz waves enable accurate communication within densified areas such as smart cities and industrial internet of things (IoT) environments.
- THz communication provides broad communication bandwidth which suits applications that handle real-time data transmission for holographic telepresence along with high-definition VR/AR services.

AI Integration:

- The roles of AI in 6G networks consist of three fundamental features: intelligent resource allocation, along with traffic prediction, and fault detection capabilities.
- Artificial intelligence automation systems enable immediate decision processes that lead to enhanced effectiveness for IoT systems.
- Using edge AI processing on 6G networks enables direct local data management which makes both the response time faster and the user data safer.

Quantum Computing:

- Secure communication becomes possible through quantum computing because it implements robust encryption which defends against future cyber-attacks.
- High-speed optimization tasks find support through this solution which must operate efficiently in massive IoT networks.
- The combination of quantum networks with 6G provides highly secure mission-critical communication links.

12.2.2 Characteristics of 6G IoT Networks

The following attributes define 6G IoT networks:

High Device Density:

- The network capacity of 6G reaches ten million devices per square kilometer which supports the expansion of IoT sensors devices and actuators [12].
- The dense distribution of network devices allows uninterrupted connectivity between devices especially in high-density areas such as urban areas and smart factories as well as autonomous transportation systems [13].

Energy Efficiency:

- Energy-efficient protocols along with optimized hardware systems extend the battery duration of IoT devices, thereby supporting sustainable device operations.
- The combination of renewable energy-based base stations together with low-power communication technologies efficiently conserves energy [14].

Real-Time Data Processing:

- 6G technology supplies below one millisecond latency which makes possible real-time communication and control operations suitable for autonomous vehicles and robotics together with remote surgical procedures.
- The convergence of edge and fog computing helps process data near the source which in turn cuts the need for centralized servers while improving system performance times.

12.2.3 Comparison of 5G and 6G IoT

Feature	5G IoT	6G IoT
Speed	Up to 10 Gbps	Up to 1 Tbps
Latency	~1 millisecond	Sub-millisecond (<0.1 ms)
Device Density	~1 million devices per km^2	~10 million devices per km^2
Spectrum	Up to millimeter wave (mmWave)	Terahertz (THz) frequencies
Energy Efficiency	Improved compared to 4G	Ultra-efficient, green communication

Feature	5G IoT	6G IoT
AI Integration	Limited (primarily centralized)	Ubiquitous, with edge AI
Security	Improved over 4G, vulnerable to future threats	Quantum-secure encryption

6G outperforms 5G across all dimensions, offering unprecedented capabilities that address the demands of next-generation IoT applications.

12.2.4 Emerging Use Cases for 6G IoT

Holographic Communication:

- Real-time holographic projection applications with high definition can be accessed through 6G networks for teleconferencing and entertainment together with remote collaboration systems.
- 6G technology depends on speed and extremely short response times to provide total immersion throughout experiences [15].

Autonomous Systems:

- 6G technology enables real-time data processing and high reliability which benefits autonomous vehicles and drones as well as robotics operations [16].
- The V2X communication standard will benefit from the capabilities of 6G to deliver secure and highly efficient transportation systems for everyone.

Intelligent Infrastructure:

- 6G technology enables smart cities to combine internet-connected devices for improving power consumption alongside traffic control and protecting citizens through public safety measures [17].
- Real-time data analytics combined with predictive maintenance through 6G networks will optimize essential infrastructure such as bridges along with power grids and water systems.

Remote Healthcare:

The enhancement of telemedicine through 6G includes operations like robotic surgeries and IoT-based real-time patient tracking that uses wearable monitoring devices.

Space Exploration and Connectivity:

- 6G IoT networks will support satellite-based remote systems to establish worldwide connectivity and environmental monitoring and disaster response tracking capabilities.
- 6G IoT technology will transform industries while restructuring communication and automation through its ability to address present weaknesses and develop unexplored opportunities.

12.3 Security Challenges in 6G IoT Applications

The developing 6G IoT networks which aim toward unmatched connectivity create major security complications. The incredibly extensive device networking along with intricate network structures and recent technological integrations highlight multiple possible security weaknesses that could produce extensive impact. The section presents the main security challenges related to 6G IoT applications as depicted in Figure 12.1.

12.3.1 Expanding Attack Surface

The massive growth of interconnected devices in 6G networks creates multiple security risks because the attack surface has become billions wide [18, 19]:

- Multiple security issues arise from the wide range of IoT devices which span from basic sensors to industrial complex machinery because devices have different security protocols which makes standardization impossible and exposes potential vulnerabilities.
- 6G IoT networks have a distributed architecture that creates numerous opportunities for attackers to access systems especially through edge and fog computing systems.
- Botnets together with DDoS attacks become possible when bad actors take advantage of unsecured devices for creating botnets which results in massive Distributed Denial of Service disruptions affecting essential infrastructure.
- Supply chain vulnerabilities emerge because hardware and software components originating from diverse vendors may have unintentional device flaws for attackers to exploit.

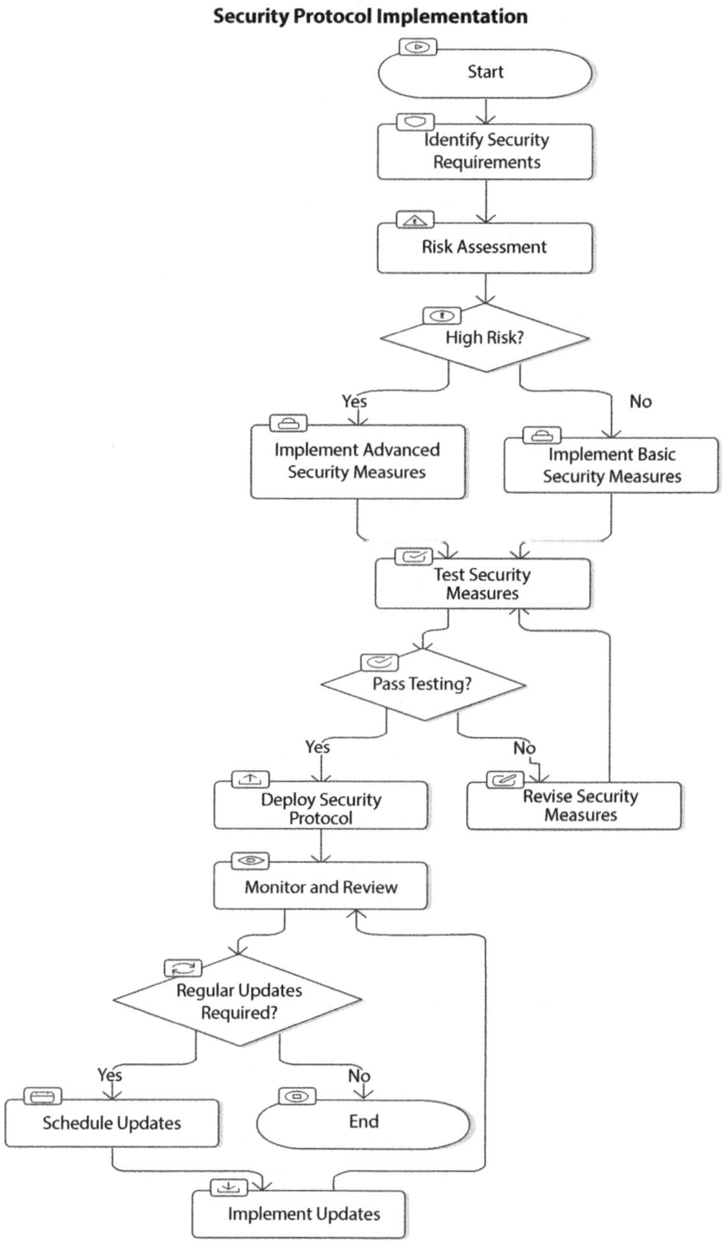

Figure 12.1 Flowchart of security protocol implementation.

12.3.2 Threats to Privacy and Data Integrity

Data privacy and data integrity concerns increase dramatically as a result of high volumes of data generation and processing in 6G IoT systems.

- The exchange of important sensitive mission data such as health records and monetary transactions becomes exposed to unauthorized interception during transmission processes.
- The combination of centralized with decentralized storage solutions creates data storage risks that include hacking incidents along with data corruption and ransomware attacks.
- Attackers can intercept and modify data through protected communication channels because of unsecure encryption protocols along with unsecured eavesdropping.
- The recent progress in data analytics technology within 6G networks raises concerns about user privacy because systems collect detailed personal data against the users' explicit permission [20].

12.3.3 Quantum Computing Threats

The modern technology of quantum computing represents a severe danger to current cryptographic systems utilized within 6G IoT networks.

- Quantum computers outpace classical computers with extreme effectiveness to solve integer factorization and discrete logarithm problems which breaks security in RSA and ECC encryption methods.
- Encrypted data transmissions from today can be stored by attackers before quantum computing reaches mainstream status making them available for decryption at that time.
- The implementation of Post-Quantum Cryptography (PQC) faces hurdles when extending it to billions of IoT devices because of performance considerations and compatibility issues [21, 22].

12.3.4 IoT Device Limitations

The security challenges increase because IoT devices normally have limited resources:

- Several IoT devices operate with insufficient processing capabilities to implement detailed encryption and authentication security standards.
- Excessive security measures reduce the operational life of IoT devices through high energy consumption.
- The inability of constrained devices to maintain updated firmware software exposes them to new security threats because they cannot perform regular updates.
- The security risk of attackers using default credentials weakens IoT devices because many manufacturers do not change these standard credentials in new devices.

Addressing the Challenges

Several security measures at different levels should be implemented to address these problems.

- Real-time threat detection through AI systems monitors 6G IoT networks while detecting abnormal behaviors across that network.
- Edge and Device-Level Security: Incorporating lightweight cryptography, secure boot processes, and tamper-resistant hardware in IoT devices.
- The incorporation of Post Quantum Cryptography performs as the first line of defense against future quantum attacks on IoT network infrastructure.
- The system should have defined procedures for implementing secure updates along with maintenance schedules to maintain devices in a working state.
- The implementation of Zero Trust Architecture represents a security model which requires authentication and complete access control for each entity with no trust by default.

Regardless of its advanced capabilities the proactive management of connected system challenges will enable 6G IoT systems to maintain security, stability, and gain trust throughout hyper-connected networks.

12.4 Enabling Secure 6G IoT Applications

Protecting 6G IoT applications from security threats remains essential to confront issues created by both hyper-connected devices along with sophisticated cyber threats facing limited resources devices. This section investigates novel technologies and methods which facilitate secure implementations for 6G IoT applications.

12.4.1 Advanced Cryptographic Techniques

Advanced cryptographic methods are essential to protect sensitive data and communication in 6G IoT applications. The various methods fulfill different needs in security by protecting against quantum vulnerabilities and maximizing resource utilization while safeguarding data privacy during calculations.

Post-Quantum Cryptography (PQC):

- The implementation of PQC uses quantum-resistant cryptographic algorithms which include lattice-based and hash-based and multivariate polynomial cryptosystems [23].
- PQC algorithms serve as a replacement for RSA and ECC methods to secure IoT devices and communication in 6G IoT applications.
- The implementation process for IoT devices with limited resources faces difficulties because optimization strategies are necessary to cut down processing requirements.

Homomorphic Encryption:

- This encryption method enables users to operate protected data while maintaining complete encryption status for all operations [24].
- The application of 6G IoT depends on secure data analytics in healthcare and finance and industrial IoT which require processing sensitive data without exposing it.
- The current implementation of fully homomorphic encryption demands better computational performance because it presents substantial operational difficulties.

Lightweight Cryptography:

- The purpose of lightweight cryptography involves developing encryption systems designed for devices that have restricted processing power with restricted memory as well as energy constraints. Secure encryption is provided by PRESENT, SPARX along with GIFT through their efficient algorithm implementations [25].
- Applications in 6G IoT: Secure communication for battery-powered sensors, wearables, and low-power IoT devices.

The main challenge exists in achieving both lightweight operational efficiency and protection against emerging security threats.

12.4.2 Distributed Trust Systems

The secure network management methods from blockchain and decentralized identity systems establish protected structures for 6G IoT networking independent from central authorities as shown in Figure 12.2.

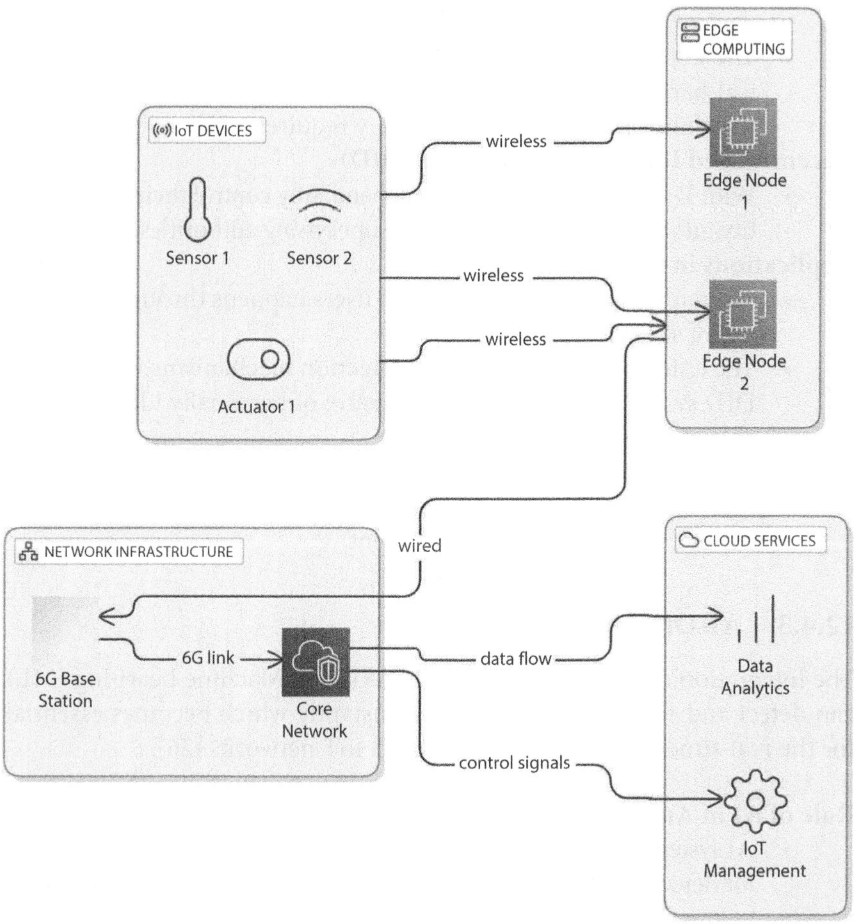

Figure 12.2 Block diagram of 6G IoT network architecture.

Blockchain:

- Secure transparent and unalterable decentralization-based data storage together with safe transactions form the core features of blockchain technology.

Applications in 6G IoT:

- Blockchain establishes trustworthy systems to verify IoT devices through its authentication protocols.
- Data Integrity ensures that transactions along with data exchanges have an unalterable audit trail.
- The automated process called smart contracts enables IoT devices to establish trustless connections for collaboration.
- The deployment of IoT systems requires resolving two critical barriers which include blockchain problems related to scalability alongside critical energy requirements.

Decentralized Identity Management (DID):

- With DID, users and devices independently control their identity information without needing supervising authorities.

Applications in 6G IoT:

- The authentication of IoT system users happens through the use of self-sovereign identities.
- The enforcement of privilege protection mechanisms within DID systems decreases the disclosure of personally identifiable information (PII).
- Standardization together with interoperability between various DID systems constitutes a main challenge in current decentralized identity management.

12.4.3 AI-Driven Threat Detection

The integration of Artificial Intelligence (AI) and Machine Learning (ML) can detect and counter security threats instantly which becomes essential for the real-time operation of dynamic 6G IoT networks [26].

Role of AI in Anomaly Detection:

- AI systems use their capacity to examine huge network data sets for detecting strange patterns that signal potential cyberattacks.

Applications in 6G IoT:

- The Intrusion Detection Systems (IDS) function with AI capabilities to detect and stop malicious activities.

- The monitoring of IoT devices through ML models detects deviations from their standard operation patterns.
- Processing robust systems through training needs extensive datasets yet adversaries can make AI systems unreliable through attacking them.

Security Automation:
Security threats receive automated responses through AI that makes the need for human intervention and response time unnecessary.

Applications in 6G IoT:

- Artificial Intelligence adjusts security policies in real-time by using dynamic assessment of threats.
- Incident response functions are achieved through automated systems which separate infected devices from the network while starting recovery protocols.
- The excessive implementation of automation systems in security functions can produce critical errors in emergencies.

12.4.4 Quantum-Resistant Communication

Traditional cryptography becomes obsolete when quantum computing reaches the market. Techniques that resist quantum attacks represent essential elements for securing 6G IoT networking connections.

Quantum Key Distribution (QKD):
QKD employs quantum mechanics to generate confidential cryptographic keys which defend communication even against quantum attacks.

Applications in 6G IoT:

- The critical systems of IoT networks require security solutions to protect healthcare together with finance and defense sectors.
- Interconnected Devices: Facilitating secure device-to-device communication.
- The implementation of QKD in IoT settings faces two main obstacles such as distance constraints and the high price tag of quantum hardware components.

Hybrid Cryptographic Approaches:
Quantum-resistant methods used alongside traditional cryptography functions as a dual-layer protective measure.

Applications in 6G IoT:

- The hybrid method allows quantum-resistant systems to transition gradually during which backward compatibility is preserved.
- Two security layers protect against both classical and quantum security threats.
- The implementation of hybrid systems for 6G IoT faces two major obstacles: system complexity management and smooth integration with existing IoT frameworks.

Secure operations of 6G IoT applications are dependent on an integrated method which unites high-tech cryptography with decentralized trust infrastructure and AI for threat detection alongside quantum-resistant communications systems. Anticipative measures targeting 6G IoT security challenges will allow the complete realization of next-generation networks along with data protection and user confidence maintenance. Secure and resilient IoT operations in the 6G era start from the innovations developed today.

12.5 Making Sci-Fi Applications a Reality with 6G IoT

6G IoT purposes futuristic concepts into everyday practical use leading to industry and daily life transformation. Using its ultra-low latency capabilities with massive connectivity and advanced communication technologies 6G IoT makes possible applications that scientists had imagined in the past.

12.5.1 Smart Cities and Infrastructure

The implementation of 6G IoT will establish smart cities through their ability to combine intelligent systems from transportation to energy management–to public safety systems.

Intelligent Transportation:

- Live V2X communication networks enable vehicles to exchange data (vehicle-to-everything) for optimizing traffic management, thereby improving both safe transportation and decreasing congestion.
- Connected bus and train systems will run independently to reduce human mistakes while improving operational efficiency.

Energy Grids:

- The integration of IoT technology in energy grids through smart grids will enable dynamic power distribution systems which effectively incorporate renewable energy sources.
- Energy Monitoring systems using sensors will supply live data about energy usage which allows better resource allocation while minimizing wastage.

Public Safety Systems:

- Networked IoT systems will provide immediate emergency data to enable quick effective disaster management.
- Advances in sensors combined with AI-based analytics systems provide better surveillance technology for security purposes and crime prevention in urban areas.

12.5.2 Holographic Telepresence

The implementation of 6G IoT technology will bring lifelike holographic telepresence which revolutionizes sector-to-sector communication methods.

Business:

- The technology enables real-time holographic conference meetings to eliminate global team members' need for physical attendance.

Healthcare:

- Through 3D holographic projection medical personnel can improve both patient access to remote care and surgical results.

Education:

- The integration of holographic technologies in educational settings will create interactive classrooms featuring full-scale interactive holographic simulations.

12.5.3 Advanced Healthcare Systems

The application of 6G IoT can transform healthcare by developing instantaneous data-based healthcare solutions which focus on patients' needs.

Remote Surgery:

- Surgeons provide remote operations assistance to robots through 6G networks because of their fast response time and dependable functionality.

Health Monitoring:

- The Internet of Things through wearable devices will track patient vital signs which will trigger healthcare provider alerts during abnormal measurements.

AI-Driven Diagnostics:

- The combination of integrated AI algorithms will process patient data to identify diseases early and develop personalized treatment choices.

Telemedicine:

- The healthcare industry will establish virtual consultations for real-time diagnostic testing to eliminate space between patients and healthcare providers.

12.5.4 Autonomous Vehicles and Robotics

The sixth generation network of the internet of things (IoT) will enable self-operating systems by delivering prompt service combined with sophisticated automated decision-making features:

Autonomous Vehicles:

- The vehicles complete quick real-time decisions through their communications with both other vehicles and surrounding infrastructure ensures security alongside operational excellence.
- Smart logistics systems using Fleet Management will track and manage autonomous fleets to decrease delivery costs while speeding up deliveries.

Robotics:

- Manufacturing procedures will become more precise through industrial automation by giving robots IoT sensors that enhance process efficiency.
- Service Robots involving IoT connectivity will provide personalized support and services to healthcare facilities and retail stores as well as hospitality establishments.

12.5.5 Immersive Entertainment and Gaming

Through the development of 6G IoT technology, the entertainment and gaming sector can achieve completely immersive experiences.

AR/VR Applications:

- The real-time interactivity of 6G technology will eliminate augmented reality (AR) and virtual reality (VR) application lag which will make them more accessible and engaging.
- Multiplayer virtual reality games involving large-scale high-definition environments will become possible when 6G networks are operational.

Holographic Entertainment:

- Under 6G technologies live performances including sports will use holographic projection systems to let viewers feel as if they are there in person.
- 360-Degree Streaming:
- High-definition 360-degree video streaming will introduce remote viewers to immersive environments through its advanced streaming technology.

Through 6G IoT technology science fiction will become a reality because it will empower new innovations in multiple industry sectors. With these advanced technologies and AI, real-time data processing through 6G IoT applications will change how people interact with the world and carry out their life activities, work processes, and social connections. Global quality of life will benefit through the breakthroughs which will simultaneously improve efficiency and enhance convenience and accessibility.

12.6 Building a Resilient Security Framework for 6G IoT

Hence, a comprehensive and elaborate security structure is required that can effectively secure 6G IoT networks which has elevated levels of integration and communication capability. This framework has to tackle threats that can occur at any level and still maintain functionality and flexibility in a volatile context.

12.6.1 Multi-Layered Security Architecture

- A layering of security incorporates protection mechanisms into layers of the IoT infrastructure to build up a system of layers against pests:

Physical Layer Security:

- Device Authenticity: This is achieved through the use of unique numbers that cannot be forged and other barriers that hinder easy physical connectivity on devices.
- System/Physical Intrusion detection: These are developed to prevent intrusion in devices or infrastructure through interferences.

Network Layer Security:

- Secure Transmission of Data: The utilization of the encrypted communication makes it difficult for the data to be intercepted by third parties.
- Anomaly Detection: The traffic pattern is supervised in real-time and alerts for threats of attacks are noted.

Application Layer Security:

- Data Encryption and Integrity Checks: This will help in protecting data which is stored and processed for preventing it from getting tampered.
- Secure APIs: APIs have secure points to avoid exploitation, which can occur when there is body-to-application contact.

12.6.2 Zero-Trust Architecture for IoT

Zero-Trust Architecture (ZTA) brings about a change of existing concept of trust because every connection needs to be authenticated.

Principles of ZTA:

- Every Request Must be Verifiable: Authentication and authorization are required at all levels of a device, user, or application.
- Restricted Access: Devices and/or users are given the least amount of access as needed for them to perform their duties in case of an attack.
- Continuous Monitoring: This makes validation of the behavior analytics continuous.

Applications in 6G IoT:

- Device-to-Device Communication: IoT devices must be authenticated before connecting to the network; all devices are monitored to avoid the spread of threats in the network.
- User Access Control: Intelligent controls are used when it comes to the user access and how the system is able to interact with the environment and new users in particular in compound environments.

12.6.3 Dynamic Access Control

With dynamic access control, there are not only structure-based but also dynamic conditions that IoT environment in 6G will require:

Context-Aware Security:

- Location-Based Access Control: This type of control has privileges that depends on the geographical location of the preferred device or the user.
- Behavioral Patterns: Deviations from typical behavior trigger additional authentication or access restrictions.
- Device State: Permission can be changed with regard to the health status, like update of firmware or abnormalities.

Adaptive Policies:

- Real-time Control: The policies of access can be modified based on the operating environment, user's role or the prevailing threat level.
- Security Measures: Violence increase and limitation during the identified threats level; for example, quarantining the contaminated devices or limiting risky procedures.

12.6.4 Secure Bootstrapping for IoT Devices

This pending issue can be addressed by using secure bootstrapping that is crucial for the IoT devices particularly those that work under constrained environments in terms of computational power and energy.

Key Components:

- Root of Trust (RoT): This is implemented through hardware or firmware; the first trust is established at the time of booting of the device.

- Mutual authentication: This is the process where device and/or networks involved in data exchange confirm each other before passing onto the other a permission to proceed with the exchange of information.
- Certificate-Based Systems: During the registration process, the service or station establishes and validates the device within a network on the basis of certificate.

Challenges in Constrained Environments:

- Limited Resources: bootstrapping protocols should not demand much computational and energy resources.
- Size: They must be capable of supporting a large number of devices running processes in the billions.

Emerging Solutions:

- Extended and Generic Bootstrap Protocols: Standard protocols, such as Lightweight Machine to Machine (LwM2M), which are optimized help in the lightweight bootstrapping.
- Integration of block chain: In the decentralized ledgers, the record of identification and onboarding of the devices is maintained and is easily checkable and tamper proof.

Therefore, the establishment of a robust security environment for the 6G IoT shall be developed in layers, zero trust model, dynamic access control, and secure bootstrapping. The aforementioned strategies can be used to counter pertinent threats and ensure that both the 6G IoT networks and other networks within the interconnected environment work securely and efficiently. This strategy not only caters for the existing threats today but also for the future changes that the organization may probably experience.

Collaborations and Standardization

As it is evident for 6G IoT to become a reality in the future, there is a need for the collaborative action on the technical, security, and operational issues emerging from cross-border emphasis. There is, therefore, the need to engage research institutions, industries, governments and standardization bodies to develop sound systems that can interconnect seamlessly. This section discusses key gaps in public and private partnerships, security and safety in the context of 6G IoT system as shown in the Figure 12.3.

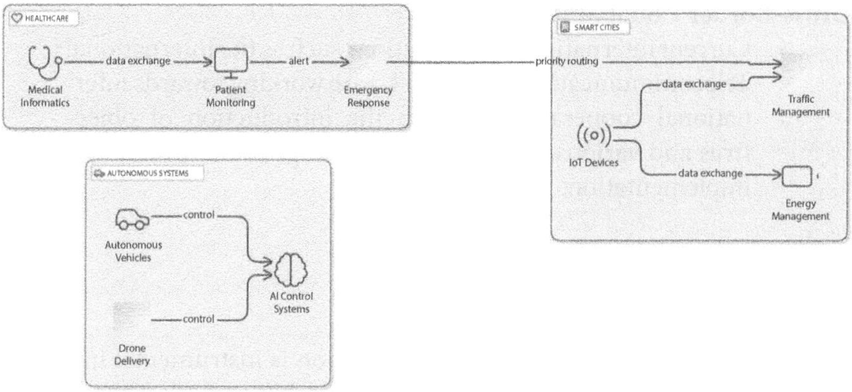

Figure 12.3 Applications diagram showcasing smart cities, healthcare, and autonomous systems.

12.7 Global Efforts in 6G Development

Research Institutions:

- Great universities and research centers initiate the evolutionary process by defining the area's main industries and technologies such as terahertz communication, quantum cryptography, or AI incorporation.
- Strategizing is also taking place by other multi-stakeholder collaborations like in the case of Europe through the Hexa-X 6G flagship projects and the emerging US 6G research programs.

Industry Contributions:

- Nokia is also among some of the global major technology companies—such as Samsung, Huawei, and Ericsson that are investing in 6G.
- Businesses are decidedly committed to creating solutions that will adhere to the standards of the 6G framework across the different components of the hardware and software.

Government Involvement:

- Currently, governments of countries are preparing to fund giant 6G test projects; for instance, the China's 6G and South Korea's 6G pilot projects.
- They're focusing on availability of spectrum resources, security and legal structures for the development of 6G.

Cross-Border Collaboration:

- Current international organizations such as the International Telecommunication Union (ITU) are working towards international cooperation through the introduction of objectives and various blueprints for the progression towards 6G implementation.

12.7.1 Security Standards for 6G IoT

Role of Standards Organizations:

It is important to argue that the standardization is instrumental in ensuring interoperability as well as security and scalability of all of the 6G IoT environment. Key organizations involved include:

International Telecommunication Union (ITU):

- ITU also creates the requirements for the 6G wireless network worldwide to ensure compatibility and security.

Institute of Electrical and Electronics Engineers (IEEE):

- Since it is the Institute of Electrical and Electronics Engineers, it plays a crucial role in identifying specific protocols that applies to wireless connection and IoT gadgets. It deals with fixed-networks with specific emphasis on secure communications on high speed low delay communication networks.

National Institute of Standards and Technology (NIST):

- As an instance, NIST has its specialization in cybersecurity; therefore, it contributes to develop core security models of 6G IoT, includes post-quantum cryptography guideline and zero-trust security architecture.

Key Security Focus Areas:

- Interconnectivity: This refers to the ability to run and communicate over devices of various manufacturers.
- Quantum-Safe Standards: Considering the risks that come with quantum computing, this a task that has to do with creating cryptographic systems are immune to the risks of quantum computing.
- IoT-Specific Frameworks: It is about creating frameworks for manufacture which targets IoT specific constraints of devices which include resource limited devices.

12.7.2 Public-Private Partnerships

Collaboration Models for Innovation:

PPPs are important in driving the development and implementation of 6G technologies by sharing risks and costs effectively.

- Innovation Hubs: Creation of organizations that foster linkages between universities, industries, and governments for conducting novel research and pilot schemes.
- Financial and Material Contributions: Through fiscal and regulatory mechanisms, the governments contribute capital and technical support which is complemented by the capital and technological advancement by private players.

Risk-Sharing Mechanisms:

- Cybersecurity Partnership: Joint efforts leadership by public and private sectors with cooperation towards developing secure protection measures against the rising threats in the digital environment.
- Standardization Contribution: Professionals in various industries develop and improve actual requirements for these international standards.

Examples of Successful PPPs:

- 5G PPP (Europe): This partnership between EU and companies was a template for advancing 5G, can be used for 6G as well.
- Top Smart Cities Initiatives: IoT solutions in smart urban settings have been successfully deployed by governments, as well as private corporations for the development of 6G applications.

One of the most imperative aspects that are closely related to the success of 6G IoT is collaboration and standardization. By initiating global activities, creating a strong security framework, and leveraging open cooperation with business actors, the stakeholders can guarantee 6G IoT networks' security, compatibility, and scalability. Such endeavors shall facilitate the actualization of 6G IoT in its potential to revolutionize industries and societies globally.

12.8 Challenges in Realizing Secure 6G IoT Applications

The advancement towards 6G and its incorporation with the Internet of Things (IoT) will make the world a new one which is full of interconnectivity between the trillions. But maintaining security within such a setting is not without a number of concerns. This paper provides a breakdown of challenges in securing 6G IoT application:

12.8.1 Scalability and Interoperability

Managing diverse devices and networks in a unified ecosystem.
Internet of things will be handled through 6G that would be far much greater than those that may be managed by 5G. The number of connected devices will be doubled in the next few years along with different communication protocols, OS and their resources rating scales which will be a challenge to manage and ineffective. Security is the issue since it has to be sustained in a context characterized by numerous and varying devices on different networks (cellular, satellites, etc.).

- Scalability Issues: This means that security solutions put into place have to support growth without a decline in performance. It means that traditional methodologies might not be effective; and hence, it becomes necessary to come with new procedures in an endeavor to secure billions of devices within the shortest time possible, with efficiency as measured by high throughput.
- Interoperability Issues: There is a need for gadgets from different manufacturers implementing dissimilar standards and protocols to operate securely. Security issues that stem from differences in security technologies can be counterproductive and that's why it is necessary to have standard and compatible IoT security features, compatible with all IoT networks.

12.8.2 Energy Efficiency in Security Implementations

Balancing robust security with minimal energy consumption.
Most IoT devices are powered by batteries; this is especially true with those in area with little or no electrical supply or in regions that lack fixed electricity supplies. The security solutions implemented should not consume much on resources, since they will cause a shorter life span of the devices and a disruption in the overall network.

- Constraints in Energy: Cryptographic algorithms and security protocols that are used are though efficient, they consume a lot of energy. This makes it necessary that their implementation is done on devices like sensors or wearable devices in a power conscious way to avoid frequent charging.
- Integration of efficiency with security: This calls for advances in areas such as lightweight cryptography, dynamic security architecture/protocols as well as security redesign to ask required computations to be offloaded to border devices and/ or cloud servers were pertinent. Both security solutions in 6G IoT environment should be efficient and involve least energy consumption.

12.8.3 Ethical and Privacy Concerns

12.8.3.1 Addressing User Consent and Data Protection

6G IoT as expected depends on a base of massive volumes of user information such as health data, position data, and even behaviors. This forms an extremely crucial concern in the realm of ethical and privacy matters.

- User Consent: It is also important for users to have control over its data; at any one point, the consent should be given and withdrawn. It is also important that the user of the program is informed about what data is being collected, and how it is going to be used; therefore, it must be done with the help of clear and comprehensible privacy policies.
- Security: The large amounts of data in the company require a secure network, User Datagram Protocol Security being one of the defenses. The IoT devices should meet the current international guidelines on data protection laws like GDPR or CAuuAA to protect the user data from unauthorized accesses or data leaks.

12.8.4 Cost and Resource Constraints

Barriers to widespread adoption of secure solutions.
The expenses of the security of IoT in 6G networks could be high, especially for the enterprises and budding nations. They indicate that high-quality security includes the use of technologies and security infrastructures that some of the stakeholders may not afford to apply.

- Resource Issues: Some of the protection methods used in information systems include encryption of data, user authentication, and real-time monitoring which are considered costly in terms of resources. Most smIoT devices are resource-scarce; and therefore, implementing such mechanisms, especially for processing, can cause a high-performance overhead.
- Cost Issues: As much as the 6G IoT needs security solutions, their implementation slows down by the amount of money it takes to develop, deploy, and maintain such solutions. This can prevent the development of the certain industries, especially in emerging markets where funding issues are often come across.

12.9 Case Studies and Prototypes

In responding to the challenges stipulated above, lessons from the use cases and pilots are important principles that capture potential secure 6G IoT scenarios. These examples aim at illustrating the journey and challenges in the early years of the 6G IoT implementation.

12.9.1 Early Implementations of 6G IoT Applications

Examples from smart cities, healthcare, and autonomous systems.

- Smart Cities: The pilots of smart cities' projects define IoT application in traffic control, safety, and energy solutions. Some of the security issues that crop up in these deployments include security of data obtained from sensors (e.g., traffic cameras or environmental sensors) as well as protection against cyber incidences that may affect the functioning of the city.
- Healthcare: Healthcare is another promising industry; various connected devices such as a remote monitoring system and wearable health trackers are being employed in the collection of the data of the patients. This means that privacy and integrity of this data are of so much importance to avoid cases of hacking of health information of people.
- Autonomous systems: On use cases, 6G IoT revolves around the use of autonomous vehicles and drones, and more. There are several procedures necessary to secure them from unauthorized access or any forms of interferences. The functionality of interacting cars and intersection with the traffic light

on the one hand and other vital traffic management systems integrated with central control centers on the other requires the real-time secure communication.

12.9.2 Security Incidents and Lessons Learned

Lessons from previous IoT attacks and its application to the protection and development of 6G cybersecurity—Studying security incidents of past networks like Mirai botnet attack which targeted IoT devices for large-scale DDoS attacks would be useful for the future 6G IoT networks.

- Vulnerabilities: Trends—such examples of trends include poor firmware updates, or execution of IoT devices with default passwords respectively. These are concerning factors that should be met in 6G networks and this can be through employing secure boot procedures, frequent software update, and better authentication.
- Lessons: It has been found that secure device provisioning, continuous monitoring, and having a zero-trust security model would be vital for the protection of 6G IoT.

12.9.3 Pilot Projects and Experimental Networks

Success stories showcasing secure 6G IoT prototypes.

- **6G-IoT Edge Computing:** One potential model that comprises edge computing in 6G IoT where security processes such as encryption will be carried out near the devices minimizing energy consumption and latency.
- **IoT security:** There are research studies that commence to implement the blockchain technology as a decentralized IoT security solution. Blockchain offers the feature of managing data and authenticating data using distributed ledger which offers generalized security to a large scale of IoT network.

12.10 Future Directions

Discussing further, toward the prospect of secure 6G IoT applications, numerous technologies and novelties are anticipated for the forthcoming IoT networks.

12.10.1 Convergence of Technologies

The paper under discussion focuses on the involvement of applications such as AI, blockchain, quantum computing and edge computing in relation to 6G IoT.

- AI: Artificial intelligence will be responsible for constant surveillance of IoT for any conflicting behavior and identification of threats that are probable to happen thereby facilitating security measures that change according to the prevailing conditions.
- Blockchain technology benefits IoT security since it can provide decentralized IoT security, where all transactions can be secure and transparent between devices apart from protecting data from breaches.
- Quantum computing: with the advancement of this computing technology, it brings in threats as well as solutions to the future security of IoT by providing challenging levels of cryptography that would need to be overcome with quantum-resistant encryption for secure data.
- Edge Computing: As opposed to sending data to centralized servers, edge computing involves processing data in a localized manner, thereby making it more secure and faster since it helps in minimizing latency and also, since strong data does not need to travel far as it is vulnerable to a potential attack.

12.10.2 Innovations in IoT Security

Adaptive security models and continuous learning systems.
It is expected that in the future, 6G IoT networks security system will be adaptive and will adapt itself according to the threat. These will then be adaptive in the sense that they will adapt to some type of context such as, the kind of device being used, location and behavior among others, and they will be able to constantly scan for possible new threats.

Vision for 6G IoT Ecosystems

- Persistent connectivity is a powerful tool that is key to the development of enduring and long-lasting networks.
- The vision of the 6G IoT is to have even more connected and robust networks that are not only capable of supporting the IoT devices or computers similar or related to IoT, but also

of supporting a new range of applications such as automated systems, smart cities, and digital twins. Making sure that such networks are secure, sustainable, and scalable will be fundamental to the positive development of 6G.

12.11 Conclusion

The experimentation from the theoretical ideas about the 6G IoT to the practical implementations could be recognized as a rather vibrant but challenging process, though the security issue is seen as the essential one. Some of the issues that arise from the use of 6G networks include scalability, interconnectivity, and data privacy that will be present due to the support of many devices than in the previous generations. Lacking security features, the billions of devices can be vulnerable to hacks, and different attacks can threaten to pry open the IoT. To pave the way for 6G's success, the possibility of creating secure transferring data from various devices made by different manufacturers will require addressing the privacy of users. To put it in a conclusive manner, enabling 6G IoT security requires developing new paradigms such as AI, blockchain, and edge computing. AI can be used to identify threats in real-time as well as prevent them. Blockchain increases data reliability and integrity, while edge computing decreases the latency and improves the local security. Furthermore, attention to past experiences in security matters and ensuring ongoing changes to implement security measures will be compulsory. To implement 6G, these technologies have to be adopted and industries have to come together and the potentiality of IoT has to be explored while keeping the domain secure, ethical, and robust.

AI disclosure statement: The author acknowledges the use of AI-based tools for minor language editing or grammatical correction. However, all intellectual contributions, analyses, and conclusions presented in this chapter are entirely the author's own.

References

1. Akyildiz, I.F. and Kak, A., 6G and beyond: The future of wireless communication networks. *IEEE Commun. Mag.*, 58, 8, 62–68, Aug. 2020.

2. Saad, W., Bennis, M., Chen, M., A vision of 6G wireless systems: Applications, trends, technologies, and open research problems. *IEEE Network*, 34, 3, 134–142, May/June 2019.
3. Zhang, Z., Xiao, Y., Ma, Z., Xiao, M., Dai, H., Li, H., 6G wireless networks: Vision, requirements, architecture, and key technologies. *IEEE Veh. Technol. Mag.*, 14, 3, 28–41, Sept. 2019.
4. Boccardi, F., Heath, R.W., Lozano, A., Marzetta, T.L., Popovski, P., Five disruptive technology directions for 5G. *IEEE Commun. Mag.*, 52, 2, 74–80, Feb. 2014.
5. Andrews, J.G., *et al.*, What will 5G be? *IEEE J. Sel. Areas Commun.*, 32, 6, 1065–1082, June 2014.
6. Wu, J., Zhang, Z., Zhang, Y., Key challenges for 6G secure IoT networks. *IEEE Internet Things J.*, 8, 9, 7419–7431, May 2022.
7. Arfaoui, M., *et al.*, Quantum-safe cryptography in 5G networks. *IEEE Commun. Stand. Mag.*, 6, 1, 72–78, Mar. 2022.
8. Kshetri, N., Blockchain's roles in strengthening cybersecurity and protecting privacy. *Telecommun. Policy*, 41, 10, 1027–1038, Nov. 2017.
9. Lu, Y. and Xu, X., AI-powered IoT: Concepts, technologies, and applications. *IEEE Trans. Ind. Inf.*, 15, 8, 4356–4368, Aug. 2018.
10. Ruan, X., *et al.*, Lightweight cryptography for IoT: Algorithms and challenges. *J. Network Comput. Appl.*, 144, 138–151, Nov. 2020.
11. Singh, K. and Misra, S., Ultra-dense networks for 6G IoT ecosystems. *IEEE Trans. Commun.*, 69, 4, 2341–2353, Apr. 2019.
12. Tang, C. and Ma, X., Edge AI integration in 6G systems. *IEEE Access*, 8, 198367–198379, 2020.
13. Khan, L.U., *et al.*, Visible light communication for IoT-enabled 6G networks. *IEEE Wireless Commun.*, 28, 4, 80–88, Aug. 2021.
14. Mao, Y., *et al.*, A survey on mobile edge computing: The communication perspective. *IEEE Commun. Surv. Tutorials*, 19, 4, 2322–2358, Dec. 2017.
15. Ali, Z., *et al.*, Real-time holographic communication: A review. *IEEE Commun. Surv. Tutorials*, 22, 4, 2354–2373, Dec. 2020.
16. Ahmed, I., *et al.*, Role of V2X communication in 6G autonomous systems. *IEEE Trans. Veh. Technol.*, 70, 2, 1512–1523, Feb. 2021.
17. Zanella, A., *et al.*, Internet of Things for smart cities. *IEEE Internet Things J.*, 1, 1, 22–32, Feb. 2014.
18. Yu, R. and Liu, Y., Blockchain for secure IoT in 6G: A review. *Future Gener. Comput. Syst.*, 117, 328–342, May 2020.
19. Wang, Y., *et al.*, IoT botnets: Characteristics, challenges, and countermeasures. *Future Internet*, 10, 7, 61, July 2018.
20. Shi, W. and Dustdar, S., The promise of edge computing. *Computer*, 49, 5, 78–81, May 2016.
21. Mosca, M., Cybersecurity in an era with quantum computers: Will we be ready? *IEEE Secur. Privacy*, 16, 5, 38–41, Sept. 2018.

22. Bernstein, D.J., *et al.*, Post-quantum cryptography: Challenges and future directions. *IEEE Trans. Inf. Theory*, 66, 8, 4853–4870, Aug. 2020.
23. Chen, L. and Childs, L., Lightweight post-quantum cryptographic protocols for IoT. *ACM Trans. Embedded Comput. Syst.*, 20, 2, 25, Feb. 2020.
24. Gentry, C., Fully homomorphic encryption using ideal lattices, in: *Proc. ACM Symp. Theory Comput*, pp. 169–178, 2009.
25. Ali, S., *et al.*, Energy-efficient cryptography for IoT: A review. *Sustainable Computing Inf. Syst.*, 28, 100413, Mar. 2020.
26. Goodfellow, I., Bengio, Y., Courville, A., *Deep learning for IoT security: An overview*, MIT Press, Cambridge, MA, 2016.

Index

Also of Interest

Check out these other related titles from Scrivener Publishing

Attacks and Defenses in Explainable Artificial Intelligence, Edited by Aml Dattatraya Vibhute, Rajesh Kumar Dhanaraj, Malathy Sathyamoorthy, and Paramasivam A. ISBN: 9781394305582. Bridge the critical gap between AI transparency and security with this essential guide to the systematic defense frameworks and ethical strategies needed to protect explainable AI (XAI) systems from sophisticated adversarial attacks.

Generative Artificial Intelligence for Next-Generation Security Paradigms, Edited by Santosh Kumar Srivastava, Durgesh Srivastava, Manoj Kumar Mahto, Ben Othman Soufiane, and Praveen Kantha, ISBN: 9781394305643. Fortify your digital defenses with this essential book, which provides a roadmap for moving beyond the limitations of traditional encryption by leveraging generative AI algorithms to proactively anticipate, detect, and mitigate the next generation of cyber threats in real-time.

Security and Privacy in 6G Communication Technology, Edited by Parita Jain, Puneet Kumar Aggarwal, Mandeep Singh, Sushil Kumar Singh, and Amit Singhal, ISBN: 9781394311002. Future-proof your knowledge and expertise in telecommunications with this essential guide, which provides a comprehensive analysis of the critical security and privacy challenges in the transition to 6G communication.

Development of 6G Networks and Technology, Edited by Suman Lata Tripathi, Mufti Mahmood, C. Narmadha, and S. Albert Alexander, ISBN: 9781394230655. *Development of 6G Networks and Technology* provides an in-depth exploration of the potential impact of 6G networks on various industries, including healthcare, agriculture, transport, and national security, making it an essential resource for researchers, scholars, and students working in the field of wireless networks and high-speed data processing systems.

Quantum Machine Learning for 6G Networks, Edited by Pallavi Sapkale, Shilpa Mehta and S. Balamurugan, ISBN: 9781394238088.

Virtual Reality and Augmented Reality with 6G Communication, Edited by B. Sundaravadivazhagan, N. Gnanasankaran, C. Pethuru Raj, and A. Saleem Raja, ISBN: 9781394336050. Stay ahead of the technological curve with this essential book, which provides a comprehensive guide to the transformative convergence of Virtual Reality (VR), Augmented Reality (AR), and 6G communication.

INTEGRATED DEVICES FOR ARTIFICIAL INTELLIGENCE AND VLSI: VLSI Design, Simulation and Applications, Edited by Balwinder Raj, Suman Lata Tripathi, Tarun Chaudhary, K. Srinivasa Rao, and Mandeep Singh, ISBN: 9781394204359. With its in-depth exploration of the close connection between microelectronics, AI, and VLSI technology, this book offers valuable insights into the cutting-edge techniques and tools used in VLSI design automation, making it an essential resource for anyone seeking to stay ahead in the rapidly evolving field of VLSI design.

DECENTRALIZED SYSTEMS AND DISTRIBUTED COMPUTING, Edited by Sandhya Avasthi, Suman Lata Tripathi, Namrata Dhanda, and Satya Bhushan Verma, ISBN: 978139420436. This book provides a comprehensive exploration of next-generation internet, distributed systems, and distributed computing, offering valuable insights into their impact on society and the future of technology.

ELECTRIC VEHICLE DESIGN: Design, Simulation and Applications, Edited by Krishan Arora, Suman Lata Tripathi, and Himashu Sharma, ISBN: 9781394204373. This book will serve as a definitive guide to conceptual and practical knowledge about the design of hybrid electrical vehicles (HEV), battery electrical vehicles (BEV), fuel cell electrical vehicles (FCEV), plug-in hybrid electrical vehicles (PHEV), and efficient EV charging techniques with advanced tools and methodologies for students, engineers, and academics alike.

INDUSTRIAL CONTROL SYSTEMS, Edited by Vipin Chandra Pal, Suman Lata Tripathi, and Souvik Ganguli, ISBN: 9781119829256. This volume serves as a comprehensive guide in the journey of industrial control systems with a multidisciplinary approach to the key engineering problems in the 21st century.

MODERN AUTOMOTIVE ELECTRICAL SYSTEMS: Theory and Applications, Edited by Pedram Asef, Sanjeevikumar Padmanaban, and Andrew Lapthorn, ISBN: 1119801047. Presenting the concepts and advances of modern automotive electrical systems, this volume, written and edited by a global team of experts, also goes into the practical applications for the engineer, student, and other industry professionals.

NANODEVICES FOR INTEGRATED CIRCUIT DESIGN, Edited by Suman Lata Tripathi, Abhishek Kumar, K. Srinivasa Rao, and Prasantha R. Mudimela, ISBN: 9781394185788. Written and edited by a team of experts in the field, this important new volume broadly covers the design of nano-devices and their integrated applications in digital and analog integrated circuits (IC) design.

EXPLAINABLE MACHINE LEARNING MODELS AND ARCHITECTURES: Real-Time System Implementation, Edited by Suman Lata Tripathi and Mufti Mahmud, ISBN: 9781394185849. This cutting-edge new volume covers the hardware architecture implementation, the software implementation approach, and the efficient hardware of machine learning applications.

MACHINE LEARNING TECHNIQUES FOR VLSI CHIP DESIGN, Edited by Abhishek Kumar, Suman Lata Tripathi, and K. Srinivasa Rao, ISBN: 9781119910398. This cutting-edge new volume covers the hardware architecture implementation, the software implementation approach, and the efficient hardware of machine learning applications with FPGA or CMOS circuits, and many other aspects and applications of machine learning techniques for VLSI chip design.

INTELLIGENT GREEN TECHNOLOGIES FOR SMART CITIES, Edited by Suman Lata Tripathi, Souvik Ganguli, Abhishek Kumar, and Tengiz Magradze, ISBN: 9781119816065. Presenting the concepts and fundamentals of smart cities and developing "green" technologies, this volume, written and edited by a global team of experts, also goes into the practical applications that can be utilized across multiple disciplines and industries, for both the engineer and the student.

DESIGN AND DEVELOPMENT OF EFFICIENT ENERGY SYSTEMS, Edited by Suman Lata Tripathi, Dushyant Kumar Singh, Sanjeevikumar Padmanaban, and P. Raja, ISBN: 9781119761631. Covering the concepts and fundamentals of efficient energy systems, this volume, written and edited by a global team of experts, also goes into the practical applications that can be utilized across multiple industries, for both the engineer and the student.

Electrical and Electronic Devices, Circuits, and Materials: Technical Challenges and Solutions, Edited by Suman Lata Tripathi, Parvej Ahmad Alvi, and Umashankar Subramaniam, ISBN: 9781119750369. Covering every aspect of the design and improvement needed for solid-state electronic devices and circuit and their reliability issues, this new volume also includes overall system design for all kinds of analog and digital applications and developments in power systems.

Printed and bound by CPI Group (UK) Ltd, Croydon, CR0 4YY

24/08/2026

14947831-0004